THE ELEMENTS OF DESSERT

THE

ELEME

OF

WILEY

JOHN WILEY & SONS, INC.

N T S

D E S S

E R T

FRANCISCO MIGOYA
THE CULINARY INSTITUTE OF AMERICA
PHOTOGRAPHY BY BEN FINK

THE
CULINARY
INSTITUTE
OF AMERICA

Cover images: © Ben Fink
Cover design: Vertigo Design NYC

Photographs © 2012 by Ben Fink

Interior design: Vertigo Design NYC

THE CULINARY INSTITUTE OF AMERICA

President	Dr. Tim Ryan '77, CMC, AAC
Provost	Mark Erickson '77, CMC
Associate Vice President–Branch Campuses	Susan Cussen
Director of Publishing	Nathalie Fischer
Editorial Project Manager	Margaret Wheeler '00
Editorial Assistant	Erin Jeanne McDowell '08

PUBLISHED BY JOHN WILEY & SONS, INC., HOBOKEN, NEW JERSEY

Published simultaneously in Canada

For general information on our other products and services or for technical support, please contact our Customer Care Department within the United States at (800) 762-2974, outside the United States at (317) 572-3993 or fax (317) 572-4002.

Wiley publishes in a variety of print and electronic formats and by print-on-demand. Some material included with standard print versions of this book may not be included in e-books or in print-on-demand. If this book refers to media such as a CD or DVD that is not included in the version you purchased, you may download this material at http://booksupport.wiley.com. For more information about Wiley products, visit www.wiley.com.

LIBRARY OF CONGRESS CATALOGING-IN-PUBLICATION DATA:

Migoya, Francisco J.
The elements of dessert / Francisco Migoya ; photography by Ben Fink.
p. cm.
Includes bibliographical references and index.
ISBN 978-0-470-89198-8 (cloth)
1. Desserts. I. Title.
TX773.M5325 2012
641.8'6--dc23
2011021010

CONTENTS

ACKNOWLEDGMENTS

I would like to thank the following people, in no particular order (except for my wife, of course; she will always be first):

My wife, Kris, for her patience, understanding, and support; and my beautiful daughter, Isabel, whose existence puts all of this into perspective.

Tom Vaccaro, Senior Director for Baking and Pastry Education, for his unwavering commitment.

Dr. Tim Ryan, president of The Culinary Institute of America, and Mark Erickson, Provost, for providing the resources and opportunities that were necessary for this book.

Maggie Wheeler, for her keen eye and attention to detail. Our third book together, how about that?

Nathalie Fischer, for putting it all together so seamlessly.

Pam Chirls from John Wiley & Sons, for believing in this project.

Bruce Ostwald, for his amazing porcelain figures (pages 466, 470, and 474) made especially for this book.

My parents, for all they provided to help me get to where I am.

My staff, especially Robert Howay, Raewyn Horton, and Justen Nickel, who assisted with the contents of this book.

The students of the CIA, for being such a great source of inspiration.

Erin McDowell, for her contributions to the production and editorial side of the book.

Ben Fink, my favorite photographer. It is always a pleasure to work with you. You make it all look so good.

Michael Nothnagel, for his help with determining a formula for making chocolate.

INTRODUCTION

Nothing is more valuable than experience when it comes to developing a dessert. But where does that experience come from? Does it come from working in a pastry kitchen for many years, and then suddenly the ideas just start flowing? Does it come from studying pastry in school? No—work and study alone are not going to produce the wonderful menu items you are hoping to make. In my opinion, dessert creation is somewhat more ambiguous in its roots, but there are certain starting points that are the pillars of creativity and production.

One of these pillars is a constant intake of information. I have an ongoing interest in what other chefs and pastry chefs are doing. I taste the recipes of others; I read as many books, magazines, and blogs as I can; and I test recipes on a continual basis. I interpret food according to my taste, textural, and visual preferences, and sometimes during that process, there is an original idea or thought.

Not everything you make can be new or never seen before. Everything comes from something, and this brings me to the creative process of making desserts, which is really quite simple. All of the ideas you have are the result of the information you have stored in your brain. Your brain creates a map of these experiences, and it is constantly working on finding places on this map, creating new roads on it as new information is stored. The bigger the map is, the more results it will churn out. This is why most of us mortals need a few years before we develop a menu we can call our own.

I believe I have a good-size food map in my brain, which helps me to develop ideas and brainstorm in the kitchen. However, having a well-developed map does not mean that every idea will work. If you test out one of your ideas and it is just plain bad, that also becomes part of the experience and builds on your personal food map. Chances are, there will be many more bad ideas than good. Finding a good idea is like finding the treasure in the map. To me, few things in life are more exhilarating than coming up with a dessert that balances it all: flavor, texture, and aesthetics.

What kick-starts the ideation process? Maybe it is a single ingredient you are curious about, or a method you saw a chef use that you had not seen before. Or maybe it is just a different approach to something you have done many times before. For the most part, I create a mental image of what I would like to see. My ideas are based initially on an aesthetic approach. I am comfortable with that because I already know that I can translate that image into something appetizing; it is just a matter of searching my mental database. But I have also created a dessert based on a beautiful dish, a new ingredient, a new method, or a new technique.

There is no single source for ideas, and it is important to realize that. Just remember, in order to come to that place where ideas just flow, you need to expose yourself to as much food (pastry and savory) as you can. When you first start out as a pastry apprentice, and even when you get your first actual pastry chef job, it is OK to emulate other pastry chef's desserts. It is not a crime. Just don't make it a constant habit; otherwise, you will not be able to develop your own style. Style is something you can truly call your own and is what will distinguish you from other pastry chefs. A unique style is easier to develop than a new dish. And, if you are the creative source for a new technique or a new dish that no one has seen before, you just might be destined for greatness. Most of the ideas that are considered innovative or revolutionary really just come from the chef taking a different approach, or looking at something in a different way than anyone else ever has. According to Vilfredo Pareto, an Italian economist and sociologist from the late nineteenth century, an idea is nothing more or less than a new combination of old elements that are related. But it is your capacity to form old elements into new combinations and your ability to see the relationships between those elements that will determine the creation of a "new" idea. Take the now

(in)famous foams, for example. These whippers were used for years exclusively for dispensing whipped heavy cream, but then there was a revolution. Ferran Adrià realized that whatever went into that whipper had to have the capacity to take air in and remain stable inside the canister, so it could be a flavored cream, or a fruit purée with a small amount of gelatin. It is people like him (and Thomas Keller and Michel Bras) who saw something others didn't see, and they are originals in their own right. It is finding the new view, the new method or technique, that will be the biggest claim to fame a chef can ever have.

You will very likely make a fair amount of mistakes, but that is part of the process. The most important lesson to be learned from this is that you cannot give up easily. In my experience, I give a dessert no more than four chances, meaning that it will only go four steps away from the original idea before I decide to drop it. When food is too overworked or overthought, it shows. Your food will look awkward and contrived and it will be hard for the customer (and even your staff) to get it. As wise as it is to not give up, it is also wise to know when to rethink your idea. You will need to decide if you give your dessert four chances or ten. It really is up to you and how much you believe in the original idea.

I want to make sure that you know and understand the most important quality aspect of a finished dessert before you get started. It is not flavor, texture, or aesthetic. The most important quality is wholesomeness. That means that whatever you make, it should be beneficial and generally good for your customers. If you work in sanitary conditions and you follow food safety principles, it will be the most important aspect of your food. After wholesomeness, then you can think of flavor, texture, and aesthetics. Here is what I explain to my staff: People are going to come to our restaurant, order our food, put the food we made into their bodies, and then pay with their hard-earned money. There is nothing more personal than that, and we should be humbled by this privilege. Think of how many people can do what we do. The trust that your customers put in you is enormous, and you need to respect that.

Ch 1

THE BASIC ELEMENTS

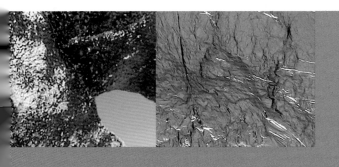

The word *dessert* comes from *desservir,* a French term that means "to remove that which has been served." Essentially, it is what is offered to the guests after everything on the table has been cleared. The meaning has evolved to an extent, but the principle has not. Once your entrée or last course has been cleared, the utensils and all glassware have been removed, and the table has been "crumbed," then the dessert is served.

It is important to understand that dessert can be presented and served in many different ways and in a variety of environments. Each setting will have a style or type of dessert that is ideal and makes the most sense to maintain the quality of the product.

Dessert is vastly more far-reaching now than it ever has been; in fact, it has become very complex and multifaceted. For all intents and purposes, dessert is the final course, but the context in which dessert can be categorized is more than something you have after your entrée. There may be courses that border the lines of sweet and savory but cannot be categorized as dessert per se. As a pastry chef, you need to really understand how far desserts can be broken down and what makes the most sense for your operation. Is your establishment high end, and does it require a large menu or a short menu? Do you offer pre-desserts or only desserts? Can your customers choose from a cake menu for a special occasion? Can you offer petits fours, and if so, how many and what is a good variety?

One of the questions asked most frequently by pastry cooks and pastry students is: How does one come up with flavor combinations? The short answer is that after a few years of manipulating and tasting food, not just where you work but in as many places as you can manage, you will come to your own conclusions and figure out what you like and dislike. This is mostly accurate, but it doesn't mean that because you like a particular flavor combination, everyone else is going to like it. This is one of the biggest reasons why some pastry chefs are successful and some are not: If your flavors work well together, people will want to eat your desserts. If they do not, they won't. We make desserts for people to eat and enjoy.

The comprehensive table of flavors on pages 61 to 84 is codified in the following way to help explain which flavors complement each other.

- **Ingredient name (ingredients are divided into categories—fruit, herbs, spices, flavorings, and so forth—and will contain some nontraditional ingredients)**

- **Type of flavor: frontal, background, or mild**

- **Flavor compatibility**

There is also a table of the most frequently used pastry preparations and components, which is meant to be used as a reference to begin the creative process. You can use this to visualize all that you can produce, and then it is just a matter of matching the components properly. Essentially, this is what you will need to know to create your own desserts:

- **The basic pastry methods**

- **The components of pastry**

- **Flavors and textures**

- **The principles of dessert composition**

- **The principles of menu composition and item enunciation**

These are all of the key points in this chapter and are the pillars or the basis of your technical knowledge. The experience part is entirely in your hands.

THE BASIC PASTRY METHODS

As with anything, pastry is all about the foundations you have acquired through experience. Once you have become comfortable with them, you should be able to move on to more elaborate and complex techniques. This is similar to what the artist Pablo Picasso did during his career. He was a master of technique. He knew how to use different materials and he also knew how to construct a canvas with his own hands. His style changed as he experimented with different theories, techniques, and ideas until he was able to start an entirely new movement. The point is, he did not jump into Cubism right away. He established a solid technical foundation beforehand. The same is true in pastry.

This section will cover all of the basic information you need to know about the most widely used pastry methods. All of these methods will be used throughout the book and have been organized alphabetically for ease of use. The recipes throughout the book will cross-reference these methods as needed.

THE BLENDING METHOD

This method is most commonly used for quick breads in which two or more ingredients are combined just until they are evenly mixed. The fat used is a liquid fat. We will be applying this method to certain sponge cakes, such as the Blackout Cake on page 303 and the Devil's Food Cake on page 256.

1. In the bowl of an electric mixer fitted with a paddle attachment, combine all of the liquid ingredients on medium speed. Some recipes require a whip instead; it depends on the density of the final mass—will it be loose like a light génoise, or dense like a *pain de gênes*?

2. Sift all of the dry ingredients together.

3. Add the dry ingredients to the liquid ingredients and mix on low speed.

4. Mix until just incorporated, scraping the bowl as necessary. Don't overmix, since this can cause gluten development in the flour and make the final product denser than intended.

5. Add the garnish at the end if needed in the recipe. The garnish is not obligatory, but in some cases a recipe will call for one. Some examples are chopped dried fruit or nuts.

THE CREAMING METHOD

Used for certain cakes (such as pound cake) and doughs (most cookies and tart doughs are made with this method), the creaming method is a mixing method in which softened fat (generally butter) and sugar are vigorously combined, either manually or mechanically, to incorporate air. This trapped air is partially responsible for the leavening of the product. The main ingredients used are sugar, fat, eggs, and flour. The sugar is granulated to assist in incorporating air into the mixture. Superfine sugar or bakers' sugar yields better results than regular granulated; the sugar dissolves better and faster into the fat because the crystals are smaller. The fat should be between 21°C/70°F and 22°C/72°F. This temperature will allow it to take air in more readily than if it were cold. Oil should not be used since it does not have the capacity to trap air with this mixing method. Vegetable shortenings and animal fats such as lard and duck fat may be used, but the end result will vary. The eggs should be warmed over a hot water bath to between 26°C/80°F and 29°C/85°F. They are usually added slowly into the butter in order to create an emulsion, and their warm temperature makes the mixing process more efficient. If the eggs are colder, the butter will seize and the emulsion will break. If the eggs are warmer, they will soften the butter too much and any trapped air would escape, resulting in a flat product. Milk, water, or fruit juices may be added to the eggs, but the eggs cannot be completely replaced. The flour that is used should be a low-protein flour, such as pastry or cake flour, but sometimes an all-purpose flour is also used. Other dry ingredients may be combined with the flour for flavor and texture, such as ground nuts, dried fruit, or cocoa powder.

THE CREAMING METHOD IS AS FOLLOWS:

1. Soften the butter. It can be left out of the refrigerator for 2 hours before using, or it can be softened in the microwave in short intervals of time until the desired temperature is reached.

2. Warm the eggs over a hot water bath to between 26°C/80°F and 29°C/85°F. Reserve until needed.

3.	In the bowl of an electric mixer fitted with a paddle attachment, mix the butter and sugar together on medium speed until there are no lumps of butter or sugar. Five to 10 minutes is appropriate for an item such as a pound cake, since this action makes the butter fluffier and aerates it as well as helps grind the sugar into the butter. If you are making a tart dough or cookie dough, simply mix the butter and sugar until both components are very well incorporated; this takes less than 2 minutes on high speed. Stop the mixer regularly to scrape down the sides and bottom of the bowl; this will ensure a homogenous mix.

4.	Add the eggs in four to six increments. After each addition, allow the mixer to turn for a minute or more to incorporate eggs; in smaller batches the time between egg additions will decrease. It is sufficient to wait for the eggs to be fully incorporated into the butter-sugar mixture.

5.	Scrape down the sides and bottom of the bowl between egg additions. Continue adding the eggs until they are fully incorporated.

6.	Stop the mixer, and then add the flour all at once. Mix on low speed to just incorporate the flour.

7.	Scrape the bowl several times to ensure thorough mixing. If you are adding a solid garnish, it is at this moment when it should be added.

8.	Do not overmix. This will cause the gluten in the flour to develop, negatively affecting the product. In cakes such as pound cake, it will produce a dense cake, and in cookies, it will cause them to spread too much when they bake.

THE CUSTARD METHOD

A custard is defined as a dairy product that is thickened with eggs (crème brûlée, crème anglaise, crème caramel, flan, quiche) or with eggs and starch (pastry cream, chocolate pudding). It is a usually sweet, very moist, tender gel of egg protein. Custards are typically classified as boiled, stirred, and baked and are grouped in this book under the boiled custard or pastry cream, baked custard, or stirred custard or anglaise methods.

A boiled custard is thickened with eggs and cornstarch over direct heat. The idea is that heat will coagulate the proteins in the starch and gelatinize the cornstarch, which will in turn thicken the liquid, which is generally milk. The mixture, in theory, will have to boil for this to happen, but as you will read in the method below, boiling is not necessary. There is a way to make a thick, smooth pastry cream without submitting it to intense heat. Because we do not need to boil this custard, it is not necessary to call it a boiled custard; we will simply call it pastry cream.

This method can get extremely complicated if you do not follow the steps to the most exact detail. It is not easier than the traditional boiled custard method; it is different and not without its complications. However, it turns out a superior-quality custard with a very smooth mouthfeel.

There are some cons to this method. The first is that there is an enzyme in the egg yolk called amylase that breaks the cornstarch in the pastry cream down into sugar (retrogradation). The only way to neutralize this enzyme is by boiling the egg yolk, which can be done with the boiled custard method. However, the custard made by the following method will not be affected within 48 hours of making the pastry cream. Making too much pastry cream is not necessarily ideal, so this method is well suited for the pastry shop. The second con is that this custard is cooked until all the proteins are just cooked and no further, which means that the addition of a flavored liquid such as rum could potentially loosen the consistency of the custard too much.

Stirred custards are similar to boiled custards in that they are cooked over direct heat, but they differ in that they do not need to boil to reach the desired consistency (between 80°C/175°F to 85°C/185°F) and are thickened only by eggs. The most common example is crème anglaise.

Baked custards use only eggs and, as the name indicates, are baked in order to coagulate the egg protein. They are usually baked inside a ramekin in a hot water bath in an oven between 135°C/275°F and 160°C/325°F.

THE BOILED CUSTARD OR PASTRY CREAM METHOD IS AS FOLLOWS:

1. Warm the eggs to 21°C/70°F in a bowl over a hot water bath. Set aside. This is an important step, since it will help the egg yolks coagulate faster than if they were refrigerator cold (see Step 5).

2. Pour the first amount of milk in a deep pot or rondeau. It should be deep enough to hold the milk when it is at a rolling boil. Add the full amount of sugar, along with any flavors (vanilla, coffee, and so forth).

3. In a small bowl, combine the cornstarch with the second, smaller amount of milk. Mix well. Whisk in the tempered egg yolks.

Warm the first amount of milk along with the sugar and any flavorings in a large deep pot. Bring the mixture to a rolling boil.

Dump the milk in one motion into the egg, second amount of milk, and cornstarch mixture, whisking vigorously for 1 minute without stopping.

The finished pastry cream will be thick, smooth, and glossy.

4. Pour through a fine-mesh sieve into a large bowl. The bowl should be large enough to hold the entire amount of milk that is in the pot, but it should not be so big that it cools down the hot milk too much once it is added to the bowl.

5. Bring the milk and sugar to a rolling boil. Let it boil for 10 seconds, and then, in one motion (very important step: It must be one dumping motion, not a slow pour), dump it into the bowl with the yolks, cornstarch, and milk while whisking vigorously (preferably another person is doing the whisking while you dump). It is imperative that you do not hesitate when dumping the milk in one motion and that you do not use a slow pour; this is necessary in order to bring the temperature of the ingredients in the bowl up high enough to coagulate the protein in the egg yolks and gelatinize the cornstarch so it will thicken. Stir for about 1 minute without stopping. This is another very important step; if you stop even for a second to switch hands because your arm is tired, it may not work out.

6. Cover the pastry cream with plastic wrap and let it cool down over an ice water bath.

NOTE *Common examples of items made from this method are pastry cream, puddings, and coconut cream pie base.*

The Baked Custard Method

There are two approaches to this method. The first should be used if the base is going to be baked right away, and the second if the base is to be reserved to cook at a different time.

METHOD 1 IS AS FOLLOWS:

1. Preheat a convection or static oven to 135°C/275°F.

2. Place the ramekins (or other vessel in which the custard will be baked) in a sheet pan or hotel pan. The ramekins or the baking vessel should be shorter than the sheet pan or hotel pan, because you will have to pour water into the pan, and the ramekin or baking vessel needs to be surrounded by water to bake the custard properly.

3. In a sauce pot, combine all of the milk (or the milk and heavy cream mix) with half the sugar and any flavorings (vanilla, cinnamon, and so forth).

4. Combine the egg yolks and the other half of the sugar in a bowl. The bowl should be large enough to hold all of the components of the recipe.

5. Bring the milk (or milk with heavy cream) to a boil. Turn off the heat, and slowly pour all of this liquid into the bowl with the egg yolks and sugar while whisking. This process is known as tempering the egg yolks, in which the eggs are brought up to a high temperature without coagulating the proteins in them, which would result in a lumpy base.

6. Pass the mixture through a fine-mesh sieve. Pour into the prepared ramekins or vessel. A funnel gun works well for portion control. Fill nearly to the top.

7. Place the sheet pan or hotel pan in the oven. Pour hot water into it, being careful not to get any into the custard base. The water should come up to the same level the custard is inside the ramekins or baking vessel. If it is too low, the "exposed" custard will overbake, since it will come into direct contact with the heat from the oven.

8. Bake until you obtain a gelatinous jiggle. This means is that if you tap or gently move the ramekins or baking vessel, the custard will jiggle. This is because the protein in the eggs has coagulated just enough to have set but is still smooth and elastic. If it still sloshes around, it means the custard needs to bake further. If it is beyond a gelatinous jiggle and the surface does not look smooth, the custard is overbaked, and at this point there is no way to fix it.

9. Once the custard has baked, take the sheet pan or hotel pan out of the oven (carefully so as to not spill any water into the ramekins), and take the ramekins or baking vessel out of the water. Place them on a clean sheet pan and let them cool at room temperature. Once they are cool, reserve refrigerated, covered well with plastic wrap. Discard after 2 days.

NOTES *Some chefs prefer to cover the hotel pan with foil, which can in fact speed up the baking process. This is not a bad practice, but it will add moisture to the surface of the custard, and that can be detrimental for items like crème brûlée, since it will be very complicated to get the sugar to caramelize over a wet surface. However, this method works well if you are pressed for time.*

METHOD 2 IS AS FOLLOWS:

1. Prepare an ice water bath. Infuse the milk (or milk and heavy cream mixture) with the desired flavor; stir in the sugar while it is hot in order to dissolve it completely. Pass through a fine-mesh sieve. Cool the liquid in the ice water bath.

2. Once it has cooled down completely, stir in the egg yolks using a whisk. Pass the custard base through a fine-mesh sieve. Reserve refrigerated in an airtight container for up to 5 days.

3. To bake the custard, follow Steps 6 through 9 of the previous method (except do not pass the custard through a fine-mesh sieve, as that has already been done).

NOTES *This second method takes longer to bake than the first method, but the advantage to it is that you can make a large amount of base ahead of time and use it as you need it. Try to refrain from making the base using the first method and then cooling it down for future use, since this will start the coagulation process in the yolks and, in the end, will not yield ideal results. The general rule is that eggs should only be heated or cooked once.*

Other baked custards, such as pumpkin pie, cheesecake, or quiche, for example, simply require that the base ingredients be mixed in well with eggs (or egg yolks alone) and then baked. These items will not require the use of a water bath, which would prevent the crust from baking properly. Common examples of custards made using this method include crème brûlée, crème caramel, and its Latin cousin, flan.

The Stirred Custard or Anglaise Method

This method refers to the stirring motion that is necessary to cook this custard over a direct heat source (flame or induction). This type of custard is fully finished in a pot on the stove top. The stirring is done with either a wooden spoon (traditionally) or a whisk. A whisk covers more area than a spoon does and thus distributes heat more efficiently and evenly.

1. Prepare an ice water bath. In a sauce pot, combine all of the milk (or the milk and heavy cream mixture) with half the sugar and any flavorings (vanilla, cinnamon, and so forth).

2. Combine the egg yolks and the other half of the sugar in a bowl. The bowl should be large enough to hold all of the components of the recipe.

3. Bring the milk (or milk with heavy cream) to a boil. Turn off the heat, and slowly pour all of this liquid into the bowl with the egg yolks and sugar while whisking.

4. Return this mixture to the sauce pot and cook over medium-low heat, stirring constantly with a whisk.

5. Stir until the base has reached a maximum temperature of 85°C/185°F. Maintain this temperature long enough to thicken the custard until it reaches what is known as the nappé stage (anywhere between 3 and 5 minutes; it depends on the size of the batch you are making). Nappé means "coated" and what it has to coat is the back of a spoon. You are supposed to be able to run a finger through the sauce and it will leave a trace. In other words, if it were not quite yet ready to come off the stove, your finger would not be able to leave a trail, the liquid on the spoon being so loose that it would cover any trace of a trail. Evaluate the custard visually—does the custard look like it has thickened from its original state? Has it reached 85°C/185°F? Temperature and consistency are your best indicators of doneness.

6. Once you have reached the correct thickness/temperature, pass the liquid through a fine-mesh sieve and cool it quickly over the ice bath.

7. Once the custard has cooled, place it in an airtight container and refrigerate it for up to 4 days.

NOTE *This method is used most notably for custard-base ice creams and crème anglaise. A citrus curd can also be considered to fall into this category, but the difference is that a curd is mixed and cooked over a hot water bath, not directly inside a pot over heat.*

FOAMED PASTRY PREPARATIONS

This method refers to the properties of an egg foam (either whites or yolks or whites and yolks) used for a batter. There are three different methods within the foaming method: the cold foaming method, the warm foaming method, and the separation foaming method. Each method has a specific purpose.

First, what is a foam? A foam is the dispersion of a gas or air in a liquid. Proteins in the egg whites and/or egg yolks are unfolded through beating at the interface between air and liquid. The main function of foamed eggs is to give volume, texture, structure, and grain to a batter. Egg whites will produce a lot more volume than egg yolks do, but sometimes a batter will call for both of these foams. Egg white can be whipped to eight times its volume, while egg yolk can be whipped to only four times its volume. The reason for this is because egg yolks contain large amounts of fat, which inhibits the intake of air. When egg yolks are whipped to their full volume, it is called the *ribbon stage*, because if you lift the whip or whisk away from them, the strand that is dripping from it will form what looks like a ribbon over the surface of the whipped yolks. The color of the yolks will also be a very pale yellow on account of all of the air that has been incorporated into them.

It is important to whip ingredients to the correct volume, especially when it comes to foamed egg whites. Underwhipped egg whites will produce a coarse batter with low volume, while overwhipped whites will curdle from extensive protein coagulation; this coarseness will prevent the foam from being uniformly and smoothly folded into other ingredients in a batter. The goal of a proper foam is to obtain the largest amount of volume for a batter that it could not achieve on its own (without the foam).

In order to obtain the ideal egg white foam, egg whites should be beaten at room temperature, but cold whites will quickly warm up through friction as they whip anyway, so letting egg whites sit out to temper before whipping them, or warming them over a warm water bath, is not absolutely necessary for a good foam. Do use a clean stainless-steel bowl (large enough to hold the foam at its full volume) and a clean whisk or whip. Plastic bowls are not recommended since they are porous and can harbor foam "enemies" such as fat and other impurities. Finally, whites should have no traces of yolk or other foreign proteins (egg shell, grease, and so forth). Tradition dictates that old egg whites whip better, since they seem thinner or more watery, and this is true to an extent, but older eggs are also alkaline (as opposed to acidic), which affects the stability of the foam; in other words, the foam won't last very long at its full volume. Acidity, which is found in fresh eggs, produces a much more stable foam. Some ingredients can be added to help with the foaming process. For example, an acid such as cream of tartar helps stabilize foams. Adding powdered egg whites also helps stabilize a foam, since it gives the whites more of the proteins that trap air, thus increasing the foam's air-trapping power. Sugar also helps with stabilizing the foam, so long as it is added at the right time. Add the sugar when the whites have reached about half their volume, and then continue to whip until they have reached their full volume. When sugar is added at the beginning, it can extend the foaming time (the time it takes for the whites to reach their full volume), which will result in what feels like a denser meringue, but this is only because the prolonged whipping time has made the air bubbles smaller than their normal size. The volume will be the same. If the sugar is added when the whites have reached almost their full volume, the sugar may not dissolve completely. This sometimes results in a meringue that weeps moisture, since the large sugar crystals pull moisture from the egg whites (the term *hygroscopic* refers to the ability that sugar and salt have to pull water away from moist ingredients), resulting in large drops of water. Meringue weeping is also caused by overwhipping the meringue; the overcoagulated proteins literally squeeze the water out of the meringue.

THE COLD FOAMING METHOD IS AS FOLLOWS:

1. Beat the egg whites until they have quadrupled in volume, then gradually add the sugar.

2. Continue beating until the egg whites have reached eight times their original volume.

3. When the whites have reached full volume, the sifted dry ingredients are gently folded in.

NOTE *Examples of items made with this method are angel food cake and French macarons.*

THE WARM FOAMING METHOD IS AS FOLLOWS:

1. Place the whole eggs and sugar in a mixing bowl over a simmering water bath and whisk until they reach 50°C/120°F. Beat this mixture until it quadruples in volume.

2. Gently fold the sifted dry ingredients into the egg mixture.

3. At this point, pour a small amount of batter into a separate bowl. Temper the melted, but cooled, butter (or oil) into the batter, and then fold this mixture into the remaining batter.

NOTE *Génoise (or sponge cake) is the most common example of an item made using this method.*

THE SEPARATION FOAMING METHOD IS AS FOLLOWS:

1. Separate the eggs.

2. Place the egg whites in the bowl of an electric mixer fitted with a whip attachment, and beat on high speed until they reach medium peaks. Slowly pour in the sugar, and continue beating until the whites reach stiff peaks.

3. Beat the egg yolks in a mixing bowl with sugar until they quadruple in volume (ribbon stage).

4. Gently fold the dry ingredients into the whipped yolks.

5. Gently fold the whipped whites into the previous mixture.

6. Fold melted, but cooled, butter (or oil) into the mix.

NOTE *Joconde, the cake used to make a classic opera cake, is made with this method.*

From all of these complicated methods, we go to an overly simple one created by Ferran Adrià. In his method, all of the ingredients are combined in a bowl with a whisk, and then they are passed through a fine-mesh sieve. This batter is placed inside a whipped cream canister, which is then filled with CO_2. This gas aerates the batter in a matter of seconds. Once the batter sits in refrigeration for a few hours, it is then portioned into plastic cups, which are heated in the microwave for about 45 seconds. The result is a very airy sponge cake, not at all like a génoise.

The downside to this method is that you can only "cook" small portions at a time. And also, it is not a replacement for any of the cakes mentioned in this method. A regular génoise tastes much better, depending on the recipe.

NOTE *The proper method for folding egg whites into a batter and anything else is as follows:*

Fold foamed whites into a mix (batter) by pushing a rubber spatula down the side of the mixer bowl, then drawing it up the center of the bowl and folding some of the lower layer on top (forming the letter "U"), while turning the bowl in the opposite direction with your other hand to optimize the amount of foamed egg that is being folded into other ingredients.

THE MERINGUE METHODS

Alphabetically, meringues should not follow the foaming method, but logistically they will. The reason for this is because we continue on the same principles, that is, the use and purpose of the foamed egg white. In this method, the foamed egg white can be used on its own, or it can be incorporated into another ingredient, either to form a batter or to make a ready-to-eat pastry preparation such as a crème Chiboust.

There are three categories of meringue: French or common, Swiss, and Italian. They are also classified as uncooked meringues (French) and cooked meringues (Swiss and Italian). In general, the ratio of egg whites to sugar for meringues will be 1:2, but this depends on what they are being used for, so it is not written in stone. The sugar will act as a stabilizer for the foam, and the more sugar, the more stable the foam.

Typically, a meringue will be whipped until it reaches its largest volume, or eight times its original volume. This is also known as the stiff-peak stage. Egg white foams can be whipped to three different stages, depending on their use. The first stage is the soft-peak stage, when the foam barely holds its shape. The second stage is the medium peak stage, when the foam can hold its shape briefly before dropping, and then there is the third and final stage, the aforementioned stiff peaks, in which the foam will completely hold a peak and not move. After this stage, the foam has been overwhipped and will look curdled.

The French Meringue Method (Uncooked Meringue)

This is the method used in the cold foaming method and the separation foaming method. It is the simplest method for making a meringue.

THE FRENCH MERINGUE METHOD IS AS FOLLOWS:

1. Place the egg whites in the bowl of an electric mixer fitted with a whip attachment. If using an acid such as lemon juice or cream of tartar (the acid will promote stability in the foam), it should be added at this time.

2. Whip the whites on high speed. When the whites have reached half their final volume (they will have quadrupled in size), slowly pour the sugar in down the side of the bowl. Ideally, granulated sugar such as superfine or bakers' is recommended, because the smaller the crystal, the faster it will dissolve into the whites.

3. Continue to whip until the whites have reached the desired volume. This desired volume is not always necessarily eight times the original volume. It could be slightly less. When a French meringue is whipped to full volume or stiff peaks, it can be difficult to fold it into another component smoothly and efficiently, since the foam will be too hard and stiff to incorporate into another equally dense or denser preparation. Whipping to maximum volume is not a problem if the meringue is to be used on its own (as a crisp meringue), but it can be an issue if the meringue is to be folded into another component. So if folding into another component, don't whip to full volume; whip until just under full volume.

NOTE *This method can be used for French macarons and soufflés, for example. Raw eggs should never be used unless the egg whites are pasteurized, and even then, this foam is not permanent unless the proteins in the egg whites have been coagulated by heat.*

The Swiss Meringue Method (Cooked Meringue)

This method requires the use of heat.

THE SWISS MERINGUE METHOD IS AS FOLLOWS:

1. Combine the egg whites with the sugar the bowl of an electric mixer. Place the bowl over a hot water bath and stir with a whisk until the mixture reaches between 57°C/135°F and 60°C/140°F. Be careful to not exceed this temperature, because doing so will coagulate the egg white proteins and result in a lumpy meringue. This process helps dissolve the sugar and makes the egg whites safe for consumption.

2. While the mixture is hot, attach the bowl to the mixer fitted with a whip attachment and beat until it has reached the desired volume. At this point, it can be folded into another preparation or dried to obtain a crisp meringue.

The Italian Meringue Method (Cooked Meringue)

This method also requires the use of heat and is the most complicated one. For Italian meringue, combine the egg whites when they have reached their full volume with sugar that has been cooked to the soft-ball stage (see cooked sugar methods on page 47). The challenge is to coordinate these two events.

THE ITALIAN MERINGUE METHOD IS AS FOLLOWS:

1. In a sauce pot, combine the sugar with enough water to moisten all of the sugar, typically 4 parts sugar to 1 part water. Turn the heat to high. Meanwhile, prepare an ice water bath. Cook the sugar to between 115°C/240°F to 121°C/250°F.

2. Beat the egg whites in the bowl of an electric mixer fitted with a whip attachment on medium speed. Before the egg whites reach their full volume, the sugar should have reached the desired temperature. If not, turn the mixer down to low speed.

3. When the sugar reaches the required temperature and the egg whites are not yet at their full volume, shock the sauce pot in the prepared ice bath for a few seconds. This is only to stop the sugar from cooking further. If, however, the sugar is at the correct temperature and the egg whites are at their full volume, just pour the sugar directly into the foamed whites. It is important to follow a few safety precautions. When pouring the sugar into the whipping whites, turn the speed of the mixer down to medium and pour the sugar down the side of the bowl. If the sugar is poured over the fast-moving whip, the hot sugar may very well splatter.

4. Continue to whip until the meringue has cooled. At this point, it can be incorporated into another preparation or dried in an oven to obtain a meringue.

NOTE *This method is used for Italian buttercream (the butter is to be added soft and while the meringue is still semi-warm so that the butter can be fully incorporated), crème Chiboust, and cooked-sugar French macarons, among other examples.*

AERATED DESSERTS UTILIZING FOAMS

This method is for preparations that contain one or up to three different foams, from egg whites, egg yolks, whole eggs, and/or heavy cream. These items include mousses, creams (which are traditionally called "Bavarois" or "Bavarian," but in this book they will be referred to as "creams"), semifreddo, parfaits, soufflés, bombes, Chiboust, diplomat, sabayon (or zabaglione), foams (or *espumas*), and Chantilly. The foams are used mainly to add lightness and a smooth texture. Some of these items can be simply refrigerated, or they can be frozen.

KEY POINTS TO CONSIDER WHEN MAKING AERATED DESSERTS:

▓ The flavor base will always be made first, before any foamed components, and can be what is known as a *bombe* (see page 16). Ideally the flavor base should be tepid or slightly warm. If adding gelatin and the base is too cold, the gelatin will set on contact; if the base is too hot, whipped heavy cream will melt when it is added.

▓ If using heavy cream, it will only whip properly if it is cold enough (between 1°C/33°F and 4°C/39°F). Any warmer and the fat in the cream will be too soft to be able to hold air bubbles. When whipping heavy cream, it is not a good idea to whip it completely stiff. If it is too stiff, you will have the same problem as you find with very stiff egg white foams. They do not combine very well with other components, and the result is not very smooth. Whip the cream to slightly under medium-stiff peaks to be able to fold it in easily and obtain a smooth end product. Once the cream has been whipped, it needs to be kept cold in order to maintain the air bubbles; if left at room temperature, the cream will soften and deflate.

▓ The consistency of the foam is crucial to an even mixture. If the egg white foam is whipped very stiff, you will not be able to fold it into the flavor base.

THE PROPER FOLDING PROCEDURE IS AS FOLLOWS:

1. As soon as the foam has reached the desired volume, it should be folded into the remaining ingredients. Do not wait to fold in the foam because even though it might be stable enough for a few minutes, you want to take advantage of the maximum volume you have obtained. The longer the foam sits, the more it will deflate, even if it isn't perceptible.

2. Place half of the foam on top of the flavor base. Bring a rubber spatula or bowl scraper down the side of the bowl, all the way down to the base, and then bring it up through the center of the bowl as you curve your hand upward. The motion will resemble the letter "J". At the same time, spin the bowl a quarter turn toward you with your free hand every time your other hand performs the "J" motion. This will maximize the amount of the foam that is folded into the flavor base and will result in the least amount of deflation. It is more effective than if you didn't turn the bowl. You have to be well coordinated to perform this action correctly, but even if you are not, practice helps.

3. Perform the same folding motion with the remaining foam. The foam is folded in two additions to prevent a decrease in volume; if you try to fold in all the foam at once, there will be a significant amount of air knocked out by the time all of the ingredients are incorporated. With two additions, the mixture will loosen up with the first addition, and the second addition will incorporate with greater ease.

4. Some recipes contain two or three foams, and many pastry shops are not fortunate enough to own two or three mixers. Ideally, all of the foams would be made at the same time and folded into each other as soon as they reach full volume. If you have only one mixer (or none), start by foaming the most stable foam, which is the heavy cream foam, and refrigerate it immediately once you have obtained the desired peaks in order to maintain its volume. Next, whip the egg yolks, and then finally the egg whites. Always fold the lightest ingredient into the heaviest (egg whites into egg yolks, then heavy cream into the previous mix or heavy cream into egg yolks).

5. Finally, portion the finished product into the desired vessel and refrigerate or freeze.

NOTE *If the recipe contains chocolate, it must be melted and then cooled to room temperature (21°C/70°F). It should be no colder than that because, if the recipe requires folding whipped heavy cream into chocolate and the chocolate is too cold, it will harden almost immediately on contact with the cold heavy cream. The result will be chocolate chunks throughout the product instead of a uniform mixture.*

Mousses

A mousse will usually contain what is known as a *pâte à bombe* or *bombe base*. A bombe is made with 60 percent yolks and 40 percent sugar that can both be combined in a bowl, heated over a water bath to 60°C/140°F while stirring with a whisk, and then whipped to ribbon stage. Alternatively, the sugar can be cooked separately to 115°C/240°F while the egg yolks whip on high speed in a mixer. When the egg yolks have reached the ribbon stage, the hot sugar is poured down the side of the bowl as the mixer whips, and then the mixture is whipped until it cools to room temperature. Bloomed gelatin is added to the bombe base while it is still warm, in order to dissolve the gelatin. Fruit purées, nut pastes, caramel, and melted chocolate can be added to this bombe base as long as they are also at room temperature. Whipped heavy cream is then folded into the base. It is crucial to refrigerate the mousse soon after it is made so that the product can set before it loses too much volume at room temperature.

There is no one method for mousse, since there are many recipes that differ with regard to using a bombe base or what kind of foamed ingredient(s) will be added. Some recipes call for a cooked meringue to be folded into it as well as whipped heavy cream. The general construction of a mousse is: bombe + flavor + heavy cream. Other additions, such as gelatin or cooked meringues, are optional.

Creams (Bavarois/Bavarian)

A cream will usually contain a custard base, and an Italian meringue and/or whipped heavy cream is folded into it. The custard base can be replaced with a fruit purée in some instances, or fruit purée can be used to make the custard base. The custard can be infused with almost any flavor. Gelatin is added to the custard while it is still warm in order to melt it. Once the custard is tepid, Italian meringue is folded into it, and then heavy cream is folded in.

Semifreddo

Semifreddo is an Italian term. Literally translated, it means "half-cold," but the Italian term should be more like *semicongelato* or *mezzocongelato*, which would translate to "half-frozen." The finished dessert is so light and airy that it barely seems to be frozen (hence the name). A semifreddo contains a sweetened, flavored egg yolk foam (bombe base) that has a meringue is folded into it (usually a French meringue, but pasteurized egg whites will need to be used since it is an uncooked meringue), and then whipped heavy cream is folded in. This dessert utilizes three foams, which is what helps give it such a light consistency.

Parfaits

Parfait means "perfect" in French. While that is a matter of personal preference, what defines a parfait is that it is a (sometimes frozen) dessert generally made with a flavored bombe base plus whipped heavy cream, and occasionally Italian meringue. Traditionally it is piped into a glass and then frozen, but it can also be piped into a mold, frozen, and unmolded.

Soufflés

In the most traditional and strict sense, a soufflé is a hot dessert in which a flavored base (crème anglaise, fruit purée, chocolate, or a combination) is combined with a French meringue *à la minute*, portioned into a ramekin, and then baked undisturbed until it rises well above the rim of the ramekin. Some chefs use a pâte à choux base or pastry cream base, which technically is cheating, since a soufflé should contain no starch (flour or cornstarch) to aid in its structure development in the oven. It must be served within a few minutes of extracting it from the oven, lest it lose its volume. This term is now very loosely used for a variety of desserts that are not even hot; in fact, they are frozen. Foams utilized in frozen soufflés can vary between pastry chefs. The only reasons they are referred to as "soufflés" are that they resemble traditional hot soufflés and they generally contain an egg white foam.

Bombe

Bombe refers more to a shape than an actual dessert. A bombe has a demi-sphere shape that apparently looks like a bomb (its translation from the French). It is similar to a parfait but contains more whipped cream, so it is lighter. This bombe is not to be confused with a pâte a bombe.

NOTE *Many desserts with the demi-sphere shape are also called bombes, even if they are not technically in this category. This dessert is often served frozen.*

Chiboust

A Chiboust is a pastry cream base that is flavored and has an amount of gelatin added to it while it is warm. An Italian meringue is then folded into it while the pastry cream is warm. This mixture is piped or poured into a mold and allowed to set in a cold environment. It is finished by browning the top in a salamander or broiler and should be served warm.

Diplomat Cream

A diplomat cream is made by folding whipped heavy cream into pastry cream. A general ratio is 1 part pastry cream to 4 parts whipped cream. This is mostly used for filling layered cakes or éclairs and for desserts such as the gâteau Saint-Honoré.

Sabayon or Zabaglione

This dessert is made with a single foam of egg yolks; the foam itself is the actual dessert and it is usually served hot with seasonal fruit. The process for sabayon combines egg yolks with sugar and often Marsala, port, Prosecco, or Champagne. These ingredients are whipped by hand over a hot water bath until they have tripled in volume. Sabayon should be served warm. As it gets cold it will lose volume and the ingredients will separate.

Chantilly Cream

Chantilly cream is a whipped heavy cream that can be plain or steeped with flavoring ingredients such as tea or spices and that is lightly sweetened and often flavored with vanilla. Alternatively, ingredients such as chocolate can be combined with the cream by bringing the cream to a boil and pouring it over the white, milk, or dark chocolate. Stir to melt the chocolate, chill the mixture, and then whip it. This closely resembles a mousse, but it is much lighter since it contains no eggs.

Foam (or Espuma)

Foam is one of the newest members of the foamed dessert club. The method consists of pouring the liquid to be aerated into an iSi siphon, closing the lid tightly, and then filling the canister with one or two charges of CO_2, which will fill the liquid with very small air bubbles. This dispersion of CO_2 that occurs throughout the liquid creates a foam-like consistency that is as light as air. The result is that the liquid will have the same consistency as though it had been whipped by hand or using a mixer. This works for some ingredients that cannot be whipped in the traditional way; the only caveat is that these liquids will require an ingredient that will be able to trap the air bubbles and keep them in place. Heavy cream, for example, contains fat, which is the component that is responsible for trapping air. But other ingredients, such as fruit juices or other liquids that are dairy-free, will require the addition of gelatin in order to trap air bubbles and create a foam.

GELLING METHODS

Not too long ago, pastry shops were limited to using gelatin and pectin, and sometimes agar-agar, as the only gelling agents. With the changes that came with modern cuisine and the popularity of new methods and techniques utilizing alternative gelling agents barely seen in small commercial kitchens, a new realm of products became readily available to most chefs. Thanks to this newfound popularity, there is an abundance of gelling agents available in quantities that are easier to purchase than they were a few years ago, when they were used exclusively by industrial manufacturers in very large amounts.

These ingredients are technically known as *hydrocolloids*. A hydrocolloid is a substance that gels in the presence of moisture. A gel can also thicken, stabilize, emulsify, and form a foam. Most hydrocolloids are of biological origin. All have been purified (refined), and some have been processed, but nevertheless the raw material used is of either marine, plant, animal, or microbial origin.

The following is a list of the most widely used and recognized hydrocolloids, along with brief descriptions of how to use them as gelling agents. There is much more information available on these ingredients, but for the purpose of practicality, this text will only describe how they are to be manipulated to form a gel.

Agar-Agar

Agar-agar requires the application of heat to fully hydrate. Combine it with a liquid while it is cold, and then bring to a boil while stirring. Boil for 10 seconds to fully hydrate the agar-agar. Pour into the desired mold and let it set. There are different varieties of agar-agar available that do not require a full boil to hydrate the agar-agar, as well as agar-agar that is mixed with other hydrocolloids to obtain a more elastic gel (see the recipe for Crème Chantilly Ribbon on page 144; see Resources, page 520). Agar-agar gels are brittle and not very smooth in texture. They also have a very present taste of the ocean that is easily detectable if they are used with liquids that are not intensely flavored. Agar-agar is a thermo-reversible gel, meaning that it can be remelted with heat. Use agar-agar with strongly flavored liquids to subdue its intrinsic taste. Refer to the mixture on page 145; it gives you the best qualities of all of those hydrocolloids.

QUANTITY USED TO GEL: VARIES DEPENDING ON USE, .4% TO 1%

Carrageenan Gum

There are three varieties of carrageenan gum: kappa, iota, and lambda. They need to be dispersed in a cold liquid and then heated to above 60°C/140°F to fully hydrate them, except for kappa, which needs to come almost to a boil to gel. It is a thermo-reversible gel. Kappa forms a strong, firm, brittle gel, while iota is a more elastic gel. They both set quickly.

QUANTITY USED TO GEL: .75% TO 1%

Gelatin

Gelatin forms a very elastic gel. It is available in powdered form or in sheets; both require cold water to hydrate. Recipes with powdered gelatin will usually call for adding the exact amount of water that is needed to hydrate the gelatin, and this water is part of the finished product. Gelatin sheets are hydrated in very cold water (usually ice water) until they have softened. This process requires only a few minutes, and the excess moisture should be squeezed off by hand. Both types of gelatin require a warm liquid to melt and dissolve them. The liquid should be above 60°C/140°F. Excessive heat can destroy the gelling properties of gelatin; above 85°C/185°F is not recommended. There are three types of sheet gelatin, which are classified according to their strength: bronze (weakest gelatin), silver (medium strength), and gold (strongest). This book will utilize silver gelatin for all of its recipes, except for the marshmallows on page 492. Gelatin sheets vary in weight, but the average is between 2.5 and 3.5 grams depending on the manufacturer. It is because of this variation that the gelatin in this book is specified by weight in each recipe and not by the sheet amount.

QUANTITY USED TO GEL: WILL VARY WIDELY DEPENDING ON THE USE, SINCE IT CAN BE USED TO FORM THE SOFTEST OF GELS AS WELL AS VERY STRONG GELS

Methocel

Methylcellulose (MC), hydroxypropylmethylcellulose (HPMC), hydroxypropylcellulose (HPC), and carboxymethylcellulose (CMC) are all derivatives of Methocel.

MC and HPMC are the most widely used; HPC and CMC are seldom used and will not be elaborated upon. Methocel is used for gelling, sheet forming ("paper"; see the recipe on page 149), and as an aerator that helps liquids take in air more readily. It forms thermo-reversible gels with a variety of textures from brittle (crisp) to soft.

There are five categories of Methocel, and within these there are different viscosities (19 total). The five categories are:

- **A (from MC): Forms firm gels; A7C is used in this book to form papers (see page 149).**

- **E (from HPMC): Forms semifirm gels; useful for forming films.**

- **F (from HPMC): Forms semifirm gels; F50 is used to make foams (see the recipe for Carrot Foam on page 367).**

- **K (from HPMC): Forms soft gels.**

- **SGA (stands for "Super-Gel"; from MC): Forms very firm gels.**

The best way to hydrate these hydrocolloids is by shearing; the liquid is placed inside a blender cup and the blender is turned on high speed, and then the powder is slowly poured in. The liquid should be cold because one of the aspects of this hydrocolloid is that it gels in the presence of heat. Depending on the category, it can gel from a temperature as low as 38°C/100°F (SGA) to one as high as 80°C/175°F (K). It is thermo-reversible in the presence of heat, but once it is cooled to its gelling temperature, it remains gelled.

Gellan Gum

There are two varieties: high acyl and low acyl. High acyl is soft and elastic, while low acyl is brittle and hard, which is why sometimes they are used in combination (25 percent high acyl to 75 percent low acyl) to obtain a hybrid.

This is the preferred hydrocolloid, since it produces gelled liquids with a very good flavor delivery, and they can be as clear as water (see the Sweet Lime Jelly on page 161). To hydrate, combine the gellan powder with a cold liquid, then whisk over high heat until the liquid is clear and the powder has dissolved. It won't necessarily need to boil. High-acyl gellan sets at about 65°C/150°F, and low-acyl gellan sets at about 40°C/105°F. It is a thermo-reversible gel, if exposed to heat for a long period of time.

QUANTITY USED TO GEL: .05% TO 1%

Guar Gum

Guar gum is used as a gel but also as an emulsifier and a thickener. Its thickening power is eight times stronger than cornstarch and sixteen times stronger than flour; for this reason it is also used in gluten-free doughs to improve their elasticity. It is also very good at preventing the formation of large ice crystals in ice cream. It can often be used interchangeably with xanthan gum because it has similar properties.

QUANTITY USED TO GEL: .2% TO .5%

Gum Arabic

Gum arabic is a gel only in very large quantities; mostly it is used as an emulsifier, and to a lesser extent as an adherent. It can be hydrated in cold or hot water through shearing. The quantities used vary widely. It is often used in combination with xanthan gum to emulsify.

QUANTITY USED TO GEL: 1% TO 40%

Locust Bean Gum (LBG)

Used as a stabilizer and as a thickener, locust bean gum is widely used in combination with other hydrocolloids, such as carrageenan. When used in combination with xanthan gum it can form a gel. It can be hydrated in cold or hot water through shearing.

QUANTITY USED TO GEL: .5% TO 1%

Pectin

Pectin is a wonderful ingredient with incredible versatility. It generally comes from apples and is not thermo-reversible. There is more than one type of pectin.

High-Methoxyl (HM) Pectin

This gels at very high temperatures (85°C/185°F). It requires an acid and heat to gel. It is used widely in jams and pâte de fruit. It is incorporated into cooked fruit once it reaches a certain temperature or degrees Brix, depending on the fruit being cooked, and it is typically added at the end of the cooking process. The pectin should be combined with a small amount of sugar in order for it not to clump when it is added to a boiling liquid. The sugar helps to evenly disperse the pectin. An acid is added after the pectin has been added in order to form the gel. The acid can be as simple as lemon juice or citric acid.

Low-Methoxyl (LM) and Low-Methoxyl Amidated (LMA) Pectin

This is also known as *universal pectin* because it can be used to gel a wider range of liquids, including dairy and other liquids with fat, which HM pectin cannot gel. It does not require an acid to gel, but it does require calcium. The calcium added is a simple solution of calcium and water, and it is added to the liquid in the same amount as the pectin. To hydrate the pectin, add the calcium solution to the liquid to be gelled, unless it happens to be a dairy product. Bring it to a boil and slowly pour the pectin in while stirring. Boil for about 1 minute while stirring constantly. LM pectin gels between 30°C/86°F and 60°C/140°F and is thermo-reversible.

Sodium Alginate

Derived from brown seaweed, sodium alginate is one of the main ingredients used for reverse spherification in this book (see the recipe on page 135). Sodium alginate requires calcium in order to gel. Sodium alginate is combined with cold water and then boiled in order for it to hydrate. It gels cold or hot, as long as there is calcium present. In this book, calcium lactate is used for reverse spherification, but other forms of calcium may be used in simpler ways, such as gently pouring a dairy product directly into a sodium alginate bath. The dairy product or the calcium lactate–laced liquid forms a gel on its surface when it is dipped in the sodium alginate bath, forming a very thin membrane that is quite similar to an egg yolk. The longer it sits in the bath, the thicker this outer membrane gets. It is a thermo-irreversible gel.

QUANTITY USED TO GEL: .5% TO 1%

Xanthan Gum

Xanthan gum is of bacterial origin and it is widely used as an emulsifier. It emulsifies cold and hot liquids under shearing, and between .2% and 1% by weight can be used for certain emulsions. It is also used as a thickener. Xanthan gum will thicken most liquids significantly, increasing their surface tension but not their texture in a very significant way when used in small quantities. In larger quantities, it can have an off-putting mucilaginous texture and appearance, which is not appetizing to see or taste in a dish.

QUANTITY USED TO GEL: .2% TO 1%

THE LAMINATION METHOD

This method is used to make items such as puff pastry, croissants, and Danish. It consists of layering dough and butter in even, consistent layers through manually extending and folding the dough and the butter together. The purpose of lamination is to develop multiple layers of dough and butter that help leaven the dough and contribute to the flaky, tender, and light characteristics of laminated products.

An entire chapter could be written about the process of lamination; this section will stick to the basic steps of the process since this book will contain only one recipe that utilizes this method: the puff pastry on page 216. The method described here will be limited to lamination and baking for puff pastry and will not cover croissant and Danish doughs, which have a separate method.

THE LAMINATION METHOD IS AS FOLLOWS:

1. Make the dough and refrigerate it. The dough is a simple dough of all-purpose flour, salt, sugar, butter (soft), and cold water, and it should be mixed just until it becomes a homogenous mass. Shape the dough into a ball, cover with plastic wrap, and let it relax for 30 minutes. When the dough is adequately rested, it must be shaped into a rectangle and refrigerated until chilled. This rectangle should be slightly larger than twice the size of the butter block.

2. Make the butter block. The butter should be at room temperature. Shape it into a rectangle. There are various ways to achieve this, but for the most part the easiest and most economical way to do this is by placing the butter on a sheet of parchment paper and manually shaping it into the desired size. Alternatively, if you make a lot of puff pastry, you may have frames made to fit the quantity of butter you need. After the butter block is made, it needs to be refrigerated so that it becomes firm again. Some chefs would say that you can use it right away, but after manipulating it to form the rectangle you need, it will be too soft. You are better off refrigerating it and then softening it again to the point where it is pliable, but not as soft as it was after shaping the block.

3. This is what the butter block needs to look like in proportion to the dough:

Place the butter block on the right half of the dough. There should be about 2.50 cm/1 in of dough around the butter block.

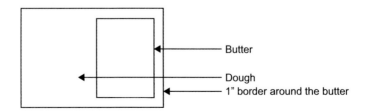

Butter

Dough
1" border around the butter

4. The butter and the dough need to be the same consistency. The dough is at the proper consistency if it is refrigerated—it should be firm but pliable. The butter also needs to be pliable. There are two ways to achieve this: One is to pull it out of the refrigerator a couple of hours before using it so that it reaches 20°C/68°F; another is to microwave it in brief intervals to reach this temperature. If you lack a microwave, you can soften it by pounding it gently with a wooden dowel. The consistency of the butter should be the same as that of the dough. The butter should feel similar to what the muscle below your thumb feels like when the thumb is flexed.

5. Place the butter block on top of the right half of the chilled dough. There should be about a 2.5-cm/1-in frame of dough around the top and right border around the butter.

6. Lift the left side of the dough over to the right side, as if you were closing a book. Push down the top and right borders using the heel of your hand in order to seal the dough around the butter using. This border ideally will be flattened by the time you are done. Be careful to not press down on the actual butter. You are simply looking to lock in the butter. Tuck the resulting flap of dough under the dough.

7. With the spine away from you and the seam facing you, roll the dough out or sheet it using a sheeter horizontally until it is 1.25 cm/.5 in thick. It should be at least two times longer than it originally was, but the width must remain the same; it is important to conserve the rectangular shape, so manually shape the dough into a rectangle if needed, without being too rough on the dough. It is crucial not to damage the dough or the butter inside it. Brush off the excess flour.

8. You will perform what is known as a book fold or single fold: Fold the left side of the dough on top of the right side of the dough. Even out the borders so that the dough remains square or rectangular. (Ideally it will be square, but a rectangle is fine as well. When it is neither of those, you need to make shaping adjustments to get the dough into shape; an even square or rectangle will ensure even layering of dough and butter. If it is oblique, rhomboidal, or oval, the even layering will be compromised.)

9. Let the dough rest for at least 15 minutes. This time can be spent in the reach-in and/or at room temperature. What is important is to keep the dough at the right consistency (which, as referenced in Step 4, should be that of your flexed thumb muscle). This means that it may spend 5 minutes in the reach-in, or the whole 15. Those 15 minutes are also important to let the dough relax. In fact, that is the only reason you let it rest between folds, but as the 15 minutes go by, the dough and butter can get soft if the ambient temperature is too warm for it, or if the dough and the butter were somewhat soft to begin with. If you do not relax it, it will pull into strange shapes when it bakes. Also, if the dough or the butter gets too hard or too soft, it is almost an irreparable mistake. If the butter portion inside the dough gets too hard from being refrigerated, you will not be able to fix this by letting the dough sit out at room temperature, since although the butter will eventually soften, the dough will get too soft. Remember, in order to achieve proper lamination, the dough and the butter should extend or stretch at the same rate. If one of them is not cooperating, your lamination will be compromised.

10. After the 15 minutes are up, perform your next book fold. Place the dough on a sheeter or work surface with the spine to your right. Sheet the dough or stretch it horizontally so that the dough is a few inches longer. Rotate the dough 90 degrees to your left, so that the spine of the dough is now away from you. Then sheet the dough or stretch it until it is 1.25 cm/.5 in thick. Brush the excess flour off the surface of the dough. Perform the book fold by folding the left side of the dough over the right side of the dough. Let it relax again for 15 minutes. You will do this three more times to obtain a total of five folds.

11. After the fifth book fold, cover the dough well with plastic wrap and then freeze it for 30 minutes. You are looking for a dough that is firm but not rock-hard. This will prevent the dough from getting damaged when you sheet it thin.

12. Sheet the dough down to the desired thickness and brush off the excess flour. Cover it well again with plastic and return it to the freezer. You may reserve it frozen for 2 months if it is well wrapped, or you can use it once it has relaxed for about 45 minutes in the freezer. The ideal consistency for working with the dough is semi-frozen, when it is slightly malleable but you can also handle it without damaging it.

13. Cut the dough into the desired shape. A wheel cutter works the best for this dough.

14. Brush the dough with egg wash and then bake it. It is also best to bake it when it is semi-frozen.

THE PÂTE À CHOUX METHOD OR THE "PRE-COOKED" METHOD

The pâte à choux method is also known as the pre-cooked method because the flour is pre-cooked before the batter is baked. Pâte à choux is an item that seems to suffer from an identity crisis. Some say it is a dough (though it is too loose to be a dough), while some say it is a batter (though it is too dense to be a batter). It will refer to it as a batter in this book, because it has more of the qualities of a batter than those of a dough. I hesitate to utilize the *pre-cooked* term for this method because there are other pastry preparations that are precooked but have nothing to do with choux, such as coconut macaroons and Florentine cookies. Because of this, it will be referred to simply as the pâte à choux method.

THE PÂTE À CHOUX METHOD IS AS FOLLOWS:

1. Preheat a hearth oven to 220°C/430°F.

2. Line a sheet pan with a nonstick rubber mat.

3. Prepare an ice water bath. It should be large enough to hold the bowl in which the choux will be mixed.

4. If using the craquelin topping (see the recipe on page 327) for the top of the choux, make sure all of the pieces are cut to the correct size.

5. Put the desired tip inside a piping bag. The tip depends on what item you are making (éclairs, religieuses or nuns, cream puffs, and so forth).

6. Boil the water with the sugar, salt, and butter over high heat. Add the milk powder and return to a boil. Turn off the heat and quickly stir in the flour. Turn the heat to medium-low (closer to low) and cook the paste for 2 minutes, stirring constantly. This is how the method gets its name; the starch in the flour is being pregelatinized at this point, moisture is evaporating, and the sugar and salt are dissolving.

7. Remove the pot from the heat and transfer the paste to a mixing bowl. Stir the choux over the prepared ice bath with a wooden spoon until cool. This method benefits the paste more than cooling it in a mixer using the paddle attachment. The paddle method seems to break the paste down into chunks and granules of paste that don't necessarily produce a smooth and even choux; in fact, this method produces a lumpy choux.

8. Add the eggs in 4 to 6 additions. Stop the mixer, drop the bowl, and scrape the sides after each addition has been fully incorporated; this will reduce the possibility of lumps in the choux. You may not need to add the entire amount of eggs. Check the consistency. If you follow the instructions precisely, the eggs should be the exact amount needed for the recipe. If there was not enough evaporation during the precooking process, the batter will require fewer eggs. If there was too much evaporation, the batter will require more eggs. Try to follow the method closely and you will avoid this problem. You should have a smooth, shiny paste.

9. Pipe the choux to the desired shapes.

10. Once they are piped, spray a fine mist of water on them and, if the recipe calls for it, place the craquelin dough on top of them.

11. Place the tray in the hearth oven and shut it down with the vents open and the door slightly ajar. Bake for 40 to 45 minutes. Check to see if they are done by breaking one open; it should be hollow or mostly hollow. The sides of the choux should be just slightly white, but the rest should have an evenly browned color.

12. Let them cool at room temperature before filling them. At this point they can be reserved frozen, wrapped tightly. When they are needed, they can be refreshed in a hot oven for a few minutes to evaporate any accumulated moisture and re-crisp the choux.

13. Finish as desired with fondant, ganache, confectioners' sugar, or other item.

NOTE *The recipe on page 327 calls for milk powder instead of whole milk, because we do not want the fat from the milk, only the flavor. Milk, because of the sugars it contains, will "soften" the choux (sugar is a tenderizer).*

THE RUBBED DOUGH METHOD OR THE CUT-IN METHOD

This method will not be widely used in this book, since it is generally used for breakfast pastries such as scones and biscuits as well as for pie dough. However, it is important to understand it as a basic pastry method. It is known as the rubbed dough method because originally this dough was made only by hand by rubbing cold pieces of butter into flour with the palms of one's hands. Now it is not limited to hand mixing; it can be done in an electric mixer using a paddle attachment to obtain the same result. The crux of this method is that the dough is made by rubbing butter into flour (and other ingredients such as cold water or heavy cream) in order to obtain a flaky dough. Flakiness is determined by how much or how little the butter is cut into the flour. The smaller the pieces of butter, the less flaky the dough will be. The larger the pieces of butter, the flakier the dough will be. Of course, there is such a thing as a piece of butter that is too large; in this case it will just melt out of the dough and not provide any flakiness.

1.   Cut the cold fat into approximately 1.25-cm to 2.5-cm/½-in to 1-in cubes.

2.   Place the fat on top of the flour.

3.   Work the fat into the flour either by rubbing it between the palms of your hands or by using an electric mixer with a paddle attachment.

4.   For a flaky dough, work the fat only until it is about the size of a walnut.

5.   Add the cold liquid to the mixture and carefully incorporate it into the dough; this will further cut the butter into the dough, making it smaller. Mix only until it is just combined and barely holds together; it will look like a shaggy mass. The final size of the butter should be about the size of a pea.

6.   Refrigerate the dough and make sure it is completely chilled and relaxed before using it. Some recipes require that the dough is rolled and folded to further incorporate the fat. Always chill the dough before baking it.

THE STRAIGHT DOUGH MIXING METHOD
(for Enriched Dough)

An enriched dough is one that contains one or more of the following: butter, milk, and/or eggs. Often these three items are found in the same dough. One of the most noteworthy examples of an enriched dough is brioche, and others, not as widely used, include sweet dough, panettone, pandoro, and kugelhopf. Brioche is one of the four "mother" doughs that are leavened with yeast (wild and/or commercially manufactured). The other three mother doughs are lean dough (baguette), sourdough, and yeast-risen laminated doughs (croissant/Danish). All doughs derive from these four doughs. Brioche is a workhorse dough that can be used in many ways, from breakfast pastries to laminated doughs, savory items, sandwich breads, or French toast.

As noble as this dough is, it needs special attention to make it as perfect as possible. This dough is essentially an emulsion, as you will see in the following procedure and the recipe on page 156.

THE STRAIGHT DOUGH MIXING METHOD IS AS FOLLOWS:

1.   Carefully weigh out all of the ingredients.

2.   Bring the milk, eggs, and butter to room temperature (21°C/70°F).

3.   Pour the milk into the bowl of an electric mixer. If using fresh yeast, it must be dissolved in this milk. If using instant yeast, mix it with the flour before pouring on top of the milk and eggs.

4.   Place 85 percent of the eggs on top of the milk. Reserve the remaining eggs to add at the end of the mixing process. They are not added at this point because eggs slow down gluten development, as the fat they contain interferes with gluten bonds.

5.   Pour the flour, salt, and sugar on top of the milk and eggs.

6.   Using a hook attachment, mix the ingredients in the bowl on low speed until they have formed a homogenous mass.

7.   Add the butter in 3 or 4 additions with the mixer on medium speed, waiting for each addition to completely combine with the dough before adding more.

8.   Mix the dough until it has reached full gluten development. This means that the dough should be able to stretch significantly without ripping. To test for this, take a piece of dough in your hands and stretch it using all of your fingers. It should form what is known as a window, which is a very thin sheet of dough that holds its shape without ripping. This should be within reason; if you pull too hard on it, it will rip, no matter how full the gluten development. At this point, turn the mixer to low speed and add the remaining eggs. Mix until a homogenous mass is obtained.

9.   The dough should be at or below 27°C/86°F; any hotter and the butter in the dough can begin to melt, thus breaking the emulsion. While this is not the end of the world, a well-emulsified brioche will yield a better product than one that is not emulsified. The crumb will be lighter and softer rather than tight and gummy.

10.   Transfer the dough to a floured surface, cover it with plastic, and bulk ferment it for 30 to 45 minutes.

11.   Punch the dough down, and then transfer it to a sheet pan (or sheet pans depending on how much dough there is) that is lined with lightly greased or floured silicone paper. Parchment paper may be used, but silicone paper has less propensity to moisten and stick to the dough. Flatten the dough with your hands and wrap the sheet pan with plastic wrap. The plastic needs to be in contact with the dough so that the dough does not form a skin on top. Refrigerate the dough until firm.

12.   Once the dough is cold and firm, it can be shaped and manipulated or reserved refrigerated for up to 48 hours before being used. It also freezes well if it is properly wrapped.

THE CHOCOLATE TEMPERING METHOD

The science behind tempering chocolate and chocolate in itself can be confounding, not to mention extensive. In this section, the information is limited to an explanation of the procedure for tempering dark, milk, and white chocolate using the seeding method. It is not relevant to explain all the methods (tabling, mechanical, ice water bath, microwave, and the use of cocoa butter powder) that are used to obtain the same result. In any method, the three most important factors are time, temperature, and agitation. Time is important because the faster you can take your chocolate from melted to set, the shinier it will be, and it will also have a better snap. When the process takes too long, especially if it takes too long to set after it has been tempered, it may yield a dull, soft chocolate that may even bloom. Temperature is important because the chocolate has to be taken up to a certain temperature, then down, and then up again in order to produce a properly tempered chocolate. When those temperatures are not respected, the chocolate will not be properly tempered. And finally agitation is important, because it helps promote the proper crystallization of fats. The fat in chocolate (cocoa butter) can crystallize in six different forms:

- **Form I (γ): Melts at 16°C/61°F to 18°C/64°F. Very unstable (present only in coating for ice creams, for example).**

- **Form II (α): Melts at 22°C/72°F to 24°C/75°F.**

- **Form III (β'2): Melts at 24°C/75°F to 26°C/79°F.**

- **Form IV (β'1): Melts at 26°C/79°F to 28°C/82°F.**

- **Form V (β2): Melts at 32°C/90°F to 34°C/93°F.**

- **Form VI (β1): Melts at 34°C/93°F to 36°C/97°F.**

Forms V and VI are the most stable, and Form V is the most widely used to make chocolate confections, décor, and so forth. It is when the cocoa butter forms hard and with good snap, is shiny, and has a good resistance to bloom. The skilled chocolatier tries to get the chocolate to Form V as quickly as possible to achieve the positive aspect of the cocoa butter in this form.

The only way to obtain this form is to properly temper the chocolate. The seeding method is the cleanest, best way to temper chocolate with precision if there are no chocolate tempering machines available.

THE METHOD FOR CHOCOLATE TEMPERING USING THE SEEDING METHOD IS AS FOLLOWS:

1. You may melt the chocolate in a bowl in the microwave for short intervals of time. The time depends on the type of microwave that you have; professional microwaves are very powerful and may burn chocolate easily. Stir the chocolate in the bowl with a rubber spatula as it melts to obtain even melting. It is preferable, however, to melt chocolate in a bowl over a hot water bath (the bowl should not touch the water), with the water simmering, not boiling. This method will give you more control over the process. The chocolate will melt faster if it is in pellet form or cut into small pieces from a block. Of course, a chocolate melter is good too. You put the chocolate in and let it melt overnight; the next day you will have a large amount of melted chocolate right at the temperature you need it. Keeping chocolate melted for long periods of time before tempering will not necessarily result in a better product. Some chocolate manufacturers promote this method for tempering their chocolates, but melted chocolate is melted chocolate, no matter how long it stays melted. Also, chocolate melters are costly.

2. Bring the chocolate to between 45°C/113°F and 50°C/112°F. Take the bowl off the simmering water bath (do not turn off the heat) or out of the microwave. Add solid chocolate to the melted chocolate. This chocolate will act as ice, cooling the melted chocolate down. A good amount to start with is about one-quarter of the amount that is in the bowl. Stir continuously, checking the temperature frequently, preferably using an infrared thermometer. A probe thermometer can get very messy and you will need to wipe the probe clean each time after you dip it in chocolate. An infrared thermometer is a no-mess guarantee.

3. Continue to stir until the chocolate reaches the desired temperature, which varies depending on the chocolate: 30°C/86°F to 32°C/90°F for dark chocolate, 29°C/84°F to 30°C/86°F for milk chocolate, and 28°C/82°F to 29°C/84°F for white and colored chocolate. You can perform a temper test, in which you dip the tip of an offset spatula or a piece of parchment paper in the chocolate and wait for it to set to see whether the chocolate is in fact well tempered. This is not a great idea, since during the time you are waiting for the chocolate to set, the chocolate in the bowl is getting colder with every second that goes by; however, it can be necessary when you first start tempering chocolate. Stick to the method detailed in these steps, as this will always result in proper tempering.

4. Use the chocolate as soon as it is tempered. In order to keep the chocolate at the right temperature, there are a few things you can do:

   ▪ Keep a separate bowl on hand with hot chocolate (at about 45°C/113°F), and add it to the tempered chocolate as it gets colder, always checking the temperature with a thermometer.

   ▪ Microwave the chocolate for brief time intervals until it is back up to the desired temperature.

   ▪ Place the bowl over a simmering water bath and stir until the chocolate is back to the desired temperature (always keep a pot with water over medium heat going as you are working with the chocolate).

NOTES *This method will not work if the chocolate's temperature goes above tempered range. If it does, you will need to restart the process.*

The room in which you work should be between 18°C/65°F and 21°C/70°F.

The ideal temperature to conserve your chocolate confections and chocolate pieces in general will be 12°C/54°F to 20°C/68°F; this will prevent the occurrence of fat bloom, which will begin to happen in environments that exceed 24°C/75°F.

MAKING YOUR OWN CHOCOLATE

Do you really have to make your own chocolate? The short answer is no. So why do it? For certain preparations, it can be an extremely special offering. Think of it: your own chocolate. There are certainly reasons why not to make it. They are the same reasons that some people don't mill their own flour or make their own ketchup. But having a bar, décor, or shell for confections made from your own chocolate is truly remarkable and unique. And potentially expensive. However, you may charge accordingly for an artisan product, which will always be much better in quality than an industrially manufactured chocolate. The equipment you will need, such as the mill to crush the beans, the juicer to make the liquor, and the mélangeur to conch the chocolate, can add up, but it is worth the investment.

An entire book, and a large one at that, could be (and has been) written about the process of making chocolate. This section is merely a general starting point. You will have to decide on the type of beans you want to use and whether you want to mix different types. The end result is up to you.

STEPS FOR CHOCOLATE MAKING

In the following section, you will read a step-by-step process for making chocolate in your shop. Bear in mind that it has slightly different steps than large-scale production (larger machines have different effects on the process and the final product), but the principles of production are essentially the same.

Selecting the Correct Beans

There is an almost limitless number of variations that can be made with microbatch chocolate depending most on the type of bean (or blend of beans) one uses, but also depending on the way it is processed. An understanding of this can only be achieved by experimenting with roasting and processing techniques, but there are a few guidelines to follow to ensure a decent finished product.

There are three basic types of beans: Criollo (considered the best-quality beans), Trinitario (considered medium-quality beans), and Forastero (also considered medium-quality beans). Decide on a location-specific cocoa bean (single origin), and the type (Criollo, Trinitario, or Forastero). There are Criollo beans that make fine chocolate and there are Criollo beans that produce terrible chocolate, in the same way that some Forastero beans can produce exceptional chocolate even though their reputation is that they are only good for flavorless, one-dimensional chocolate. It depends on the quality of the fruit tree and how the beans were handled on the journey from the tree to their final destination. Mold is one of the most common defects found in fermented cocoa beans.

This is similar to what occurs with wine; the exact same grape growing in two different regions can produce very different wines. Cocoa beans also depend on this same terroir to define their potential quality as a chocolate.

Following are general flavor guidelines for commonly used beans from different areas of the world:

- **South American beans are known to have fruity, floral characteristics.**

- **African beans are best known for simple, straightforward chocolate flavors.**

- **Madagascar beans are intensely fruity and highly acidic, with a unique flavor.**

To begin thinking about the formulation process, it is important to generally understand a few numbers and concepts with regard to cocoa beans. Cocoa beans can range from 53 percent to 59 percent cocoa butter (fat) content, but for the sake of consistency in formulation, the recipes assume that cocoa beans contain 55 percent cocoa butter as a constant, and the rest of the bean (45 percent) is cocoa solids. In a bag of cocoa beans, all beans could potentially have a different fat percentage, but it will not be lower than 53 percent or higher than 59 percent.

Finished chocolates containing 38 percent or more cocoa butter are considered couverture. This is achieved by adding additional cocoa butter; otherwise it would be an extremely high-percentage chocolate that is too bitter for most uses and very unpleasant to eat.

Cleaning

Care must be taken to ensure that no foreign matter is mixed in with the cocoa beans before processing. It is not uncommon to find small rocks, twigs, and small pieces of metal in a bag of cocoa beans. These foreign objects can be detrimental to the final flavor of the chocolate, but they can also damage the cocoa mill and mélangeur.

The cleaning process is as follows:

1. **Place the cocoa beans in a perforated container or colander. Use a shop vacuum to suck away any dust and small fibers from the batch. Conversely, the beans can be shaken in a drum sieve to remove the dust.**

2. **Spread the beans on a sheet pan and visually inspect them to make sure that there are no foreign objects, especially rocks. Remove any that you see. You must go one by one. This can be tedious, but it is necessary.**

3. **A small, powerful magnet can be waved over the beans to attract any small pieces of metal that may be present.**

Roasting

Cocoa bean roasting completes the development of flavors that we associate with cocoa and chocolate that was begun during the bean's fermentation.

There are two methods that a microbatch chocolate manufacturer can employ to roast cocoa beans in a conventional oven (a convection oven is ideal, but the temperature will need to be adjusted accordingly):

■ **Whole bean roasting: This method is the most common.**

■ **Nib roasting: Roasting times and temperatures will be different based on several factors, including the type of bean and the desired results. While there is no binding set of rules, Forastero beans, also known as *bulk cocoa,* will generally produce chocolate with less complexity and more straightforward "cocoa" flavor. These beans can take a darker roast to accentuate those characteristics. Some Trinitario and Criollo beans, also known as *fine cocoa* or *flavor cocoa,* generally have more complexity and light, fruity notes that are best cultivated with a lighter roast.**

GENERAL ROASTING TIMES

Roast the beans in a 160°C/325°F oven for 10 minutes and then at 135°C/275°F for 10 minutes longer, stirring every 5 minutes. Turn off the oven and leave the beans inside for 10 minutes. Roasting for the first few minutes at a relatively high temperature helps to puff the husk away from the bean itself by vaporizing some of the residual moisture in the bean. This makes the husk much easier to remove when winnowing. The remaining roast time ensures an even roast.

A NOTE ON POPPING WHILE ROASTING *When you notice some of the cocoa beans beginning to split open (again from air expansion), this is a good indicator that the roast is near completion, except in the case of finer, Criollo-type beans, where this is a sign that they may be overroasted. Ideally, with Criollo beans, you will be able to determine the exact time and temperature required to produce an ideal toasting and not rely on looking for the skin to split. This time and temperature is something you will have to determine through trial and error until you are satisfied with the final result.*

Winnowing

Winnowing is the act of removing the husk from the bean. Once the cocoa beans are roasted and cooled to room temperature, pass them through a cocoa mill (a grain mill adapted to handle cocoa beans; see Resources, page 520). This breaks the bean into fairly uniform sizes while pulling the husk away from the nib. Having nibs the same size helps to make the winnowing much more efficient because less nib is blown away.

Use a good-quality blow dryer to blow away the husk and leave the nibs remaining. Toss the nibs up with one hand and point the blow dryer toward the nibs you are tossing; this will help make it easier for the husks to blow off. Surround the area in which you will be winnowing with large plastic bags, or do it outdoors, because the small flecks of husk can make a huge mess. Trial and error will determine the ideal distance to position the blower from the nibs to most efficiently blow away husk but not nib as you pick up, drop, and agitate the contents of the bowl.

After successfully winnowing away most of the husk, spread the nibs on a sheet pan and return them to a hot oven (163°C/325°F) for a few minutes. This will make sure that any mold or bacteria on the husk that may have contaminated the nibs is neutralized. Also, warm nibs will pass through the juicer more easily.

Grinding

Pass the warm nibs through the juicer (see Resources, page 520). It is important to use this specific juicer since it separates the liquor from the waste—unlike other juicers—catching the liquor in one container and the waste in another. Pass the waste through the juicer several times until almost nothing is coming out.

Some of the benefits of using the juicer to grind the nibs into liquor are that it filters out any remaining husk and produces a fairly smooth chocolate liquor that requires less refining than if the liquor were processed in a Robot Coupe.

Refining

Make sure the bowl and rollers of the mélangeur are warm (see Resources, page 520, for the mélangeur). Add the liquor and begin refining. Keep a hot blow dryer pointed into the top opening to help maintain the temperature of the chocolate. Slowly add the predetermined amount of sugar over the course of an hour or so. These slow additions prevent the motor and rollers of the mélangeur from becoming bogged down.

Allow the chocolate to refine for at least 36 hours and up to 48 hours. Generally after 24 hours, a very fine and smooth chocolate is produced, but longer will certainly not hurt the chocolate and will in fact make it a better product.

Conching

Conch comes from the word *concha*, which means "shell" in Spanish. In this process, the flavor and texture of chocolate is refined by warming and grinding the cocoa beans, either in a traditional concher or between rollers. The characteristic taste, smell, and mouthfeel of chocolate are developed at this stage.

Spread the cocoa beans in an even layer on a sheet pan and sort through them to remove any undesirable objects.

After the beans have been roasted, run them through a cacao mill to loosen the husks from the cocoa nibs.

Use a blow dryer to winnow the husks from the nibs.

Pass the cocoa nibs through a juicer to obtain a smooth paste (cacao liquor).

After the liquor has been extracted, the chocolate must be refined and conched to achieve a smooth texture.

Finished chocolate will have excellent flavor, texture, and shine.

Conching on the commercial scale is performed in very specialized machines, but on the microbatch scale, this process is performed in the same mélangeur and occurs simultaneously when refining the chocolate. You will need to suspend the blow dryer over the opening of the mélangeur. The addition of heat and hot air circulation provided by the blow dryer helps to blow away many of the undesirable volatile compounds that are responsible for chocolate's sometimes harsh, tannic, acidic properties. Leave the blow dryer on in 2-hour intervals, shutting it down for 30 minutes between intervals so that it cools down, and if necessary, turn it off overnight if no one can supervise it. Any remaining moisture left in the chocolate is also allowed to evaporate into the hot blowing air.

Conching improves the flow of the chocolate. It ensures that all of the sugar and cocoa particle are evenly coated with fat. The act of conching may also smooth out the refined particles, improving flow and mouthfeel. Keep in mind that this is a micro-batch process. Industrial manufacturers have specialized machinery that do all of this automatically.

ADDING LECITHIN AND COCOA BUTTER

Adding cocoa butter or lecithin will depend on the cocoa percentage you are looking for; this is not always necessary. If choosing to include additional cocoa butter and lecithin, make sure to add it at the end of conching. Both will slow the evaporation of excess moisture from the chocolate, so do not add them too early.

Cocoa butter lowers viscosity, improves flavor release, and helps increase snap in tempered chocolate; in large quantities it can dilute the cocoa flavor, but this is rarely a concern. Cocoa butter should be added when it is melted, and ideally at 45°C/115°F.

Lecithin, most notably an emulsifier derived from soybeans, acts a viscosity reducer. Think of it as an intermediary between the cocoa and sugar particles, which don't naturally flow past each other easily; covering the particles with lecithin allows them to flow much more easily around each other. Up to .45 percent lecithin (in powder form) can be added, although .35 percent is usually enough to make a chocolate with a good working viscosity. Using more than .5 percent will begin to thicken the chocolate, thus negating the lecithin's benefits.

DARK CHOCOLATE FORMULATION

What is left after grinding is the cocoa liquor. The weight of that along with the percentage of cocoa is what will determine the formula. This will determine how much cocoa butter and sugar need to be added to the liquor in order to achieve the desired cocoa percentage and fat percentage.

The following formula was determined in conjunction with Professor Michael Nothnagel, math professor at The Culinary Institute of America in Hyde Park, New York.

VARIABLES

C% = desired cocoa percentage (as a decimal)

F% = desired fat percentage (as a decimal)

L = weight of chocolate liquor

B = weight of cocoa butter

S = weight of sugar

Note that C%, F%, and L will be known (or chosen) for a particular recipe.

This is what it would look like in diagram form, which makes is somewhat easier to visualize the process and understand the parts that will make up the final process:

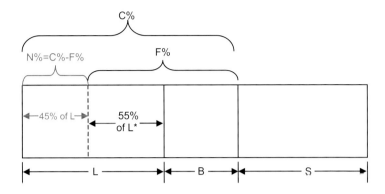

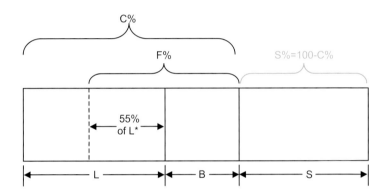

L* is the constant fat percentage determined in Step 1. Of the total weight of the cocoa liquor, 55% of it will be fat, no matter how much cocoa liquor there is.

Step 1: Calculate the total weight of the chocolate that will be produced.

Subtract the fat percentage from the cocoa percentage to calculate the solids percentage, which will be called N% (in red in the diagram that follows): Divide the weight of the solids by its percentage to calculate the total weight, which we will call T:

Total weight = weight of liquor solids/solids %

T = .045 x L/N%

Step 2: Calculate the weight of the sugar to be added.

Subtract the cocoa percentage from 100% to calculate the sugar percentage, which we will call S% (in green in the diagram that follows): Multiply the sugar percentage by the total weight calculated in Step 1:

Sugar weight = total weight x sugar percentage

S = T x S%

Step 3: Calculate the weight of the cocoa butter to be added.

Add the weight of the solids to the weight of the sugar, then subtract from the total weight calculated in Step 1:

Cocoa butter weight = total weight – (liquor weight + sugar weight)

B = T – (L+S)

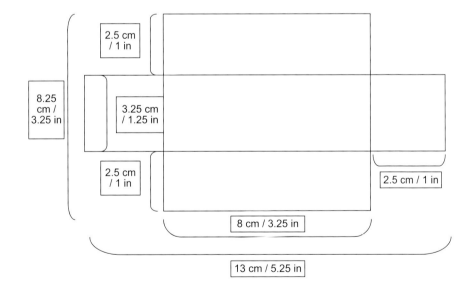

DARK CHOCOLATE FORMULAS

60 PERCENT DOMINICAN REPUBLIC

YIELD: 2 KG/4 LB 6.55 OZ

INGREDIENT	METRIC	U.S.	%
Cocoa liquor	974 g	2 lb 2.36 oz	48.7%
Superfine or bakers' sugar	797 g	1 lb 12.1 oz	39.84%
Cocoa butter, heated to 45°C/115°F	221 g	7.8 oz	11.07%
Lecithin powder	8 g	.28 oz	.4%

63 PERCENT VENEZUELA

YIELD: 2 KG/4 LB 6.55 OZ

INGREDIENT	METRIC	U.S.	%
Cocoa liquor	1.11 kg	2 lb 7.04 g	55.33%
Superfine or bakers' sugar	737 g	1 lb 10 oz	36.85%
Cocoa butter, heated to 45°C/115°F	148 g	5.23 oz	7.41%
Lecithin powder	8 g	.28 oz	.4%

66 PERCENT MADAGASCAR

YIELD: 2 KG/4 LB 6.55 OZ

INGREDIENT	METRIC	U.S.	%
Cocoa liquor	1.24 kg	2 lb 11.73 oz	61.99%
Superfine or bakers' sugar	677 g	1 lb 7.89 oz	33.86%
Cocoa butter, heated to 45°C/115°F	75 g	2.65 oz	3.75%
Lecithin powder	8 g	.28 oz	.4%

70 PERCENT PAPUA NEW GUINEA

YIELD: 2 KG/4 LB 6.55 OZ

INGREDIENT	METRIC	U.S.	%
Cocoa liquor	1.4 kg	3 lb 1.44 oz	70.08%
Superfine or bakers' sugar	591 g	1 lb 4.83 oz	29.53%
Lecithin powder	8 g	.28 oz	.39%

NOTE *This recipe has a high percentage of cocoa liquor and does not require any additional cocoa butter since there is a sufficient amount in the cocoa liquor to obtain a 70% chocolate.*

MILK CHOCOLATE FORMULAS

40 PERCENT MILK CHOCOLATE

YIELD: 2.01 KG/4 LB 6.9 KG

INGREDIENT	METRIC	U.S.	%
Superfine or bakers' sugar	900 g	1 lb 15.75 oz	44.78%
Whole milk powder	260 g	9.17 oz	12.94%
Cocoa liquor	300 g	10.58 oz	14.93%
Cocoa butter, heated to 45°C/115°F	500 g	1 lb 1.64 oz	24.88%
Vanilla powder	20 g	.71 oz	1%
Salt	20 g	.71 oz	1%
Lecithin powder	10 g	.35 oz	.5%

1. Grind the sugar in a coffee grinder until it is very fine and powder-like. Do the same with the whole milk powder.

2. Warm the cocoa liquor to 45°C/115°F. Place the warm cocoa liquor and the cocoa butter in the mélangeur.

3. Slowly add the whole milk powder and the sugar (20 percent of each at a time, alternating).

4. Refine for 24 hours, adding the vanilla, salt, and lecithin during the last 2 hours of refining.

NOTES *Be sure to use whole milk powder and not fat-free milk powder.*

This percentage (40 percent) is the most common when it comes to milk chocolate.

45 PERCENT MILK CHOCOLATE

YIELD: 2 KG/4 LB 6.55 OZ

INGREDIENT	METRIC	U.S.	%
Superfine or bakers' sugar	905 g	1 lb 15.92 oz	45.2%
Whole milk powder	260 g	9.17 oz	12.99%
Cocoa liquor	330 g	11.64 oz	16.48%
Cocoa butter, heated to 45°C/115°F	505 g	1 lb 1.81 oz	25.22%
Vanilla powder	1 g	.04 oz	.05%
Salt	.5 g	.02 oz	.02%
Lecithin powder	.8 g	.03 oz	.04%

Follow the same procedure as for 40 percent milk chocolate.

55 PERCENT MILK CHOCOLATE

YIELD: 2.02 KG/4 LB 7.25 OZ

INGREDIENT	METRIC	U.S.	%
Cocoa liquor	520 g	1 lb 2.34 oz	25.74%
Whole milk powder	380 g	13.4 oz	18.81%
Cocoa butter, heated to 45°C/115°F	540 g	1 lb 3.05 oz	26.73%
Superfine or bakers' sugar	550 g	1 lb 3.4 oz	27.23%
Lecithin powder	10 g	.35 oz	.5%
Salt	20 g	.71 oz	.99%

Follow the same procedure as for the 40 percent milk chocolate, but leave out the vanilla powder.

NOTE *This is my favorite variety of milk chocolate, which is borderline dark but still with some dairy notes.*

WHITE CHOCOLATE AND OTHER VARIETIES OF WHITE CHOCOLATE

YIELD: 2.01 KG/4 LB 6.9 OZ

INGREDIENT	METRIC	U.S.	%
Superfine or bakers' sugar	780 g	1 lb 11.51 oz	38.81%
Whole milk powder	400 g	14.11 oz	19.9%
Lecithin powder	10 g	.35 oz	.5%
Cocoa butter, heated to 45°C/115°F	820 g	1 lb 12.92 oz	40.8%

1. Grind the sugar and the milk powder separately in a coffee grinder as finely as possible.

2. Pour the cocoa butter in the mélangeur and then add 20 percent of the sugar. Turn on the mélangeur. Add 20 percent of the milk powder. Alternate additions of sugar with the milk powder (20 percent each time) until they are all in the mélangeur.

3. Let it refine for 12 to 18 hours, adding the lecithin 2 hours before the refining time is over.

NOTES *Use milk powder with fat (whole milk powder); most common milk powders are fat-free.*

Making white chocolate is much easier since it does not require cocoa liquor. It simply requires cocoa butter, sugar, milk powder, and lecithin. White chocolate is technically not chocolate since it contains no cocoa liquor. Technically it should be called couverture.

You can make flavored chocolates, such as the Matcha or Earl Grey white chocolate on page 512. Use 2 percent to 4 percent of the total weight of the chocolate; you will want to taste as you go and add more if needed as it refines. Powdered flavors should be ground as finely as possible in a coffee grinder and added at the beginning of the refining process. Alternatively, the milk powder may be replaced by ingredients such as dried coconut (fresh or toasted) and freeze-dried vegetable or fruit powders (substitute the same amount: about 20 percent of the total weight). You may also substitute the milk powder with goat's milk powder, yogurt powder, quark powder, heavy cream powder, or sour cream powder.

MAKING CHOCOLATE DÉCOR

Chocolate décor should be shiny and have a snap; it should be thin but not see-through thin. Thin décor shows finesse and craftsmanship; it shows that he or she who made it has a hand and a way with chocolate, which is acquired only through much practice and proper instruction. Those thick pieces of décor you see here and there were either made by someone who is not quite adept or, highly likely, purchased from a manufacturer. These pieces are on the thick side because they are made to withstand transportation and also because they are made by machines; machines cannot replicate a finely crafted piece of chocolate.

You should not forget that chocolate décor is partially intended for decoration purposes, which means that it is part of embellishing a dessert, but it should also make sense with the dessert. It should be a part of the dessert and lend a supporting role; it is not the dessert in and of itself. The flavor profile needs to be there. Often, décor is used in excess, as an easy way to make a dessert look nice while completely disregarding flavor profile. The elements of your dessert need to make sense with each other, and visual appearance will not work as the guiding creative force if you cannot make the flavors play well together.

1. Prepare your work area. Typically, to make shiny pieces of décor, the chocolate should be spread on plastic (acetate) sheets, because it is a flexible material that is shiny, and tempered chocolate reflects the surface it sets on. Anchor the sheet down to a flat surface, which does not necessarily have to be marble. Because marble holds temperatures longer than most materials, a flat sheet of Plexiglas or even wood can work to your advantage. If the shop is on the cold side, then the chocolate may set almost on contact with the marble. To anchor the acetate, use a mister to spray water on the work surface, and then place the sheet of acetate on top. Flatten it down with a paper towel to prevent smudging the surface and to eliminate any bubbles that may be under the sheet. You can also use nonstick oil spray, but it is more complicated to clean up. If you will be making many chocolate décor pieces, you may need to prepare many work surfaces. You may also be working on individual pieces of décor, so make sure you have your pieces of acetate cut and ready to go.

2. You will need an offset spatula, a ruler (depending on what you are cutting), and a cutting instrument (paring knife, ring cutter).

3. Pour the chocolate on the surface of the acetate. Try to drizzle it on the entire surface instead of letting it puddle in the center of the sheet, because the latter makes it harder to spread it out evenly. The quantity is something you will have to work on getting right through trial and error. How much is enough to cover the surface of an entire sheet of acetate in a thin layer? You could weigh it for consistency, but this could be a waste of time considering that your chocolate is tempered.

4. Spread the chocolate using an offset spatula at a 45-degree angle. Try to get the chocolate in an even layer from one side of the acetate to the other. This will determine an even layer of chocolate without bumps. It's fine if some chocolate spills over the side of your sheet.

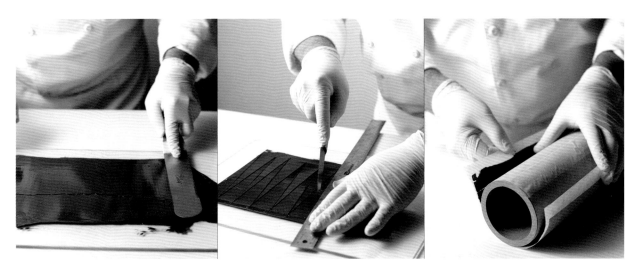

Spread the chocolate at a 45-degree angle into a thin, even layer on a sheet of acetate.

When the chocolate is halfway crystallized, cut the chocolate using a shaped cutter or the back of a paring knife and a ruler if necessary.

If you are going to shape the decor, do it quickly just after cutting it—before it sets completely.

5. Let the chocolate set halfway. If you try to cut it before that, you will have a mess on your hands. If you are cutting straight shapes, using a ruler and the back of a paring knife, make notches where you need to cut, then make your cuts. If you are using a shaped cutter, simply make the cuts.

6. The chocolate should still be malleable at this point. If you are going to shape it, do it at this moment; it is crucial to work quickly to keep the chocolate from setting.

7. Let the chocolate set completely. If you are not using the décor right away, it is a good idea to let the pieces stay on the acetate as long as possible. This helps protect their integrity.

NOTE *There are many ways with and variations on décor, such as using transfer sheets, texture sheets, two or three types of chocolate, brushing one color of chocolate on and then pouring another over, using gold leaf, and so on, but the basic principles remain the same.*

GANACHE METHOD

Ganache is mostly an emulsion and, to a lesser extent, a suspension. It combines a liquid (water) and a fat (chocolate) to form a smooth-textured chocolate and liquid mix. It is this smoothness that is the most desirable quality of a ganache; the more liquid there is, the smoother the ganache will be, and the more chocolate there is, the denser it will be. Obtaining a smooth ganache is not very complicated so long as the proper steps are followed.

THE SIMPLE GANACHE METHOD IS AS FOLLOWS:

1. The chocolate should be broken down into small pieces (about 1.5 cm/.5 in). This can be a tedious task, but fortunately, most chocolates are available in small pellets or pistoles, which eliminate the task of cutting chocolate into tiny pieces. Reserve the chocolate in a bowl.

2. Bring the liquid to a boil. This liquid may be anything from cream to fruit juices to beer, and it can contain corn syrup, glucose, or sorbitol. Sorbitol is a type of alcohol used to reduce the water content of a ganache, thus extending its shelf life.

3. Pour one-third of the boiling liquid into the chocolate and stir with a rubber spatula. It will dissolve most of the chocolate.

4. Return the liquid to a boil, pour another one-third of it into the chocolate, and stir until it has been incorporated completely.

5. Bring the remaining liquid to a boil and pour it into the bowl. Stir until the chocolate has completely dissolved. Some pastry chefs opt to add the liquid all at once, and while it yields a good result, it is not as good an emulsion as when the liquid is added in three additions. The stirring motion and the slow addition of liquid create a smoother texture.

6. Some recipes call for the addition of butter. If so, the softened butter should be added when the previous mixture of chocolate and cream reaches 30°C/86°F, and it is added to the chocolate in small pieces. It is rubbed in with the rubber spatula by pressing the butter against the side of the bowl. The butter is not necessarily stirred into the ganache, since at this point the butter and the ganache are very similar in texture, and stirring can cause unwanted air bubbles to form as well as crystallization.

7. Pipe the ganache into the desired shell for molded chocolates and candy bars or into a frame for cutting and then dipping (see Step 8). Ideally, a ganache is made when it is needed; making excess ganache to get ahead does not yield very good results. Once the ganache sets, it has to be re-softened without breaking the emulsion, and it just becomes more complicated than it has to be. More often than not, the ganache breaks, and it takes even longer to bring it back to a proper emulsion. Making a ganache takes just as long as softening one and even less time than fixing one that is broken.

8. When making a ganache for hand-dipped (or enrobed) chocolates, pour the ganache, just as it is made, into a frame to set. The ganache should be pourable and fill in the frame easily. This frame is typically made of steel bars, like those used for caramels. These bars are strong and heavy enough to contain the pressure that a hot, fluid caramel can exert on them. They can be used to form many different sizes of squares/rectangles, and they are available in different thicknesses. In this book, the frames measure 30 cm/12 in wide by 45 cm/18 in long by 1.25 cm/.5 in deep, and they will hold about 2 kg/4 lb 6.4 oz of ganache. The final yield will depend on how the ganache is cut. The bars will need to be placed over a flat surface that can be moved from one place to another (in other words, not a static work surface, unless you can give up that space for more than 12 hours). Try to use a marble or granite surface that fits inside a sheet pan. The marble should be lined with a nonstick rubber mat, and then the bars are placed on top of the mat. Once the ganache is made, pour it into the frame, spread it out evenly with an offset spatula, and then even out the surface with a long Plexiglas or steel bar. It is important to let the ganache set at room temperature and not refrigerated.

NOTES *There are a variety of methods for making ganache, and which you use depends on the intended use or the desired final consistency. For example, the method just described is mostly useful for fluid ganaches that are to be piped into chocolate shells or truffle shells. But if the proportion of liquid and solid ingredients is changed to more solid than liquid, the ganache can be poured into a frame and then cut with a guitar and dipped. Alternatively, there are recipes that call for the chocolate component of the ganache to be tempered before other ingredients are added to it. This is generally used for "slab" ganache (ganache that will be cut and dipped). In this case, the cream or liquid is warmed to 38°C/100°F and then stirred into the tempered chocolate before pouring it into a frame. Again, it all depends on the desired final result. What is undeniable is that the ganache has to be properly emulsified in order to yield a smooth result that is palatable and not grainy. Graininess is the sign of an improperly made emulsion.*

The shelf life of a ganache is directly related to the following factors:

a) *Water activity (a_w) or water content. The lower the water content, the longer the shelf life. The water content is the sum of all of the water in the ingredients in a recipe. The water activity can be measured with an a_w meter. It is measured on a scale from 0 to 1 (1 being the highest). Ideally, the water activity is below .85. To put things in context, a chocolate mousse has about .9 a_w, and a hard caramel has a a_w of .4.*

b) *Sugar helps extend the lifespan of a ganache. On average, a ganache with a minimum of 30 percent total sugar total is recommended.*

c) *Fat from cocoa butter also helps extend the shelf life of a ganache; 21 percent (total) minimum is recommended. Fat from dairy can range from 0 percent to 15 percent.*

d) *The pH should be under 5. This is easily measured with a pH meter.*

MOLDED CHOCOLATES

Molded chocolates differ from hand-dipped chocolates in several ways. Molded chocolates are generally made using sturdy polycarbonate molds. Polycarbonate is a very shiny clear plastic that is almost impossible to deform. This is crucial since chocolate, when properly tempered, will reflect the surface of whatever surface it is crystallizing on. The shinier the surface, the better. You cannot really obtain very shiny chocolate when hand dipping, unless you place a sheet of acetate or other plastic over its surface just after dipping the piece in tempered chocolate and before the chocolate crystallizes. There are many possibilities with molded chocolates with regard to garnishing the mold, using techniques and methods that are not possible with hand-dipped chocolates. The method for hand-dipped chocolates is best suited for mass-quantity production utilizing an enrober, which is a very expensive piece of equipment.

THE METHOD FOR MOLDED CHOCOLATES IS AS FOLLOWS:

1. If it is the first time you are using a particular mold, wash it with hot water and soap, using a cloth towel to wash them, not a rough scrub pad.

2. Rinse the molds well and dry them quickly with a lint-free towel to prevent water marks on the surface.

3. Polish the molds using a lint-free cloth or cotton swabs. The squeaking sound you hear is a good thing.

4. Temper the chocolate and pour it into the mold. At this point, don't fuss too much about what you are doing. New molds always need to be filled once before you start using them. What this does is a fine layer of cocoa butter on the mold, which will make the subsequent molded chocolates shinier. The first pass is a loss. Let the chocolate set, and then turn it out of the mold, tapping gently to release the chocolate. Polish it again.

5. Set up your *mise en place* using the following:

    - A wire rack to hold your molds upside down. It should be placed over a nonstick rubber mat or sheet of parchment paper to catch any dripping chocolate.

    - Two putty knives made of stainless steel. They should be wider than the chocolate molds.

    - A ladle, large enough to hold the chocolate you will pour into your molds. If possible, the ladles should be large enough to hold all the chocolate needed for a mold, so that you won't have to pour the chocolate twice.

    - Enough sheet pans to hold the molds once they have been scraped, and once they have been filled and capped.

    - A source of heat to keep the chocolate in temper: a simmering water bath, microwave, or a bowl of hot chocolate.

    - An infrared thermometer (or other thermometer).

    - Paper towels for cleanup.

    - Moist towels for cleanup.

- A blow dryer or propane torch to clean up chocolate on your work area when you are done. Ideally, you should clean it as you go, but you will not believe how quickly you can have a huge mess on your hands, literally.

6. If you are garnishing your mold, begin with this step (if you are not, skip to Step 7). In the picture on page 44, the mold is being coated with a thin layer of colored cocoa butter. To do this, simply melt the cocoa butter and airbrush it into the mold. It need not be tempered, since the cold air that expels it through the airbrush performs that task of cooling it down before it hits the mold. If you are hand-brushing the colored cocoa butter or if you are piping, drizzling, or brushing on a different colored or type of chocolate into the mold, it should be tempered. Tempering cocoa butter is similar in principle to tempering chocolate, but the process is not as strict and finicky. Simply melt the cocoa butter and cool it with some unmelted cocoa butter until it is cool to the touch. It will set quickly. If you have a mold with many details and nooks and crannies, hand-brush some tempered chocolate or cocoa butter in first. It can be the same type of chocolate you are using to cast the mold, but it doesn't matter; what matters is preventing the formation of air pockets. Brushing chocolate in fills in any tight corners or spots.

7. Once the molds are prepared, you are ready to cast your molds. Dip the ladle into your tempered chocolate and pour it completely onto the molds. Use one hand to pour and the other to hold the mold. Put the ladle back in the bowl. Tap the side of the mold with your putty knife (this brings many air bubbles to the surface), then flip the mold over onto the bowl of tempered chocolate. Some pastry chefs do not subscribe to this method, since they claim it cools the tempered chocolate down, and therefore they turn the filled molds over onto another bowl, which has the sole purpose of collecting chocolate from the molds and is to be reused to fill other molds. It does in fact cool the chocolate down, but not too dramatically. This why you must check the temperature of the chocolate frequently and adjust it with a heat source (see Step 5). Turn the mold back up and tap it again. The smaller bubbles will have an easier time coming up through a smaller amount of chocolate than when the mold was full. At this point you can tap the mold on a flat surface to ensure the release of bubbles from inside the mold.

8. Turn the mold back over again and tap it with the putty knife. This will get the chocolate from the bottom of the mold to pour down the side of the mold and create an even layer of chocolate in your mold, which is a sign of a quality molded chocolate. When this is not done correctly, the chocolate tends to settle at the bottom of the mold, and this will give you a shell with thin walls and a thick top when the molded chocolate comes out of the mold. Excess chocolate will be dripping out of the mold. Scrape it off with the putty knife and clean your knife on the side of the tempered chocolate bowl.

9. Place the mold on top of the wire rack to set the chocolate. Clean your putty knife by scraping the excess off with your second putty knife. It is crucial to keep your tools and work area as clean as possible. Repeat the process with your other molds, checking the temperature of your chocolate frequently and making the temperature adjustments you need with your chosen heat source. After two or three molds, return to your first cast mold. It may have some chocolate dripping out of the mold, but at this point it will be semi-set; scrape that excess off with your putty knife. If it has hardened too far, it will damage the shell of the molded chocolate. Since it won't come off easily, it will crack off. Try to prevent this from happening.

10. Once your shells are completely set, fill them with their respective fillings to just under the top. A quality molded chocolate has a thin bottom layer that is just as thin as the entire shell.

Garnish the mold as necessary. Here, a mold is being sprayed with a thin layer of colored cocoa butter.

Ladle tempered chocolate generously into the mold, and tap it vigorously to remove any air bubbles.

Flip the mold over a bowl of tempered chocolate.

Scrape the mold with a putty knife to remove any excess chocolate before it crystallizes completely.

Let the chocolate crystallize, then fill the mold with the desired filling. Cap off the mold using the same technique used previously.

The finished molded chocolates should release easily from the mold. They will have a shiny surface and an even shell throughout.

11. To cap the chocolate, temper the chocolate. You will need the same mise en place that you did to cast the molds (see Step 5), plus a hair dryer or mild heat source and enough sheets of acetate or textured acetate for all of your molds. The sheets should be the same size as the entire surface of the chocolate mold.

12. Before you cap a mold, apply warm air to the surface of the mold using a blow dryer set on the cool setting, which softens the shell just enough to allow the base and the shell to bind perfectly. Do not use the warm or hot settings, which will melt the chocolate. Without this step the base will have a cracked look and won't be even and smooth.

13. Pour the chocolate onto the mold as soon as you have warmed it, making sure you get all the pieces covered. Put the ladle down and scrape the excess off with a putty knife, making sure it is flush with the mold so you get a clean scrape. Immediately after (and before the chocolate sets), place the sheet of acetate on top of the chocolate, and with a clean putty knife smooth out the surface so it is perfectly flat on the base of the chocolate mold.

14. Let the chocolate set completely. The molds can be placed in the refrigerator for 5 minutes to ensure a clean release. Longer times may create condensation on the surface of your chocolates and make the chocolate brittle to the point where it may crack when you turn them out of the mold.

15. On a clean surface, gently turn the mold over as close to the work surface as possible, since being higher up will damage your pieces as they fall out. If you did everything correctly, the pieces will slide out. They might need a little tap on the top of the mold, for which the putty knife can be useful, just a little nudge to let them slide out.

16. Handle your pieces with powder-free gloves or cotton gloves to avoid leaving smudges on the surface of the chocolate.

17. Keep the chocolates in a cool, dry place away from light, preferably in a closed environment where there will be little to no dust particles. The lifespan of a chocolate depends on what it is filled with.

HAND-DIPPED CHOCOLATES

This type of confection is almost completely different in nature from molded chocolates, where the shell is determined by the filling. The filling can be a layer of ganache, caramel, marzipan, pâte de fruit, or marshmallow, or it can be two or three of these items stacked. The filling is poured into a frame just after it is made, and then it is left to set at room temperature (see Step 8 of the ganache on page 41).

THE METHOD FOR HAND-DIPPED CHOCOLATES IS AS FOLLOWS:

1. Using a paint roller, paint tempered chocolate on the surface of the item to be cut and dipped (ganache, caramel, and so forth). Let it set, and then turn it over and apply a coat of tempered chocolate in the same way.

2. Ideally, cut the slab with a guitar cutter to the desired shape; a cutter of this kind is expensive, but cutting by hand will definitely show. You can also use a ring cutter for round shapes; dip the cutter in hot water and pat it dry before cutting the product.

3. Set up your *mise en place* using the following:

   - Dipping fork(s).

   - Flat surface lined with an acetate sheet or nonstick rubber mat. Using a textured mat on the surface makes the dipped chocolate a little more special than placing it straight on a rubber mat. If you are using an acetate sheet, with or without texture, moisten the surface you will be placing it on first with a water mister. You can also use nonstick oil spray, but this is harder to clean up and it may make the acetate cling a little too much to the surface it is on. Place the acetate on the surface, and then rub it with a paper towel using your hand to smooth out the surface.

Place the item to be dipped on a dipping fork and submerge it into the tempered chocolate. Scrape the bottom of the tool against the rim of the bowl to remove excess chocolate.

Use a second fork to transfer the chocolate to a surface to set, taking care not to create a foot.

If you are garnishing the chocolate with a textured transfer sheet, apply it before the chocolate has completely crystallized.

▨ Garnishes for the chocolates, other forks and tools to create a texture on the dipped chocolate's surface, individual acetate squares with or without texture and with or without a transfer image.

▨ Source of heat to keep the chocolate tempered (microwave, simmering water bath, or a bowl with hot chocolate).

▨ Tempered chocolate.

4. Place the item to be dipped on a dipping fork and dip it into the tempered chocolate, completely submerging it into the chocolate.

5. Scrape the bottom of the dipping tool against the rim of the bowl to remove the excess chocolate. One of the attributes of quality dipped chocolates is that they do not have any feet at their base. It should be a sharp corner. Feet develop when there is still too much chocolate left on the piece and it is not scraped off properly.

6. Transfer each piece to the prepared surface to set. Before it sets you will need to apply the desired garnish. If it is an edible component like salt, a pinch of cinnamon, or cocoa nibs, it should be applied before the chocolate sets so that it will adhere to the piece. Otherwise it will fall off. If you are looking for a textured design, this should also be created before the chocolate sets, but not if it is still too wet; otherwise the texture will not stay and the chocolate will puddle back to a flat surface. You can use a dipping fork for this or an offset spatula. If you are applying a square of acetate on the sheet, you should also apply it before the chocolate sets so that it will stick; only remove it once the chocolate sets completely.

NOTES *The ideal temperature for conserving chocolates is in a low-moisture room with temperature control set to 12°C/54°F to 20°C/68°F. The ideal temperature to taste chocolates is the same.*
A chocolate confection is ideally tasted in small pieces rather than a single bite.
Chocolate should never be acidic, acrid, or astringent.
Always use the highest-quality ingredients.
A chocolate confection should have a slight snap. Otherwise, the chocolate was not tempered correctly.

The shell of a molded chocolate and a dipped chocolate should be thin, but not see-through thin. A molded chocolate should have a glossy shine. A hand-dipped chocolate will have a much more muted shine, since it is not always setting against a shiny surface such as a polycarbonate mold. A glossy shine in a hand-dipped chocolate will only be achieved if it is topped with a piece of acetate before it sets.

COOKED SUGAR

Cooked sugar is used for a large variety of products. It is very versatile but can also be very temperamental, which is why it is crucial to understand what you are doing before you get started.

There are two ways to cook sugar for practically any preparation that requires cooked sugar: the wet method and the dry method.

THE WET METHOD FOR COOKING SUGAR IS AS FOLLOWS:

1. Make sure that you use a pot that is very clean. Any debris or grease will crystallize the sugar. Copper works very well but is expensive and hard to keep clean. Stainless steel also works very well. If you have copper pots and are willing to spend the time maintaining them, then all the better, but the cooking time is only reduced by a fraction.

2. Make sure to use the correct size pot. If you are making a caramel, when you add the hot heavy cream into the bubbling sugar, it will increase in volume greatly due to the production of steam. If the pot is too short, it will bubble over.

3. Combine the sugar in a sauce pot with enough sugar to hydrate all of the sugar crystals. A common ratio is 4 parts water to 1 part sugar, but you can use a lot less water to fully hydrate sugar. This reduced amount of water also helps cook the sugar faster. The more water there is, the longer the sugar will take to reach the temperature you are looking for, because the additional water takes longer to evaporate. Water is the vessel that will get the sugar hot and start the cooking process, but once the water evaporates, the sugar will continue to cook on its own. Make sure that all of the sugar has been fully hydrated. Any dry crystals will crystallize all of the sugar.

4. Make sure that there are no sugar crystals on the side of the pot. These crystals can crystallize the rest of the sugar. Use a clean brush dipped in water to clean the inside of the pot. This brush should be a brush that is not used for anything other than this purpose. Pastry brushes with grease will drip grease into the pot and contaminate the sugar, crystallizing it.

5. The optimal heat source for cooking sugar is an induction burner, since it heats from the bottom to the top. Flame heat can affect the cooking of the sugar negatively, causing it to cook unevenly. However, if you are using a copper pot, you will need to use a flame. Always cook sugar over the highest heat possible to prevent crystallization.

6. Cook the sugar to the correct temperature; always use a thermometer.

NOTE *This method is used for a variety of preparations, such as Italian meringue, nougat, caramels, and so forth. It can also be used in combination with other forms of sugar, such as glucose and corn syrup. The principles are the same, while the results will vary.*

Cooked Sugar Temperatures

STAGE	TEMPERATURE
Pearl	106°C/223°F
Thread	108°C/228°F
Blow or soufflé (or soft bubble)	110°C/230°F
Soft ball	115°C/240°F
Firm ball	117°C/242°F
Hard ball	120°C/248°F
Soft crack	125°C/257°F
Middle crack	141°C/286°F
Hard crack	155°C/310°F
Caramel	160°C/320°F
Light brown caramel	170°C/340°F
Medium brown caramel	180°C/360°F
Dark brown caramel	190°C/380°F
Black jack (actually, *burnt* is a more appropriate name for this stage)	205°C/410°F

THE DRY METHOD FOR COOKING SUGAR IS AS FOLLOWS:

1. Place the sugar in a stainless-steel pot or copper pot.

2. Cook over high heat, stirring frequently with a wooden spoon. The sugar goes from crystalline form to caramelized with no points in between to speak of. The heat is very intense, and speed in stirring is crucial.

3. If the sugar is getting too dark in some spots and you still have other spots where the sugar hasn't caramelized at all, you may lower the heat to even out the caramelized sugar.

4. Stir until all of the sugar has cooked and caramelized.

NOTE *This method is used for preparations such as pralines and caramel sauce.*

FROZEN DESSERT METHODS

This section will focus on five methods. Two methods will be explained for ice cream (the egg-free ice cream method, the modern ice cream method), one for granités (granitas), and two for sorbet and sherbets (the classic method and the modern method). A classic ice cream method is exactly the same as the stirred custard method (see page 8), and methods for still-frozen desserts are the same as the aerated dessert methods. Many of those desserts can be served frozen as well.

ICE CREAM METHODS

The modern ice cream method is for ice creams that are not made by the stirred custard method. This method is for ice creams that contain ingredients such as stabilizers, milk powder, and glucose and/or invert sugar, among others. These types of ice creams have a much better shelf life during service. They are less susceptible to heat shock (melting and-re-freezing) than stirred custard bases, since they have stabilizers that help with their texture and structure. All stabilizers are hydrocolloids (see page 18); come directly from natural sources such as plants, sea algae, and sometimes animals (gelatin); and are minimally processed. The trick is not to use too much. These recipes use between .3 percent and .4 percent of the total weight of the recipe in stabilizers.

THE EGG-FREE ICE CREAM METHOD IS AS FOLLOWS:

1. To begin the egg-free method, combine all of the ingredients in a sauce pot or other adequately sized cooking vessel.

2. Place the sauce pot over high heat and whisk continuously until the mixture reaches 85°C/185°F. Turn the heat down to medium-low.

3. Continue whisking the base for 2 more minutes in order to homogenize it. It is not necessary to bring the base to a boil because the purpose of this method is to combine all the ingredients properly and to dissolve all of the solids, which consist mainly of sugar. Since these bases lack eggs, milk powder is often added to bind the excess liquid in the mixture in order to prevent the formation of large ice crystals.

4. Strain the base through a fine-mesh strainer to filter out any unwanted solids such as infused flavors (vanilla pods and so forth).

5. Immediately after straining, cool the base down in an ice water bath. Let the base age for at least 4 hours before churning it.

6. Before churning, give the base a good stir.

7. Churn to −4°C/25°F.

8. Place the churned product in a −10°C/14°F freezer. Reserve for service.

1. Scale all of the ingredients accurately. Mix 10 percent of the sugar with the stabilizer. The stabilizers should not be added to the liquid without mixing them with the sugar, since adding them alone will cause them to clump. These clumps are impossible to break down and will render the stabilizer/emulsifier properties at least weaker than they would be in a soluble powder form, if not useless.

2. Place the milk in a pot over high heat.

3. At 25°C/77°F, add the milk powder and flavoring if it is a steeped flavoring (such as vanilla, spices, or other flavoring). From this point on, whisking should be constant to prevent any of the ingredients from settling to the bottom of the pot.

4. At 35°C/95°F, pour in and mix all of the sugars until dissolved. This refers to any type of sugar, either in solid (granulated) or liquid form (glucose or invert sugar, for example). Some recipes might contain egg yolks. If so, they should be whisked in at this temperature.

5. At 45°C/113°F, add the heavy cream, if using.

6. Before the mixture reaches 50°C/122°F, add the stabilizer-sugar mixture in a slow, pouring motion while whisking constantly.

7. Bring the mixture up to 85°C/185°F, take off the heat, and cook for 2 more minutes while whisking constantly to pasteurize and homogenize the mixture.

8. If there are any solid or liquid ingredients, such as chocolate or nut pastes, fruit purées, or liquors, add them at this moment.

9. Pass the mixture through a fine-mesh sieve and chill to 4°C/39°F as quickly as possible using an ice water bath.

10. Let the mixture age for at least 4 hours or ideally for 12 hours before churning.

11. Before churning, give the base a good stir.

12. Churn to −4°C/25°F.

13. Place the churned product in a −10°C/14°F freezer. Reserve for service.

THE GRANITÉ METHOD

This is a method that is used for the flavored shaved ices known as granité or granita, depending on where you are from. It can also be used to make flavored solid ices.

THE GRANITÉ METHOD IS AS FOLLOWS:

1. Place the main ingredient in a stainless-steel bowl. This is usually a fruit or vegetable juice, an infused or flavored liquid, or a wine. The infused or flavored liquid can be a dairy product, generally milk, and is not exclusive of water or juice.

2. Make sure that the temperature of the main ingredient is 20°C/68°F. If not, temper it. This will give you an accurate reading on a refractometer. Colder or warmer liquids will not provide an accurate reading.

3. Add some 65° Brix simple syrup that is at a temperature of 20°C/68°F. Speaking in very general terms, a good starting point is 1 part simple syrup to 4 parts of the main ingredient. The ° Brix refers to the sugar density of the simple syrup. A 65° Brix syrup is a syrup that is 65 percent sugar and 35 percent water. You can also use a 50° Brix simple syrup, but you will need more of it in your base, and it may dilute the flavor.

4. Whisk the mixture thoroughly. Take a reading with the refractometer. It should read between 16° Brix and 19° Brix. My personal preference is 17° Brix, which is not too sweet but sweet enough. Always taste to make sure the flavor is to your liking. It is good to trust a refractometer, but you should be able to trust your taste buds as well. A pinch of salt is recommended, to round out the flavors of your base.

5. Pour the granité base into a stainless-steel hotel pan. The size will depend on the desired amount.

6. Place the pan in a −18 C°/0°F freezer.

7. After 45 to 60 minutes, remove the pan from the freezer and scrape the ice crystals that will have formed around the rim of the pan.

8. Repeat this process every 30 minutes, always scraping in a circular motion to ensure even crystal formation.

9. Once all the liquid has frozen, transfer the granité to a size-appropriate hotel pan and cover. Reserve for service in a −18°C/0°F freezer. This freezer needs to be colder than one that holds sorbets or ice creams, so that the ice crystals do not melt. This type of frozen dessert is more susceptible to heat shock since there is very little to protect the ice from melting.

   NOTE *You can use this method up until Step 4 to make solid flavored ices.*

THE CLASSIC SORBET METHOD (also used for sherbets)

This is the simplest and most straightforward method for making sorbets and sherbets; it is also the most widely used when there are limited resources and equipment. The results can be just as good as with modern methods, but the margin of error and the care these items require is higher since they are less stable and more susceptible to temperature changes.

THE CLASSIC SORBET METHOD IS AS FOLLOWS:

1. Place the main liquid, which is the flavor of your sorbet, in a stainless-steel bowl. This main liquid should be free of solid particles and previously strained through a fine-mesh sieve. It can be a fruit or vegetable juice, purée, infused liquid, or wine. In the case of a sherbet, it can be a dairy product, such as milk, buttermilk, or yogurt, which can also be flavored.

2. If the main liquid was refrigerated, temper it to 20°C/68°F; this will give you an accurate reading on a refractometer. Colder or warmer liquids will not provide an accurate reading. To temper the main liquid, place the bowl in a larger bowl that is filled halfway with water at 40°C/104°F. Stir until the main liquid reaches 20°C/68°F.

3. Pour in some simple syrup that is at 20°C/68°F as well and combine with a whisk. The simple syrup amount should be the equivalent of 20 percent of the weight of the main liquid.

4. Take a reading with the refractometer. If the refractometer reads below 25° Brix, add more simple syrup. If you have gone above the desired Brix level, simply add more of the main liquid. Acidic or bitter liquids will require more simple syrup than "sweeter" ones, unless a more savory result is desired. Once the desired degrees Brix is reached, the sorbet or sherbet base can be refrigerated, up to 3 days in most cases, or churned.

5. Churn the sorbet base and transfer to a −10°C/14°F freezer.

6. Let the sorbet harden in the freezer for 2 to 4 hours before serving. Reserve for service.

THE MODERN SORBET METHOD (also used for sherbets)

This method is similar in nature to the classic sorbet method in which a sweetener is added to a base ingredient/flavor of sorbet, but this method yields a much more service-friendly product. The base is usually a mix of fruit or vegetable juice or purée or infused liquid or wine, or a flavored dairy product for sherbets, with water (not always; it depends on the main ingredient) and a special sorbet syrup (recipe follows) that contains a variety of sugars and sorbet stabilizers, which are what make the end product so service friendly.

1. Bring your main ingredient and the sorbet syrup up to 20°C/68°F. If the liquid you are making the sorbet out of is thick in nature (such as a fruit purée), add 10 percent of its weight in water. The water should also be tempered.

2. Add 10 percent of the weight of the main ingredient in sorbet syrup. Check the Brix degrees with a refractometer. It should read 30° Brix to 32° Brix. If it does not, continue to add sorbet syrup until it does.

3. Once you have combined the sorbet mixture with the main ingredient and water, let it "mature" or age for at least 2 hours and up to 6 hours, which is ideal. This will give the stabilizers and sugars time to bind with the main ingredient to produce a high-quality sorbet.

4. Churn the sorbet base and transfer to a −10°C/14°F freezer.

5. Let the sorbet harden for 2 to 4 hours before serving.

6. Reserve for service.

SORBET SYRUP

YIELD: 5 KG/11.02 LB

INGREDIENT	METRIC	U.S.	%
Sorbet stabilizer	35 g	1.23 oz	.7%
Sugar	2.1 kg	4 lb 10.07 oz	42%
Water	1.96 kg	4 lb 4.96 oz	39.1%
Glucose powder	910 g	2 lb .1 oz	18.2%

1. Combine the sorbet stabilizer with 10 percent of the sugar. Mix thoroughly.

2. Place the water, the remaining sugar, and the glucose powder in a pot over high heat. Stir constantly using a whisk.

3. When the mix reaches 40°C/104°F, slowly pour in the sorbet stabilizer mixture as you stir. If the mixture is poured in too quickly, the stabilizer will clump up and therefore not work.

4. Continue stirring until the mixture reaches 85°C/185°F. At this temperature, the stabilizers will fully hydrate and the sugars will dissolve completely.

5. Take the pot off the heat and transfer the liquid mixture to an ice water bath. Let the mix cool completely before you add it to the main ingredient

6. Reserve refrigerated. Discard after 2 months. If there is still sorbet syrup in the refrigerator after 2 months, you have either made too much or you are not making enough sorbet. Make enough to last for 1 week, if that.

THE COMPONENTS OF PASTRY

The following information is meant to be used as a visual reference to aid you in the ideation of desserts. How you use it and which items you choose to use are up to you. Sometimes we may forget about certain components or overlook them, and this list is meant to help remind you. There are some preparations that are very rare or that may not suit most applications. Those have been omitted from this list. Some preparations will be repeated in different categories due to their nature. For example, in chocolate preparations there will be chocolate sauce, and under sauces, there will be chocolate sauce as well. Savory preparations have not been included, since this book focuses on pastry preparations.

This list also includes a listing of available ingredients. Sometimes all it takes to get an idea is to see a flavor you want to use, and that can set you off thinking about a series of products you can make with that ingredient. Not every ingredient is in this listing. As with the pastry preparations, some are too specific to an area or are very hard to obtain.

CHOCOLATE PREPARATIONS

COATING

Ganache

Glaze

Tempered chocolate (hand-dipped confection)

Tempered chocolate shell/vessels and confections

Velvet spray (coating)

FILLING FOR A CAKE OR INDIVIDUAL DESSERT

Bavarian cream

Crémeux

Ganache

Mousse

Panna cotta

INSERT

Bubble chocolate or aerated solid chocolate

Meringue

FROZEN

Bombe (frozen and chilled)

Frappé

Frozen bubbles

Frozen yogurt

Granité

Ice

Ice cream

Parfait (frozen and chilled)

Semifreddo

Sherbet

Sorbet

Soufflé (hot and frozen)

GARNISH

Atomized chocolate (powdered chocolate, which is different from cocoa powder)

Bubble chocolate or aerated solid chocolate

Chantilly

Crème anglaise

Croquant

Décor

Flexible ganache

Foam (can be frozen)

Meringue

Powder (with tapioca maltodextrin)

Sauce

Shaved chocolate

Soil

Solid chocolate pieces

Tuile

DOUGH/BAKED ITEM

Angel food cake

Biscotti

Brioche

Brownies

Cookies (a very large variety)

Devil's food cake/Blackout cake

Flourless chocolate cake

Génoise

Macarons

Meringue

Pain de gênes

Pound cake

Sablé dough (cookies and tart shells)

Shortbread

Tuiles

OTHERS

Caramel

Chocolate pudding

Crème brûlée

Crème caramel

Drinking chocolate

Hand-dipped confections and molded chocolates

Pastry cream

Pot de crème

Puff pastry

Spread

Truffles

CUSTARDS

STIRRED

Crema catalana

Crème anglaise

Curds

Rice pudding

Tapioca pudding

BAKED

Bread pudding

Cannelé

Certain pies (pumpkin, for example)

Cheesecake

Clafouti

Crème brûlée

Crème caramel

Flan

Pot de crème

Royale

BOILED

Cream pies

Crema catalana

Pastry cream

AERATED DESSERTS

HOT

Chiboust

Foams (using a cream whipper; can be also refrigerated)

Parfait (can be refrigerated or frozen)

WARM

Sabayon or zabaglione

Soufflé

REFRIGERATED

Bombe

Chantilly

Cream (Bavarian)

Cream (diplomat)

Foamed flavored milk (fresh or dehydrated)

Foamed liquids (non-egg foamed, foamed using a whisk or electric mixer with a whip; can be frozen and sometimes warm depending on the additive used as aerator)

Mousse

Parfait

FROZEN

Semifreddo

Bombe

Frozen bubbles

Mousse

Parfait

Soufflé

COATINGS

Atomized chocolate

Buttercream

Chocolate plaques

Chocolate shell

Cocoa powder

Coconut

Confectioners' sugar

Cooked sugar

Dextrose

Fondant (poured and rolled)

Frosting or icing

Ganache

Gelled liquid

Glaze

Marzipan

Meringue/foams

Mirror glaze or clear glaze

Nuts (toasted or candied)

Shaved chocolate

Velvet spray

Whipped cream

DOUGHS (PASTRY SPECIFIC)

Beignet

Biscotti

Brioche

Cookies

Craquelin

Doughnut (can be brioche based)

Filo

Gaufrettes

Gingerbread

Kataifi

Laminated (puff, croissant, Danish)

Linzer dough

Mochi

Pâte brisée

Pâte sablée

Pâte sucrée

Pie dough

Pizzelle

Sablé breton

Shortbread

Soil

Speculoos

Streusel

Strudel

Sugar cookies (1-2-3 cookie dough)

BATTERS (PASTRY SPECIFIC)

Almond cream

Angel food cake

Baumkuchen

Blini

Brownie/Blondie

Brownies

Cake doughnut

Cannelé

Chiffon

Crêpe

Dacquoise

Financier

Flourless cake

Frangipane

Fruit sponge cake

Frying batter

Funnel cake

Gâteau basque

Gâteau breton

Génoise

Japonaise

Joconde

Lace tuiles

Ladyfingers

Macarons

Madeleine

Marjolaine

Micro génoise

Muffin

Pain de genes

Pâte à choux

Pound cake

Savarin

Tuile

COOKED SUGAR PREPARATIONS

Blown sugar

Brittle

Brûlée (a finishing method
more than a preparation)

Cajeta

Candied fruit

Caramel (light or dark)

Cooked sugar décor

Cooked sugar macarons

Cotton candy

Croquant

Dragées

Dulce de leche

Flaky confections (cooked
sugar poured into chocolate,
see the recipe on page 323)

Fondant

Fudge

Hard candies

Italian buttercream

Italian meringue

Jelly

Liquor bonbons

Marmalade

Marshmallow

Marzipan

Mousseline

Nougat

Nougatine

Pâte de fruit

Popping candy

Praline (smooth or chunky)

Preserved nuts (marrons glacés)

Preserves

Pulled sugar

Pulled sugar cellophane

Solid cooked sugar pieces
for showpieces

Spun sugar

Syrup

Toffee

SUGAR PREPARATIONS (UNCOOKED)

Coating (truffles, pâte de
fruit, crystallized fruit)

Compacted for sugar showpieces

Crystallized fruit, flowers, and herbs

Dusting (confectioners'
sugar/dextrose)

French meringue

Garnish (pearl sugar)

Pastillage

Royal icing

FRUIT PREPARATIONS

Battered and fried

Blanched

Braised

Butter

Candied

Caramelized

Carbonated

Compote

Compressed sous vide

Confit

Cooked sous vide

Coulis

Crystallized

Dehydrated

Freeze-dried (whole or pulverized)

Fresh

Fritters

Frozen desserts (virtually all)

Gelée

Infusion

Jam

Jelly

Juice

Macerated

Marmalade

Nitrogen frozen (shaved or grated)

Paper

Paste

Pâte de fruit

Poached

Preserved

Pulp

Purée

Rendered

Roasted

Sautéed

Steamed

Water

SAUCES

Caramel (clear to dark)

Chocolate based

Coulis

Custard based sauces (anglaise)

Fluid gels

Purée

Reductions (juice, purée,
cooking liquid, infusions, etc.)

Syrup

Thickened juices/purées

Thickened liquids/infusions

NUT-BASED PREPARATIONS

All frozen desserts (even
sorbet and ices)

Candied

Coconut

Dacquoise

Dragées

Financier

Gianduja

Joconde

Macarons

Marzipan

Nougat

Nut butter

Pain de gênes

Praline (smooth or chunky)

Toasted

Turrón (torrone)

CARAMEL PREPARATIONS

Coating

Confection

Filling

Frozen desserts

Fruit poaching medium

Garnish

Glaze

Inclusion or insert

Sauce

Soaking liquid

Spread

HYDROCOLLOID PREPARATIONS

Aerated liquids (non–egg based)

Any dough or batter

Bubbles

Clarified liquids (through filtration)

Coating

Creams (bavarois)

Crispy foams

Egg-free "custards"

Emulsions

Film (gelatin)

Flexible chocolate ganache

Flexible curd

Fluid gel

Foams

Gels (gelées, jellies)

Glaze

Jellies

Marshmallows

Mousse (some types)

Noodles

Panna cotta

Paper

Pâte de fruit

Powders (fat-based ingredients)

Reverse-spherification

Spaghetto or tubes

Spherification

Sponges

Suspensions

Thickened liquids

Veils

Warm foams

Warm gels (gelées, jellies)

MERINGUES

Dacquoise

Egg white powder–aerated liquids

Egg yolk

French

Italian

Non–egg white aerated liquids (see Note)

Swiss

NOTE *Almost any liquid can be whipped if it contains a protein. A liquid that contains gelatin can be whipped; for an example, see the egg-free marshmallows on page 492. Other ingredients, such as Methocel F50, can whip egg-free liquids as well. Liquids with fats are almost impossible to whip in this style, because the fat molecules prevent air bubble from being trapped. Heavy cream is not in the same category.*

FROZEN DESSERTS

Bombe

Bubbles

Custard-based ice cream

Dry ice (frozen)

Foam

Frappé

Frozen yogurt

Gelato

Granité (granita)

Ice pops

Ices

Mousse

Nitrogen (frozen)

Non–custard based ice cream

Parfait

Semifreddo

Shaved ices

Sherbet

Sorbet

Soufflé

Spoom

HERB, TEA, INFUSION, FLOWER, AROMATICS, AND SPICE PREPARATIONS

Candied

Crystallized

Dehydrated

Distilled

Freeze dried/powdered

Fresh (some types)

Gelled

Infused

Macerated

Preserved

Suspended

GRAIN PREPARATIONS

Caramelized puffed rice

Cereals

Cream of wheat

Feuilletine

Freeze-dried corn

Horchata (rice milk)

Mochi

Polenta

Popcorn

Pudding (rice, tapioca)

Puffed grains (rice, quinoa, corn)

Puffed rice coated in chocolate

Rice "chicharrón" (fritter)

Tapioca film

Wafer paper (rice-based)

FLAVORS AND TEXTURES

Each of the sections in this chapter is meant to build upon the previous one. The methods have been covered and the most common preparations were charted. The next logical step is to look into flavors and textures in order to put together a dessert.

What is flavor? Flavor can be explained simply as the combination of taste and smell. Flavor is 80 percent aroma. When you taste a lemon, what you are tasting is its acidity, sourness, and, to a much lesser extent, saltiness. What you smell, however, is aroma, and that is what signals to the brain that it is a lemon. When both of these factors (aroma and taste) are combined, the result is flavor. This is why when you have a cold you cannot taste your food very well and also why when you are hungry your sense of smell gets stronger. We can only perceive three aromas at a time. Any more than that is too much and the aromas will become muddled and not distinct. The same goes for tastes. More than three different tastes cannot be identified clearly. Try to keep your desserts within those parameters.

Understanding flavors and textures and how they can be used, as well as how ingredients can be manipulated into different textures, will contribute to developing your own map of ideas for dessert development. However, a dessert is not only flavor and texture. Food is one of the only things in the world that combines all of the senses. The senses are the windows to the

the method for tasting food

There is such a thing as a correct method for tasting. The following method was inspired by the method used for tasting wine. In wine tasting, you swirl the wine in the glass to stir around the volatile aroma compounds, which are released from the wine and aspirated by the nose through agitation. The wine is then drunk, and then an inward whistling is used to oxygenate the wine and release volatile compounds. This amplifies the way a wine will taste in order to appreciate it to its fullest. Based on that, this is the method for tasting food correctly:

1. **If you are going to taste food, don't just taste a little pinch of food. You must put all of the components of the dish in the spoon or fork in order to fully appreciate it. You cannot come to a conclusion about the dessert if you only take a morsel of one of the components.**

2. **Everything that is chilled or frozen tastes better when it is tempered. Try to plan accordingly.**

3. **Place the food in your mouth and start chewing with your mouth open. This is going to oxygenate the food that is in your mouth. If you are shy about this, then cover your mouth with your hand.**

4. **As you are chewing, rub what you are tasting with your tongue against your soft palate. This will help oxygenate the food even further, it will warm the food up (which helps with taste perception), and it will combine it/dilute it with saliva. This also helps with textural perception. Your tongue and soft palate are extremely sensitive.**

5. **The volatile aromatic compounds travel around the oral cavity and then go up through your nose from behind as you swallow and exhale. Think about what is in your mouth. Is the flavor profile there? Is it present enough, or does it need fine-tuning?**

Tasting all of your food is a crucial component to be being a successful pastry chef. What happens if, for example, one of your cooks oversalts a dough? You are the last line of defense. You must catch these mistakes before they go out into the dining room.

body. Keeping those factors in mind will determine the success or failure of a finished product. Much of that success can also be attributed to context or, more accurately, *terroir* and not just to the body's five physical senses.

Culture can also have very strong influences on taste preference because much of what you ate at home or growing up is highly likely to remain your taste preference for pretty much your entire life, with some additions here and there. Some tastes can be acquired. Many say that beer, caviar, and Champagne, for example, are acquired tastes. The preferences that are acquired early on are what can make peoples' tastes so different. Aversions to food are hard to explain, although they can become clearer when it comes to such items as very fragrant (stinky) cheese. Although the not-so-ordinary aversions, such as to chocolate, are less common, they do occur, and that is just a matter of personal taste. If two people are sitting at the same table having the same food, there will still be two completely different perceptions of the meal. You should pretend that every single customer is a chef or restaurant critic, perhaps more knowledgeable than you. Because you never know, do you? If one customer likes it, chances are that most other people will like it as well, but don't forget that you cannot make everyone happy all of the time. Maintaining a sensory contrast and a sensory balance is the biggest challenge for anyone preparing food. It is a skill that is honed with time and with practice.

Other factors, such as mood, state of mind, tiredness, and so on, can also influence one's sensory perception of food, and unfortunately, none of them are under your control. One could argue that what is good is good, no matter what, but that is not true. Each person is different, and one person can have a very different perception of a dish than another. In fact, the same person can have a different perception of the exact same dish on different days. In the end, cooking is an art that cannot be substituted by science, and in reality, all that is in your control is the quality of your food, the quality of your service staff, and the environment in which you serve your food.

Texture is another determining factor that needs close attention. Not only are some textures preferred over others, but your customers also may have certain expectations for texture. If a fresh, raw apple is soft, the signal to your brain is: Something is wrong here. But if it is crisp and juicy, then all is good so long as the flavor is appropriate.

There are general texture preferences. The following list is in order, from the most preferred to the least, but in the end it really depends on the nature of the food at hand (one does not expect a mousse to be crispy; it should be creamy and smooth), and again, personal preference. This is merely a list of general food texture preferences. Following it is another list that is made up of undesirable textures.

DESIRABLE TEXTURES

- Crunchy
- Chewy
- Crispy
- Creamy
- Smooth
- Juicy
- Spongy (this applies mostly to bread)

Having more than one texture in your dessert from the list above is a good idea. Textural contrasts are desirable.

▓ Watery	▓ Soggy	▓ Lumpy	▓ Grainy
▓ Sticky	▓ Slimy	▓ Tough	
▓ Greasy	▓ Icy	▓ Hard	

The tables that follow are broken down by category or type of ingredient. This is by no means a list of every single ingredient in pastry, but it is large enough to cover the most readily available products. Within each ingredient, the table will note if it has a frontal, background, or mild flavor. Is it an intense, easily perceptible flavor; more of a background flavor that plays more of a supporting role to push other flavors forward; or is the ingredient mild and better eaten on its own? The tables also show what other flavors it combines well with or "flavor compatibility." The tables do not note unusual or uncommon flavor pairings, since that is something that you can get to once you know how to group flavors together. The following flavor combinations are reliable and only meant to be suggestions, but they work very well with the ingredients in question.

In the third column, there is also a list of flavors that serve to play a supporting role. If the supporting flavor is then listed as a main ingredient in the first column, the original ingredient it was paired with will not repeat in its third column, since this reciprocal pairing does not always apply. The ingredient will always be the main focus flavor; the flavors it combines with are secondary flavors, and sometimes when those secondary flavors are given a lead role, they cannot be paired with their original partner.

Fruits

Fruits have an incredible versatility and can be used and cooked in a large variety of ways. Often they can be used without cooking, although some fruits, such as apricots, benefit tremendously from cooking. Other fruits, like Asian pears, are best kept raw. An entire dessert can be built around a fruit or a variety of fruits; however, it is important to know how to manipulate them to bring the best out of them and also to know how to combine them with other fruits or components. Only use fruit that is in season because that is when it is at its best, and also because it is less expensive. You can choose not to use fresh fruit. There is no rule that says that you should have fresh fruit on your menu year-round. You can use dried fruit or you can put away fresh fruit throughout the main produce months in your area by either freezing them (whole or puréed) or preserving them. Of course, this requires large storage spaces in your freezer and in your pantry; this can increase your food costs tremendously during those in-season months but greatly reduce them in the winter. You can also stick to other flavors, such as chocolate, spices, or nuts. It is the resourceful pastry chef who will succeed in pleasing customers throughout the year.

INGREDIENT	TYPE OF FLAVOR: FRONTAL, BACKGROUND, OR MILD	FLAVOR COMPATIBILITY
Apples	Frontal to mild, easily overpowered if too much sugar or too many spices are used	Vanilla Butter Heavy cream Most spices (cloves, nutmeg, ginger, grains of paradise, cinnamon) Fennel Anise Caramel White chocolate Milk chocolate Dark chocolate Most nuts (pecans and walnuts at the forefront) Apple liquors and derivatives (cider, vinegar) Cheese (cheddar, Ekte Gjetost, Emmentaler, cream cheese) Currants Honey Maple syrup/sugar Oats Molasses Brown sugar Sour cream Clotted cream Crème fraîche Saffron
Apricots	Frontal; much more pronounced when cooked than when raw. Dried apricots also have a good concentrated flavor that is preferred over raw apricots.	Most nuts (almonds, pecans, pistachios) Wheat beers, Sauternes, and Alsatian wines Vanilla Verjus Butter Caramel Ginger Ice cream (vanilla, nut based, chocolate) Heavy cream Crème fraîche Clotted cream Lavender Marzipan Elderflower
Asian pears	Mild; mostly used raw	Vanilla Bergamot Chamomile Aromatic wines (Alsatian and dessert wines) Lemons, limes Elderflower Litchis

INGREDIENT	TYPE OF FLAVOR: FRONTAL, BACKGROUND, OR MILD	FLAVOR COMPATIBILITY
Bananas	Frontal	Caramel Vanilla Spices: cinnamon, anise, cloves, nutmeg Peanut butter Milk chocolate (dark and white as well, to a lesser extent) Tropical fruits: coconut, pineapple, mango Butter Rum Brown sugar Crème fraîche Heavy cream Strawberries
Blackberries	Frontal	Vanilla Heavy cream Cinnamon Orange peel Clotted cream Crème fraîche Lemon peel Almonds White chocolate
Blueberries	Mild	Vanilla Lemons Cinnamon Mascarpone Peaches Butter Buttermilk Cream Raspberries Strawberries
Cherries	Mild; more pronounced when they are cooked than when they are raw	Vanilla Pistachios and almonds Marzipan Cinnamon Dark chocolate Red wine Heavy cream Crème fraîche Orange peel
Citrus Fruit Varieties	Frontal. The acidity gives it a pronounced taste.	
Blood oranges/ Oranges/Navel oranges/Tangerines/ Mandarin oranges/ Clementines		Vanilla Cinnamon Dark chocolate White chocolate Cranberries Mint Grenadine Campari

INGREDIENT	TYPE OF FLAVOR: FRONTAL, BACKGROUND, OR MILD	FLAVOR COMPATIBILITY
Grapefruits/Pomelos	Frontal	Mint Campari Vanilla Asti Spumante Pomegranates
Kaffir limes/leaves	Frontal	Ginger Cream Lemongrass Basil
Kumquats	Frontal	Vanilla Cinnamon Cream Carrots Meringue
Lemons/Meyer lemons	Frontal	Huckleberries Raspberries Blueberries Blackberries Honey Poppy seeds Vanilla Milk chocolate Dark chocolate White chocolate Mint Tarragon Meringue Beer, especially lager, pilsner, and wheat
Limes/Key limes	Frontal	Coconut Vanilla Rum Butter Dark chocolate White chocolate Mangoes Mint
Yuzus	Frontal	Vanilla Passion fruit Lemongrass Black sesame paste White chocolate Green tea Tapioca Litchi Caramel Mint Basil

INGREDIENT	TYPE OF FLAVOR: FRONTAL, BACKGROUND, OR MILD	FLAVOR COMPATIBILITY
Black, red, or white currants	Frontal	Almonds Heavy cream Vanilla Dark chocolate
Cranberries	Frontal	Oranges Cinnamon Vanilla Lemons Almonds Pecans Maple syrup Quince Currants Cloves
Dates	Mild	Caramel Dark chocolate Milk chocolate Coffee Maple Mascarpone Pistachios Butter Almonds Marzipan
Dried fruits Used as is or rehydrated provides two very different intensities of flavor. Rehydrated dried fruits have a very pronounced flavor.	Frontal (rehydrated), mild (as is)	Spices (cinnamon, cloves, star anise) Chocolate Nuts Vanilla
Figs	Mild	Cinnamon Balsamic vinegar reduction (sweet) Marsala Red wine Port Marzipan Almonds Cheeses (blue, Gorgonzola, Explorateur, goat, ricotta) Pistachios Vin santo Oranges Currants Honey Mascarpone Cream Sherry

INGREDIENT	TYPE OF FLAVOR: FRONTAL, BACKGROUND, OR MILD	FLAVOR COMPATIBILITY
Grapes: Concord/ Varietal grapes	Frontal	Peanut butter Cheese (blue, goat's milk) Eucalyptus Mint Lemons Buttermilk Cashews Walnuts
Guavas	Frontal	Vanilla Meringue Hibiscus Tamarind Cheddar, manchego, and cream cheese (guava paste only) Bananas Coconut
Huckleberries	Frontal	Vanilla Lemons Meringue Butter Almonds Corn
Litchis	Frontal	Elderflower Rose Raspberries Almonds Coconut Lemons Milk chocolate Basil Mint
Mangoes	Background	Mint Coconut Limes Bananas Oranges Rum Cream Pineapple
Melons	Mild	Vanilla Lemons Limes Mint Port Beaumes de Venise (sweet wine) Yogurt Prosecco/Champagne/Asti Spumante Raspberries

INGREDIENT	TYPE OF FLAVOR: FRONTAL, BACKGROUND, OR MILD	FLAVOR COMPATIBILITY
Papayas	Mild	Mint Limes Oranges Passion fruit
Passion fruit	Frontal	Vanilla Mascarpone Coconut Pineapple Mint Basil Champagne/Prosecco/Asti Spumante Tequila White rum Caramel White chocolate Lime zest Bananas
Peaches/Nectarines	Mild	Almonds Vanilla Sauternes Ice wine Blueberries Cinnamon Cream Lemons Crème fraîche Butter Mint Champagne/Prosecco/Asti Spumante Moscato d'Asti Honey Verjus Elderflower Caramel

INGREDIENT	TYPE OF FLAVOR: FRONTAL, BACKGROUND, OR MILD	FLAVOR COMPATIBILITY
Pears	Mild	Vanilla Almonds Marzipan Cranberries Honey Cream Butter Caramel Cinnamon Cloves Lemons Mascarpone Dark chocolate Milk chocolate Blue cheeses Chestnuts Walnuts Crème fraîche Red wine Star anise Maple syrup Amaretto Frangelico Hazelnuts Elderflower
Persimmons	Mild	Cinnamon Vanilla White chocolate Cream Honey Lemons Pomegranates
Pineapple	Frontal	Vanilla Dark rum Caramel Coconut (raw and toasted) Almonds Bananas Star anise Limes Mangoes Butter Tequila Macadamia nuts
Plums	Mild	Almonds Vanilla Cinnamon Brandy Oranges Lemons Honey Cream

INGREDIENT	TYPE OF FLAVOR: FRONTAL, BACKGROUND, OR MILD	FLAVOR COMPATIBILITY
Pomegranates	Frontal	Oranges Apples Vanilla Yogurt Cardamom Ginger
Prunes (dried plums)	Mild	Armagnac Brandy Cinnamon Walnuts Dry red wine Allspice
Pumpkins/Butternut squash	Mild	Cinnamon Cloves Nutmeg Vanilla Allspice Ginger Sour cream/crème fraîche Caramel Milk chocolate Butter Cream Brown sugar Maple syrup Sage Pumpkin seeds
Quince	Frontal	Cinnamon Cloves Ginger Vanilla Apples/apple cider Pears Manchego or goat cheese Maple syrup
Raisins	Mild	Rum Bananas Oatmeal Cinnamon Red wine Port Quince Dark chocolate Almonds Pecans

INGREDIENT	TYPE OF FLAVOR: FRONTAL, BACKGROUND, OR MILD	FLAVOR COMPATIBILITY
Raspberries	**Mild**	Vanilla Cream Lemons Oranges Blueberries Strawberries Almonds Dark chocolate White chocolate Crème fraîche Meringue Yogurt Marzipan
Rhubarb	**Frontal**	Strawberries Crème fraîche Cream Butter Almonds Angelica Oranges/blood oranges Caramel
Strawberries	**Frontal**	Vanilla Bananas Cream Meringue Crème fraîche Dark chocolate White chocolate Lemons Mascarpone Oranges Raspberries Blueberries Rhubarb Balsamic vinegar Black pepper
Watermelon	**Mild**	Lemons Limes Tomatoes Basil Vanilla

Herbs

Herbs are not necessarily used as a primary component in a dessert, although often they can function as a main flavor or as the determining flavor profile around which a dessert is built. Herbs aren't generally pleasant to eat in large quantities. They are mostly used to accompany or enhance other flavors. Herbs that have a strong presence (frontal flavor) should be used in moderation, since they can often overwhelm to the point of numbing any other flavors on the dish, including their own. Think of herbs as enhancers or secondary notes.

Some herbs can be used fresh, and others, categorized as resinous, are used to flavor foods and may not be entirely pleasurable to chew on, like rosemary or bay leaves. The latter should be used while cooking so that it can release its flavors and then it should be removed. Fresh herbs, like mint or basil, are better when they are not cooked. Herbs that are traditionally used in savory cooking are not included in this listing, such as chervil, cilantro, chives, and parsley. However, this doesn't mean they cannot be used in desserts.

INGREDIENT	TYPE OF FLAVOR: FRONTAL, BACKGROUND, OR MILD	FLAVOR COMPATIBILITY
Angelica	Frontal	Anise Apricots Ginger Lavender Oranges Rhubarb Strawberries
Anise hyssop Regular hyssop is not commonly used in desserts. It does combine well with cranberries, thyme, and rosemary.	Frontal	Peaches Rhubarb Butter Honey Lemons Blueberries Strawberries Raspberries Melons Apricots Watermelon
Basil (sweet, Thai, purple) There are many other varieties of basil, such as lemon, chocolate, and cinnamon. Those namesake flavors are also their flavor compatibility. They can be used with some of the flavors in the third column above.	Mild	Coconut Pineapple Mangoes Pine nuts Almonds Blueberries Raspberries Strawberries Honey Citrus fruits Watermelon

INGREDIENT	TYPE OF FLAVOR: FRONTAL, BACKGROUND, OR MILD	FLAVOR COMPATIBILITY
Bay leaf	Mild	Quince Caramel Vanilla Figs Rice Thyme
Fennel fronds/ Fennel bulb	Frontal	Apples Caramel Bay leaf Anise Lemons Oranges Mint Pernod Thyme Almonds Honey Sambuca
Hierba santa (a.k.a root beer leaf)	Frontal	Root beer Vanilla Caramel Molasses Saffron Cream
Lavender	Frontal	Honey Almonds Cream Vanilla Plums Peaches Cherries Lemons Raspberries Thyme Strawberries
Lemon balm	Mild	Fennel Peaches Nectarines Ginger Melons Mint
Lemongrass	Mild	Coconut Black sesame paste Litchis Basil Vanilla Cream

INGREDIENT	TYPE OF FLAVOR: FRONTAL, BACKGROUND, OR MILD	FLAVOR COMPATIBILITY
Lemon verbena	Mild	Peaches Nectarines Apricots Lillet Blanc Blueberries Verjus Black currants
Mint	Mild to Frontal	Practically all fruits Dark chocolate Milk chocolate Heavy cream Honey Lavender Lemongrass Lemon verbena Yogurt Buttermilk
Peppermint	Frontal	Heavy cream Dark chocolate Lemons
Rosemary	Frontal	Heavy cream Lemon Lavender Honey Apples Quince Pears Strawberries
Saffron	Frontal	Apples White chocolate Heavy cream Vanilla Rice Cardamom Cinnamon
Sage	Frontal	Pumpkin Butter Butternut squash Cinnamon Cloves Nutmeg Heavy cream Sour cream Cherries Rosemary Thyme

INGREDIENT	TYPE OF FLAVOR: FRONTAL, BACKGROUND, OR MILD	FLAVOR COMPATIBILITY
Shiso leaf	Mild	Licorice Mint Miso Strawberries Sake Oranges Lemons Apricots
Tarragon	Frontal	Lemons Oranges Meyer lemons White chocolate Poppy seeds Fennel Grapefruits Melons
Thyme	Frontal	Vanilla Lemons Heavy cream Pears Almonds Caramel Honey Pine nuts Olive oil Rosemary

Spices

Spices are meant to be used almost in the same capacity as herbs. They contribute flavor mostly, and on some occasions they contribute texture, but this is not a desirable quality. Spices tend to be on the hard side and are generally unpleasant to chew on, let alone swallow. Spices can be toasted before they are used to increase their strength. Heat releases the aromas that are particular to a spice; when using them raw (that is, not toasted), they are not as flavorful. Spices can be combined with other spices to produce successful and appealing flavors, but it is important to know how to use them in combination for the results to be harmonious. One spice can easily overpower another one if they are not used in the correct proportion.

Quality can vary from one source to another. Using higher-quality spices means that you don't need to use as much, as the flavor is usually more potent. As with herbs, typically savory spices are not included in this listing, including achiote, celery seeds, black pepper, and cayenne pepper.

INGREDIENT	TYPE OF FLAVOR: FRONTAL, BACKGROUND, OR MILD	FLAVOR COMPATIBILITY
Allspice Allspice has this name because it tastes like cinnamon, cloves, ginger, and juniper berry all put together, and while they are not all the spices by any means, they are certainly plenty.	Frontal	Pumpkin Butternut squash Cinnamon Ginger Cloves Quince
Anise seeds (also star anise)	Frontal	Pineapple Rye bread Fennel seeds Quince Pears Apples Coffee Milk chocolate Cinnamon Ginger Vanilla
Cardamom Black cardamom is considered slightly sweeter than regular cardamom	Frontal	Espresso Heavy cream Cinnamon Dates Ginger Oranges Milk chocolate Plums Cherries

INGREDIENT	TYPE OF FLAVOR: FRONTAL, BACKGROUND, OR MILD	FLAVOR COMPATIBILITY
Cinnamon Cinnamon can produce a mucilaginous texture when it is heated and combined with a liquid, especially when using powdered cinnamon.	**Frontal**	Apples Pears Bananas Espresso Dark chocolate White chocolate Cherries Peaches Vanilla Heavy cream Butter Cream cheese Dried fruits (figs, raisins, currants, apricots, prunes) Oats Rice Pecans Almonds Blueberries Cloves Ginger Maple Nutmeg Oranges Cranberries Pumpkin Butternut squash Caramel Cardamom Sour cream Crème fraîche Buttermilk
Cloves	**Frontal**	Apples Pineapple Bananas Pumpkin Butternut squash Quince Pears Vanilla Currants Cinnamon Ginger Lemons Oranges Red wine Prunes Dates

INGREDIENT	TYPE OF FLAVOR: FRONTAL, BACKGROUND, OR MILD	FLAVOR COMPATIBILITY
Ginger (fresh)	Frontal	Coconut Apples Basil Dark chocolate Cinnamon Vanilla Heavy cream Honey Mint Molasses Limes Lemons Pears Bananas Yuzus Oranges Pineapple Coconut
Ginger (ground)	Frontal	Gingerbread Lemons Pumpkin Butternut squash Acorn squash Butter
Grains of paradise	Frontal	Apples Butter Strawberries Hazelnuts Pineapple
Juniper berries	Frontal	Lemons Oranges Cinnamon Licorice
Licorice	Frontal	Cardamom Oranges Grapefruits Vanilla Heavy cream Mint Coffee Fennel Gingerbread Milk chocolate
Mace	Frontal	Nutmeg Butter Heavy cream Pumpkin Acorn squash Butternut squash Milk chocolate

INGREDIENT	TYPE OF FLAVOR: FRONTAL, BACKGROUND, OR MILD	FLAVOR COMPATIBILITY
Nutmeg It is especially important to use high-quality nutmeg; lower-quality nutmeg has a metallic flavor.	Frontal	Pecans Ginger Apples Cinnamon Cloves Mace Pumpkin Butternut squash Acorn squash Butter Maple Brown sugar Caramel
Vanilla You may have noticed that vanilla is in almost every single "Flavor Compatibility" column for every ingredient. The reason for this is because using vanilla is almost like using sugar or salt. It rounds out other flavors and is a great flavor enhancer for them—always present but never too loud and never in the way.	Background	Practically everything, but these are especially suitable: Passion fruit Dairy (cream, crème fraîche, yogurt, mascarpone) Caramel Milk chocolate Pineapple Rum Most citrus fruits (oranges in particular) Berries (blueberries in particular)

Coffee and Chocolate

This can potentially be a very large list, since chocolate goes with many different flavors, but in reality, there are some flavors that it goes better with than others. The following list includes only those flavors that are ideal with a particular chocolate. For example, it doesn't mean that raspberries do not go well with dark chocolate (some strongly disagree), but that they simply are more agreeable with white chocolate. This table refers to chocolate in its solid form and no other forms (such as syrup, powder, cocoa, couverture, and so on).

INGREDIENT	TYPE OF FLAVOR: FRONTAL, BACKGROUND, OR MILD	FLAVOR COMPATIBILITY
Coffee (espresso)	Frontal	Dark chocolate Milk chocolate Mint Peppermint Lemons Oranges Caramel
Dark chocolate	Frontal	Caramel Espresso Cardamom Oranges Pecans Cashews Mint Cherries Port Figs Ginger Heavy cream Butter Hazelnuts Coconut Earl Grey tea Bergamots Raisins Currants Toasted bread Olive oil Salt

INGREDIENT	TYPE OF FLAVOR: FRONTAL, BACKGROUND, OR MILD	FLAVOR COMPATIBILITY
Milk chocolate	**Frontal to background**	Bananas Lemons Almonds Coffee Walnuts Peanuts Peanut butter Almond praline Yuzus Grapefruits Dates Cinnamon Pistachios Passion fruit Jasmine tea
White chocolate	**Mild**	Raspberries Strawberries Vanilla Heavy cream Peaches Apricots Blackberries Blueberries Peppermint Tarragon Limes Macadamia nuts Elderflower Litchis Rose Mangoes Candied apples Saffron

Nuts, Legumes, and Seeds

In this section, nuts and their relatives are covered, including seeds and legumes, the family to which peanuts belong. It is important to note that nuts, peanuts, and seeds should always be toasted in order to bring out their flavor. When they are raw and untoasted, they don't really have much flavor. To toast nuts and peanuts, it is advisable to coarsely chop them before toasting them. This will toast more surface than if the nuts were whole, but this will also depend on the nut's use. Perhaps chopping them is not visually what you had in mind. In order to get an even toasting for all of these types of ingredients, it is a good idea to stir them around the pan every few minutes while they toast in a hot oven so that they brown evenly. Some chefs say that they gauge the extent of the toasting of a nut, peanut, or seed by smelling them. As soon as they perceive the nuts' toasted aroma coming out of the oven, the nuts are ready. When you can smell them, yes, they are in fact becoming aromatic, but a golden browning on the surface takes a little longer than from when you first smell the aroma. The color is the best gauge. This also gives them a better visual appeal.

Nuts

INGREDIENT	TYPE OF FLAVOR: FRONTAL, BACKGROUND, OR MILD	FLAVOR COMPATIBILITY
Almonds	Frontal	Apricots Peaches Cherries Plums Huckleberries Dark chocolate Milk chocolate Maple Vanilla Cinnamon Coconut Caramel Heavy cream Figs Honey
Amaretto (derived from almonds)	Frontal	Dark chocolate Dr. Pepper Almonds Apricots Marzipan Espresso/coffee Cherries Peaches Heavy cream
Brazil nuts	Mild	Coconut Bananas Caramel Milk chocolate Kaffir lime leaves Lemongrass Pineapple Vanilla

INGREDIENT	TYPE OF FLAVOR: FRONTAL, BACKGROUND, OR MILD	FLAVOR COMPATIBILITY
Cashews	Mild	Butter Grapes Bananas Milk chocolate Coconut Condensed milk Raisins Apricots Dried cherries
Chestnuts	Mild	Rum Armagnac/cognac Heavy cream Vanilla Butter Walnuts Almonds Pears Pumpkin Caramel
Coconut	Background	Passion fruit Pineapple Rum Vanilla Lime zest and juice Dark chocolate Almonds Litchis Caramel Basil Cilantro Rice Lemongrass
Hazelnuts	Frontal	Pears Dark chocolate Milk chocolate Honey Praline Gianduja Caramel Peaches Dried figs Frangelico Dried cranberries

INGREDIENT	TYPE OF FLAVOR: FRONTAL, BACKGROUND, OR MILD	FLAVOR COMPATIBILITY
Macadamia nuts	Mild	White chocolate Milk chocolate Caramel Butter Pineapple Rum Mangoes Vanilla
Marzipan	Frontal	Dark chocolate Almonds Apricots Peaches Cherries Black currants Vanilla Praline
Pecans	Background	Dried currants Cherries Peaches Apples Butter Brown sugar Maple Honey Cinnamon Vanilla Toffee Butterscotch Caramel Heavy cream
Pine nuts	Frontal	Oranges Honey Basil Dark chocolate Butter Caramel Lemons Cream

INGREDIENT	TYPE OF FLAVOR: FRONTAL, BACKGROUND, OR MILD	FLAVOR COMPATIBILITY
Pistachios	Frontal	Cherries Peaches Apricots Milk chocolate Huckleberries Vanilla Pine nuts Almonds Honey Oranges Kumquats
Praline	Frontal	Milk chocolate Dark chocolate Grapefruits Almonds Amaretto Meyer lemons Caramel
Walnuts	Mild	Bananas Milk chocolate Dark chocolate Coconut Apples Caramel Maple Pumpkin Acorn squash Cinnamon Prunes Quince Honey Pears Raisins

Legumes

INGREDIENT	TYPE OF FLAVOR: FRONTAL, BACKGROUND, OR MILD	FLAVOR COMPATIBILITY
Peanuts and peanut butter	Frontal	Milk chocolate Bananas Concord grape jelly Honey Caramel Coconut Dark chocolate Vanilla

Seeds

INGREDIENT	TYPE OF FLAVOR: FRONTAL, BACKGROUND, OR MILD	FLAVOR COMPATIBILITY
Poppy seeds	Mild	Butter Lemons Vanilla Heavy cream
Pumpkin seeds	Background	Pumpkin Dark chocolate Milk chocolate Caramel Dried cranberries
Sesame seeds (black)	Frontal	Bananas Lemongrass Litchis Coconut
Sesame seeds (white)	Mild	Honey Bananas Caramel Vanilla Cinnamon

NOTE *Sunflower seeds, while arguably good to eat on their own, are rarely used for pastry products.*

THE PRINCIPLES OF DESSERT COMPOSITION

All of the previous information in this chapter comes together in this section. Once you know most pastry preparations, flavors, textures, and ingredients, you can attempt the composition of a dessert. The more you work with food, the fewer mistakes you will make, at least most of the time. It is important for you to remember that from failure you can also learn, and what you learn is not to make the same mistake again.

As you will see in the following chapters of this book, the definition of dessert extends beyond that of a plated dessert. It is pre-desserts, cakes (entremets), passed desserts, buffet desserts, and mignardises. They are all different in their form of delivery, and specific principles for each category will be elaborated on in their respective chapters. However, there are a few common principles that apply to all of them. Here are a few key points to keep in mind.

Serving Size

First of all, you must always keep in mind that dessert in any form is served at the end of a meal. Obvious, of course, but what is often forgotten or not considered is that the person who is about to have dessert may not have much room left. It should leave a pleasurable feeling afterward, not a feeling of discomfort. Keep this in mind if you are in the type of establishment that serves a pre-dessert, dessert, and mignardises. That is three more courses for someone who has had at least two courses before that.

The Relationship with the Executive Chef/Chef de Cuisine/Owner

Ideally, you and the chef have developed a harmonious cooking relationship where your desserts make sense with his or her food. Often there can be a large disconnect between both kitchens, with is a discrepancy in style and finished product. The most successful restaurants share a common vision and ways of thinking about food. An ideal relationship between the chef and the pastry chef is not often born from the start; it takes time working together, but it doesn't hurt to start off by sharing a similar way of thinking about food.

Trends

It is important to understand trends, and they should be approached carefully. A technique like spherification is going to stick around for a while, but there are other techniques that are more fads than trends. The problem with trends is that if you are not one of the first to hop on the bandwagon (or better yet, be the person who sets the trend), you are seen as a copycat. Approach each trend, if you must approach, with caution and in small doses. After all, you want to be the keeper of your own style and not of another's.

Finding the Right Plate

This is completely subjective and up to personal preference, but there is no doubt that a high-quality porcelain is preferable over low-end china. The right plate can make your dessert, and the opposite is also true. If you put a beautiful dessert on a thick brown dinner plate, it can destroy it. A plate can show you possibilities and dimensions and particular ones may inspire you to build a dessert around it.

The Place of Business

Where are you? What is your type of business? This is important for you to understand since it is what will determine the type of food you make. Is it casual or high-end? Hotel or restaurant? In the Northeast or in the West? Understand your environment and you will understand the customer.

The Staff

The kitchen staff member in your shop are not the only ones responsible for your food; you must also consider the service staff. Listen to them. What are they saying about your food? What do the customers say? Are they well trained to deliver your food and answer questions, or are they just there to carry food to the table? Motivating the staff to sell your desserts is not complicated. Often all you need to do is have them taste your food on a regular basis so that they can fully comprehend what they are selling, and most important, so that they know how to sell it. It becomes more familiar that way than if they just read it off the menu. If they can see it and they can taste it, they will sell it.

The Ten Principles of Dessert Composition

So far, you may have read about all of the methods, pastry preparations, flavors, and textures that are available. Based on that, these are ten points you must keep in mind when composing a dessert.

1. Bells and whistles are just that. They are not necessary. Keep it simple, but not too simple. Less is more, and more is just more.

2. Think about what you want to convey. What is your vision? What do you want the guests to experience? What is it that they will take away from your dessert?

3. Use three frontal flavors maximum: No one can detect more than that. You can use mild or background flavors to enhance the frontal flavors, but don't get too carried away. Too many mild flavors can turn into one big muddled flavor.

4. Use two textures at least, unless the nature of your dessert is that of a single texture such as a hot soufflé or a tiramisù, both of which are soft desserts. A wide variety of textures is extremely pleasant to the palate.

5. If possible, incorporate more than one temperature. Hot and cold or freezing are very desirable contrasts, but only when they are done correctly and if they make sense.

6. Tempered food has the most pronounced flavor. What happens when you chew food, besides breaking it down and combining it with saliva, is that your mouth brings the temperature of what you are eating down or up to your body temperature. Hot foods or cold or freezing foods will not offer their peak flavor until they are tempered. Having said that, if you can temper your cold and frozen desserts (but not so much that they are not frozen any more) for a few minutes before serving them, you will be doing your guests a great favor.

7. Rein in the sugar. Sugar can overwhelm and disguise flavors—and mistakes, too. Overly sweet desserts are not desirable.

8. Use what is in season. It is more economical, and the product will be at its best.

9. Keep it small. Keep pre-desserts even smaller.

10. Make sure your desserts make sense with your environment, your chef, and your style.

THE PRINCIPLES OF MENU COMPOSITION AND ITEM ENUNCIATION

The proper way to describe an item is almost an art unto itself, since you do not want to write too much information or too little information on the menu. The following rules should be adhered to when writing a menu.

The Ten Principles of Menu Composition

1. Try to not repeat ingredients. This means that if you have bananas in one item, keep it that way. Why have two desserts with the same ingredient?

2. Always have one dark chocolate dessert, and if you must have another chocolate dessert (see point number 1), make it a different chocolate, such as milk, white, or a variation of chocolate such as gianduja or caramelized white chocolate. Chocolate desserts are always the top-selling menu item, unless you put something strange in them like beets, which kind of works but turns most people off. If you have a second chocolate dessert, it takes the pressure off the other chocolate dessert. Place the chocolate desserts at the end/bottom of the menu, so that the customers will see the other options and perhaps decide upon a non-chocolate dessert. When a person looks at a menu, statistically, the eye is always drawn to the top right-hand side of a page. Place whatever you want to draw attention to there. Do not place a chocolate dessert there because the customer will see it and then not even look at what else you have to offer.

3. You don't always have to use fruit. As mentioned before, if you live in an area that does not produce fruit (or vegetables, for that matter) during the late fall, winter, and early spring, utilize other ingredients.

4. When it's in season, use the fruit. It is a great way to showcase an ingredient that people want to taste after a year of not having it. Using fruit will also lower your food costs, and you will have an ingredient that requires little manipulation.

5. Not every dessert has to have a frozen component. Often there are menus that have eight different items, and they all have some sort of ice cream or sorbet.

6. How many dessert items are on the menu depends on how much you can handle reasonably during a busy service without shooting yourself in the foot and compromising the customer's experience. This is also determined by the type of establishment. But in reality, why have twenty desserts on a menu? No one needs that many options. Five to eight items is a good, reasonable average number.

7. Keep the wording simple and straightforward (see the enunciation advice that follows).

8. Proofread your menu. Spell Check is a useful tool. Use it. If there is a foreign word on your menu, look for the correct spelling.

9. Your name does not necessarily have to be on the menu.

10. Not everyone will understand your humor, so be cautious when including it on the menu. In fact, some might confuse humor for something completely different.

Menu consultants might place menu items into one of four categories:

- Star: These are popular items with high profits. Customers will pay more money than they have to for these items.

- Puzzle: These are highly profitable dishes that are not popular.

- Plow horse: These are the opposite of puzzles, that is, highly popular and unprofitable.

- Anchor: These are not very commonly used items, but typically this is a very expensive item that is used to make everything else around it look like a bargain, even if it isn't.

Menu composition can truly be a science, but don't trick your customers into buying one item or another. They can certainly be persuaded by the service staff. If, for example, there is an item on your menu that is not moving, ask your staff to pitch it to your guests. Even with all of this, people will order what they want. Sometimes a dessert goes out to the dining room, and the tables around the guest who ordered it see it, and they will almost always order it. This can change all of the careful planning you had done for the night for having sufficient mise en place. Based on probability and sales history, you produce a certain amount of each dessert for each service, and if a not-so-popular item suddenly and without warning sells more than you expected, you may have to eighty-six it before service is over. This won't happen with buffet desserts that are all on display or passed-around desserts, but for pre-desserts and plated desserts it almost certainly will.

Desserts that are offered at the beginning of a meal are almost a sure sell. An example of this is a soufflé. Soufflés are offered as a menu option at the beginning of a meal because they take time to make and they take time to bake, and no one wants to wait 40 minutes after their entrée has been cleared for a dessert. Never underestimate the power of suggestion. Murphy's Law would say that if you somehow figure out a way to not offer that dessert at the beginning of a meal and also succeed in not having your customers wait for it too long, the number of orders will be significantly reduced.

Dessert Enunciation

There aren't very many rules here, but there is one that is unchangeable. The main component in the dessert should be named first. The main component is usually the largest component on the plate, dessert, or cake, and it is what the dessert is built around, texture-wise and flavor-wise. If you think of the way ingredients are listed on the back of a box of cookies you buy at the store, they are listed in order of quantity, the first ingredient being the largest quantity, and the last one being the least quantity. That is how you should think of a menu item, as a general parameter.

Also keep in mind the length of the description. Here is an example of too much information. This is not taken from an actual menu; it is merely to show an example:

Bell Weather Farm Organic Strawberry Ice Cream, Tahitian Vanilla Bean–Scented Creamy Mascarpone "Panna Cotta," Warm Twice-Baked "Brioche" and Almond-"Frangipane" with a side of Sweet Thai Basil "Granité," served with fresh, wild "Fraises des Bois" on the side

It is tiring to read and a mouthful. Too much information. Too many hyphens. Too many quotation marks. It conforms to the recommended rules of flavor and textural quantities, but it's too much to read. By the time the customer is done reading the remaining desserts on your menu, a few long minutes will have gone by and interest will dwindle.

Here is the opposite end of the spectrum using the same dessert example as above, but with no information, just the ingredients:

Strawberry-Vanilla-Mascarpone-Brioche-Thai Basil

While this makes your menu look clean and tight, it will require a lot of interaction between the wait staff and the customer. It may take even longer for the wait staff to explain the menu than for the customer to read the first, overly long description. Of course, all of this can be debunked by another theory, which is equally valid, and that is that the customer will decide on a dessert by looking at the flavors alone, because no matter what it is, he or she likes those flavors and will choose based on flavor preference and not component preference. They trust that the chef will have done something exceptional with those flavors.

There are two solutions to an adequately enunciated dessert. The first is that you can use a combination of both descriptions above, without getting too carried away:

STRAWBERRY-VANILLA-MASCARPONE-BRIOCHE-THAI BASIL (title of the dessert)
Strawberry sorbet, vanilla-mascarpone panna cotta, warm toasted brioche with frangipane, Thai basil granité, and fraises des bois (description of the dessert)

The wait staff, if asked to elaborate on the dessert, can explain that the strawberries are organic and from a local farm, that the vanilla is Tahitian, that frangipane is an almond cream that is baked on top of the brioche, that Thai basil is slightly sweeter than regular basil, and that *fraises des bois* are small wild strawberries that really pack flavor.

Or you can use a reduced version of the enunciation above, without the title or as the title:

Organic Strawberry Sorbet, Vanilla-Mascarpone Panna Cotta, Warm Toasted Brioche with Frangipane, Thai Basil Granité, and Fresh Wild Strawberries

This type of enunciation can also be used on signs for dessert buffets, placed at the front of the dessert. A little more information may be required; it's up to you and also the availability of wait staff that is close to the dessert table and who may be able to interact with the guests.

RESTAURANT BREADS

While it is not mandatory to make your own bread, it isn't impossible to make it either. It all depends on what you are capable of doing with the environment you have at your disposal. Some bread, such as brioche, can (and should) be baked in a convection oven, but most other breads should not. Sourdough, for example, should only be baked in a hearth oven for the best results. You can rig a static oven to act as a hearth, but there is only so much bread you can bake in a static oven. (For an example on how to completely bypass a hearth oven to bake sourdough, see the recipe on page 100.) Therefore, the ovens that you have to bake with are truly what will determine your bread-baking capacity. Other equipment, such as electric mixers (many restaurants are equipped with 12- or 20-qt electric mixers) and workbenches, are easier to come by. Remember that bread has been made for the past 5000 years without much more than a pair of hands and a heat source.

This is absolutely not a book on how to bake bread, and you should not expect to know all you need to know about bread from these next few pages, but this fundamental information will show you how to make basic varieties of bread. Should you want to learn more, there are many publications that can assist with the subject. However, there is nothing that will teach you more than to actually get your hands in the dough and work it.

The size of the bread you are making is one of the principal starting considerations. The larger the loaf, the more flavorful and complex it will be in the end. This is because a larger loaf needs longer to ferment; this improves the flavor of the bread because yeast cells have more time to do the work they need to do without being rushed. Large loaves will also need more time in the oven to bake than a small roll, and this creates a longer, more pronounced Maillard reaction on the crust, which translates into a more complex flavor and better crust. That is not to say that smaller pieces cannot be flavorful as well. It all depends on what you are looking for. With bread, it must be a long and slow process in order to obtain the best results.

This section will cover the broadest variety of bread without getting extremely complicated. Always keep in mind that bread can be very complicated. Most breads, but not all of them, use what is known as a pre-ferment or poolish. This is a "seed" that helps ferment the bread and also contributes to its final flavor. There are many different types of pre-ferments, but the most important consideration is that you will need to plan ahead and establish a working schedule to make sure that your bread will be ready on time. Work backward from your deadline to establish this schedule. If your bread needs to be completely baked and cooled by 5:30 P.M., at what time must your pre-ferment be ready to use? How long will it take your bread to mix, bulk ferment, shape, proof, and bake?

Note: Baker's percentages are different from the percentages in pastry recipes. The percentages are based on the flour (or combination of types of flour), and that percentage is always set to 100 percent, even if the other ingredients weigh more than the flour. You can round out the quantities to the closest whole number.

SQUID INK EPI

YIELD: ABOUT 70 MINI EPIS

PRE-FERMENT (POOLISH)   YIELD: 1.49 KG/3 LB 4.56 OZ

INGREDIENT	METRIC	U.S.	%
Yeast, instant dry, red label	3 g	.12 oz	.45%
Bread flour	743 g	1 lb 10.24 oz	100%
Water, at 21°C/70°F	743 g	1 lb 10.24 oz	100%

Mix the yeast into the flour, and then add to the water. This can be mixed by hand in a bowl and should be left to ferment at room temperature (21°C/70°F) for at least 4 hours and ideally 12 to 18 hours before you need it.

SQUID INK LEAN DOUGH   YIELD: 3.7 KG /8 LB 2.51 OZ

INGREDIENT	METRIC	U.S.	%
Water, at 21°C/ 70°F	732 g	1 lb 9.82 oz	51.83%
Squid ink	37 g	1.3 oz	2.62%
Bread flour	1.41 kg	3 lb 1.81 oz	100%
Poolish	1.47 kg	3 lb 3.96 oz	104.31%
Yeast, instant dry, red label	3 g	.12 oz	.23%
Salt	43 g	1.51 oz	3.02%

1. The desired dough temperature (or DDT) is 24°C/75°F. This is the final temperature you want the dough to be at when it is done mixing.

2. Mix the water with the squid ink.

3. Combine the flour, poolish, and yeast in the bowl of an electric mixer fitted with the dough hook. Mix for 3 minutes on speed 1.

4. Cover the dough with a plastic bag and let it rest for 15 minutes. Add the salt and mix for 5 minutes on speed 1. If you are making larger amounts of dough, the dough will require more mixing time during the second mixing. The dough should be mixed just enough to reach full gluten development—check the gluten "window" (see page 93).

5. Transfer the dough to a floured wooden table and let it bulk ferment for 45 minutes covered with a plastic bag.

6. Punch the dough down, and fold it onto itself. Keep it covered.

7. Bulk ferment the dough for another 45 minutes.

8. Divide the dough into 50 g/1.76 oz pieces.

9. To pre-shape the dough, push it down with the heel of your hand and brush off the excess flour from the dough. Roll the dough in toward you vertically, pushing the dough down with your fingertips as you roll it up to tighten the roll and to help de-gas it. Make sure that there isn't too much flour on the dough; brush it off if you can see it. Roll each piece out into a 10-cm/4-in oblong with slightly tapered ends.

10. For the intermediate fermentation, allow the dough to rest for 15 minutes covered with plastic wrap.

11. **For the final shape:** Roll each piece of dough out to 15 cm/6 in. Try to get an even roll with ends that are tapered. Place a linen (*couche*) on a wood board, coat the couche with some bread flour, and start placing the epis on the linen with the seam facing the linen, making sure that you pull the linen in to "cradle" each row of pre-shaped epis; this will keep them separate from each other and will also keep them straight.

12. Proof for 1 to 1½ hours at room temperature inside a plastic bag; alternatively, proof the dough in a proof box for 45 to 60 minutes at 30°C/86°F with 80 percent humidity.

13. Set a hearth oven to 250°C/482°F. Flip each piece of dough onto a wooden paddle by pulling on the side of the linen. You can get up to four pieces on the paddle since the dough will be in a row on the couche. Flip the dough onto a loader with the seam of the baguette at the bottom. Once all of the pieces of dough are on the loader, cut the dough with a pair of scissors in five evenly spaced pieces at a 45-degree angle; be careful to not cut all the way through the dough. All of the cuts should be evenly spaced and the same size. While you are cutting the dough, take one tip and turn it to one side gently, take the next tip and pull it in the opposite direction, and so on.

14. Load the epis into the oven and press the steam button for 5 seconds. Bake for 10 to 15 minutes, then open the vent and bake for 5 more minutes. Take the bread out of the oven with a peel and slide onto a metro shelf to cool. Discard after 24 hours.

NOTES

The two-stage mixing process is known as autolysis, *and it was discovered by Professor Raymond Calvel in France, who realized this rest period improves the links between starch, gluten, and water and improves the extensibility (stretchiness) of the dough. As a result, when mixing is resumed, the dough forms a mass and becomes smooth more quickly, reducing mixing time by about 15 percent. This produces bread with more volume, better crumb, and better structure. Mixing the dough for too long can also cause it to oxidize, turning it a pale white.*

This is a very special bread that is based on basic lean dough. Lean dough is the type that is used to make baguettes. Epi refers to the wheat-like shape of the bread.

BRIOCHE AND CARAMELIZED ONION CUBE

YIELD: ABOUT 40 LOAVES/CUBES (4 to 6 servings per cube); 140 KG/30 LB 13.82 OZ

INGREDIENT	METRIC	U.S.	%
Caramelized Onions			
Canola oil	400 g	14.11 oz	10%
Vidalia onions (or any other yellow onions)	3.6 kg	7 lb 14.98 oz	90%
Brioche			
Milk, at 21°C/70°F	1.09 kg	2 lb 6.28 oz	23.16%
Eggs, at 21°C/70°F	1.88 kg	4 lb 2.21 oz	40.06%
Bread flour	4.69 kg	10 lb 5.27 oz	100%
Salt	122 g	4.33 oz	2.62%
Sugar	698 g	1 lb 8.64 oz	14.91%
Yeast, instant dry, gold label	56 g	1.98 oz	1.2%
Butter, pliable	2.36 kg	5 lb 3.15 oz	50.31%
Caramelized Onions	3.12 kg	6 lb 14 oz	66.55%
Gold leaf sheets	40	40	

1. **For the caramelized onions:** Heat the oil in a rondeau over high heat. When the oil begins to shimmer, add the onions and turn the heat down to medium-low.

2. Cook until the onions are completely caramelized, stirring frequently, about 1 hour. Cool at room temperature.

3. Pour the milk and eggs into a 20-qt mixer bowl, and stir to combine. Pour the bread flour, salt, sugar, and yeast on top. Mix on low speed until just incorporated.

4. Add one-third of the butter and switch the mixer to medium speed. Mix until that butter has been incorporated, and then add another equal amount of butter. Mix until that has been completely mixed in, and then add the last third of butter.

5. Continue to mix on medium speed until full gluten development occurs. To check for gluten development, perform a "window" test. Take a small amount of dough and stretch it with your hands. It should be elastic enough to be pulled until it is very thin and you can see through it without it ripping. At this point, the final dough temperature should not exceed 27°C/80°F.

6. Remove 6 kg/13 lb 3.64 oz of the dough from the mixer bowl and put it on a sheet pan lined with a sheet of silicone paper; cover with plastic wrap.

7. Add the caramelized onions to the dough in the mixer bowl and mix for a few seconds to evenly incorporate them with the dough. Remove the dough from the bowl and place it on a sheet pan lined with silicone paper. Cover with plastic wrap. Let both doughs bulk ferment for 45 minutes.

8. After bulk fermentation, refrigerate the dough. The dough is ready to be shaped when it is has firmed up and relaxed for at least 1 hour. At this point, it can be either reserved in the refrigerator for 12 hours before shaping or frozen for later use.

9. Lightly grease forty 10-cm/4-in stainless-steel cube molds with nonstick oil spray. Place 10 molds on each of 4 sheet pans lined with silicone paper.

10. Divide the onion brioche into 200-g/7.05-oz pieces and shape them round. Reserve covered with plastic wrap in the refrigerator.

11. Divide the plain brioche into 150-g/5.3-oz pieces and shape them round. Refrigerate them covered with plastic wrap to firm them up again, and then roll them out into 30-cm/12-in diameter disks using a rolling pin.

12. Brush the disks with water. At the center of each disk, place a piece of caramelized onion brioche. Close the disk of plain dough around it, sealing the seams by pinching them shut.

13. Place the brioche inside the prepared cubes with the seam side down, facing the sheet pan.

14. Proof at 30°C/85°F and 60 percent humidity for 2½ to 3 hours or until the dough is almost doubled in size. You can also proof them by sliding each sheet pan in a large plastic bag and closing it with a knot. This dough will take close to 4 hours to proof at room temperature.

15. Meanwhile, set a convection oven to 175°C/350°F.

16. Once the brioche is proofed, put a sheet of silicone paper on top of each sheet pan and then stack all of the sheet pans on top of each other. Make enough room in the convection oven to fit all 4 sheet pans stacked together; remove all of the racks except the lowest one. Place 3 empty sheet pans on top of the top sheet pan.

17. Bake for 20 to 30 minutes; the brioche is done when the internal temperature is 90°C/195°F.

18. Take the brioche out of the oven and quickly remove it from the mold; otherwise it will collapse onto itself and look deflated. Cool at room temperature.

19. Once they have cooled, apply a sheet of gold to the top of each cube. Reserve in a cool, dry place. Discard after service.

NOTE

This is a cube-shaped brioche loaf with caramelized onions that is meant to be shared by the table. It is pre-sliced just before it is served and is kept in cube form by tying a ribbon around the loaf.

TEFF PITA BREAD

YIELD: 2 KG/4 LB 6.55 OZ

WHY THESE
FLAVORS WORK

INGREDIENT	METRIC	U.S.	%
Water	570 g	1 lb 4.11 oz	134.12%
Teff flour	425 g	14.99 oz	100%
Bread flour	425 g	14.99 oz	100%
Duck fat	60 g	2.12 oz	14.12%
Yeast, instant dry, gold label	5 g	.18 oz	1.18%
Salt	17 g	.6 oz	4%
Malt	8 g	.28 oz	1.88%
Poolish (page 91)	490 g	1 lb 1.28 oz	115.29%

1. Bring the water to a boil, stir in the teff flour, and allow to cook over medium heat until the teff has completely gelatinized and is pulling away from the sides of the pot. Cover with plastic wrap and allow to cool to room temperature.

2. Place the teff paste and all of the remaining ingredients in the bowl of an electric mixer fitted with the dough hook. Mix on speed 2 until full gluten development is achieved.

3. Place the dough in an oiled bowl and bulk ferment for 1 hour, with a four-fold at the 30-minute mark. For a four-fold, punch the dough down and fold it onto itself twice.

4. Roll down on a sheeter to 4 mm/.18 in.

5. Place the dough on a floured sheet pan and allow it to relax in the freezer for 30 minutes.

6. Once the dough is chilled and relaxed, cut it into either disks measuring 10 cm/4 in round or rectangles measuring 5 cm/2 in wide by 10 cm/4 in long. Place on a floured couche/linen and allow to proof for 30 minutes at 30°C/85°F and 75 percent humidity.

7. Meanwhile, preheat a hearth oven to 260°C/500°F. Alternatively, set a static oven to the same temperature; you will need to have a baking stone in the oven.

8. Bake until fully puffed, about 10 minutes. Cool at room temperature.

NOTE

Teff is a cereal crop grown in Ethiopia that can be obtained whole or ground as fine as whole wheat flour. It is an ancient grain that is not commonly used but is being rediscovered and used by many artisan bakers. It is a very flavorful grain that is nutty with intense molasses sweetness and whole wheat and brown rice flavors. It has a dark brown color.

STEAMED TRUFFLE BUNS

YIELD: ABOUT 70 BUNS; 3.7 KG/8 LB 2.51 OZ

INGREDIENT	METRIC	U.S.	%
Bread flour	1.43 kg	3 lb 2.31 oz	100%
Poolish (page 91)	1.49 kg	3 lb 4.48 oz	104.3%
Water, at 21°C/ 70°F	739 g	1 lb 10.08 oz	51.83%
Yeast, instant dry, red label	3 g	.12 oz	.23%
Truffle salt	43 g	1.52 oz	3.03%
Black truffles, sliced thinly with a mandoline or truffle slicer	150 g	5.3 oz	

1. Assemble Cryovac bags measuring 10 cm/4 in by 15 cm/6 in. Grease the interior with a light film of extra-virgin olive oil. Use about 2 g/.07 oz per bag for a total of 140 g/4.94 oz. Be careful to not get any grease close to the top of the bag (inside and outside); otherwise it won't seal. You will also need a heat sealer.

2. The desired dough temperature (or DDT) is 24°C/75°F. This is the final temperature you want the dough to be at when it is done mixing.

3. Combine the flour, poolish, water, and yeast in the bowl of an electric mixer fitted with the dough hook. Mix for 3 minutes on speed 1.

4. Cover the dough with a plastic bag and let it rest for 15 minutes. Add the salt and mix for 5 minutes on speed 1. If you are making larger amounts of dough, the dough will require more mixing time during the second mixing. The dough should be mixed just enough to reach full gluten development—check the gluten "window" (see page 93).

5. Transfer the dough to a floured wooden table and let it bulk ferment for 45 minutes covered with a plastic bag.

6. Punch the dough down, and fold it onto itself. Keep it covered.

7. Bulk ferment the dough for another 45 minutes.

8. Divide the dough into 50 g/1.76 oz pieces.

9. To pre-shape the dough, push it down with the heel of your hand and brush off the excess flour from the dough. Roll the dough in toward you vertically, pushing the dough down with your fingertips as you roll it up to tighten the roll and to help de-gas it. Make sure that there isn't too much flour on the dough; brush it off if you can see it. Roll each piece out into a round ball.

10. Bench rest the dough for 15 minutes.

11. Reshape the buns and place each one inside a bag with a slice of truffle. Heat-seal the bag closed.

12. Proof for 1 to 1½ hours at room temperature, or in a proof box for 45 to 60 minutes at 30°C/86°F with 80 percent humidity.

13. Meanwhile, turn on a steamer to 100°C/212°F.

14. Once the buns are proofed, make a small incision on the top right corner of each bag using a pair of small, sharp scissors. This will help the bun expand inside the bag, and it will also be the section of the bag where it can be torn open by the customer to eat.

15. Steam for 10 minutes until the dough expands to fill the bag completely. Cool to room temperature. Reserve refrigerated and well covered.

16. To pick up, place the dough in a steamer for 2 minutes before serving.

HERB GRILLED SOURDOUGH BOULE

Sourdough is one of the most complex doughs to make, especially because of the pre-ferment it uses. The white sour starter takes 5 days to get going, but once it is made all you have to do is feed it every day.

This bread will not be baked in an oven; it will be placed directly on a grill when it is fully proofed. The herbs are "glued" to its surface and bake into the crust while it is cooking on the grill. Cooking bread this way is similar to how bread was originally cooked over direct flames in the more primitive forms of bread baking. It gives it a different character and depth of flavor than if it were baked directly in a hearth oven.

WHITE SOUR STARTER

A white sour starter takes 5 days to make, but once you have it you can keep it alive by feeding it every day, and this way it can be used for daily bread production. Many bakeries have had their white sour starter for years, some for decades, and some for even longer than that; however, the age of the sourdough does not translate into better flavor. This starter uses wild yeast, which is why it takes so many days to make.

DAY 1

INGREDIENT	METRIC	U.S.	%
Bread flour	200 g	7.05 oz	100%
Water, at 30°C / 86°F	200 g	7.05 oz	100%

Mix the flour and water together. Let it sit overnight at room temperature, covered.

DAY 2

Stir the mixture from day 1.

INGREDIENT	METRIC	U.S.	%
Day 1 mix	200 g	7.05 oz	100%
Water, at 30ºC / 86ºF	200 g	7.05 oz	100%
Bread flour	200 g	7.05 oz	100%

Weigh out the necessary amount of Day 1 mix and discard any left over. Stir in the water. Mix in the flour. Reserve overnight at room temperature, covered.

INGREDIENT	METRIC	U.S.	%
Day 3 mix	400 g	14.11 oz	100%
Water, at 30ºC / 86ºF	200 g	7.05 oz	100%
Bread flour	200 g	7.05 oz	100%

Weigh out the necessary amount of Day 3 mix and discard any left over. Stir in the water. Mix in the flour. Reserve at room temperature, covered.

DAY 5

INGREDIENT	METRIC	U.S.	%
Day 4 mix	200 g	7.05 oz	33.33%
Water, at 30ºC / 86ºF	400 g	14.11 oz	66.66%
Bread flour	600 g		100%

Weigh out the necessary amount of Day 4 mix and discard any left over. Stir in the water. Mix in the flour. Reserve at room temperature, covered. The starter can be used the day after this step is done, and it must be fed every 24 hours. Typically it is fed soon after the quantity you need for the recipe is taken out of the starter.

FOR THE DAILY FEEDING

INGREDIENT	METRIC	U.S.	%
Water, at about 9ºC/49ºF	1.45 kg	3 lb 3.15 oz	100%
White sour starter	251 g	8.87 oz	17.33%
Bread flour	1.45 kg	3 lb 3.15 oz	100%

1. Place the cold water (from the tap) in a mixing bowl and dissolve the sour starter in it.

2. Add the flour and mix until you have obtained a homogenous mass.

3. Leave at room temperature (21ºC/70ºF).

4. Make sure you feed this white sour starter 18 hours before you mix the dough and on a daily basis.

SOURDOUGH

YIELD: 140 KG/30 LB 13.82 OZ (40 LOAVES; 350 G/12.35 OZ EACH)

INGREDIENT	METRIC	U.S.	%
White sour starter	3.27 kg	7 lb 3.32 oz	58.45%
Bread flour	5.59 kg	12 lb 5.29 oz	100%
Whole wheat flour	654 g	1 lb 7.06 oz	11.69%
Medium rye flour	654 g	1 lb 7.06 oz	11.69%
Water, at 21°C/70°F	3.59 kg	7 lb 14.81 oz	64.28%
Salt	235 g	8.29 oz	4.2%
Sage stems	80	80	
Thyme stems	120	120	
Rosemary stems	40	40	

1. Make sure to feed the white sour starter 18 hours before mixing the dough.

2. **For the dough:** Add the white sour starter, all of the flours, and the water to the mixer bowl. Mix on low speed for 3 minutes, and then let rest for 15 minutes covered with plastic. Add the salt and mix for 5 more minutes on low speed. The dough should achieve full gluten development; check the gluten development by performing a "window" test (see page 93).

3. Transfer the dough to a floured wooden work table and bulk ferment for 1 hour. Punch the dough down and fold it onto itself. Bulk ferment for 1 more hour.

4. Fold the dough onto itself one more time and bench rest for 15 minutes.

5. Divide the dough into forty 350-g/12.35-oz pieces.

6. Round the dough into a ball, pulling it toward you to tighten it. Transfer to heavily floured boule baskets (see Resources, page 520). The smooth top goes into the basket first; the seam should face upward. Bulk ferment at room temperature for 2 hours, covered with plastic wrap. Place in the refrigerator to rest and retard the yeast overnight.

7. Pull the dough out of the refrigerator 1 to 2 hours before you intend to grill it and check the proof. The dough should spring back when you apply gentle pressure with your fingertips.

8. Turn a grill on as high as it can go. Preheat a convection oven to 160°C/325°F.

9. Brush water over the surface of the dough while it is in the basket.

10. Apply 2 sage, 3 thyme, and 1 rosemary stem to each loaf. Push gently into the dough.

11. Turn the baskets, one at a time, over on top of the grill. Gently ease the dough out of the basket. Once you have pronounced grill marks on one side, after about 6 minutes, flip the dough over and grill to obtain grill marks on that side as well, 5 to 6 more minutes.

12. Check the internal temperature of the dough. It should read 95°C/205°F. If it has not reached this temperature and it already has pronounced grill marks, place the loaf in the preheated convection oven to finish cooking.

13. Cool on a wire rack or metro shelf. Reserve at room temperature. Serve at room temperature. One loaf will serve 4 to 6 people.

Ch²

PRE-DESSERTS

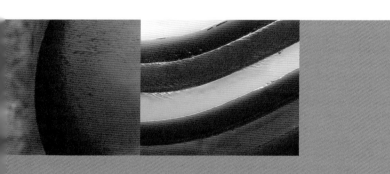

The term *pre-desserts* sounds like a choppy mash-up of words, but it does in fact express the meaning of this category perfectly. A luxury that is typically served at high-end establishments, a pre-dessert, to put it simply, is a dessert that is served before the main dessert; it can be compared to an appetizer served before the main course. The comparison is not only correct to describe the order in which it is served, but it is also parallel with regard to size. There are no written rules when it comes to portion size, but sense dictates that it should be smaller than the course that follows. Two or three bites (four at the very maximum) should suffice. It must be small, but does not necessarily need to be sweet. You can think of pre-desserts as a bridge between the last savory course and the sweet items to come. It can fill the gap, prepare the guest for dessert, and ease him or her into sweetness.

In most cases, restaurants only have one, two, or up to three different pre-desserts; more is not unheard of but quite hard to maintain. A pre-dessert is not necessarily part of what a customer will choose; they may be on the menu, but as a set item. Often the pre-dessert is not mentioned on the menu, and is given to the customer before the ordered dessert arrives. This can have a very positive impact, since it can be seen as a complimentary course. Have more than one pre-dessert available and up to three because, if you are serving a two- or three-top, each person can have a different pre-dessert. If you have a four-top, you can do 2 x 2 x 2 (two identical pre-desserts for each two people times two), and for a six-top 3 x 3 x 2 (three different desserts for each three people times two). With odd numbers from 5 and above, it can be more challenging because with the previous system, two pairs will have the same dessert and one person will have a unique dessert. In cases like this, I suggest that everyone receive the same dessert. In any case, it is important for the wait staff to ask if there are any dietary restrictions, and your pre-desserts should be able to skirt any food allergies. For example, have a nut-free option, a gluten-free option, or a vegan option, but maybe not all three. It is practically impossible to have a menu that satisfies all food allergies and supports all types of dietary choices.

There are a few considerations you need to think about before you decide whether to serve pre-desserts. The customer assumes that it is free, and in fact you do not typically charge for a pre-dessert. This means that you have to find a way to cover the cost of the pre-dessert, either in your desserts or in the savory courses, because in reality it is not free. It is also a course that takes a few minutes to eat, and if your restaurant is in the business of turning tables quickly, then you should definitely skip this course. Also consider that, as suggested on page 164, if desserts need to be on the small side, pre-desserts should be even smaller, and ideally, simpler. Pre-desserts are also an opportunity to blur the line between savory and sweet if you are so inclined and can do it correctly; a good example of this is cheese. Cheese is often the last course in some countries, especially European countries, and you can find ways to incorporate this into a pre-dessert. In fact, the cheese can do most of the work, and all you need to do is find a way to make it more enjoyable with one or two added components. There are of course other options besides cheese, and savory ingredients are not indispensable.

Do not think of pre-desserts as being a palate cleanser. I understand the intention—the idea is that it clears any flavors that linger in the mouth to clear the area out for new ones. This situation does not require that your palate be cleansed; it simply requires the use of flavors that are completely different from the last savory course and completely different from the dessert course to follow. This difference in flavors will be easily perceived by the senses.

As much as a pre-dessert should be a shift in flavors between the last savory course and dessert, it should also be different in temperature from the dessert course, if possible. For example, if there is ice cream in most of your desserts, do not use ice cream or other frozen components in the pre-dessert. It is easier to get away with not having frozen components in the pre-dessert than in a dessert. It is also a good idea to use different types of ingredients from the desserts in the pre-dessert. If your pre-dessert is built around berries, you should not have berry desserts. Keep strong flavors as part of the dessert menu and not the pre-dessert offering(s), since an ingredient like coffee or chocolate can overwhelm and mask or mute the flavor of the dessert to come.

Plating should be fast and uncomplicated. Keep in mind that the customer has his or her mind set on the dessert, and a pre-dessert should be a minor interlude. It should also be fast and uncomplicated because you need to not overwhelm your service and your line. If there is an item on the plate that is cooked, baked, or fried to order (which is not impossible or even out of the question), it had better be done quickly, since you need to get to work on the next course in addition to the other tickets you have up on your board.

MILK CHOCOLATE AND LIME CURD | LEMON SODA SPHERE | CRYSTALLIZED VERBENA LEAF

YIELD: 10 SERVINGS

WHY THESE FLAVORS WORK	Milk chocolate's sweetness is enhanced by the sour-bitter tastes of the lime. They are frontal flavors, very pronounced and identifiable, yet in this preparation they are both texturally smooth and creamy: opposite tastes/one texture. The lemon soda sphere has more of a background citrus flavor. The crystallized verbena has mostly citrus and floral notes. The verbena leaf is a brief note that is friendly with the other flavors without imposing. Milk chocolate and citrus get along very well.
COMPONENTS	**Milk Chocolate and Lime Curd** (page 134) **Lemon Soda Sphere** (page 135) **Crystallized Verbena Leaf** (page 136)
PLATING PROCEDURE	1. Using an offset spatula, place the curd disk on the plate. 2. Gently place a carbonated lemon soda sphere on top of the disk. 3. Put a crystallized verbena leaf on top of the sphere. Serve immediately.

COCONUT ICE CREAM | BLACK SESAME SEED SAUCE

YIELD: 10 SERVINGS

WHY THESE FLAVORS WORK

Coconut is a mild to background flavor that is present but not as much as black sesame paste, which is a frontal flavor; this is why the coconut is used here in a larger amount than the black sesame seed paste. The coconut supports the strength of the black sesame paste without fading into the back completely.

COMPONENTS

Black Sesame Seed Sauce (page 139)

Coconut Ice Cream (page 138)

Passion Fruit Gel (page 139)

Small basil leaves

PLATING PROCEDURE

1. Dip the tip of a 25-cm/10-in offset spatula in the black sesame seed sauce and spread about 15 g/.5 oz on a plate.

2. Place a coconut ice cream rectangle over the sauce.

3. Spoon a small drop of passion fruit gel on top of the coconut ice cream. Place a small basil leaf on top of the gel. Serve immediately.

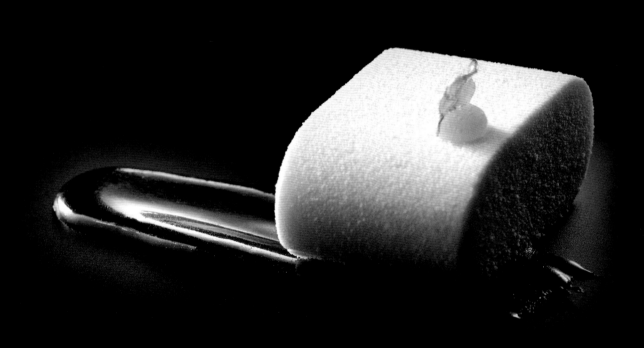

LITCHI | ROSE | RASPBERRY JELLIES | ROSE PETAL CAKE CRUMBS

YIELD: 10 SERVINGS

WHY THESE FLAVORS WORK

I had originally seen this flavor combination in one of Pierre Hermé's macarons, the Ispahan. It seemed unusual to me, but when I was able to taste these flavors I realized that they play off of each other almost seamlessly. It is important to use natural, organic roses and to make an infusion out of them to obtain a proper rose flavor; do not use rose flower extract since some people have an aversion to that aroma/flavor. This dessert is mostly pure flavor and less so texture, since all three jellies have relatively the same consistency. The cake crumbs add some solid texture but to a lesser degree. This dessert is more about the interaction of these flavors and the vessel of a gelled liquid.

COMPONENTS

Litchi Jelly (page 140)

Rose Jelly (page 140)

Raspberry Jelly (page 140)

Rose Petal Cake Crumbs (page 141)

PLATING PROCEDURE

1. Place the jelly rectangles in the following order on a plate: litchi, then rose, then raspberry. Repeat one more time.

2. Spoon 45 g/1.5 oz of rose petal cake crumbs around the jellies. Serve.

FROZEN FENNEL MERINGUE | DISTILLED GRANNY SMITH APPLE JUICE GELÉE | APPLE MOLASSES | CRYSTALLIZED ANISE HYSSOP LEAF

YIELD: 10 SERVINGS

WHY THESE FLAVORS WORK	Fennel is a fresh, aromatic flavor that pushes the crisp sour-sweet flavor of a Granny Smith apple forward. The molasses is a direct product of reducing the apple juice and concentrating its flavor, which becomes that of a dark caramel with apple notes; caramel goes very well with apples. The anise hyssop leaf has a flavor that is very similar to fennel but with more intense notes of anise.
COMPONENTS	**Apple Molasses** (page 142) **Distilled Granny Smith Apple Juice Gelée** (page 143) **Frozen Fennel Meringue** (page 142) **Crystallized Anise Hyssop Leaf** (page 136)
PLATING PROCEDURE	1. Using a syringe without a needle, inject about 2 g/.07 oz of the apple molasses onto the gelée in a grid pattern. 2. Cut out a piece of the frozen fennel meringue with an ice pick to obtain an organic shape; the piece should be about 5 cm/2 in square. Place it on top of the gelée. 3. Place a crystallized anise hyssop leaf in front of the frozen fennel meringue. Serve immediately.

APPLE TATIN ICE POP | CRÈME CHANTILLY RIBBON | APPLE CHIP

YIELD: 10 SERVINGS

WHY THESE FLAVORS WORK	These flavors work for the same reason that a classic apple Tatin with whipped cream works. The tart, sour, and sweet flavors that come from the slowly cooked apples and sugar is tempered and rounded out by the sweet cream. While the apples on their own are good enough, the cream adds a rich dairy dimension that goes so well with apples.
COMPONENTS	**Apple Tatin Ice Pops** (page 143) **Crème Chantilly Ribbon** (page 144) **Apple Chips** (page 145)
PLATING PROCEDURE	1. Remove the frozen apple pops from the freezer. 2. Carefully wrap a strand of crème Chantilly ribbon around the frozen pop. Trim any excess off if the ribbon is too long for the tube. 3. Place on the plate. Place a small apple chip between the first two loops of the crème Chantilly ribbon. Serve immediately.

CLEAR COFFEE JELLY STAINED WITH POMEGRANATE JUICE | LICORICE SAUCE | PAIN D'ÉPICES FROZEN BUBBLES

YIELD: 10 SERVINGS

WHY THESE FLAVORS WORK

Licorice is a flavor that people either love or hate; there is little ambivalence when it comes to preference. I happen to like it very much. It has a very fresh flavor similar to fennel and mint, but it also has a toasted, Maillard-like flavor, which makes it unique. It pairs well with coffee since it shares the toasted notes and the warmth of its flavor. The pain d'épices is a mixture of spices (cinnamon, nutmeg, ginger, clove, black pepper, anise seeds, and orange zest) that enhance the dominant flavor of the licorice and the coffee. The pomegranate adds an acidic note that pushes the bitterness from the coffee forward.

COMPONENTS

Licorice Sauce (page 147)

Clear Coffee Jelly Stained with Pomegranate Juice (page 147)

Candied Orange Zest (page 148)

Pain d'Épices Frozen Bubbles (page 146)

PLATING PROCEDURE

1. Place the frozen licorice sauce on the plate; turn on a heat gun and thaw the sauce using the lowest heat setting on the heat gun.

2. Trim both ends of the coffee jelly using a thin sharp knife. This will show the clarity of the jelly but will also highlight the visual aspect of the bright red ring around the jelly.

3. Place the clear coffee jelly next to the licorice sauce. Place a single strand of candied orange zest on top of the coffee jelly.

4. Cut a piece from the frozen pain d'épices foam using a small offset spatula. It should be an organic shape, no larger than 5 cm/2 in long and wide. Place it next to the jelly. Serve immediately.

OLD CHATHAM CAMEMBERT CHEESE | FIG PAPER ENVELOPE | CANDIED DANDELION | ORGANIC HONEYCOMB | CARAMELIZED HONEY

YIELD: 10 SERVINGS

WHY THESE FLAVORS WORK

Cheese and fruits typically go well together. Now, this does not apply to all cheeses and all fruits. Camembert and figs are a good example of a proper match. Figs are sweet but not too sweet. They balance the funk and the salt from cheese. The honey components (sauce and comb) add a sweet note and also a floral flavor. The candied dandelion is also a floral flavor, which ties in with the other floral notes from the wildflower honey. The fig paper is crispy, and so is the candied dandelion; therefore there is a good balance of textures, from soft to crispy.

COMPONENTS

Old Chatham Camembert cheese (see Resources, page 520)

Caramelized Honey Sauce (page 148)

Organic honeycomb (see Note)

Candied Dandelion (page 149)

Fig Paper Envelopes (page 149)

PLATING PROCEDURE

1. Cut out 10 rectangles of parchment paper measuring 5 cm/2 in wide by 10 cm/4 in long. You will need two blocks of Old Chatham Camembert cheese. This cheese comes in squares measuring about 7.5 cm/3 in by 2.5 cm/1 in deep. Cut the cheese into .75-cm/.25-in-wide slices, leaving the rind on (or take it off, if you prefer). Cut the slices by dipping a thin, sharp knife into hot water, drying it, and then quickly cutting down through the cheese. Ideally this cheese is cut when it is cold (from the refrigerator) in order to get a clean cut; on the other hand, it tastes best when it is tempered (as most cheeses do). Once you have cut the cheese, place it on a parchment paper rectangle cutout. Put the cheese on a flat half sheet pan and keep it covered and at room temperature during service. Discard any that is left over after service.

2. Sauce the plate with the caramelized honey. Cut out 2.5-cm/1-in cubes of organic honeycomb using a thin, sharp knife. Dip the knife in hot water first and then dry it in order to get a clean cut. Place the honeycomb on top of the sauce. Lean the candied dandelion in front of the honeycomb. Do not cut the honeycomb in advance since the honey tends to seep out of the comb, leaving the comb without the honey.

3. Open the dehydrator door where the fig paper sheets are stored. Place a rectangle of cheese on top of the fig paper while still in the dehydrator; otherwise the paper will harden when it cools, making folding it without cracking impossible. Fold the fig paper over the cheese. Place the package onto the plate, seam facing back, on top of the caramelized honey sauce, in front of to the honeycomb and candied dandelion. Serve immediately.

NOTES

Honeycombs are edible. The comb part is what some consider to be inedible, but it is fine to eat. It is considered a nonnutritive substance.

The paper gets soft if it is in contact with moisture for even a few minutes; therefore, speed is essential in delivering this dish to the table.

GOAT CHEESE BAVARIAN CREAM | BEET JELLY | DATE POUND CAKE CRUMBS

YIELD: 10 SERVINGS

WHY THESE FLAVORS WORK

Beets and goat cheese enjoy a pleasant relationship on the plate because the deep, earthy flavor of the beet and the barn-like flavor of the cheese are so well aligned and balance each other so well; each has a unique personality that is hard to miss. The date cake is a fruit component that is tempered and subdued and adds a simple note of refined sweetness that does not interrupt what the other flavors have to say. The micro lovage is a grassy-tasting herb, slightly minty, that pairs well with the goat cheese.

COMPONENTS

Date Pound Cake Crumbs (page 151)

Goat Cheese Bavarian Cream (page 152)

Beet Jelly Sheets (page 152)

Micro lovage

PLATING PROCEDURE

1. Spoon 45 g/1.5 oz of date pound cake crumbs on a plate.

2. Place a tube of goat cheese Bavarian cream on a rectangle of beet jelly. Gently roll the beet jelly and the goat cheese Bavarian together to wrap the Bavarian with the jelly completely.

3. Place over the crumbs.

4. Put 3 leaves of micro lovage on the cake crumbs. Serve immediately.

LIQUID CHOCOLATE ORB | VANILLA CREAM VEIL | BURNT SUGAR

YIELD: 10 SERVINGS

WHY THESE FLAVORS WORK	Although chocolate and vanilla are often considered opposites, and they are in fact very distinct and different flavors, they get along very well. Chocolate will always dominate vanilla, but the vanilla helps enhance the flavor of chocolate, much like salt does. The burnt sugar adds a bitter note that rounds out the chocolate flavor and the creaminess of the vanilla veil as well.
COMPONENTS	**Vanilla Cream Veil** (page 154) **Encapsulated Liquid Chocolate Orb** (page 153) **Burnt Sugar Décor** (page 155)
PLATING PROCEDURE	1. Place the vanilla cream veil on a plate. 2. Place a single orb on top of one end of the veil. 3. Cover the orb with the opposite end of the veil, folding it over the orb. 4. Place a burnt sugar décor plaque on top of the veil. Serve.

ROBIOLA BOSINA CHEESE | CHERRY JAM | WARM TOASTED BRIOCHE

YIELD: 10 SERVINGS

WHY THESE FLAVORS WORK

Robiola Bosina is a soft cheese from the Langhe region in northern Italy that is made from sheep's milk and cow's milk. It has a semifirm rind. Its creamy, mild flavor is enhanced by the sweet and slightly sour cherry jam. The sage leaf adds a floral, herbal note that adds emphasis to the cheese. The brioche adds a buttery rich note of flavor that gets along well with the other flavors. To me there are few things as good as a warm, thick slice of crispy brioche; it almost doesn't need anything else. This dessert must be eaten while the cheese is warm and soft and the bread is warm and crisp. The jam should preferably be tempered (not cold and not warm).

COMPONENTS

Warm Toasted Brioche (page 156)

Clarified butter, as needed

Robiola Bosina cheese slices

Fried Sage Leaves (page 157)

Cherry Jam Tube (page 155)

PLATING PROCEDURE

1. Turn a griddle onto 175°C/350°F right before service.

2. Cut four 2.5-cm/1-in-thick slices from the loaf of brioche. Brush both sides generously with clarified butter.

3. Toast the brioche on each side until golden brown, about 2 minutes on each side.

4. Meanwhile, cut a 1.25-cm/.5-in wide slice of Robiola Bosina cheese. Place it on a room temperature plate. Using a heat gun set on the lowest temperature, warm the cheese for about 10 seconds. The rind will keep the soft center in place.

5. Place a fried sage leaf on top of the cheese.

6. Place the toasted brioche slices on the plate, immediately followed by the cherry jam tube. Serve immediately. The cheese and the brioche must be eaten while warm.

MAPLE TAPIOCA | VANILLA PANNA COTTA

YIELD: 10 SERVINGS

WHY THESE FLAVORS WORK	Vanilla's flavor is one that is very well aligned with most other flavors, since it does in fact have a flavor of its own; it can do double duty as a flavor enhancer, pushing other flavors forward—like maple in this case—without muting its own. This is a soft-textured dessert, but it has two different types of soft textures—one that is melt-in-your-mouth smooth (panna cotta) and one that is soft and chewy (tapioca).
COMPONENTS	**Maple Tapioca** (page 158) **Vanilla Panna Cotta** (page 158)
PLATING PROCEDURE	Spoon 15 g/.5 oz of maple tapioca on top of the vanilla panna cotta, using a slotted spoon to drain the excess liquid off the tapioca pearls. Make sure the tapioca is mounded, not flat, on top of the panna cotta. Serve.
NOTE	*If possible, temper the panna cotta for about 20 minutes before serving. This will give it a smoother mouth feel. You can pull this panna cotta out of the refrigerator when the main course goes out, but make sure to communicate with your front-of-the-house staff.*

BLOOD ORANGE CURD | DULCE DE LECHE | MACARON MORSELS | BLACK OLIVE CHOCOLATE TILE

YIELD: 10 SERVINGS

WHY THESE FLAVORS WORK

The acidity of the curd is tamed by the sweetness of the dulce de leche, which is not just sweet, but also contributes Maillard flavors and a smooth texture. The curd is acidic in taste but is also rich and creamy, producing a very pleasant mouth feel. The macaron is mostly textural, since its main flavor (almond) is very subtle and gets lost with the dominant flavors of blood orange and dulce de leche. Chocolate adds a flavor that ties into the citrus and caramel flavors, enhancing them without taking away from them.

COMPONENTS

Macaron Morsels (page 159)

Candied Blood Orange Zest (page 159)

Blood Orange Curd (page 159)

Dulce de leche (see Note)

Black Olive Chocolate Tile (page 160)

Blood Orange Zest Powder (page 160)

PLATING PROCEDURE

1. Place 15 g/.52oz of macaron morsels on the plate. Keep them close to each other.

2. Spoon 10 g/.35 oz of candied blood orange zest on top of the macaron morsels.

3. Spoon 40 g/1.4 oz blood orange curd on top of the macaron morsels.

4. Spoon 18 g/.63 oz of dulce de leche on top of the curd.

5. Place the black olive chocolate tile on top of the dessert.

6. Sprinkle a pinch of blood orange zest powder next to the finished dessert. Serve.

NOTE

Dulce de leche can be made or purchased as is. There are many very high-quality examples of dulce de leche that far surpass anything one could make. I do not recommend making dulce de leche for the same reason I wouldn't recommend making your own ketchup; some industrially manufactured products are just better. See Resources, page 520.

PRESSED WATERMELON | SWEET LIME JELLY | BLACK SEA SALT | LIME ZEST | EXTRA-VIRGIN OLIVE OIL

YIELD: 10 SERVINGS

WHY THESE FLAVORS WORK	Watermelon's sweetness is enhanced by two other tastes/flavors: the acidity of the lime and the salt. Lime and watermelon are very often seen together, and the extra-virgin olive oil is used to wrap all of those flavors together.
COMPONENTS	**Pressed Watermelon** (page 161) **Sweet Lime Jelly** (page 161) **Black sea salt** **Lime zest** **Extra-virgin olive oil**
PLATING PROCEDURE	1. Place the pressed watermelon on the plate. 2. Place a rectangle of the sweet lime jelly directly over the watermelon. 3. Put 2 g/.07 oz of black sea salt on the right side of the watermelon. 4. Zest one-eighth of a fresh lime over the left side of the lime jelly using a rasp (Microplane). 5. Drizzle a few drops of extra-virgin olive oil around the jelly (about 3 g/.1 oz). Serve.

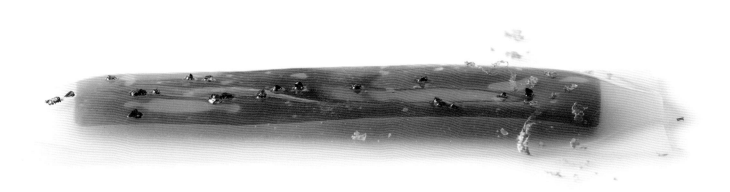

MILK CHOCOLATE DISKS

YIELD: 150 G/5.29 OZ

INGREDIENT	METRIC	U.S.
Milk chocolate, tempered	150 g	5.29 oz

1. Review the steps for making chocolate décor on page 38.

2. Spread the chocolate into a thin, even layer using an offset spatula.

3. When the chocolate is semi-set, use a 5-cm/2-in ring cutter to cut out at least 10 disks. If there are additional disks, reserve them for future use.

4. Place a sheet of parchment paper over the disks and place a flat weight over them, such as a cutting board, so that they set flat.

5. Reserve in a cool, dark place. Use as directed for the Milk Chocolate and Lime Curd dessert.

MILK CHOCOLATE AND LIME CURD

YIELD: 600 G/1 LB 5.16 OZ

INGREDIENT	METRIC	U.S.	%
Sugar	110 g	3.88 oz	18.33%
Lemon juice	70 g	2.47 oz	11.67%
Lime juice	40 g	1.41 oz	6.67%
Eggs	110 g	3.88 oz	18.33%
Milk chocolate, melted	120 g	4.23 oz	20%
Butter	150 g	5.29 oz	25%

1. Prepare two flexible silicone mats that each have eight disks, 6 cm/2.5 in diameter by 1.25 cm/.5 in deep (to obtain the 10 pieces; these mats are quarter sheet mats). Place these mats onto a flat half sheet pan.

2. Combine the sugar, lemon juice, lime juice, and eggs in a bowl and whisk to obtain an even mixture. Place over a hot water bath and stir until the curd has thickened; the temperature will be between 80°C/175°F and 85°C/185°F.

3. Add the melted chocolate and whisk until the mixture forms a homogenous mass.

4. Stir in the butter completely and pass the mixture through a fine-mesh sieve.

5. Pour the contents into a piping bag and pipe it into the silicone molds, evening out the top with an offset spatula. Place a milk chocolate disk over the top of the curd and press down gently to ensure that they adhere to one another.

6. Freeze until hardened. Coat with velvet spray when ready to serve.

    NOTE *This recipe uses lemon juice and lime juice to control the acidity of the final product; if only lime juice is added, it can be too sour to eat.*

VELVET SPRAY

YIELD: 605 G/1 LB 5.34 OZ

INGREDIENT	METRIC	U.S.	%
White chocolate coins	300 g	10.58 oz	49.58%
Cocoa butter	300 g	10.58 oz	49.58%
Lime green–colored cocoa butter	5 g	.18 oz	.83%

1. Combine 150 g/5.29 oz of the white chocolate and 150 g/5.29 oz of the cocoa butter over a hot water bath and stir to melt. Set aside.

2. Repeat with the remaining white chocolate, cocoa butter, and colored cocoa butter.

3. Unmold the curd disks from the silicone mold and place over a flat surface lined with a nonstick rubber mat. Return to the freezer.

4. Set up a spray station, a surface that should be covered with plastic to keep the shop clean where you can spray the curd disks with the chocolate velvet spray.

5. Fill a compressor canister with the white chocolate spray first (think of it as a primer). Spray the milk chocolate and lime curd disks with an even coating of spray.

6. Return to the freezer, then clean the spray gun and pour in the green velvet spray.

7. Spray the disks with green velvet spray to coat completely. Keep the compressor gun at least 60 cm/24 in from the disks to obtain a velvety smooth look.

8. Place the sprayed disks on a clean half sheet pan lined with a nonstick rubber mat and reserve in the refrigerator for service. Discard leftover disks after service.

LEMON SODA SPHERE

YIELD: 4.27 KG/9 LB 6.62 OZ

INGREDIENT	METRIC	U.S.	%
Sodium Alginate Bath			
Water	4 kg	8 lb 12.96 oz	93.68%
Sugar	250 g	8.82 oz	5.85%
Sodium alginate	20 g	.71 oz	.47%
Lemon Soda Base			
Lemonade	205 g	7.23 oz	82.58%
Sugar	35 g	1.23 oz	14.1%
Calcium lactate	7 g	.25 oz	2.82%
Xanthan gum (.5%)	1 g	.04 oz	.5%
Simple syrup, at 50° Brix	1 L	1.04 qt	
Lemonade	200 g	7.05 oz	

1. **For the sodium alginate bath:** Combine the water, sugar, and sodium alginate in a pot and bring to a boil.

2. Remove the pot from the heat, and allow the mixture to cool to room temperature. Store, refrigerated, overnight. Discard this mixture after 10 days of use.

3. **For the lemon soda base:** Combine the lemonade and the sugar in a narrow bain-marie. Pour in the calcium lactate and shear with a handheld blender.

4. Continue to shear and add the xanthan gum, pouring it in slowly. Shear for 45 seconds to 1 minute.

5. Pour this liquid mixture into the cavities of a 1.5-cm/.75-in diameter silicone dome mold and freeze. Meanwhile, warm up the sodium alginate bath to 80°C/175°F. Warm a large water bath for rinsing the spheres to the same temperature, and warm the simple syrup to hold the spheres.

6. Once the domes are frozen hard, remove them from the mold and place them inside the hot sodium alginate bath for 1 minute. They will still be frozen at the core.

7. Take the spheres out of the sodium alginate bath using a slotted spoon and rinse each one in the hot water. Place the spheres in the hot simple syrup. Allow it to cool before refrigerating. Discard after 36 hours.

8. Place the spheres and the lemonade inside a soda siphon. Alternatively, you can use a cream siphon (see the sidebar on page 137). The charges for soda siphon and cream siphons are interchangeable between both apparatus, but for carbonation for the soda siphon, you will need CO_2 (cream uses N_2O chargers).

9. Close the lid on the siphon tightly and load two charges if using a 1-liter siphon. There are no smaller versions of the soda siphon; there are, however, smaller versions of the cream siphon, in which case you will need only one charge. Let it sit refrigerated overnight. The CO_2 needs to permeate the spheres.

10. Just before service, release the pressure from the siphon before opening the lid. Transfer the carbonated spheres to a vacuum-seal canister (see Resources, page 520) and vacuum seal it. This will preserve the carbonation in the spheres during service. You will have to do this (vacuum seal) after each dessert is served; otherwise the carbonation in the sphere will decrease. Reserve the spheres in multiple canisters (about 10 spheres per canister). This canister can also be used with the more economical vacuum sealers; the canister comes with a tube attachment that can be connected to the sealer to extract the air from the canister. Discard the carbonated spheres after service. No matter how well it is sealed, it will lose its carbonation by the next day.

NOTES *Prepare the sodium alginate bath, preferably the day before you need it, to fully hydrate the sodium alginate. This recipe yields a large amount; it is always best to have much more than you need so that the liquid to be turned into spheres has plenty of space and no spheres come in contact with each other while in the bath, since they will stick to each other.*

These spheres tighten and get rounder after sitting in the simple syrup for 12 hours. When they are just thawed, they are somewhat flat oval disks. The hot bath, water, and syrup contribute to its outer gel membrane's tightening. This rest time also allows the spheres' bubbles to coalesce into large bubbles, which is visually desirable.

Always use a high-quality, natural lemonade, or better yet, make your own with fresh lemon juice, sugar, and water.

CRYSTALLIZED VERBENA LEAF

YIELD: 10 LEAVES

INGREDIENT	METRIC	U.S.	%
Verbena leaves (see Note)	10	10	
Egg whites, pasteurized	50 g	1.76 oz	9.09%
Superfine sugar	500 g	1 lb 1.6 oz	90.91%

1. Using a small brush, brush both sides of the leaves with a very thin layer of egg whites.

2. Immediately afterward, place the leaves on top of the sugar and cover them with more sugar. Gently pick up the leaves and place them on a sheet pan lined with a nonstick rubber mat. Let dry for 24 hours.

3. Once dry, the leaves can be held in an airtight container with silica gel packs for more than 1 year.

NOTE *Verbena leaves should not be confused with lemon verbena leaves.*

VARIATION *For crystallized anise hyssop leaves, substitute an equal amount of small anise hyssop leaves for the verbena.*

the iSi cream whipper and the soda siphon

These are two different pieces of equipment with different uses but similar principles, which are to incorporate air into a product. The cream whipper does so with N_2O-filled (nitrous oxide) chargers, and the soda siphon uses CO_2 (carbon dioxide) chargers.

The cream whipper has many uses other than its original intended use, which was simply to make whipped cream to top off your coffee. It wasn't until Ferran Adrià realized its potential and started using it to make cold foams, and eventually hot foams, that this thing just caught like wildfire. This book uses it for one item only (technically two if you count the micro génoise in the process shots for the Volcano Vaporizer, see page 209), and that is to make bubble chocolate. This is one of my favorite ways to eat chocolate with nothing more added to it than a little oil and air. There is really no other way to incorporate air into chocolate in our kitchen environment than with the cream whipper.

I mentioned the micro génoise above, which is also a creation of Ferran Adrià and is frankly a brilliant idea. You put batter components in a canister and then aerate it with the N_2O chargers instead of having to whip the eggs with a mixer and then fold the dry ingredients in by hand. Now, it is a great concept and the finished product is visually arresting, but some feel that the flavor is not as good when compared with a regular génoise.

The soda siphon is also used in this book, once, to carbonate an encapsulated sphere of lemon soda (see page 209). The idea was to make a gel of lemon soda, which would lose its carbonation eventually, and resolve that issue by re-carbonating it using the soda siphon. Theoretically you can carbonate anything that is moist. It doesn't mean that you should carbonate everything you come across (fizzy oysters, anyone?), but carbonating a Champagne gelée is a terrific idea. Carbonated drinks do not stay carbonated for long once their containers are opened. You can keep a gelée carbonated in a siphon for many hours. Now that is a desirable texture.

COCONUT ICE CREAM

YIELD: 1 KG/2 LB 3.27 OZ

INGREDIENT	METRIC	U.S.	%
Coconut Ice Cream Base			
Skim milk	300 g	10.58 oz	30%
Coconut milk	320 g	11.29 oz	32%
Heavy cream	105 g	3.7 oz	10.5%
Powdered milk	42 g	1.48 oz	4.2%
Sugar	160 g	5.64 oz	16%
Ice cream stabilizer	3 g	.11 oz	.3%
Egg yolks	70 g	2.47 oz	7%
White chocolate, melted	100 g	3.5 oz	

NOTE *You will have more ice cream than you need for 10 servings, but it is not very effective to make and churn smaller amounts. Make the whole amount and churn it; what you do not use you can remelt and churn one more time. Or better yet, make more than the 10 pieces this recipe calls for and reserve them frozen.*

1. **For the coconut ice cream base:** See Modern Ice Cream Method on page 50. Combine the skim milk and coconut milk. Add them in Step 3 and add the heavy cream in Step 6 when it reaches 45°C. Age the base for at least 4 hours.

2. Meanwhile, line a flat surface such as a Plexiglas or a half sheet pan with a nonstick rubber mat. Place 10 (or more; see Note) rectangular molds that measure 6 cm/2.5 in long by 5 cm/2 in wide by 2.5 cm/1 in deep on top of the mat.

3. Line the inside of each mold with a strip of acetate 22.5 cm/9 in long by 1.25 cm/.5 in wide. Freeze this setup.

4. Churn the coconut ice cream base, and then fill each rectangular mold. Even out the tops with an offset spatula. Return to the freezer to harden.

5. Once hardened, remove the frame and the acetate strip and return to the freezer.

6. Remove the ice cream from the freezer. Turn the ice cream up so it stands with the length side horizontally and the width side vertically. Apply a thin layer of chocolate to the top of the ice cream, acting quickly to spread it in an even layer. This will be the "foot" of the ice cream, or what it will be standing on eventually.

WHITE VELVET SPRAY

YIELD: 300 G/10.58 OZ

INGREDIENT	METRIC	U.S.	%
White chocolate	150 g	5.29 oz	50%
Cocoa butter	150 g	5.29 oz	50%

1. Combine the white chocolate and cocoa butter in a bowl and melt over a hot water bath.

2. Transfer to an airtight container and reserve at room temperature for up to 1 year.

3. Set up a spray station, a surface that should be covered with plastic to keep the shop clean where you can spray the ice cream with the white velvet spray.

4. Stand the ice cream on the chocolate foot.

5. Fill a compressor canister with the velvet spray and spray the disks with an even coating of spray. Keep the compressor gun at least 60 cm/24 in from the ice cream to obtain a velvety smooth look.

6. Transfer the sprayed ice cream to a clean sheet pan lined with a nonstick rubber mat (ideally frozen beforehand to keep the ice cream from melting).

7. Reserve frozen and covered for service. Discard after 3 days.

BLACK SESAME SEED SAUCE

YIELD: 225 G/7.94 OZ

INGREDIENT	METRIC	U.S.	%
Black sesame paste	150 g	5.29 oz	66.67%
Superfine sugar	75 g	2.65 oz	33.33%

1. Stir the sesame paste well before pouring it out of the container it is held in. The oil tends to separate from the solids if it sits for too long without being stirred.

2. Combine both ingredients in a bowl and stir using a small whisk until the sugar is dissolved. Adjust the sweetness as necessary; if it is too sweet, add more paste, or if it is not sweet enough, add more sugar.

3. Reserve at room temperature. Discard after 1 week. Always stir before using.

PASSION FRUIT GEL

YIELD: 227 G/8 OZ

INGREDIENT	METRIC	U.S.	%
Simple syrup, at 50° Brix	150 g	5.29 oz	65.93%
Passion fruit puree	75 g	2.65 oz	32.97%
Agar-agar	3 g	.09 oz	1.1%

1. Combine all of the ingredients in a small sauce pot. Bring them to a boil over high heat while stirring constantly with a whisk. Once the liquid boils, let it boil for 10 seconds.

2. Pour the liquid into a half hotel pan and let it set in the refrigerator until it has gelled.

3. Purée it in a blender until smooth.

4. Reserve refrigerated in an airtight container for up to 4 days.

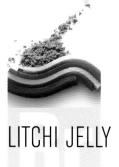

LITCHI JELLY

YIELD: 201 G/7.1 OZ

INGREDIENT	METRIC	U.S.	%
Litchi purée	140 g	4.94 oz	69.51%
Water	40 g	1.41 oz	19.86%
Sugar	20 g	.71 oz	9.93%
Gellan gum, low acyl	1 g	.05 oz	.7%

1. Make a rectangular frame (stainless-steel bars or plastic) that measures 9 cm/3.5 in long by 5 cm/2 in wide by 1.25 cm/.5 in deep over a flat surface (see Resources, page 520).

2. Combine all of the ingredients in a small sauce pot using a whisk. Bring to a boil and then pour the liquid into the prepared frame. Let it set in the refrigerator.

3. Once it is set, remove the frame using the back of a paring knife, and cut with a sharp thin slicing knife vertically into slices .75 cm/.25 in wide.

4. Reserve in the refrigerator covered with plastic wrap. Discard after 36 hours.

ROSE JELLY

YIELD: 201 G/7.1 OZ

INGREDIENT	METRIC	U.S.	%
Rose Infusion			
Water	350 g	12.35 oz	
Organic red roses, petals only, coarsely chopped	4	4	
Rose infusion	175 g	6.17 oz	86.89%
Sugar	25 g	.88 oz	12.41%
Gellan gum, low acyl	1 g	.05 oz	.7%

1. Bring the water to a boil and pour over the chopped rose petals. Allow to steep for 5 minutes and then strain.

2. Cool in an ice water bath. Make the jelly following the procedure for the litchi jelly, replacing the litchi purée and water with the rose infusion.

RASPBERRY JELLY

YIELD: 201 G/7.1 OZ

INGREDIENT	METRIC	U.S.	%
Raspberry purée	165 g	5.82 oz	81.93%
Sugar	35 g	1.23 oz	17.38%
Gellan gum, low acyl	1 g	.05 oz	.7%

Make the jelly following the procedure for litchi jelly, replacing the litchi purée and water with the raspberry purée.

ROSE PETAL CAKE CRUMBS

YIELD: 1.01 KG/2 LB 3.52 OZ

INGREDIENT	METRIC	U.S.	%
Rose Petal Purée			
Rose petals (about 6 roses)	90 g	3.17 oz	23.38%
Water	250 g	8.82 oz	64.94%
Sugar	40 g	1.41 oz	10.39%
Lemon juice	5 g	.18 oz	1.3%
Sponge Cake			
Butter, melted	110 g	3.88 oz	10.89%
Eggs	100 g	3.53 oz	9.9%
Rose petal purée	220 g	7.76 oz	21.78%
Crème fraîche	30 g	1.06 oz	2.97%
Elderflower liqueur	50 g	1.76 oz	4.95%
Sugar	240 g	8.47 oz	23.76%
All-purpose flour	220 g	7.76 oz	21.78%
Beet powder	30 g	1.06 oz	2.97%
Baking powder	10 g	.35 oz	.99%

1. **For the rose petal purée:** Simmer the rose petals in the water until the roses are tender, about 15 minutes.

2. Add the sugar and lemon juice and simmer for an additional 5 minutes.

3. Purée in a blender until smooth. Cool in an ice water bath. If not using right away, reserve in an airtight container in the refrigerator. Discard after 4 days.

4. **For the sponge cake:** Lightly spray a half sheet pan with nonstick oil spray. Line it with a nonstick rubber mat.

5. Preheat a convection oven to 160°C/325°F.

6. Make sure all liquids (butter, eggs, rose petal purée, crème fraîche, elderflower liqueur) are at 21°C/70°F.

7. Sift the dry ingredients together.

8. Whisk the butter into the eggs in a bowl large enough to fit all the ingredients in the recipe. Pour the butter in slowly while whisking to create an emulsion.

9. Whisk in the rose petal purée, crème fraîche, and elderflower liqueur.

10. Stir in the dry ingredients. Mix until just combined and you have obtained a homogenous mass.

11. Pour into the prepared sheet pan and even it out using an offset spatula.

12. Bake for 12 to 15 minutes. Test for doneness with a toothpick or alternatively, press the center of the cake with your fingers; if it springs back, it is done.

13. Let the cake cool at room temperature.

14. Place the cake in a dehydrator set to 65°C/150°F. Once it is dry, after 3 to 4 hours, break it up into pieces and grind in a Robot Coupe until finely ground cake crumbs are obtained. If they feel slightly wet, return the crumbs to the dehydrator to dry completely.

15. Once they are dry, reserve them in an airtight container in a cool, dry place. Discard after 4 days.

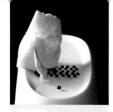

FROZEN FENNEL MERINGUE

YIELD: 500 G/1 LB 1.64 OZ

INGREDIENT	METRIC	U.S.	%
Fennel Juice			
Ascorbic acid	5 g	.16 oz	.76%
Salt	1 g	.04 oz	.08%
Fennel bulbs, fronds and stems trimmed, bottoms trimmed, cut into eighths (about 2 bulbs)	600 g	1 lb 5.12 oz	91.53%
Superfine sugar	50 g	1.76 oz	7.63%
Meringue			
Fennel juice	320 g	11.29 oz	63.94%
Egg white powder	18 g	.63 oz	3.6%
Sugar	75 g	2.65 oz	14.99%
Water	75 g	2.65 oz	14.99%
Gelatin sheets, silver, bloomed in cold water, excess water squeezed off	3 g	.09 oz	.50%
Absinthe	10 g	.35 oz	2%

1. **For the fennel juice:** Place the ascorbic acid and the salt in a one-sixth pan. This will be the pan into which the fennel juice will be pouring as it comes out of the juicer.

2. Juice the fennel. Stir the juice with a spoon or whisk so that the ascorbic acid and the salt dissolve.

3. Strain the liquid through a fine-mesh sieve, then pass it through a fine-mesh bag (commercially known as a Superbag; see Resources, page 520). Stir in the sugar until it has dissolved.

4. **For the meringue:** Line a half hotel pan with a sheet of acetate. Pour the fennel juice into a small electric mixer bowl.

5. Pour the egg white powder over the fennel juice and mix on low speed.

6. Meanwhile, make a syrup with the sugar and the water by combining them in a small sauce pot and bringing them to a boil. Turn off the heat and make sure that all of the sugar has dissolved. Add the gelatin and stir until it has dissolved. Let it cool to room temperature.

7. Add this syrup to the juice and egg white powder mixture when it has reached half the maximum volume (it will have tripled in size). Whip on high speed until the mixture reaches full volume (it will have increased in volume six times from its original volume), and then pour in the absinthe. Mix for 10 more seconds, and then pour the foam into the prepared hotel pan and place in the freezer to harden.

8. Once hardened, reserve frozen for service or wrap tightly and reserve frozen. Discard after 1 week.

DISTILLED APPLE JUICE/APPLE MOLASSES

YIELD: 600 G/1 LB 5.44 OZ

INGREDIENT	METRIC	U.S.	
Apple Juice			
Granny Smith apples	1.6 kg	3 lb 8.48 oz	88.88%
Superfine sugar	200 g	7.05 oz	11.12%

1. **For the juice:** Cut the apples in half and then each half into 4 wedges. Juice the apples using a juicer (see Note).

2. Place the juice in the distiller (see Resources, page 520) and turn it on.

3. When most of the liquid has been distilled (95 percent), there will be a thick, dark brown liquid left at the bottom of the distiller; this is the apple molasses. Reserve this liquid for service in an airtight container at room temperature. It will keep indefinitely if stored properly in a cool, dry area.

4. Add the sugar to the distilled apple juice and stir until it has dissolved. Proceed with the gelée.

NOTE *The Champion juicer is the best machine for this particular use.*

DISTILLED GRANNY SMITH APPLE JUICE GELÉE

YIELD: 600 G/1 LB 5.44 OZ

INGREDIENT	METRIC	U.S.	
Apple Gelée			
Distilled apple juice	600 g	1 lb 5.12 oz	98.52%
Gelatin sheets, silver, bloomed in cold water, excess water squeezed off	9 g	.02 oz	1.48%

1. **For the gelée:** Set up 10 bowls over a flat sheet pan. Combine 10 percent of the distilled apple juice with the gelatin in a small sauce pot. Place over medium-low heat and stir until the gelatin has dissolved.

2. Pour the liquid into the remaining apple juice and stir to combine.

3. Pour the liquid into a sauce gun, and portion 60 g/2.17 oz into each bowl.

4. Transfer the sheet pan with the bowls into the refrigerator and let them set. Ideally, this should be done at least 2 hours before service to let the gelatin set. Once the gelatin is set, cover the bowls. Discard after service if any are left over.

APPLE TATIN ICE POPS

YIELD: 717 G/1 LB. 9.28 OZ

INGREDIENT	METRIC	U.S.	%
Tatin Base			
Sugar	200 g	7.05 oz	24.91%
Ground cinnamon	3 g	.11 oz	.37%
Golden Delicious apples, peeled, cored, cut into quarters	600 g	1 lb 5.12 oz	74.72%
Gelatin sheets, silver, bloomed in cold water, excess water squeezed off	17.5 g	.62 oz	2.44%

1. **For the Tatin base:** Preheat a convection oven to 150°C/300°F.

2. Make a dry caramel (see method on page 48) with the sugar in a small sauté pan over high heat.

3. Pour it into a cake pan 20 cm/8 in diameter by 7.5 cm/3 in deep; swirl the sugar around to coat the bottom of the pan.

4. Sprinkle the cinnamon over the sugar in an even layer.

5. Place the apple quarters side by side next to each other, overlapping them slightly. All of the quarters should fit snugly in the pan. Cover the pan with foil.

6. Bake for about 20 minutes. When the apples are tender and cooked through, remove the foil, turn the oven down to 120°C/250°F, and bake for another 20 minutes. The apples should have an amber-brown coloring. Turn the apples out of the pan into a hotel pan.

7. Line ten PVC cylinders 19 cm/7.5 in long by 2.5 cm/1 in diameter with a square of acetate plastic. It should fit snugly inside the tube. Place the tubes in a standing position on top of a half sheet pan lined with a nonstick rubber mat.

8. Place the warm cooked apples in a small bain-marie. Place the gelatin sheets on top of the hot apples. The apples must be hot or the gelatin will not melt; if the apples have cooled off, flash them in a hot oven for a few minutes to heat them back up.

CRÈME CHANTILLY RIBBON

YIELD: 254 G/8.96 OZ

9. Purée the apples using a handheld blender until smooth. Transfer the purée to a piping bag and pipe into the prepared tubes.

10. Place the tubes in the freezer to harden. Once hardened, remove the apple purée from the tubes but keep them wrapped in the acetate. Reserve in an airtight container in the freezer. Discard after 5 days.

INGREDIENT	METRIC	U.S.	%
Heavy cream	120 g	4.23 oz	47.24%
Sugar	30 g	1.06 oz	11.81%
Milk	100 g	3.53 oz	39.37%
Agaroid RS-507 (see Note)	4 g	.14 oz	1.57%

1. Set up an ice water bath with equal parts of about 2 kg/4 lb 6.4 oz water and ice in a bowl.

2. Have a heavy cream whipper filled with two chargers on hand (see Resources, page 520). Place a small nozzle attachment on the whipper's spout. This nozzle will fit snugly on the spout and will have a small tip that will fit into food-grade plastic tubes. Alternatively, if you have a compressor, it can work just as well. You will have to attach a needle to the air spout; this needle should be able to fit inside the food-grade tubes.

3. Warm up the heavy cream and the sugar in a microwave oven or on the stovetop. The sugar should be completely dissolved. Keep the mixture hot.

4. Combine the milk with the Agaroid in a 960-mL/1-qt sauce pot and whisk to combine. The Agaroid should be poured in slowly while whisking to avoid clumping.

5. Place the liquid over medium-high heat and bring to a boil while whisking constantly. Boil for 5 more seconds while stirring to hydrate the agar. Stir in the hot cream (the cream needs to be kept hot, or otherwise the Agaroid will set on contact with a cold liquid).

6. Fill a squeeze bottle with the hot cream mixture.

7. Fill 10 food-grade tubes that measure 100 cm/40 in long by .4 cm/.16 in diameter using the squeeze bottle with the hot agar mixture; each time you fill a tube, drop it in the ice water bath so the agar gels.

8. Once the agar is gelled and you are ready to extract it, place inside a warm (not hot) water bath for 10 seconds. Place one end of a plastic tube on the spout of the whipper and make sure the nozzle is snug inside the tube. Gently press on the whipper's release to push

APPLE CHIPS

the Chantilly onto a nonstick rubber mat. If you are using a compressor, turn it out, introduce the needle into the tube, and let the compressed air push the tube of gelled Chantilly out. Reserve the tubes in an airtight container in the refrigerator for up to 4 days.

NOTE *Agaroid RS-507 is a mixture of agar-agar, locust bean gum, xanthan gum, and carrageenan gum that is premixed (see Resources, page 520). This mixture provides an agar gel that is smooth and elastic and easy to manipulate and wrap around the apple tatin tube without breaking. If you cannot find it, make your own mix, with 60 percent agar-agar, 20 percent locust bean gum, 10 percent xanthan gum, and 10 percent carrageenan.*

INGREDIENT	METRIC	U.S.	%
Simple syrup, at 50° Brix	400 g	14.11 oz	99.26%
Ascorbic acid	3 g	.11 oz	.74%
Granny Smith apple	1	1	

1. Combine the simple syrup and the ascorbic acid in a small sauce pot and bring to a boil. Remove the pot from the heat.

2. The apple should be sliced as thinly as possible on a mandoline or electric slicer (1 to 2 mm/.04 to .08 in maximum). As the apples are being sliced, place them inside the hot syrup mix.

3. Let the sliced apples cool in the syrup and sit in the syrup overnight in the refrigerator.

4. The following day, cut disks out of the slices using a 2.5-cm/1-in ring cutter. Pat the disks dry with a paper towel to absorb excess syrup. Place the disks on a nonstick rubber mat and dry in a dehydrator set to 65°C/150°F for at least 2 hours, or until completely dry. Alternately you can dry them in a very low temperature oven (less than 100°C/212°F if possible) for about 1 hour.

5. Once the apple disks are dry, gently take them off the rubber mat and place them in an airtight container at room temperature. Discard after 1 week; check for crispness daily and refresh in a dehydrator or low-temperature oven as needed.

   NOTE *This recipe will yield more chips than what you need for 10 portions, but it is what a whole apple will yield; using a whole apple is necessary in order to make this item correctly.*

PAIN D'ÉPICES FROZEN BUBBLES

YIELD: 10 SERVINGS

INGREDIENT	METRIC	U.S.	%
Pain d'Épices Spice Mixture			
Ground cinnamon	5 g	.18 oz	33.33%
Ground ginger	3 g	.12 oz	23.33%
Ground nutmeg	1 g	.04 oz	6.67%
Ground cloves	1 g	.04 oz	6.67%
Black pepper, freshly ground	1 g	.04 oz	6.67%
Ground anise seeds	2 g	.07 oz	13.33%
Orange zest	1 g	.05 oz	10%
Bubbles			
Skim milk	150 g	5.29 oz	68.73%
Pain d'épices spice mixture	2 g	.09 oz	1.15%
Sugar	20 g	.71 oz	9.16%
Acacia honey	45 g	1.59 oz	20.62%
Xanthan gum	1 g	.03 oz	.34%

1. **For the spice mixture:** Combine the cinnamon, ginger, nutmeg, cloves, black pepper, anise seeds, and orange zest in a coffee grinder and grind until you obtain an even mix. Reserve in an airtight container at room temperature for up to 6 months.

2. You will need a 2.1-L/2.25-qt vacuum canister, also known commercially as a Quick Marinator (see Resources, page 520). Lightly spray the interior of the canister with a coat of nonstick oil and line the inside of the canister with plastic wrap. Turn the dial on the lid to "vacuum."

3. **For the bubbles:** Combine the milk, spice mixture, sugar, and honey in a blender cup and blend until it becomes an even mixture.

4. Pour the xanthan gum in slowly on medium speed. Let it hydrate while mixing for 1 minute.

5. Pour the mixture into the vacuum canister, and put the lid on it. Vacuum seal it on medium using a Cryovac machine. This will expand the bubbles trapped in the liquid and will fill the canister to capacity. Turn the dial on the lid to "closed."

6. Place in a freezer until hardened. The hardening time depends on the quality of the freezer; if available, use a blast freezer.

7. Reserve frozen for service; the servings will be cut to order. As long as it is kept covered, it can be used for up to 3 days.

CLEAR COFFEE JELLY STAINED WITH POMEGRANATE JUICE

YIELD: 652 G/1 LB 6.88 OZ

INGREDIENT	METRIC	U.S.	%
Coffee	1 kg	2 lb 3.2 oz	
Distilled coffee	500 g	1 lb 1.64 oz	75.9%
Sugar	150 g	5.29 oz	22.77%
Gellan gum, low acyl	3 g	.1 oz	.43%
Calcium lactate	6 g	.21 oz	.91%
Pomegranate juice	1 L	1.04 qt	

1. Place the coffee in the distiller (see Resources, page 520) and distill completely. Ideally this should be very strong coffee. A French press will provide the strongest brew. Espresso, while it may seem like a good idea, will result in a very bitter product.

2. Reserve the resulting liquid in the refrigerator for up to 5 days.

3. Place 10 cylindrical glasses that have a diameter of 4 cm/1.5 in and are at least 5 cm/2 in tall on a flat surface. It is imperative that the glasses be straight and not tapered at the base in order to obtain an even cylinder. They should also have a flat bottom (not concave).

4. Combine the distilled coffee and sugar in a small sauce pot and whisk to dissolve the sugar. Adjust the sweetness as necessary. Stir the gellan gum and calcium lactate into the liquid while it is cold.

5. Bring to a boil to hydrate the gum and dissolve the calcium, and let boil for 5 seconds.

6. Remove from the heat and pour into the glasses, filling each one with about 60 g/2.12 oz. Refrigerate.

7. Once set, remove the jelly from the glasses very carefully. Reserve in the refrigerator and discard after 1 day.

8. Place the gelled coffee in a one-sixth pan with the pomegranate juice and soak for 1 hour.

9. Remove the gelled coffee from the juice and pat it dry with a clean paper towel.

NOTES *Make the gelled coffee the day you need it.*

For the best results, stain a few of these gelled coffee cylinders every hour or so. The stained look is best when it has been done recently. As time passes, the stain penetrates the cylinder more and more, taking away the visual impact of a bright red ring.

LICORICE SAUCE

YIELD: 470 G/1 LB .48 OZ

INGREDIENT	METRIC	U.S.	%
Licorice	150 g	5.38 oz	31.91%
Water	320 g	11.36 oz	68.09%

1. Bring both ingredients to a boil together in a small sauce pot over high heat and then turn the heat down so that the mixture is simmering. Continue to cook until the licorice has dissolved. Purée using a handheld blender, and then pass through a fine-mesh sieve.

2. Pour the hot liquid into a piping bag and pipe into rectangular shaped molds (see Resources, page 520); only fill one-third of the way. To avoid air pockets, brush some of the sauce in first, if needed, then pipe the sauce into the molds. Freeze until hardened. Once hardened, remove from the mold. Reserve frozen in an airtight container for up to 3 weeks.

NOTE *If possible, use Finnska licorice bites for the licorice in the sauce.*

CANDIED ORANGE ZEST

YIELD: 220 G/7.76 OZ

INGREDIENT	METRIC	U.S.	%
Orange peel	20 g	.71 oz	9.09%
Simple syrup, at 50° Brix	200 g	7.05 oz	90.91%

1. For the orange peel, use a peeler to peel the skin off of an orange, peeling it from top to bottom. Remove the pith using a knife.

2. Cut the peel into a fine chiffonade.

3. Boil the peel in a small sauce pot with enough water to just cover the peel. Repeat this process two more times, changing the water each time. This will remove any bitter taste.

4. Cook the peel with the simple syrup in a small sauce pot on medium heat until the peel is translucent. Drain the simple syrup from the peel and cool the peel as soon as possible; it may crystallize if you do not.

5. Once the candied zest has cooled, transfer it to an airtight container and reserve in the refrigerator. Discard after 5 days.

   VARIATION *For candied citron, substitute citron peel for the orange peel.*

CARAMELIZED HONEY SAUCE

YIELD: 1.4 KG/3 LB 1.28 OZ

INGREDIENT	METRIC	U.S.	%
Wildflower honey	1 kg	2 lb 3.2 oz	71.43%
Water	400 g	14.11 oz	28.57%

1. Place the honey in a 3.84-L/4-qt sauce pot over high heat. Bring to a boil, and then turn the heat down to medium. Meanwhile, bring the water to a simmer. Let the honey simmer until reduced to a dark amber brown, about 30 minutes. It will reduce by 75 percent; it will also thicken, and therefore water needs to be added to make it lighter.

2. Once the honey has reduced, slowly stir in the hot water. You may not need to add all of it. The intention is to have a thick syrup that will act as a sauce. It it's too thick, it will not be a very good sauce to eat.

3. Cool at room temperature and reserve in an airtight container at room temperature. If stored in these conditions, the sauce will keep indefinitely.

FIG PAPER ENVELOPES

YIELD: 253 G/8.95 OZ

INGREDIENT	METRIC	U.S.	%
Fig purée	250 g	8.82 oz	98.52%
Methocel A7C	2 g	.09 oz	.99%
Xanthan gum (.5%)	1 g	.04 oz	.49%

1. Ideally, this paper is made at least 8 hours before service or even the day before. This will allow it to fully dry in the dehydrator and become crisp and brittle when it is taken out of the dehydrator.

2. Cut 10 stencils from of a thin acetate sheet with the dimensions below using a ruler and a sharp cutter.

3. Pour the fig purée into a blender cup. Turn the blender on to medium speed. Slowly pour in the Methocel A7C, and then slowly pour in the xanthan gum. It will form a thick purée.

4. Using a small offset spatula, spread it onto the cut-out acetate pieces in a thin, even layer.

5. Place each piece inside the dehydrator set to 65°C/150°F. Let dry for at least 8 hours or overnight. These can be kept in the dehydrator for up to 2 days. After 2 days, they become very hard to handle and excessively brittle.

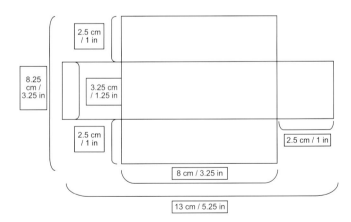

CANDIED DANDELION

YIELD: 10 FLOWERS

INGREDIENT	METRIC	U.S.
Dandelion flowers	10	10
Simple syrup, at 50° Brix	500 g	1 lb 1.6 oz

1. Make sure you are using organic dandelions. They grow wild practically everywhere, but you have to make sure that they are not taken from an area that has been sprayed with pesticides or where house pets roam freely. Remove the stems.

2. Line a sheet of Plexiglas large enough to hold the dandelions (a 12.5-cm/5-in square should be sufficient) with a square of acetate that is the same size. Lightly spray the Plexiglas first with a light coating of nonstick oil spray; this will help the acetate cling to it. Once it is sprayed, wipe the surface of the Plexiglas with a paper towel to spread the oil evenly on the surface. Place the square of acetate on top of the Plexiglas and smooth it out with a clean cloth or paper towel to obtain a flat surface.

3. Turn a dehydrator on to 50°C/120°F.

4. Warm the simple syrup to a low simmer over medium heat.

5. Put the dandelions in and simmer them for about 2 minutes; any longer than that will damage them.

6. Remove the flowers from the syrup and put them on the prepared acetate. Spread them out with your hands, face down.

7. Dry them in the dehydrator for at least 2 hours.

8. Once they are dried, take them off the acetate carefully so as to not break them.

9. Keep them in an airtight container with silica gel packs to keep them from getting soft. If there are any left over after service, it is a good idea to re-dry them for about 30 minutes on a daily basis.

cheese as dessert

There are two approaches to cheese as dessert. One is to have a cheese cart with options for your customers to choose from, and another is to compose a dish that showcases a cheese (see page 126 for Robiola and Cherry Jam with Toasted Brioche). Either way is acceptable, but you need to understand what each style entails.

The variety to offer on a cheese cart is a difficult decision. Before you even get started, it is important to know a lot about cheese. What types of milk are used? The cheese could be made from buffalo, cow, ewe, goat, or a combination of these milks. How is cheese categorized by type and texture? They could be blue, hard, semihard, semisoft, soft, soft pâte, soft washed, soft white. How long will this cheese keep? What is affinage? (Answer: This French word refers to the process of maturing and ripening cheese.) This is an educational process that takes time; taste as many cheeses as possible and learn as much as you can about them before you commit to a cheese program. You can have a simple cheese selection or offer every type of cheese there is; it all depends on what you are looking for and what your staff is trained to do. Now, it doesn't mean that the pastry chef is responsible for developing a cheese program, but it is within the realm of possibility that you may want to take on such a responsibility, since theoretically cheese, as well as dessert, is eaten at the end of a meal. Consider also that offering cheese means there will be one more plate of food that might keep customers from ordering one of your actual desserts.

Composed cheese plates can be a smart alternative to a cheese cart since you can limit these to just a few choices (two or three cheeses, for example, each one with its own garnish, sauce, and so forth). This type of offering is a terrific transition between the last course and dessert (or pre-dessert), since you can combine savory components with sweeter ones.

Note: Cheese carts need to be kept covered during service to prevent any flying insects or other unwanted matter from coming in contact with the cheese, but also to keep the cheese from drying out too much, which may happen once you start cutting into it, depending on the cheese.

DATE POUND CAKE CRUMBS

YIELD: 1.04 KG/2 LB 3.36 OZ

INGREDIENT	METRIC	U.S.	%
Water	315 g	11.11 oz	31.37%
Dates, pitted	175 g	6.17 oz	17.43%
Baking soda	5 g	.18 oz	.5%
All-purpose flour	185 g	6.53 oz	18.43%
Baking powder	2 g	.07 oz	.2%
Salt	2 g	.07 oz	.2%
Butter	60 g	2.12 oz	5.98%
Sugar	140 g	4.94 oz	13.94%
Eggs, at room temperature	120 g	4.23 oz	11.95%
Cocoa powder	45 g	1.5 oz	

1. Preheat a convection oven to 160°C/320°F.

2. Lightly spray the interior border of a half sheet pan with a nonstick oil spray. Line it with a nonstick rubber mat.

3. Bring the water and dates to a boil. Lower to a simmer and cook until soft, about 5 minutes. Remove from the heat.

4. Add the baking soda. Let sit for 20 minutes. Purée the mixture in a blender until smooth.

5. Sift together the flour, baking powder, and salt.

6. Cream the butter and sugar in a mixer fitted with a paddle attachment until the butter is soft and light, about 3 minutes.

7. Turn the machine down to low speed and add the eggs in 4 additions, waiting for each addition to fully incorporate before adding the next.

8. With the machine stopped, add the flour mixture and then turn on to low speed. Mix until just incorporated. Repeat with the date purée.

9. Spread the batter into the prepared sheet pan in an even layer using an offset spatula.

10. Bake until done or until the cake springs back when gentle pressure is applied with the fingertips at the center of the cake, 7 to 10 minutes.

11. Cool to room temperature.

12. Cut into cubes of about 2.5 cm/1 in; they don't need to be exact.

13. Freeze until hardened.

14. Once hard, grind in a Robot Coupe until the crumbs are small. Freeze again and grind again to make smaller crumbs. Coat the crumbs in the cocoa powder by tossing them together in a bowl.

15. Reserve refrigerated in an airtight container. Discard after 3 days.

BEET JELLY SHEETS

YIELD: 202 G/7.16 OZ

INGREDIENT	METRIC	U.S.	%
Beet juice	200 g	7.05 oz	98.57%
Salt	2 g	.07 oz	.74%
Gellan gum, low acyl	1 g	.04 oz	.69%

1. Have a flat plastic sheet pan on hand that is the same dimensions as a half sheet pan, if possible.

2. Combine all of the ingredients in a small sauce pot and stir using a whisk.

3. Bring to a boil and then remove from the heat. Skim the surface.

4. Pour onto the plastic sheet pan and move it around to even out the liquid.

5. Let it set and then cool it down in the refrigerator.

6. Using a ruler and then the back of a paring knife, cut out rectangles measuring 7.5 cm/3 in wide by 8 cm/3.25 in.

7. Reserve well covered and refrigerated until ready to use. Discard after 3 days.

GOAT CHEESE BAVARIAN CREAM

YIELD: 506 G/1 LB 1.85 OZ

INGREDIENT	METRIC	U.S.	%
Goat Cheese Anglaise			
Milk	130 g	4.59 oz	36.62%
Goat cheese, soft	130 g	4.59 oz	36.62%
Sugar	45 g	1.59 oz	12.68%
Egg yolks	50 g	1.76 oz	14.08%
Bavarian Cream			
Goat Cheese Anglaise	300 g	10.58 oz	59.29%
Heavy cream	200 g	7.05 oz	39.53%
Gelatin sheets, silver, bloomed in cold water, excess water squeezed off	6 g	.21 oz	1.19%

1. **For the goat cheese anglaise:** See the crème anglaise method on page 8. Combine the milk and goat cheese and mix thoroughly with a handheld blender. Make the Bavarian cream; follow the method for aerated desserts on page 14.

2. Line 10 PVC tubes measuring x 2.5 cm/1 in wide by 7.5 cm/3 in long with acetate sheets. Place the tubes on a flat sheet pan lined with a nonstick rubber mat.

3. Pipe the cream into the prepared tubes; even out the top with an offset spatula and freeze to harden.

4. Once hardened, remove the frozen cream from the tubes and remove the acetate.

5. Reserve on a sheet pan lined with a nonstick rubber mat, loosely covered with plastic wrap and refrigerated during service. Wrap tightly after service.

6. Discard after 2 days.

ENCAPSULATED LIQUID CHOCOLATE ORB

YIELD: 215 G/7.58 OZ

INGREDIENT	METRIC	U.S.	%
Chocolate Base			
Water	80 g	2.82 oz	37.21%
Sugar	60 g	2.12 oz	27.91%
Cocoa powder	25 g	.88 oz	11.63%
Heavy cream	50 g	1.76 oz	23.26%
Encapsulating Gel			
Water	625 g	22.05 oz	89.29%
Sugar	50 g	1.76 oz	7.14%
Genutine 400-C (see Note)	25 g	.88 oz	3.57%
Simple syrup, at 50° Brix, chilled	200 g	7.05 oz	

1. **For the chocolate sauce:** Boil the water and sugar in a 960-mL/1-qt sauce pot over high heat until the sugar is dissolved.

2. Turn off the heat and stir in the cocoa powder with a whisk until it is dissolved.

3. Return the pot to high heat and bring to a boil again; add the cream and turn the heat down to a simmer.

4. Cook until thickened, about 15 minutes, stirring frequently.

5. Cool over an ice water bath. The sauce will keep for 4 days in the refrigerator.

6. Pour into 2.5-cm/1-in diameter silicone sphere molds; you will need a total of 10 spheres.

7. Freeze until hardened. Reserve in the molds until use.

8. **For the encapsulating gel:** Combine the water and the sugar in a small sauce pot.

9. Shear the Genutine into the water and sugar mixture using a handheld blender.

10. Bring to a boil over high heat while stirring.

11. Cool to about 50°C/120F° at room temperature.

12. Unmold the spheres. Keep 5 in the freezer covered with plastic to maintain their temperature.

13. Stab a sphere on its flat end, using a scribe or long needle. Dip it in the warm gel for 2 seconds and pull it out quickly. The reason it is important to keep the spheres inside the mold until the last minute is that if you don't, there will be a layer of condensation that forms on the sphere; when you dip it in the warm gel, the gel will set and slide off the sphere like a sock.

14. When you pull the sphere out of the gel, quickly turn the scribe to point upward so that the excess gel trickles down the scribe and you can form an even-looking sphere, without strange-looking bumps.

15. Dip the sphere into the cold simple syrup. This will make the gel set completely. Gently push the encapsulated sphere off the scribe using your fingers. There will be a very small hole left from the scribe, but do not worry; the liquid chocolate is not very fluid and will not seep out of the sphere.

16. Store the spheres in the simple syrup. Discard after 3 days.

NOTE *Genutine 400-C is a commercially available product that is a mixture of carrageenan (kappa) and locust bean gum; see Resources, page 520. If you are not able to obtain it, you can mix your own: 60 percent kappa carrageenan (30 g/1.06 oz) and 40 percent locust bean gum (20 g/.7 oz).*

VANILLA CREAM VEIL

YIELD: 407 G/14.36 OZ

INGREDIENT	METRIC	U.S.	%
Half-and-half	350 g	12.35 oz	86%
Sugar	50 g	1.76 oz	12.29%
Vanilla paste	5 g	.18 oz	1.23%
Universal pectin (or pectin NH 95) (see Note)	2 g	.07 oz	.49%

1. Lightly grease the back of a half sheet pan with non-stick oil spray. Spread the oil evenly over the back of the pan using a paper towel. Line the back of the pan with a sheet of acetate. Smooth out the surface with a clean paper towel to eliminate any bubbles trapped under the surface.

2. If available, place a 3-mm/.2-in-deep frame on top of the acetate. The frame should be slightly smaller than the back of the sheet pan. These frames are made of Plexiglas and can be made to order (see Resources, page 520). Otherwise, you can use caramel bars (heavy stainless-steel bars). Tape the outside of the frame onto the sheet pan to prevent any liquid from seeping. Alternatively, you can use a flat plastic tray lined with acetate that is at least 3 mm/.2 in deep. Once the veil is made, it can be poured directly into the tray.

3. Bring the half-and-half, 80 percent of the sugar, and the vanilla paste to a boil. Meanwhile, combine the remaining sugar well with the pectin.

4. Once it reaches a boil, shear the pectin mixture into the boiling liquid using a handheld blender. Boil for 1 more minute to hydrate the pectin.

5. Let the liquid cool to 50°C/120°F. If you pour the liquid into the frame while it is hot, it will warp the acetate and result in an uneven sheet.

6. Pour the liquid into the frame, let it set for about 20 minutes at room temperature, and then transfer it into the refrigerator.

7. Once it has set, remove the frame by passing the back of a paring knife around the inside border of the frame.

8. Using a warm, thin, sharp knife (dip the entire blade in a hot water, then dry it), cut out strips measuring 2.5 cm/1 in wide by 12.5 cm/5 in long. Each time you cut a strip, put it on a new half sheet pan lined with another half sheet of acetate. Keep all of the strips separated. Cover them well with plastic wrap and keep them refrigerated during service. Discard after 2 days.

NOTE *This type of pectin requires calcium to gel, which is found in the half-and-half. Regular pectin requires an acid.*

BURNT SUGAR DÉCOR

YIELD: 500 G/1 LB 1.6 OZ

INGREDIENT	METRIC	U.S.	%
Sugar	500 g	1 lb 1.64 oz	50%

1. Cook half of the sugar in a sauce pot over high heat, stirring frequently, until the sugar turns black. Be aware that there will be a large amount of smoke as a result of burning the sugar. Cool the hot sauce pot by shocking it in a bowl with cold water (not ice water) to stop the cooking and burning of the sugar.

2. Pour the hot sugar over a lightly greased marble surface to cool. Once it has cooled, chop it into small pieces.

3. Grind the burnt sugar in a Robot Coupe. Grind it further in a coffee grinder with the remaining sugar to obtain an even mix.

4. Preheat a convection oven with the fan off (otherwise the sugar will be blown all over the oven) to 160°C/325°F or a static oven to 150°C/300°F.

5. Line a half sheet pan with a nonstick rubber mat. Using a 5-cm/2-in square stencil, sprinkle the sugar into the stencil. Make a total of 10, trying to make an even layer of sugar.

6. Bake the sugar until it has formed a solid sheet, about 5 minutes.

7. Cool the sugar décor to room temperature. Once it has cooled, transfer it to an airtight container with silica packs to keep the it dry. Stored this way, it will keep indefinitely.

CHERRY JAM TUBE

YIELD: 406 G/14.32 OZ

INGREDIENT	METRIC	U.S.	%
Calcium Solution			
Calcium lactate	2 g	.07 oz	1.8%
Water	120 g	4.23 oz	98.2%
Cherry Jam			
Cherry purée (see Notes)	350 g	12.35 oz	86.21%
Sugar	50.g	1.76 oz	12.32%
Calcium Solution	4 g	.14 oz	.99%
Universal pectin (pectin NH 95)	2 g	.07 oz	.49%

1. **For the calcium solution:** Combine both ingredients using a handheld blender to dissolve the calcium. Reserve refrigerated.

2. **For the cherry jam:** Boil the cherry purée, 80 percent of the sugar, and the calcium solution in a small sauce pot. In the meantime, combine the remaining sugar with the pectin to obtain an even mixture.

3. Add the pectin-sugar mixture to the jam by shearing it in with a handheld blender.

4. Return to a boil for 1 minute while stirring with a whisk.

5. Pour the hot jam into a half hotel pan to cool at room temperature.

6. Once it is cool, fill each of the 10 tubes with 30 g/1.06 oz of the jam. See Note below.

7. Close the tubes and reserve them at room temperature if using for that day's service. If not, keep them refrigerated for up to 2 weeks.

NOTES *Make the calcium solution first. This jam is gelled with universal pectin (pectin NH 95), which requires calcium to gel. This is much more than what you need, but it is not reasonable to make only 4 g/.07 oz. The remainder keeps very well once refrigerated.*

The tubes are food grade aluminum with a 45 g/1½ oz capacity. See Resources, page 520.

WARM TOASTED BRIOCHE

YIELD: 2.4 KG/5 LB 4.64 OZ

INGREDIENT	METRIC	U.S.	%
Milk, at 10°C/50°F	240 g	8.47 oz	21.63%
Eggs, at room temperature	415 g	14.64 oz	17.26%
Bread flour	1.03 kg	2 lb 4.48 oz	43.04%
Salt	27 g	.95 oz	1.12%
Sugar	155 g	5.47 oz	6.45%
Yeast, instant dry, gold label	12 g	.44 oz	.52%
Butter, at 21°C/70°F	520 g	1 lb 2.24 oz	21.63%
Egg Wash			
Egg yolks	20 g	.7 oz	24.69%
Whole eggs	50 g	1.8 oz	61.73%
Milk	10 g	.35 oz	12.35%
Salt	1 g	.03 oz	1.23%

1. Pour the milk and 311 g/10.97 oz of the eggs into a 5.76-L/6-qt mixer bowl fitted with a dough hook and stir to combine. Pour the bread flour, salt, sugar, and yeast on top. Mix on low speed until just incorporated.

2. Add 173 g/6.1 oz of the butter and switch the mixer to medium speed. Once that butter has been incorporated, add another 173 g/6.1 oz of butter. Wait until it has been completely mixed in, and then add the remaining butter.

3. Continue to mix on medium speed until full gluten development is achieved. To check for gluten development, perform a "window test" (see page 93); stretch a small amount of dough with your hands. It should be elastic enough to be pulled until it is very thin and you can see through it without it ripping.

4. Add the remaining eggs and mix until just incorporated. At this point, the final dough temperature should not exceed 27°C/80°F.

5. Remove the dough from the bowl and place it on a floured surface. Cover with plastic wrap and let it bulk ferment for 45 minutes.

6. Transfer the dough to a sheet pan lined with silicone paper or greased parchment paper to prevent it from sticking. Wrap the sheet pan with plastic wrap and refrigerate. The dough is ready to be shaped when it is has firmed up and relaxed for at least 1 hour. At this point, it can be reserved in the refrigerator for 12 hours before shaping, or it can be frozen for later use.

7. Coat the interior of 3 half-cylinder terrine molds measuring 5 cm/2 in wide by 40 cm/16 in long by 4 cm/1.5 in deep with a light coat of nonstick oil spray, and then line them with silicone paper.

8. Divide the dough into three 300-g/10.6-oz pieces. This is all that is needed for 10 servings; the remaining dough can be frozen. Making smaller amounts of brioche is not only inefficient, but you will also not be able to obtain a properly mixed dough. It is a dough that keeps very well in the freezer if it is well wrapped.

9. Flatten the piece of brioche with the heel of your hand, using some flour on the work surface and on the brioche to keep it from sticking. Using a rolling pin, roll it out to 10 cm/4 in wide by 37.5 cm/15 in long. Place the dough in front of you, with the long side horizontally placed. Roll the dough toward you, packing it tightly with your fingertips every time it comes full circle. When you reach the seam, seal it tight by pinching it sealed to the body of the dough. Flatten the dough again, making sure the seam is facing up.

10. Transfer the dough to the prepared mold with the seam facing down. Flatten the tube of dough.

11. Combine all of the ingredients for the egg wash in a small bowl using a whisk, then pass the mixture through a fine-mesh sieve. Brush the dough with the egg wash.

12. Proof the dough for 1 hour and 45 minutes, or until doubled in size, in a 32°C/89°F environment. The dough can also be proofed for 3 hours at room temperature (21°C/70°F); if using this method, keep the dough covered with a plastic bag, making sure the plastic bag does not touch the surface of the dough.

13. Preheat a convection oven to 160°C/325°F.

FRIED SAGE LEAVES

YIELD: 10 LEAVES

14. Once the dough is proofed, brush it again with the egg wash and, using a sharp pair of scissors, snip small incisions in a straight row across the crown (the highest point of the middle section of the dough) of the dough.

15. Bake until dark golden brown, about 13 minutes.

16. Remove the dough from the oven and quickly extract it from the mold. It will collapse onto itself if it is left to cool in the mold.

17. Once it has cooled off completely, it can be used for service.

    NOTE *This dough can also be kept frozen after it is baked, as long as it is well wrapped with plastic.*

INGREDIENT	METRIC	U.S.
Peanut oil	200 g	7.05 oz
Sage leaves	10	10

1. Heat the oil in a small sauce pot to 185°C/365°F.

2. Fry the leaves 2 at a time. They are done frying when they no longer release bubbles while they are in the hot oil; make sure to turn them over once while frying.

3. Take the leaves out of the oil and let them drain on top of a clean paper or cloth towel.

4. Reserve them uncovered during service at room temperature in a cool, dry place. Discard after service.

VANILLA PANNA COTTA

YIELD: 1.04 KG/2 LB 4.8 OZ

INGREDIENT	METRIC	U.S.	%
Heavy cream	950 g	2 lb 1.12 oz	90.69%
Tahitian vanilla pods, split, beans scraped	2	2	
Sugar	90 g	3.17 oz	8.59%
Gelatin sheets, silver, bloomed in cold water, excess water squeezed off	7 g	.26 oz	.72%

1. Combine the heavy cream, vanilla pods and seeds, and the sugar in a 1.92-L/2-qt sauce pot. Bring to a boil and then strain through a fine-mesh sieve.

2. Stir in the bloomed gelatin with a whisk until it dissolves.

3. Using a funnel gun, portion the panna cotta into 30-g/1-oz tins, filling them halfway. There will be panna cotta left over, which you can hold in the refrigerator for up to 5 days.

4. Let the panna cotta set in the refrigerator. Reserve refrigerated. Discard after 2 days. Once it is portioned into the tins, it will develop a skin on the surface over time, even when wrapped, since the wrap will not be directly on the surface of the panna cotta.

MAPLE TAPIOCA

YIELD: 750 G/1 LB 10.4 OZ

INGREDIENT	METRIC	U.S.	%
Tapioca, small pearl	150 g	3.53 oz	5.36%
Cold water 1	450 g	15.87 oz	16.07%
Cold water 2	2 kg	4 lb 6.4 oz	71.43%
Maple syrup	180 g	6.35 oz	6.43%
Maple sugar	20 g	.71 oz	.71%
Salt	.1 g	.003 oz	0%

1. Combine the tapioca and the first amount of water in a 3.84-L/4-qt sauce pot. Bring to a boil over high heat while stirring with a wooden spoon. When it thickens, strain it through a fine-mesh sieve and rinse it under cool water. The objective is to strain the mucilaginous liquid that has formed from the tapioca starch.

2. Cook the tapioca in the second amount of water over high heat at a rolling boil. The tapioca will be completely cooked when the pearls are almost completely translucent, 20 to 25 minutes. Strain the pearls through a fine-mesh sieve and cool them under cold running water.

3. Combine the pearls with the maple syrup, maple sugar and salt, stirring to dissolve the sugar. Reserve in the refrigerator during service. The pearls should not be held after service. Tapioca goes from being nicely chewy to waterlogged (an undesirable texture) and crumbly when it is stored in a moist environment.

BLOOD ORANGE CURD

YIELD: 645 G/1 LB 6.72 OZ

INGREDIENT	METRIC	U.S.	%
Blood orange juice	110 g	3.88 oz	17.05%
Sugar	150 g	5.29 oz	23.26%
Eggs	110 g	3.88 oz	17.05%
Gelatin sheets, silver, bloomed in cold water, excess water squeezed off	5 g	.18 oz	.78%
Butter, pomade (softer than room temperature)	270 g	9.52 oz	41.86%

1. Combine the blood orange juice, sugar, and eggs in a bowl and cook them over a hot water bath until thickened while whisking constantly; the mixture should reach 85°C/185°F.

2. Add the gelatin, stirring until it dissolves completely.

3. Stir in the butter (it is necessary to have the butter very soft in order for it to mix in well with the other ingredients).

4. Cool at room temperature covered with plastic wrap. After it has cooled, then refrigerate it. Discard after 1 week.

MACARON MORSELS

Make a one-quarter batch of macarons using the recipe and procedure on pages 342 and 344. Once the macarons have cooled, chop them into small morsels using a knife. Reserve in an airtight container at room temperature. Discard after 6 days.

CANDIED BLOOD ORANGE ZEST

See the recipe and method for candied orange zest on page 148. Substitute blood orange zest for the orange zest.

BLOOD ORANGE ZEST POWDER

YIELD: 20 G/.71 OZ

INGREDIENT	METRIC	U.S.
Blood orange zest	20 g	.71 oz

1. Dry the zest in a dehydrator set to 50°C/120°F for about 2 hours.

2. Once the zest is dry, grind it to a fine powder in a coffee grinder.

3. Reserve in an airtight container at room temperature. If kept dry, it will keep and be fully aromatic for up to 6 months.

BLACK OLIVE CHOCOLATE TILE

YIELD: 10 RECTANGLES

INGREDIENT	METRIC	U.S.
Black Olive Chocolate (page 511)	200 g	7.05 oz

1. Temper the black olive chocolate and spread it into a thin layer over a textured transfer sheet with lines through it.

2. When the chocolate is semi-set, cut out 10 rectangles measuring 6 cm/2.5 in wide by 9 cm/3.5 in long using a ruler and the back of a paring knife.

3. Place another sheet of acetate on top of the chocolate and put a flat surface such as a sheet of Plexiglas on top of it to keep it flat, plus a weight to keep it down, such as a heavy cutting board (or two). The intention is to keep the chocolate flat and for it to remain flat once it is set; otherwise it will warp as its sets.

4. Reserve in a cool, dry area. It will keep for up to 1 year if stored properly.

PRESSED WATERMELON

YIELD: 500 G/1 LB 1.64 OZ

INGREDIENT	METRIC	U.S.
Seedless watermelon, rind removed	500 g	1 lb 1.64 oz

1. Slice the watermelon into 1.25-cm/.5-in-thick slices.

2. Place each slice inside a vacuum-seal bag and vacuum seal it in a Cryovac machine on the highest setting.

3. Refrigerate the watermelon for 4 to 5 hours.

4. Remove the watermelon from the bags and pat them dry with a clean, heavy-duty paper towel.

5. Cut into rectangles measuring 4 cm/1.5 in wide by 12.5 cm/5 in long.

6. Reserve in an airtight container in the refrigerator. Discard after service.

SWEET LIME JELLY

YIELD: 507.6 G/1 LB 1.91 OZ

INGREDIENT	METRIC	U.S.	%
Water	150 g	5.29 oz	29.55%
Lime juice	200 g	7.05 oz	39.4%
Simple syrup, at 50° Brix	150 g	5.29 oz	29.55%
Gellan gum, high acyl	2 g	.06 oz	.32%
Agar-agar	6 g	.21 oz	1.18%

1. Have 3 flat plastic trays available; they should each measure about 30 cm/12 in square and be at least 1.25 cm/.5 in deep. Do not line the trays with acetate.

2. Combine all of the ingredients in a small sauce pot.

3. Bring the liquid to a boil over high heat and let boil for 10 to 15 seconds. Divide the liquid among the 3 trays. Move the trays around after each pour so that the liquid can coat the entire surface of the tray with a thin film of gel. If you wait to move the liquid after pouring it into all of the trays, the liquid might gel prematurely in the trays.

4. Once the liquid is gelled, cut into rectangles measuring 7.5 cm/3 in wide by 15 cm/6 in long while still on the trays; keep covered and refrigerated during service. Discard after 2 days.

Ch ³

PLATED DESSERTS

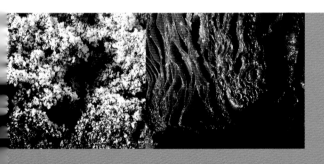

There is no rulebook that says that a plated dessert must be this way or that way. But there are a few guiding principles that have helped to define this course and that act as a foundation to determine the final product.

First and foremost, a plated dessert should not overwhelm the diner. It's unnecessary to serve a customer a large amount of food for the final course. Restraint is recommended and will be greatly appreciated, especially if you serve pre-desserts and petits fours. Keep in mind that you are trying to provide a pleasurable experience, not a punishment.

However, this principle can be applied to other courses of a meal, so what is it that makes a plated dessert a plated dessert? The obvious is that it is sweet, it is plated, and that it is the last course unless you serve petits fours. But for me, the primary defining factor is that it must have an *à la minute* component or an element that is to be consumed within minutes of being plated or else its quality will suffer. For example, a hot element that can get cold, a toasted element that can soften, a fruit paper that is crisp but can become soggy, a frozen component that can melt, bubbles that can pop, and so forth.

There is often a blurred line between a dessert that should be in a display case or a buffet line and one that is on a plate. A dessert for a buffet is supposedly completely finished and ready to be eaten. There are occasions when the pastry chef takes this dessert and simply adds ice cream and a sauce or some chopped fruit. This becomes a plated dessert in strict technical terms, but I would also say that it is closer to a buffet dessert with ephemeral elements added to it.

Plated desserts are the original form of contemporary desserts. Classically, the dessert cart arrived at your table after dinner. This practice has been phased out for the most part (some restaurants still use it), although I wonder why. If it is done well, it can be a great experience for the customer. But in restaurants today, you normally order an appetizer, an entrée, and a dessert. At some restaurants that I worked at during the beginning of my career, this was the menu structure, and it was typically a prix fixe (you pay a certain amount for the three courses). In those situations, where the dessert is already included in the price, most customers order dessert, since, well, it's already paid for. In restaurants where desserts are paid for separately, they "mysteriously" drop in popularity.

A plated dessert should appear simple—not overly handled or contrived. This is, of course, a matter of personal preference. Clean, straight lines, uncluttered surfaces, and clearly defined flavors and textures are my guiding principles. This is what "simple" means to me. True simplicity in this form is very hard to pull off properly.

When you are developing a plated dessert, always ask yourself the following questions:

- **Is it complicated to pick up? How long does this dessert take to plate? Is it service-friendly? How involved is it? How many components are there? Are there different temperature components?**

- **Will my staff understand what my vision is? Can I explain this dessert to the wait staff? Can the wait staff explain it to the customers? Is it too conceptual?**

- **Most important, does it taste good? Well, second most important, because remember the most important thing: Is it wholesome?**

PLATING SEQUENCE

Plating sequence refers to the order in which the components of a dessert are put on a plate and applies to pre-desserts as well as plated desserts. The order is determined by the lifespan of each component; in other words, what can hold the longest at its peak condition will go onto the plate first, and you will continue to place items on the plate in descending order of longevity. The last item you plate is often the most fragile and time-sensitive/temperature-sensitive component. Often this will be a frozen component, but not always; it could also be a soufflé. Alternatively, there could be a garnish that goes on top of the frozen component, in which case the garnish will not technically be the last item to go on the plate. You will have to make use of your common sense. Oftentimes you will have two or more components with a similar lifespan, in which case it doesn't matter in which order they are plated.

Apply chilled components that can hold for longer periods to the plate first.

Sauces are another component that can be added early in the plating process.

Next, a base for the frozen component can be added to keep it in place on the plate.

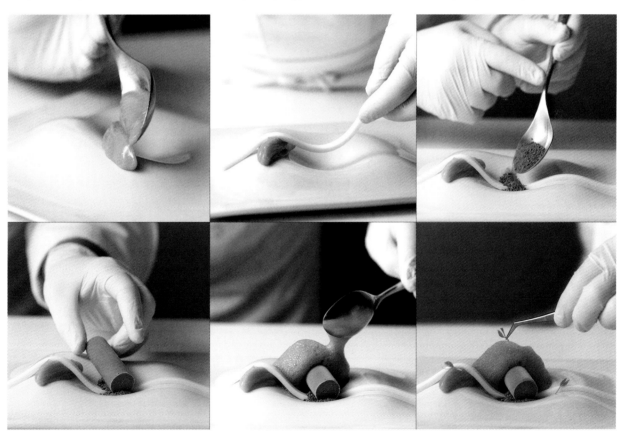

Frozen components should be placed quickly and carefully on top of the base.

Foams or other fragile components can be added toward the end of plating.

Garnishes or other final touches can be added the moment the plate is ready to go to the dining room.

BACON ICE CREAM | QUEBEC MAPLE SYRUP–FLAVORED KATAIFI | BROWN BUTTER PANNA COTTA | BURNING HAY SCENT

YIELD: 10 SERVINGS

WHY THESE FLAVORS WORK

Bacon and maple have been paired together for many years. The very salty flavor of the bacon balances out the very sweet flavor of the maple, with neither taste becoming overwhelming. The caramelized white chocolate has a caramel/Maillard flavor that adds depth of flavor to the bacon and the maple; the same goes for the brown butter in the panna cotta, which truly emphasizes the Maillard flavors of the dessert.

COMPONENTS

Quebec Amber Maple Kataifi (page 211)

Brown Butter Panna Cotta (page 208)

Caramelized White Chocolate–Covered Slab Bacon Ice Cream (pages 208, 210)

Burning hay scent

PLATING PROCEDURE

1. Place the maple kataifi on top of the panna cotta.

2. Place the white chocolate–covered bacon ice cream over the kataifi. Using the Smoking Gun, scent the interior with burned hay smoke (see Notes). Temper the ice cream for 2 to 3 minutes before serving, so that it is smooth enough to eat. Serve.

   This is not a scooped ice cream; it comes right out of the freezer, and therefore it is harder than a scooped ice cream, which is softened somewhat by the scoop or spoon that is being used.

NOTES

The Smoking Gun is an apparatus created by Polyscience (see Resources, page 520), which burns dry matter such as wood chips or spices, and in this case hay, in a controlled environment. It has a flexible rubber hose attached to the spout where the smoke comes out so that you can control where the smoke goes as the hay burns. In this case it will be inside the glass. Once it is smoked, the tube should be removed and the lid put in its place to keep the smoke in.

DARK CHOCOLATE: CAKE | SORBET | LIGHT GELÉE

YIELD: 10 SERVINGS

WHY THESE FLAVORS WORK	There is but one flavor here, chocolate, and obviously chocolate will work with chocolate. The difference here is that the chocolate is found in three different textures: a moist cake, a smooth sorbet, and a light gelée. The textural differences make this an interesting dessert.
COMPONENTS	**Dark Chocolate Light Gelée Sauce** (page 213) **Dark Chocolate Sorbet** (page 211) **Dark Chocolate Cake coated in White Velvet Spray** (page 212)**, hollowed out**
PLATING PROCEDURE	1. Place a rectangle of frozen chocolate gelée sauce on the plate; pass a warm blow dryer over it for a few seconds to thaw. 2. Remove the sorbet from the freezer (it should be in a piping bag) and gently soften it with your hands by rolling it on a flat surface. 3. Pipe about 40 g/1.4 oz of the soft sorbet into the hollowed-out cavity of the chocolate cake. 4. Place the filled cake next to the sauce. Serve immediately.

WARM COCONUT TAPIOCA PUDDING | FROZEN MANGO PARFAIT IN CRISP FEUILLES DE BRICK | ALOE AND HIBISCUS GELÉE

YIELD: 10 SERVINGS

WHY THESE FLAVORS WORK	Fruits that are from a particular region typically go well together. In this case, it is tropical fruits: mango and coconut, with a flower from a tropical area, hibiscus. The aloe, while not tropical, adds some acidity and brightness to the sweeter components on the plate. The three flavors—aloe, coconut, and mango—are not frontal, but they are all distinct. Coconut is mellow, but it enhances the mango. The aloe brings freshness to the coconut and mango. The hibiscus is definitely frontal, dominating in strength of flavor but not in quantity. The wheatgrass is very subtle, but it adds an herbal flavor that ties in well with all the other components.
COMPONENTS	**Frozen Mango Parfait in Crisp Feuilles de Brick** (page 215) **Warm Coconut Tapioca Pudding Liquid** (page 214) **Aloe and Hibiscus Gelée** (page 213) **Wheatgrass blade**
PLATING PROCEDURE	1. Place the frozen mango parfait on the plate, or preferably in a bowl. Let it temper. 2. Meanwhile, combine 50 g/1.75 oz of the prepared tapioca pearls with 40 g/1.4 oz of the warm liquid pudding in a bowl and place over a boiling water bath to bring the tapioca pearls up to temperature. 3. Place a stainless-steel rectangle measuring 7.5 cm/3 in high by 5 cm/2 in long by 2.5 cm/1 in wide over the frozen mango parfait. Spoon the warm coconut tapioca pudding into the rectangle. Place a rectangle of aloe gelée on top of the tapioca. Garnish with a single blade of wheatgrass, horizontally across the top of the gelée. Serve immediately.
NOTE	*This dessert is taken to the table and placed in front of the customer, where the server will remove the ring and the contents will then "fall" into the bowl.*

CARAMELIZED CHOCOLATE PUFF PASTRY | VANILLA CRÈME CHANTILLY | BUTTER POWDER

YIELD: 10 SERVINGS

WHY THESE FLAVORS WORK	The chocolate puff pastry, which contains a large percentage of butter, contributes more of a flaky texture (the result of the layering of butter and dough) than a butter flavor. This component adds a baked pastry flavor (Maillard) that ties in well with the whipped vanilla crème Chantilly. The moist creaminess of the Chantilly together with the brittle flakiness of the puff pastry is sometimes all you need in a dessert.
COMPONENTS	**Caramelized Chocolate Puff Pastry** (page 216) **Vanilla Crème Chantilly** (page 216) **Butter powder**
PLATING PROCEDURE	1. Remove a rectangle of baked puff pastry from the dehydrator and place on a plate. 2. Spoon a 60-g/2-oz quenelle of crème Chantilly next to the puff pastry. 3. Sprinkle 2 g/.07 oz of butter powder on top of the quenelle (you will need a total of 20 g/.7 oz of butter powder for 10 servings; see Resources on page 521). Serve immediately.

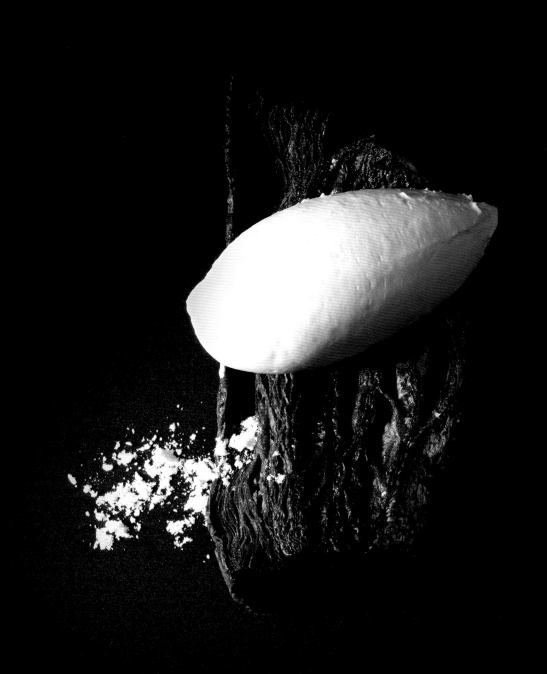

FIG LEAF ICE CREAM | SCOTTISH SHORTBREAD CRUMBS | JASMINE TEA CAKE | MELTING CHOCOLATE BOX

YIELD: 10 SERVINGS

WHY THESE FLAVORS WORK

Fig leaf has a green, herby flavor with some fig notes. The shortbread has background Maillard and butter flavors that do not overpower the fig leaf. The high flavor note will also come from the jasmine and the chocolate, which are used in a balanced proportion so as to not overwhelm the fig leaf.

COMPONENTS

Chocolate Sauce Rectangle (page 217)

Fig Leaf Ice Cream Cylinder (page 217)

Scottish Shortbread Crumbs (page 218)

Jasmine Tea Cake Rectangles (page 218)

Chocolate Box (page 219)

PLATING PROCEDURE

1. Using a 11 cm/4.5 in long by 1.25 cm/.5 in wide rectangular stencil, spread the chocolate sauce on a plate.

2. Warm the fig leaf ice cream cylinder gently in your hands, using gloves, and coat it in the Scottish shortbread crumbs.

3. Wrap a jasmine tea cake rectangle (each rectangle measures 5 cm/2 in wide by 10 cm/4 in long by 5 mm/.25 in thick) around the crumb-coated ice cream. Place it on the plate with the seam facing down to prevent the cake from unwrapping itself from the ice cream.

4. Place the chocolate box on top of the ice cream. It will conceal the entire dessert.

5. Using a paint stripper (heat gun) set to the lowest setting, warm the chocolate to soften it. Focus the heat on one corner of the cube until it just starts to melt, then turn the gun off.

6. Serve immediately. It is crucial that the chocolate is not setting into a solid state again when it gets to the customer so that it is easier to cut through with a fork. It should still be shiny from the heat.

BLACKBERRY AND ROSE SORBET | STRAWBERRY JELLY | GOAT'S MILK WHITE CHOCOLATE TILE | ROSE PETAL CAKE

YIELD: 10 SERVINGS

WHY THESE FLAVORS WORK

The flavors of rose and strawberry play off of each other; each is clearly distinguished, but they also enhance each other. Both flavors are frontal, which means they are clearly detected by the tongue. The blackberry flavor is frontal as well, but it is also an aromatic fruit with slightly floral notes from the rose petal. In this case, it is not used in equal proportion to the other flavors; it is used in a larger proportion and is the focus flavor of the dessert. The goat's milk white chocolate is a background flavor, which merely pushes the other flavors forward but has a distinctive goat's milk flavor; goat's milk cheeses go very well with most fruit. The ash, which is flavorless, is typically used in cheese making, mostly for soft goat cheese, which is why it makes sense in this dessert.

COMPONENTS

Rose Petal Cake (page 221)

Rose Hip Honey and Water Soaking Liquid (page 221)

Blackberry and Rose Sorbet Tube (page 220)

Goat's Milk White Chocolate Tile (page 219)

Strawberry Jelly Tube (page 220)

Ash spatter (see Resources, page 520)

PLATING PROCEDURE

1. Place the rectangle of rose petal cake on the plate.

2. Brush only the surface of the cake with rose hip honey and water soaking liquid (about 10 g/.35 oz per cake).

3. Place the tube of blackberry sorbet on top of the cake.

4. Lean the goat's milk chocolate tile on top of the sorbet.

5. Put the strawberry jelly tube on top of the chocolate tile.

6. Sprinkle a pinch of ash on top of the dessert (about .2 g/.007 oz per order).

7. Allow the sorbet to temper for about 2 minutes before serving.

FROZEN ESPRESSO BOMBE | LEMON CURD | MILK FROTH

YIELD: 10 SERVINGS

WHY THESE FLAVORS WORK	The combination of espresso, lemon, and milk is considered a classic flavor profile. In many coffee shops, when you order an espresso you automatically get a lemon zest twist with it. The flavor of the lemon enhances the bitterness of the espresso even further but in a pleasant way, and the milk helps cut down the bitterness and adds richness to the dessert, smoothing out the bitter flavors.
COMPONENTS	**Frozen Espresso Bombe** (page 222) **Lemon Curd** (page 223) **Espresso Paste** (page 224) **Milk froth**
PLATING PROCEDURE	1. Place the espresso bombe on the plate. Let it temper for 3 to 5 minutes. Always check before serving it; you do not want to send it out if it is rock-hard. It may take more than 5 minutes. 2. Place one end of the lemon curd on top of the bombe; the other end will be directly on the plate. Spoon 10 g/.3 oz of espresso paste on this end of the curd. 3. Using an espresso machine steamer probe or a milk frother, steam whole milk and spoon it onto the bombe. Serve immediately.

PEAR ICE CREAM | CARAMEL-POACHED SECKEL PEAR | CARAMELIZED ALMOND GENOA BREAD | CHOCOLATE VEIL

YIELD: 10 SERVINGS

WHY THESE FLAVORS WORK

This is another classic flavor combination: pear, almond, and chocolate. The pear contributes floral notes, enhanced by the nuttiness of the almond bread, which also has Maillard notes. Chocolate binds these two flavors together. They are all distinct flavors that harmonize well without overpowering each other. The chocolate is the frontal flavor, while the pear is a semi-frontal flavor. The almond is a background flavor, as are the caramel flavors from the caramelized cake and the caramel and pear stock, all working as enhancers for the frontal flavors.

COMPONENTS

Caramel-Poached Seckel Pear (page 225)

Hot Caramel and Pear Stock (page 225)

Sugar, as needed

Almond Genoa Bread (page 224)

Chopped toasted almonds

Pear Ice Cream (page 225)

Chocolate Veil (page 226)

Gold leaf

Chocolate Décor Curved Triangle (page 226)

PLATING PROCEDURE

1. Cut a poached pear into quarters. Drop one-quarter of the pear in the hot caramel and pear stock to warm it up.

2. Place 100 g/3.5 oz sugar in a small sauté pan. Make a dry caramel over high heat, and then turn the heat down to low. This caramel can be replenished with new sugar as needed and used throughout service. Keep it warm (it stays liquid) in the sauté pan over very low heat so that you do not have to repeat the entire process each time you get an order.

3. Place a rectangle of almond Genoa bread on the sugar, then turn it after 10 seconds. Repeat until the entire cake is coated in sugar. This coat should be very thin so that it is easy to eat, not thick, which can cause dental damage. It is meant to be eaten with the caramel hardened on the cake to give textural contrast with the soft cake under it. Place the cake on a plate.

4. Place 3 g/.1 oz of chopped and toasted almonds next to the cake, and spoon a quenelle of pear ice cream onto the chopped almonds.

5. Place the chocolate veil over all of the components that are already plated with the shiny side facing up. The shiny side of the veil is the side that is facing the tray, not the exposed surface. Using a small offset spatula, slide under a corner of the veil and pick it up gently

without damaging it. Using a paring knife, make a small slit where the ice cream is, about 2 cm/.75 in long.

6. Remove the hot pear from the liquid and pat it dry with a paper towel; place it next to the cake; put a small piece of gold leaf on the pear.

7. Place the triangle décor on top of the dessert. Serve immediately.

FROZEN LANDSCAPE

YIELD: 10 SERVINGS

WHY THESE FLAVORS WORK

These flavors were paired through association: rice milk to saffron to blood orange to pistachio. (Rice = rice dish = paella = Spain = saffron = orange = blood orange = Italy = Sicilian pistachio = pistachio) Fortunately the association could go either way, which means all the flavors go well with each other. This is because the only frontal flavor, blood orange, merges with and is enhanced by the other flavors, which are all background and do not interrupt each other. They are all clearly distinguishable without getting in each other's way.

COMPONENTS

Blood Orange Sorbet Base (page 227)

Rice Milk Sorbet Base (page 227)

Pistachio Ice Cream Base (page 227)

Saffron Ice Cream Base (page 228)

PLATING PROCEDURE

1. Place the serving plates (or other containers for the frozen desserts) in a freezer.

2. Churn all of the bases separately. Pour them into separate piping bags fitted with different piping tips. Use a #6 open fluted tip for the blood orange, a #4 closed fluted tip for the rice sherbet, a #6 plain tip for the pistachio, and a #4 plain tip for the saffron ice cream. Try to keep the frozen bases in the warmest section of your freezer so that they do not harden too quickly. If they are too hard to pipe, simply put them in a refrigerator for a few minutes until they are of piping consistency.

3. Pipe the frozen desserts onto the frozen serving plates, alternating flavors to create a random pattern. Place the desserts in the freezer. Keep the serving plates frozen at -10°C/14°F or slightly warmer if possible. This dessert should not be rock-hard for service. If you can adjust your freezer to -5°C/23°F, it will be better.

4. When an order comes in, temper the cube for at least 5 minutes before serving. If you do not have the luxury of waiting 5 minutes, microwaving the cube on the "defrost" setting for a few seconds usually helps soften the ice cream without melting it. Discard any leftover cubes after service.

PUMPKIN MOUSSE | BROWNED BUTTER AND CRANBERRY SHORTBREAD | PUMPKIN SEED AND MILK CHOCOLATE BAR | CRANBERRY JUICE FROTH

YIELD: 10 SERVINGS

WHY THESE FLAVORS WORK

Pumpkin is a very mellow flavor that needs a lot of help to get noticed; often people identify the flavor of the spice that the pumpkin is mixed with as the actual flavor of pumpkin. For example, pumpkin pie usually smells mostly of the spice mix used in the custard, not necessarily of the pumpkin itself. This is why we are using roasted pumpkin in this recipe with absolutely no spices to mask its flavor. A useful tip for flavor combination is this: Produce that is harvested during the same period of time will usually taste good together, and even more so if it's from the same part of the world. This is why pumpkin and cranberry can work well together. Cranberries have a tart fruitiness that can act as salt does, enhancing the mellow pumpkin. As for the pumpkin seeds—well, they're from the pumpkin, therefore it is a natural pairing, but interestingly enough, pumpkin seed paste has a much more pronounced flavor than pumpkin flesh. This is why seeds are used in a smaller proportion in this dessert. The star is the pumpkin, and the other flavors play merely a supporting role.

COMPONENTS

Pumpkin Seed and Milk Chocolate Bar (page 228)

Pumpkin Mousse Square (page 230)

Cranberry Juice Froth (page 232)

Cranberry powder (see Resources, page 520)

PLATING PROCEDURE

1. Place the pumpkin seed and milk chocolate bar on the plate. Put the pumpkin mousse on the bar and let it temper for about 5 minutes if possible.

2. Spoon the cranberry juice froth onto one corner of the mousse.

3. Sprinkle a pinch of cranberry powder onto the mousse. Serve.

WARM DARK CHOCOLATE TART | CLOTTED CREAM

YIELD: 10 SERVINGS

WHY THESE FLAVORS WORK

This dessert warrants an explanation, since the first impression is that it is just melted chocolate with caramel, shortbread, and some cream. Here's what makes it special: The chocolate used is a very high-fat, high-viscosity, low-fluidity chocolate that does not run when it is melted, but rather holds its shape. Therefore one gets the impression that the chocolate is incredibly shiny, but it is in fact melted. It also gives the textural impression of a ganache, but again, it is just chocolate. The salted caramel adds Maillard flavor but also salt, which enhances all flavors involved. Chocolate and caramel are frequently seen together, since their flavors play off each other quite well. The shortbread contributes additional Maillard flavors, but more important, a crunchy texture to an otherwise soft dessert. The real flavor contrast is with the clotted cream, which has a very intense, rich dairy flavor that complements the chocolate. It also has a second and equally important role, and that is to slightly set the melted chocolate when it is in your mouth. How is this? Well, the chocolate is warm, the cream is cold, and therefore the cold cream will momentarily harden the chocolate in the mouth; the chocolate will soon after soften again, creating a ganache of sorts. The atomized chocolate is the third chocolate component, and its role is really just to keep the cream in place.

COMPONENTS

Warm chocolate

Salted Caramel (page 232)

Scottish Shortbread Crumbs (page 218)

Clotted cream

Black Chocolate Tile (page 233)

PLATING PROCEDURE

1. Turn a dehydrator on and set it to 35°C/95°F. Place a solid 650-g/22.9-oz block of Peter's chocolate (see Resources, page 521) in a half hotel pan inside the dehydrator. It should be in there at least 30 minutes before service so that it softens completely.

2. Spoon 60 g/2.12 oz of the softened chocolate on a plate.

3. Spoon 20 g/.7 oz of the salted caramel on top of the chocolate.

4. Spoon 20 g/.7 oz of the shortbread crumbs on top of the caramel.

5. Spoon a 35-g/1.23-oz quenelle of clotted cream next to the soft chocolate.

6. Place a tile of chocolate on top of the previous components to cover them completely. Serve immediately.

NOTE   *You can use Devon cream or even crème fraîche as a replacement, but the flavor of clotted cream
        is unique and, if you can obtain it, it is definitely worth trying.*

CRISPY MILK | BAGUETTE ICE CREAM | CARAMELIZED WHITE CHOCOLATE SPIRAL | CAJETA | MALDON SEA SALT

YIELD: 10 SERVINGS

WHY THESE FLAVORS WORK

All of the flavors in this dessert are considered background flavors. The dominant flavor comes from the Maillard reactions that occur in the cajeta (with a goat's milk flavor as well) and the caramelized white chocolate spiral. With that thread in common, these components are bound to get along very well, with the salt added to enhance these flavors. The crispy milk is a dehydrated milk foam that is toasted; the foam contributes an intense dairy flavor.

COMPONENTS

Crispy Milk (page 233)

Cajeta

Maldon sea salt

Caramelized White Chocolate Spiral (page 234)

Baguette Ice Cream (page 234)

PLATING PROCEDURE

1. Place the crispy milk piece on the plate.

2. Spoon 20 g/.7 oz of cajeta on top of the crispy milk, so that it trickles down to the plate.

3. Sprinkle 1 g/.03 oz of Maldon sea salt on top of the cajeta.

4. Place a caramelized white chocolate spiral in front of the crispy milk.

5. Spoon a 60-g/2-oz quenelle of baguette ice cream behind the crispy milk. Serve immediately.

HUCKLEBERRY COMPOTE | MEXICAN VANILLA CREAM | LEMON JOCONDE CRUMBS | LEMON STREUSEL

YIELD: 10 SERVINGS

WHY THESE FLAVORS WORK

Huckleberry and lemons are a classic flavor combination; the lemon flavor enhances the huckleberry flavor, which is very intense and similar to wild blueberries but with citrus notes. Vanilla acts as the background flavor that complements the frontal flavors. The anise hyssop adds a light anise flavor, which enhances the huckleberry and lemon further.

COMPONENTS

Lemon Streusel (page 237)

Huckleberry Compote (page 235)

Mexican Vanilla Cream (page 236)

Lemon Joconde Crumbs (page 237)

Encapsulated Huckleberry Compote (page 235)

Anise hyssop leaves

PLATING PROCEDURE

1. Spoon 30 g/1.06 oz of lemon streusel into a bowl.

2. Using a slotted spoon, scoop out 20 g/.71 oz of huckleberry compote from the cooking liquid and place it on top of the streusel.

3. Pipe 60 g/2.12 oz of vanilla cream into the bowl, on top of the streusel. Tap the bowl to even out the surface.

4. Spoon 20 g/.71 oz of lemon Joconde crumbs on top of the cream and even them out with the back of a spoon.

5. Put the encapsulated huckleberry compote near the center of the bowl, on top of the crumbs.

6. Place 1 anise hyssop leaf on top of the sphere. Serve immediately.

FROZEN EARL GREY FOAM | BERGAMOT SORBET | BERGAMOT CHOCOLATE SHELL | EARL GREY GÉNOISE

YIELD: 10 SERVINGS

WHY THESE FLAVORS WORK

Earl Grey is traditionally a black tea with flavor added from bergamot orange oil; therefore, this flavor combination is essentially tied together by tradition, but also because the bitterness of the black tea and the floral, citrus notes of the bergamot pair very well. The flavors of chocolate, citrus, and black tea are aligned for similar reasons and are frequently found together in many dessert preparations.

COMPONENTS

Frozen Earl Grey Foam in Chocolate Shell Tube (page 240)

Chocolate Letter "B" (page 239)

Yellow Chocolate Plaques (page 238)

PLATING PROCEDURE

1. Place the assembled frozen Earl Grey foam tube on a plate, seam facing down.

2. Using a cornet (parchment paper cone filled with melted chocolate), attach the letter to the chocolate tube. Attach 1 square yellow chocolate plaque to each side of the shell, shiny side facing out. Serve immediately.

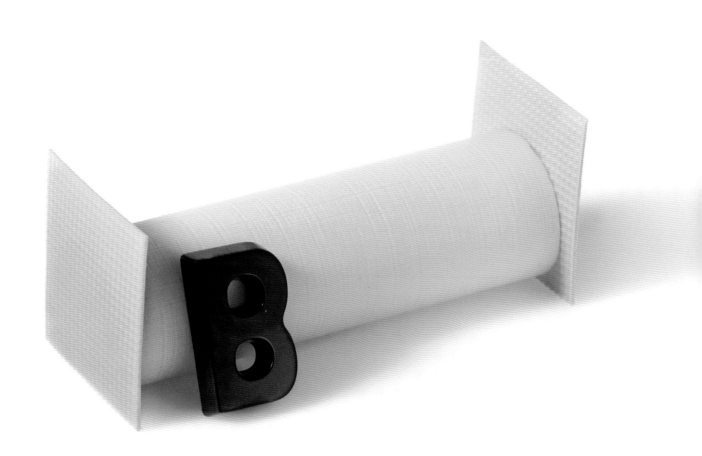

WARM JASMINE RICE PUDDING | VIETNAMESE COFFEE ICE CREAM TRUFFLE

YIELD: 10 SERVINGS

WHY THESE FLAVORS WORK

Jasmine rice has a very floral and aromatic flavor that is not necessarily sweet, but it is a flavor that is very agreeable with desserts. Vietnamese coffee makes sense here because it is also very aromatic; it can share this quality with the jasmine without overwhelming it. There is also a wonderful temperature difference in this dessert that comes from combining the hot pudding with the ice cream.

COMPONENTS

Vietnamese Ice Cream (page 241)

Melted dark chocolate (72 percent) for coating

Warm Jasmine Rice Pudding (page 241)

Coffee Jelly Tube (page 242)

Instant Vietnamese coffee powder (see Resources, page 520)

PLATING PROCEDURE

1. Unmold a half-sphere of Vietnamese ice cream from the silicone mold. Carefully and quickly dip it in the melted chocolate.

2. Place the chocolate-covered ice cream in the middle of a bowl.

3. Pour 113 g/4 oz of the warm jasmine rice pudding on top of the ice cream.

4. Place a tube of coffee jelly partially on the side of the bowl and partially on the pudding.

5. Sprinkle a pinch of instant Vietnamese coffee on top of the rice pudding in a straight line across the jelly. Serve immediately.

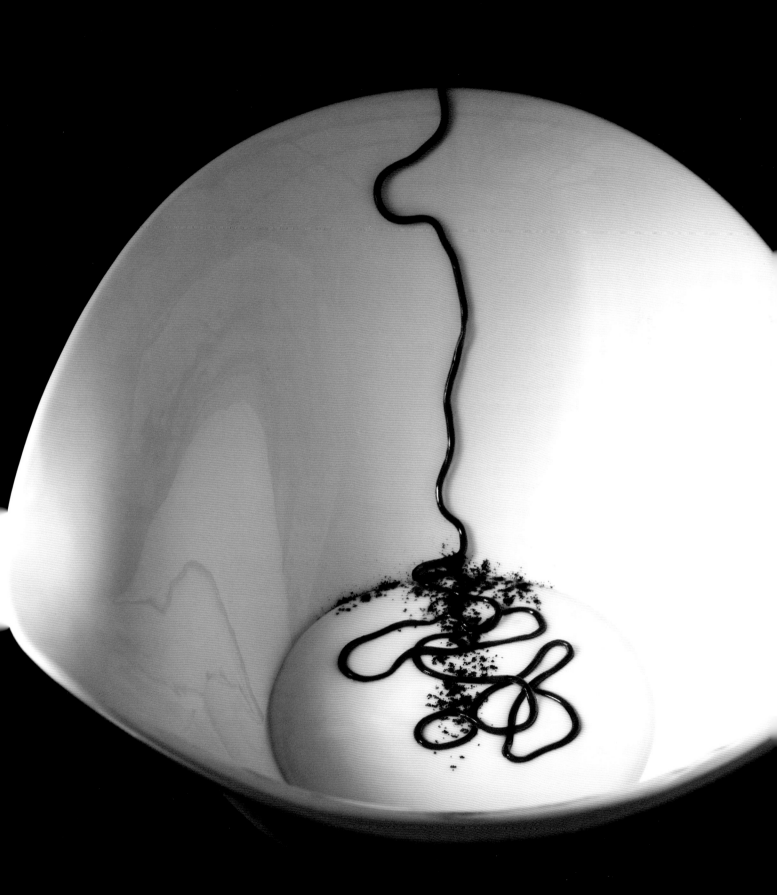

WARM PANDAN LEAF–INFUSED CARAMELIZED CREAM | BLACK SESAME GENOA BREAD | HIBISCUS GLAZE | POPCORN SHOOT

YIELD: 10 SERVINGS

WHY THESE FLAVORS WORK

The pandan cream and the popcorn may seem not to have anything in common, but in my opinion, pandan tastes very much like popcorn, and so do popcorn shoots. The popcorn flavor binds itself well to the black sesame, which is subtle but with some intermittent intensity. The hibiscus adds a note of acidity, which acts as a flavor enhancer.

COMPONENTS

Pandan Leaf–Infused Caramelized Cream Tube (page 242)

Hibiscus Glaze (page 244)

Black Sesame Genoa Bread (page 243)

Powdered Popcorn (page 244)

Popcorn shoot

Turbinado sugar

PLATING PROCEDURE

1. Prior to service, place a 960-mL/1-qt sauce pot filled halfway with water over low heat. Keep it covered.

2. When an order comes in, drop the pandan tube into the hot water to heat it up.

3. Spread 20 g/.7 oz of hibiscus glaze on a plate.

4. Place 1 thin rectangle of black sesame Genoa bread over the glaze.

5. Spoon 5 g/.17 oz of powdered popcorn on one side of the Genoa bread. Put a popcorn shoot on top of the popcorn.

6. Remove the pandan tube from the water carefully; pat it dry with a clean paper towel. Place it on a wire rack. Sprinkle 5 g/.17 oz of turbinado sugar on top of the tube and caramelize it using a blowtorch.

7. Transfer the tube to the plate, onto the Genoa bread, on the opposite side of the powdered popcorn.

WORMWOOD ICE CREAM | 72% CHOCOLATE CAKE | QUARK CHOCOLATE TILE

YIELD: 10 SERVINGS

WHY THESE FLAVORS WORK

The basic flavor profile is comprised of bitter flavors and the way they interact with each other. Wormwood has a flavor reminiscent of Angostura bitters. It is also one of the ingredients in the original absinthe liqueur and is often maligned as a substance that induces hallucinations. Extracts contain a much smaller proportion of thujones (the component that may be toxic in large quantities) and are harmless. The bitterness from the chocolate is more familiar. These two flavors play off each other with a unifying theme but are clearly distinct. The quark chocolate has more of a sweet-sour dairy note that helps bind all of the flavors together and adds texture with its snap.

COMPONENTS

Velvet Coated Wormwood Ice Cream (page 245)

Quark Chocolate Tile (page 246)

Fried Mint Leaf (page 247)

PLATING PROCEDURE

1. Place the wormwood ice cream on the plate; let it temper for a few minutes.

2. Place a quark chocolate tile on top of the ice cream.

3. Put the fried mint leaf in front of the ice cream. Serve immediately.

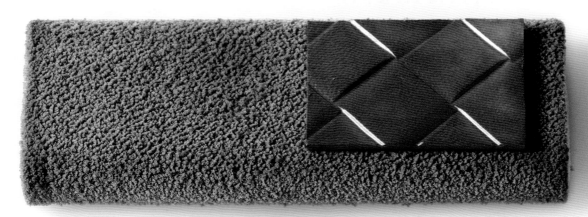

LILAC ICE CREAM | MINI VIOLET MACARONS | MINT POUND CAKE | RHUBARB AND ELDERFLOWER GELÉE

YIELD: 10 SERVINGS

WHY THESE FLAVORS WORK

The main flavor in this dessert is the lilac, which is a pronounced floral flavor. It is similar to the elderflower and violet in this regard, and the tartness of the rhubarb helps enhance these floral components. The herbal flavor of the mint helps round out the floral notes.. The verbena flowers are meant to resemble small lilac flowers and are not necessarily contributing heavily to the flavor. The macarons add a textural component.

COMPONENTS

Lilac Ice Cream (page 247) **coated in Pink Velvet Spray** (page 248)

Mint Pound Cake coated in Green Velvet Spray (page 248)

Rhubarb and Elderflower Gelée (page 249)

Mini Violet Macarons (page 250)

Pressed verbena flowers

PLATING PROCEDURE

1. Place the lilac ice cream on the plate; it is a molded ice cream and may need to temper for a few minutes before it is served.

2. Place the mint pound cake on top of the ice cream.

3. Place a slice of rhubarb and elderflower gelée half on top of the ice cream and half on the plate.

4. Put 3 mini violet macarons around the ice cream. Put 3 verbena flowers around the ice cream. Serve immediately.

BUTTERNUT SQUASH AND CINNAMON ICE CREAM | TRUE RED VELVET CAKE | BLACK CURRANT "PAPER" | INDONESIAN CINNAMON BUBBLES | SILVER HONEY SAUCE

YIELD: 10 SERVINGS

WHY THESE FLAVORS WORK

Butternut squash has an affinity for spices like cinnamon, clove, ginger, and vanilla. Butternut squash has a flavor that is so subtle that if you are not careful, the only noticeable flavor the dessert will have is that of the cinnamon. That is why, in this case, the ice cream base has large quantity of butternut squash and just a hint of cinnamon. The cinnamon makes the flavor of the squash come out. The "true" velvet cake refers to the fact that this cake is made in the original way, that is, without food coloring. True velvet cakes are just slightly red (more like a reddish-brown), and this is because originally they were made with natural cocoa powder rather than Dutch-process (alkalized) cocoa powder, which reacted with the leavener (baking soda) to create the red tinge in the cake. Its chocolate flavor is a great addition to the squash since it will not cover it up, but balance well with it. It helps that they are different temperatures, different textures, and contain different fats. To punch these flavors up, the thin sheet of black currant adds a tart fruit note that acts almost like salt, pushing flavors forward. The cinnamon foam will be a subtle but welcome addition to the cinnamon in the ice cream. The silver honey sauce is simply honey with silver powder, the honey adding its particular and subtle flavor to the mix.

COMPONENTS

Silver Honey Sauce (page 253)

True Red Velvet Cake (page 252)

Butternut Squash and Cinnamon Ice Cream (page 251)

Black Currant "Paper" (page 253)

Indonesian Cinnamon Bubbles (page 254)

PLATING PROCEDURE

1. Spoon 5 g/.2 oz of silver honey sauce around the plate.

2. Place the red velvet cake at the center of the plate.

3. Place the butternut squash ice cream on top of the cake.

4. Place a square of black currant "paper" on top of the ice cream.

5. Spoon a dollop of Indonesian cinnamon bubbles onto the paper. Serve immediately.

TOASTED MILK PANNA COTTA COVERED IN CARAMELIZED MILK CHOCOLATE | CRISP CROISSANT CROUTON | DEVIL'S FOOD CAKE SOUP

YIELD: 10 SERVINGS

WHY THESE FLAVORS WORK	There are three components in this dessert that have Maillard flavors: the toasted milk panna cotta, the caramelized milk chocolate, and the crisp croissant. That alone brings them together. The devil's food cake soup, which is a purée of chocolate cake, acts as a flavor binder for all the other components.
COMPONENTS	**Croissant Crouton** (page 255) **Toasted Milk Panna Cotta** (page 254) **covered in Caramelized Milk Chocolate Velvet Spray** (page 255) **Golden Caramelized Milk Chocolate Décor** (page 257) **Devil's Food Cake Soup** (page 256)
PLATING PROCEDURE	1. Place the croissant crouton on the plate. 2. Put the frozen milk panna cotta on top of the crouton. 3. Pour 90 g/3.17 oz of the devil's cake soup in the center of the panna cotta. 4. Place the décor at the center of the bowl, on top of the soup. Wait for the panna cotta to soften for 2 to 3 minutes, then serve.

SALTED PEANUT BUTTER ICE CREAM | RAISIN JELLY VEIL | TOASTED VIRGINIA PEANUT GENOA BREAD | CELERY FROTH | PEANUT BRITTLE

YIELD: 10 SERVINGS

WHY THESE FLAVORS WORK

I would never have thought to combine raisins with peanuts, never mind celery. Crunchy celery with smooth peanut butter and sweet raisins does work, although nothing in my mental flavor map can reasonably tell me why. However, if it didn't taste at least a little bit good, no one would enjoy it and it would not have become the popular snack it is today. In this dessert I have taken those flavors and manipulated the textures. The raisin is infused with cola and then gelled. Cola tastes like raisins (or prunes). The peanut butter flavors the ice cream and is used to make a sponge cake (Genoa bread); peanuts are also used to make a crispy brittle. The celery is juiced and then blended to make it foamy, so it contributes flavor and not texture as in its original form.

COMPONENTS

Celery Froth (see Note)

Toasted Virginia Peanut Genoa Bread (page 257)

Salted Peanut Ice Cream Bar (page 258)

Raisin Jelly Veil (page 259)

Peanut Brittle (page 259)

PLATING PROCEDURE

1. Juice a whole celery stalk with a juicer. It will produce a natural froth when it is juiced.

2. Place the toasted Virginia peanut Genoa bread on the plate.

3. Put the salted peanut ice cream on top of the Genoa bread.

4. Cover the ice cream with the raisin veil.

5. Spoon a dollop of celery froth on the left side of the raisin veil.

6. Place a piece of peanut brittle on the right side of the veil. Serve immediately.

NOTE

To make the celery froth, juice a celery stalk for each portion in a professional juicer. This produces a natural froth that does not require any additives and results in a very pronounced celery flavor. You will only need the froth, though; reserve the juice for other uses such as celery granité or sorbet.

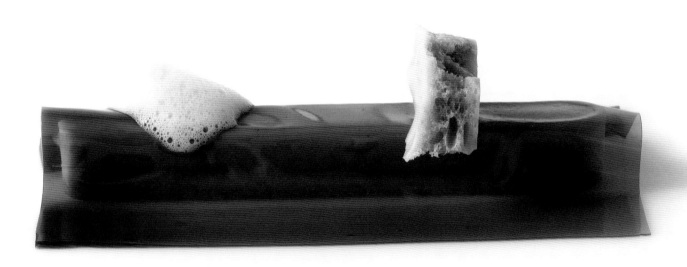

BROWN BUTTER PANNA COTTA

YIELD: 618 G/1 LB 5.76 OZ

INGREDIENT	METRIC	U.S.	%
Brown Butter Solids			
Milk powder	300 g	10.58 oz	42.86%
Butter	400 g	14.11 oz	57.14%
Panna Cotta			
Heavy cream	375 g	13.23 oz	60.68%
Sugar	60 g	2.12 oz	9.71%
Brown Butter Solids	175 g	6.17 oz	28.32%
Gelatin sheets, silver, bloomed in cold water, excess water squeezed off	8 g	.28 oz	1.29%

1. **For the butter solids:** Combine the milk powder and butter in a sauce pot and cook over high heat. The heat will brown the milk powder, creating an amplified brown butter flavor. Butter on its own will not provide much brown butter flavor due to the small amount of milk solids in it. If more milk solids are added, then the resulting mixture will have more of that flavor.

2. Cool in a hotel pan at room temperature.

3. **For the panna cotta:** Combine the cream, sugar, and brown butter solids in a 960 mL/1 qt sauce pot and bring to a simmer to dissolve the sugar and brown butter solids. Pass through a fine-mesh sieve.

4. Add the bloomed gelatin and stir until it has dissolved.

5. Portion 20 g/.70 oz into the desired bowl.

6. Let set uncovered in the refrigerator for at least 3 hours before service. Once it has set, cover loosely with plastic wrap. Discard after 2 days.

SLAB BACON ICE CREAM

YIELD: 1 KG/2 LB 3.2 OZ

INGREDIENT	METRIC	U.S.	%
Bacon-Infused Milk			
Milk	1 kg	2 lb 3.2 oz	58.82%
Slab bacon, cut into 2.5-cm/1-in cubes, fat rendered off	250 g	8.82 oz	14.71%
Ham hock	450 g	15.87 oz	26.47%
Ice Cream			
Bacon-Infused Milk	650 g	1 lb 6.88 oz	65%
Heavy cream	87 g	3.09 oz	8.75%
Powdered milk	40 g	1.41 oz	4%
Sugar	150 g	5.29 oz	15%
Ice cream stabilizer	3 g	.09 oz	.25%
Egg yolks	70 g	2.47 oz	7%

1. **For the bacon-infused milk:** Combine all of the ingredients in a sauce pot. It needs to be small enough to hold the bacon and the hock completely submerged in the milk.

2. Bring to a boil over high heat, then turn the heat down to a simmer for 2 minutes. Turn off the heat and cover the pot. Let the bacon and hock infuse for 30 minutes.

3. Strain the bacon and hock out of the milk. Cool the milk and proceed with the ice cream base.

4. **For the ice cream:** Follow the modern ice cream method on page 50. Reserve the base in the refrigerator until ready to churn.

the volcano vaporizer

This machine, which sounds like it took its name from a Star Trek volcano destruction device, is used to scent food through vapor. It is an electromechanical device that produces vapor by gently heating plant matter to the point where the essential oils responsible for flavor are vaporized. The body of the machine produces hot air with a temperature level that can be adjusted to suit a specific ingredient, since not all ingredients will require the same amount of heat. There is a fan that forces the hot air through the ingredient, thus releasing its aromatic compounds.

The machine has two attachments that the vapor can be passed through. One is called a *collection balloon,* which is a cellophane balloon that is attached to the volcano's spout; the company calls the other a *mixology attachment,* which is a food-grade, heat-resistant hose that can be attached to the volcano's spout on one end, and the scented vapor comes out the other end. This is the attachment that was used for the scented desserts in this book (see Slab Bacon Ice Cream on page 208, Cassis Sponge Cake on page 437, and Bacon Praline on page 514). This hose allows you to funnel the vapor to any container you choose.

This is a great piece of equipment because it helps add aromas to desserts to influence their flavor without necessarily using the actual ingredient that is used to produce the aroma. For example, the hay that was used to scent the bacon ice cream on page 208 is an ingredient that wouldn't necessarily be used as a component that is to be eaten (although it is not out of the question), and so in this case we are just getting the scent of the hay. The results that the Volcano Vaporizer produces are much different than those you obtain from a tool such as the Smoking Gun, which relies on fire and smoke to scent food. That has its place, but they produce two very different results.

Some products that work well with the Vaporizer are lavender, cinnamon, clove, vanilla, star anise, Earl Grey tea, hops, tobacco, sage, thyme, and eucalyptus. There is a temperature guide for each type of ingredient on the Volcano Vaporizer's Web site (see page 520).

Fill the chamber of the vaporizer with crushed dried herbs or other aromatic ingredients.

Place the tube inside the container you are infusing with scent.

The finished dessert will be scented with the vaporized aromatic particles of the chosen aromatic ingredient.

CARAMELIZED WHITE CHOCOLATE SHELL

YIELD: 605 G/1 LB 5.28 OZ

INGREDIENT	METRIC	U.S.	%
White chocolate coins	500 g	1 lb 1.6 oz	82.64%
Cocoa butter, melted	50 g	1.76 oz	8.26%
Canola oil	55 g	1.94 oz	9.09%

1. Preheat a convection oven to 115°C/240°F.

2. Place the chocolate in a half hotel pan and place inside the oven. Stir every 30 minutes, using a wooden spoon, for 3 hours or until fully caramelized. It will be a medium amber brown, similar to caramel sauce.

3. Remove the caramelized white chocolate from the oven and stir in the melted cocoa butter. At this point, the chocolate can be reserved in a cool, dry area and used as you would use regular white chocolate; however, in this case you will not be using it as such. You will need to add the canola oil in order for it to become a shell. The addition of oil will make the chocolate softer so that when it is cut into with a spoon or fork, it will yield to gentle pressure and not be cumbersome to eat.

4. Let the chocolate cool to 30°C/86°F and pour into the desired mold (see Note). Let it sit for 5 minutes, then pour the excess chocolate out. Scrape the base of the mold to even it out and let the shell set in the refrigerator. Once it has set, it can come out of the mold. Reserve frozen if using soon; the bacon ice cream will be piped into the shell and it must be frozen to keep the ice cream from melting. If not using soon, reserve in a cool, dry place for up to 1 year.

NOTE *The mold used in this photo is an antique mold that is not commercially available. Many of these molds can be found online (see Resources, page 520).*

CARAMELIZED WHITE CHOCOLATE VELVET SPRAY

YIELD: 500 G/1 LB 1.64 OZ

INGREDIENT	METRIC	U.S.	%
Caramelized White Chocolate (page 316)	250 g	8.82 oz	50%
Cocoa butter	250 g	8.82 oz	50%

1. Combine both ingredients in a bowl and melt them over a hot water bath. If using soon, keep the spray liquid by keeping it warm (above 40°C/105°F) over a warm water bath. If not, reserve in an airtight container at room temperature for up to 1 year.

2. To fill the molds, make sure the chocolate shells are frozen.

3. Churn the ice cream base to medium smoothness, not all the way; otherwise, it cannot be piped into the mold and will not fill it completely. Pour it from the machine directly into a piping bag.

4. Pipe the ice cream into the shells and fill them to the top. Even out the top with an offset spatula. Reserve all of the filled shells frozen at -10°C/14°F.

5. Let the ice cream harden for at least 2 hours. Meanwhile, set up a spray station, a surface that should be covered with plastic to keep the shop clean where you can spray the chocolate velvet spray.

6. Fill a compressor canister with the caramelized white chocolate spray. Spray the ice cream–filled shells with an even coating of spray. Keep the compressor gun at least 60 cm/24 in from the shells to obtain a velvety smooth look.

7. Keep the shells well covered to prevent frost from forming on their surface. Make sure that you do not touch the surface of the shells with either plastic wrap or your hands, however, since it will scuff the velvet. Discard after 3 days.

QUEBEC AMBER MAPLE KATAIFI

YIELD: 220 G/7.76 OZ

INGREDIENT	METRIC	U.S.	%
Butter	50 g	1.76 oz	22.73%
Quebec amber maple syrup	50 g	1.76 oz	22.73%
Kataifi (see Note)	100 g	3.53 oz	45.45%
Maple sugar	20 g	.71 oz	9.09%

1. Preheat a convection oven to 160°C/325°F.

2. Line a full sheet pan with a nonstick rubber mat.

3. Melt the butter with the maple syrup in a small sauce pot. Reserve melted.

4. Weigh out 10 g/.35 oz bundles of kataifi. Spread each bundle into a 7.5-cm/3-in square, using your hands to do so.

5. Using a spoon, drizzle about 10 g/.35 oz of the melted butter and maple syrup on each kataifi bundle. Sprinkle 2 g/.07 oz of maple sugar evenly over each bundle.

6. Bake until golden brown, about 10 minutes.

7. Let cool on the sheet pan at room temperature.

8. Reserve the bundles exposed during service, but covered, as they might soften with moisture. Be careful when handling them, as they are extremely delicate. Any left over can be reserved in an airtight container. Refresh them the following day in a warm oven for a few minutes, if needed. Only perform this refreshing once. If you have the same refreshed pieces left over for a third day, you are making too many and need to reduce your par stock.

NOTE *Kataifi is very thinly shredded filo dough, purchased as is (see Resources, page 520).*

DARK CHOCOLATE SORBET

YIELD: 1 KG/2 LB 3.2 OZ

INGREDIENT	METRIC	U.S.	%
Sugar	30 g	1.06 oz	3%
Sorbet stabilizer	5 g	.18 oz	.5%
Bottled water	605 g	1 lb 5.28 oz	60.5%
Invert sugar	120 g	4.23 oz	12%
Dark chocolate coins 61%	240 g	8.47 oz	24%

1. Combine the sugar and the sorbet stabilizer; mix well.

2. Combine the water and invert sugar in a 1.89-L/2-qt sauce pot; heat to 40°C/105°F.

3. Pour the sugar–sorbet stabilizer mix in while whisking vigorously.

4. Heat the liquid up to 85°C/185°F and pour over the dark chocolate into a bowl.

5. Using a handheld immersion blender mix well until all the chocolate is melted.

6. Cool over an ice water bath and let the base age for at least 2 hours before churning.

7. Churn the base and pour into a piping bag. Reserve frozen at -10°C/14°F during service.

8. Thaw any left over after service to re-churn the next day. Discard the base after 5 days and refrigerate.

DARK CHOCOLATE CAKE

YIELD: 2.19 KG/4 LB 13.28 OZ

INGREDIENT	METRIC	U.S.	%
All-purpose flour	303 g	10.69 oz	13.82%
Cocoa powder	123 g	4.34 oz	5.61%
Salt	9 g	.32 oz	.41%
Baking soda	15 g	.53 oz	.68%
Baking powder	12 g	.42 oz	.55%
Sugar	600 g	1 lb 5.15 oz	27.37%
Eggs	250 g	8.82 oz	11.41%
Buttermilk	370 g	13.05 oz	16.88%
Cold coffee	340 g	11.99 oz	15.51%
Butter, melted but cool	170 g	6 oz	7.76%
White Velvet Spray (page 429)	400 g	14.11 oz	

1. Preheat a convection oven to 160°C/325°F.

2. Lightly grease a half hotel pan with nonstick oil spray, and line it with a half sheet of parchment paper.

3. Sift all of the flour, cocoa powder, salt, baking soda, and baking powder and place in the bowl of an electric mixer.

4. Combine the eggs, buttermilk, and coffee in a bowl and whisk together to obtain a homogenous mix.

5. Place the bowl with the dry ingredients on mixer fitted with the paddle attachment. Mix on low speed and slowly pour in the egg mixture.

6. Once the liquid has been completely incorporated, pour in the butter and mix until it has combined completely.

7. Pour the batter into the prepared pan. Bake until the cake springs back when it yields to gentle pressure, 20 to 30 minutes. Or perform a knife test by introducing the tip of a knife down the center of the cake; if it comes out dry, it is done baking.

8. Cut the cake into cubes that are about 6.5 cm/2.5 in. The shape can be somewhat organic; it needn't be a perfect cube, but it should at least have a flat base to sit on.

9. Using a #40 ice cream scoop, hollow out the cake cubes from the bottom (the flat side). Freeze the cakes for about 45 minutes.

10. Meanwhile, melt the white spray. Set up a spray station, a surface that should be covered with plastic to keep the shop clean where you can spray the cake with the white velvet spray.

11. Fill a compressor canister with the white velvet spray and spray the cake with an even coating of spray. Keep the compressor gun at least 60 cm/24 in from the bombes to obtain a velvety smooth look.

12. Reserve the cakes in the refrigerator until needed. Wrap tightly with plastic wrap, trying to not damage the surface of the cake. The velvet may come off; to prevent this you may place the cakes inside a 10-cm/4-in deep hotel pan and then wrap the pan to protect the cakes. If refrigerated, they will keep in peak condition for 3 to 4 days. If frozen, they will keep for no longer than 1 month.

DARK CHOCOLATE LIGHT GELÉE SAUCE

YIELD: 642 G/1 LB 6.56 OZ

INGREDIENT	METRIC	U.S.	%
Water	240 g	8.47 oz	37.35%
Sugar	175 g	6.17 oz	27.24%
Cocoa powder	70 g	2.47 oz	10.89%
Heavy cream	150 g	5.29 oz	23.35%
Gelatin sheets, silver, bloomed in cold water, excess water squeezed off	7.g	.26 oz	1.17%

1. Boil the water and sugar in a 960-mL/1-qt sauce pot over high heat until the sugar is dissolved.

2. Turn off the heat and stir in the cocoa powder with a whisk until it is dissolved.

3. Return the pot to high heat and bring to a boil again; add the cream and reduce the heat to a simmer.

4. Cook until thickened, about 20 minutes; stir frequently. Add the bloomed gelatin. Pour 30 g/1.06 oz into each cavity (measuring 2.5 cm/1 in wide by 7.5 cm/3 in long by 3 cm/1.25 in deep) of a silicone rectangular mold and freeze. Reserve the remaining gel for later use. Discard after 1 week.

5. Once the gel has frozen hard, unmold the pieces and reserve frozen for service in an airtight container.

ALOE AND HIBISCUS GELÉE

YIELD: 242 G/8.55 OZ

INGREDIENT	METRIC	U.S.	%
Aloe juice (Shirakiku brand, see Resources, page 520)	200 g	7.05 oz	82.51%
Gellan gum, low acyl	1 y	.05 oz	.50%
Hibiscus extract (see Resources, page 520)	1 g	.04 oz	.41%
Hibiscus syrup (see Resources, page 520)	40 g	1.41 oz	16.5%

1. Have ready a 10-cm/4-in square stainless-steel frame on a flat Plexiglas surface lined with acetate; it is crucial that this surface be completely flat. Surround the base frame that comes in contact with the acetate and Plexiglas base with a small tube of rolling fondant. Press down well.

2. Combine the aloe juice and the gellan gum in a sauce pot while cold. Bring the mixture to a boil and let boil for 10 seconds. Let it cool slightly.

3. Pour the contents of the sauce pot onto the frame and let it cool without moving the tray. Once it has set, cool the gelée down further in the refrigerator.

4. Once it has completely set, carefully remove the frame by passing a warm, sharp paring knife around the inside border of the frame. Dip the knife into hot water, dry it with a clean paper towel, and cut out 1-cm/.4-in wide batons. You should have exactly 10 pieces. Dip the knife in hot water and dry it each time you cut. Make sure you cut as straight as possible. Keep the pieces on the Plexiglas with the acetate.

5. Combine the hibiscus extract with the hibiscus syrup. Fill a long-needled syringe with the liquid.

6. Insert the needle on top of the gelée halfway in, and then inject the liquid as you pull the needle out. It should leave a thin line of hibiscus inside the gelée. Repeat until you obtain between 18 and 20 hibiscus "streaks" in each gelée.

7. Keep the gelées covered during service. Discard after service, since the hibiscus will stain the gelée too much, making the thin line disappear.

WARM COCONUT TAPIOCA PUDDING LIQUID

YIELD: 1.01 KG/2 LB 3.84 OZ

INGREDIENT	METRIC	U.S.	%
Tapioca			
Tapioca, small pearl	150 g	5.29 oz	5.77%
Cold water 1	450 g	15.87 oz	17.31%
Cold water 2	2 kg	4 lb 6.4 oz	76.92%
Coconut Pudding Liquid			
Coconut milk	400 g	14.11 oz	55.55%
Sugar 1	100 g	3.53 oz	13.81%
Heavy cream	200 g	7.05 oz	27.78%
Salt	.5 g	.02 oz	.05%
Universal pectin	7 g	.25 oz	.97%
Sugar 2	12 g	.42 oz	1.66%

1. **For the tapioca:** Combine the tapioca and the first amount of water in a 3.84-L/4-qt sauce pot. Bring to a boil while stirring with a wooden spoon. When it thickens, strain it through a fine-mesh sieve and rinse it under cool water. The objective is to strain the muci-laginous liquid that forms from the tapioca starch.

2. Cook the tapioca in the second amount of water over high heat at a rolling boil. The tapioca will be completely cooked when the pearls are almost completely trans-lucent, 20 to 25 minutes. Strain the pearls through a fine-mesh sieve and cool them down with cold running water.

3. Covering the cooked pearls directly with plastic, reserve at room temperature. You may add some corn syrup to keep the pearls from clumping up with each other. This item must be made the day it is needed and as close to the time of service as possible. Tapioca, as other starches do, will go from being pleasantly chewy to waterlogged and crumbly in a period of 12 hours or less.

4. **For the coconut pudding liquid:** Make this as close as possible to service. Combine the coconut milk with the first amount of sugar, the heavy cream, and salt. Bring to a boil, ideally using an induction burner. Gas burners can easily scorch the bottom of a pot.

5. Meanwhile, combine the pectin with the second amount of sugar, mixing them well.

6. When the liquid comes to a boil, add the pectin-sugar mixture by shearing it in with a handheld blender. Return to a boil and boil for 1 minute.

7. Turn the heat down as low as possible. Reserve at 50°C/120°F for service in a small sauce pot over very low heat. Keep the liquid covered during service. This is crucial; otherwise the liquid will evaporate and the smooth custard-like texture will be compromised. Discard any left over after service.

NOTE *The benefit to using universal pectin, which is thermo-reversible (melts with heat) is that you can keep this warm for extended periods of time without the texture of the liquid deteriorating. If this were an egg-based cus-tard, it would be practically impossible to hold this pud-ding warm for any length of time without compromising its texture, not to mention the fact that harmful bacteria would propagate.*

FROZEN MANGO PARFAIT IN CRISP FEUILLES DE BRICK

YIELD: 1 KG/2 LB 3.2 OZ

INGREDIENT	METRIC	U.S.	%
Feuille de Brick Tubes			
Butter, melted	100 g	3.53 oz	96.15%
Vanilla paste	4 g	.14 oz	3.85%
Feuilles de brick sheets	3	3	
Frozen Mango Parfait			
Heavy cream	420 g	14.82 oz	42%
Sugar 1	120 g	4.23 oz	12%
Egg yolks	160 g	5.64 oz	16%
Sugar 2	40 g	1.41 oz	4%
Mango purée	257 g	9.07 oz	25.7%
Gelatin sheets, silver, bloomed in cold water, excess water squeezed off	3 g	.11 oz	.3%

1. **For the feuille de brick tubes:** Preheat a convection oven to 160°C/325°F; turn the fan off if possible.

2. Lightly spray the exterior of 10 metal tubes measuring 7.5 cm/3 in long by 2.5 cm/1 in diameter with non-stick oil spray. Place them on a sheet pan in a standing position.

3. Combine the melted butter with the vanilla paste; reserve warm.

4. Cut out 20 pieces of silicone paper. Ten should measure 7.5 cm/3 in wide by 7.5 cm/3 in long, and 10 should measure 7.5 cm/3 in wide by 10 cm/4 in long. Line the sprayed tubes with the smaller rectangles of silicone paper. Brush a small amount of the butter and vanilla paste mixture around each parchment-lined tube.

5. Using a ruler and a paring knife, cut out strips of brick dough measuring 5 cm/2 in wide by 7.5 cm/3 in long. Wrap the brick dough around the prepared tubes. The length of the dough should make it overlap itself twice and create a 5-cm/2-in long tube.

6. Wrap each tube with the longer sheets of silicone paper; keep the paper in place using a paper clip. Return the tubes to a standing position. If the oven fan cannot be shut off, lay the tubes down with the paper clip facing down; this will help keep the tubes from rolling around while the fan blows in the oven.

7. Bake until the dough is golden brown, 8 to 10 minutes with the fan on or 12 to 15 minutes with the fan off.

8. Once the tubes have cooled, gently remove the silicone paper from the tubes and slide the baked brick tubes from the mold. Reserve in an airtight container at room temperature. Discard after 3 days.

9. Place the baked brick tubes on a flat sheet pan lined with a nonstick rubber mat.

10. **For the frozen mango parfait:** Combine the heavy cream and the first amount of sugar in the bowl of an electric mixer fitted with a whip attachment. Whip to medium peaks. Reserve refrigerated.

11. Combine the egg yolks with the second amount of sugar in mixer bowl and cook over a hot water bath until the mixture reaches 60°C/140°F while stirring constantly with a whisk. Stir for 2 minutes at this temperature. Place the bowl on the electric mixer and whip on high speed to quadruple the volume of the yolks (ribbon stage). Meanwhile, combine the mango purée with the bloomed gelatin in a bowl and melt over a warm water bath. Do not let this mixture get too hot.

12. Fold the egg yolk mixture (pâte à bombe) into the mango and gelatin mixture.

13. Fold a small amount of the whipped cream into the egg-mango mixture, then fold in half of the whipped cream. Once this amount has been folded in completely, fold in the remaining whipped cream.

14. Transfer to a piping bag. At least 2 hours and up to 8 hours before service, pipe the mango parfait into the baked brick tubes. Even out the top with an offset spatula and freeze. Once frozen, cover them well with plastic wrap and reserve frozen at −10°C/14°F.

CARAMELIZED CHOCOLATE PUFF PASTRY

YIELD: 1.5 KG/3 LB 4.9 OZ

INGREDIENT	METRIC	U.S.	%
All-purpose flour	515 g	1 lb 2.17 oz	34.29%
Salt	12 g	.42 oz	.8%
Cocoa powder	50 g	1.76 oz	3.33%
Butter, melted	50 g	1.76 oz	3.33%
Pretacao cocoa paste	50 g	1.76 oz	3.33%
Cold water	300 g	10.58 oz	19.97%
White vinegar	25 g	.88 oz	1.66%
Butter (block)	500 g	1 lb 1.64 oz	33.29%
Egg Wash (page 156)	50 g	1.75 oz	
Corn syrup	50 g	1.75 oz	

1. Combine the flour, salt, and cocoa powder in the bowl of an electric mixer fitted with the dough hook.

2. Turn the mixer on low speed and slowly pour in the melted butter. Mix until just combined.

3. Add the cocoa paste and mix until combined evenly.

4. Combine the water and vinegar, add to the dough, and mix until just combined. The dough does not require any gluten development.

5. Let the dough rest covered on a half sheet pan lined with well-floured parchment paper for 30 minutes.

6. Press the dough down to fit inside the half sheet pan so that it will be rectangular. Wrap the dough and refrigerate for at least 2 hours so that it firms up.

7. Proceed with the lamination procedure on pages 22–24.

8. Sheet the dough down to 5 mm/.2 in thick. Let it relax for 30 minutes in the freezer.

9. Preheat a convection oven to 160°C/325°F.

10. Once the sheet of dough is semi-frozen, use a wheel cutter and a ruler to cut out 10 strips 2.5 cm/1 in wide by 12.5 cm/5 in long. Brush each piece with egg wash, making sure the egg wash does not trickle down the sides of the dough because this can hinder the dough from its full expansion. Place them on a sheet pan lined with a nonstick rubber mat. The dough should still be very firm and semi-frozen before it is put in the oven; if not, return the dough to the freezer for a few minutes. Semi-frozen dough bakes much better than soft dough.

11. Bake the puff pastry until it is crisp, 12 to 15 minutes. It may require more time than this, though; check for crispness.

12. Remove the puff pastry from the oven and brush each piece with corn syrup on the top and sides. Bake for 5 minutes longer. Let cool at room temperature.

13. Reserve in a dehydrator set to 50°C/120°F. Discard any pieces that are left over after service.

NOTE *This recipe yields more dough than you will need, but it is always good to make plenty of puff pastry because it is very labor-intensive and it is better to get a large batch made than to have to repeat this every day you need it. Besides, puff pastry dough freezes very well.*

VANILLA CRÈME CHANTILLY

YIELD: 680 G/1 LB 7.98 OZ

INGREDIENT	METRIC	U.S.	%
Heavy cream	600 g	1 lb 5.15 oz	88.24%
Superfine sugar or bakers' sugar	70 g	2.47 oz	10.29%
Vanilla paste	10 g	.35 oz	1.47%

1. Combine all of the ingredients in the bowl of an electric mixer fitted with a whip attachment. Whip on high speed until the mixture achieves stiff peaks.

2. Reserve refrigerated. Re-whip as needed throughout service.

FIG LEAF ICE CREAM CYLINDER

YIELD: 1.07 KG/2 LB 5.6 OZ

INGREDIENT	METRIC	U.S.	%
Whole milk	500 g	1 lb 1.64 oz	46.73%
Heavy cream	250 g	8.82 oz	23.36%
Fig leaves, stemmed	5	5	
Sugar	170 g	6 oz	15.89%
Egg yolks	150 g	5.29 oz	14.02%

1. Prepare an ice water bath.

2. Combine the milk and cream in a sauce pot and bring to a simmer. Turn off the heat and add the fig leaves. Stir them in and cover the pot with plastic wrap. Let steep for 4 to 5 hours.

3. Strain the leaves out, squeezing them well to get as much flavor out of them as possible.

4. Add half of the sugar to the flavored milk-cream mixture. Add the remaining sugar to the egg yolks in a bowl. Proceed with the classic custard method on page 5.

5. Cool the base down over an ice water bath and age it for at least 4 hours before churning it.

6. Meanwhile, line 10 PVC rings (or stainless steel if available) with acetate. Place them on a flat half sheet pan lined with a nonstick rubber mat. Place this setup in the freezer.

7. Churn the base and pour it into a piping bag.

8. Pipe the ice cream into the frozen prepared molds, and even out the top with an offset spatula. Return to the freezer to harden.

9. Take the ice cream out of the molds; leave the acetate on. Reserve frozen in an airtight container for service.

10. Melt down and re-churn after 24 hours in the freezer. The ice cream can be re-churned only once, so make sure to keep track of the ice cream that has been churned once and those that have been churned twice. This base contains no stabilizers, so it has a short lifespan in the freezer.

CHOCOLATE SAUCE

YIELD: 635 G/1 LB 6.4 OZ

INGREDIENT	METRIC	U.S.	%
Water	240 g	8.47 oz	37.80%
Sugar	175 g	6.17 oz	27.56%
Cocoa powder	70 g	2.47 oz	11.02%
Heavy cream	150 g	5.29 oz	23.62%

1. Bring the water and sugar to a boil in a 1.92 L/2 qt sauce pot over high heat and boil until the sugar is dissolved.

2. Turn the heat off and stir in the cocoa powder with a whisk until it is dissolved.

3. Return the pot to high heat and bring to a boil again. Add the cream and turn the heat down so that the sauce maintains a simmer.

4. Cook until thickened, about 30 minutes, stirring frequently.

5. Cool the sauce over an ice bath. The chocolate sauce will hold for four days in an airtight container in the refrigerator.

JASMINE TEA CAKE RECTANGLES

YIELD: 496 G/1 LB 1.44 OZ

INGREDIENT	METRIC	U.S.	%
Eggs	220 g	7.76 oz	44.35%
Sugar	125 g	4.41 oz	25.2%
Salt	1 g	.04 oz	.2%
All-purpose flour	125 g	4.41 oz	25.2%
Ground jasmine tea	5 g	.18 oz	1.01%
Butter, melted but cool	20 g	.71 oz	4.03%

1. Lightly spray a half sheet pan with nonstick oil spray. Line it with a nonstick rubber mat.

2. Preheat a convection oven to 160°C/325°F.

3. Make the cake using the warm foaming method on page 11.

4. Bake for 6 to 7 minutes (check for doneness by pressing gently at the center of the cake; it should spring back if it is fully baked).

5. Let cool at room temperature.

6. Refrigerate for 2 hours.

7. Cut into rectangles measuring 5 cm/2 in wide by 10 cm/4 in long by 5 mm/.25 in thick.

8. Reserve at room temperature during service. If they are cold, they will be too brittle and will not be able to be wrapped around the ice cream without breaking. Discard any left over after service.

VARIATION *For **Earl Grey Génoise**, replace the jasmine tea with Earl Grey tea. Once the cake is chilled, cut it into rectangles measuring 2 cm/.75 in wide by 12.5 cm/5 in long by 5 mm/.25 in thick. Reserve frozen in an airtight container until use. Discard after 5 days.*

SCOTTISH SHORTBREAD CRUMBS

YIELD: 600 G/1 LB 5.12 OZ

INGREDIENT	METRIC	U.S.	%
Butter, soft	210 g	7.41 oz	35%
Sugar	105 g	3.7 oz	17.5%
All-purpose flour	245 g	8.64 oz	40.83%
Rice flour	35 g	1.23 oz	5.83%
Salt	5 g	.18 oz	.83%

1. Line a half sheet pan with a nonstick rubber mat.

2. Cream the butter with the sugar in an electric mixer fitted with a paddle attachment until it is light and fluffy.

3. Stop the mixer and add all the flours and salt. Pulse the mixer until a homogenous mass is obtained.

4. Spread it evenly onto the prepared sheet pan until it is about 6 mm/.25 in thick.

5. Freeze the dough until hard, about 30 minutes.

6. Meanwhile, preheat a convection oven to 160°C/325°F.

7. Score the dough using a fork.

8. Bake it until golden brown, 10 to 13 minutes.

9. Let cool at room temperature.

10. Once it is cool, grind it in a Robot Coupe until fine. Pass it through a drum sieve; grind what was left in the sieve and pass it through the sieve.

11. Reserve in an airtight container at room temperature for service. Discard after 3 days. The excess may be reserved frozen for up to 1 month.

NOTE *For the Caramelized White Chocolate Mousse, Toasted Baguette Purée, Scottish Shortbread, Caramelized Milk Chocolate Leaf, and Quenelle of Sweet Crème Fraîche on page 282, add 150 g/5.3 oz melted butter to the recipe. After grinding the shortbread in the Robot Coupe to obtain crumbs, add the melted butter while the Robot Coupe is working and mix just until it is incorporated. Spread the shortbread to a thickness of 2 mm/.07 in between 2 sheets of parchment paper using either a rolling pin or a sheeter. Freeze to harden. Once hardened, remove the parchment paper. Cut out 10-cm/4-in squares. Reserve frozen. Discard after 1 month.*

CHOCOLATE BOX

YIELD: 1.6 KG/3 LB 8.32 OZ

INGREDIENT	METRIC	U.S.
Dark chocolate, tempered (preferably 64% or higher)	1.6 kg	3 lb 8.32 oz

1. Brush the inside of cube molds measuring 5.5 cm/2.25 in square by 7.5 cm/3 in deep (see Resources, page 520) with the tempered chocolate (to prevent bubbles in the corners of the molds). Pour the chocolate into the molds. Let sit for about 1 minute, then turn the molds over and empty out the excess chocolate out. Let the molds sit on a cooling rack to allow the excess chocolate to pour out.

2. Scrape the bottom of the molds with a putty knife.

3. Cool the chocolate in the refrigerator.

4. Once the chocolate looks like it has released from the mold, try to pull it out. Since this mold is straight, sometimes it is hard to pull the chocolate out. You may need to freeze the molds for a few minutes, and then let them sit at room temperature for a few more minutes and then try to release the chocolate. Always make more than you need, since there is a good chance that some cubes will crack.

5. Reserve the molds in a cool dry area, preferably enclosed. Discard after 1 year.

NOTE *This is much more chocolate than you will actually need, but this will be enough to fill the molds completely and then empty them to leave a well-formed shell.*

GOAT'S MILK WHITE CHOCOLATE TILE

YIELD: 400 G/14.11 OZ

INGREDIENT	METRIC	U.S.
Tempered goat's milk white chocolate (page 38; replace powdered milk with powdered goat's milk)	400 g	14.11 oz

1. Assemble 10 crinkled aluminum plaques (food-grade aluminum sheets, cut to 7.5 cm/3 in wide by 15 cm/6 in long). The crinkled look is obtained by bending the aluminum with a pair of needle-nose pliers. Make sure the aluminum pieces are well washed, sanitized, and polished with a lint-free cloth before using.

2. Dip the plaques into the tempered chocolate. Let the excess drip off and wipe the chocolate off of the border of the plaques using your fingertips. It is crucial that this be a very thin piece of chocolate because of its large size.

3. Let the chocolate set in a cool, dry place, and then unmold the chocolate tiles. Reserve in a cool, dry place. Discard after 6 months.

BLACKBERRY AND ROSE SORBET TUBE

YIELD: 1 KG/2 LB 3.2 OZ

INGREDIENT	METRIC	U.S.	%
Water	120 g	4.23 oz	12%
Red rose petals, large, organic	10 to 12	10 to 12	
Blackberry purée, seeds strained out	580 g	1 lb 4.32 oz	58%
Sorbet Syrup (page 53)	300 g	10.58 oz	30%

1. Bring the water to a boil and then add the petals. Turn off the heat and cover the pot with plastic wrap. Let steep for 4 to 5 hours. Strain the petals out and remeasure the water; you should have 120 g/4.23 oz. Let it cool completely.

2. Meanwhile, line 10 PVC tubes measuring 15 cm/6 in long by 1.25 cm/.5 in diameter with acetate plastic sheets. The acetate should protrude from both ends of the PVC tube because they will be easier to pull out of the PVC than if they were the same size as the tube.

3. Place them on a sheet pan in the freezer to get cold.

4. Combine the rose petal water with the blackberry purée and the sorbet syrup using a whisk.

5. Churn the sorbet base and pour it into a piping bag. Pipe the sorbet into the frozen PVC tubes. Return the tubes to the freezer to harden, about 2 hours.

6. Once they have hardened, remove the frozen sorbet, acetate and all, from the PVC tubes. Reserve the acetate-wrapped tubes frozen. If you want to get ahead, trim the ends of the sorbet using a sharp, thin knife so that the tube measures exactly 15 cm/6 in long. Keep the tubes covered while frozen. They may be kept in the freezer for up to 4 days. After that, melt them down and re-churn them. Sorbets can be re-churned more often than ice creams.

STRAWBERRY JELLY TUBE

YIELD: 254 G/8.96 OZ

INGREDIENT	METRIC	U.S.	%
Strawberry Water			
Strawberries, stemmed	1 kg	2 lb 3.2 oz	100%
Jelly Tube			
Strawberry water	220 g	7.76 oz	86.61%
Superfine sugar	30 g	1.06 oz	11.81%
Agaroid RS-507 (see Resources, page 520)	4 g	.14 oz	1.57%

1. **For the strawberry water:** Place the strawberries in a bowl, and then place the bowl over a boiling water bath.

2. After about 10 minutes, take the bowl off the boiling water. Pass the liquid through a fine-mesh sieve. Reserve the strawberries for another product such as sorbet, ice cream, or jam.

3. **For the jelly:** Set up an ice water bath with equal parts of about 2 kg/4 lb 6.4 oz water and ice in a bowl.

4. Have a heavy cream whipper filled with two chargers on hand (see Resources, page 520). Place a small nozzle attachment on the whipper's spout. This nozzle will fit snugly on the whipper's spout and will have a small tip that will fit into food-grade plastic tubes. Alternatively, if you have a compressor it can work just as well. You will have to attach a needle to the air spout; this needle should be able to fit inside the food-grade tubes.

5. Combine all of the ingredients in a small sauce pot.

6. Bring the mixture to a boil over medium-high heat while whisking. Once it comes to a boil, let it boil for about 5 seconds.

7. See the procedure for Crème Chantilly Ribbon on page 144. Continue with Steps 6 through 8 of the method. Reserve in the refrigerator until service. Discard after 3 days.

NOTE *For more information on Agaroid RS-507, see the note under the Crème Chantilly Ribbon recipe on page 144.*

ROSE HIP HONEY AND WATER SOAKING LIQUID

YIELD: 130 G/4.59 OZ

INGREDIENT	METRIC	U.S.	%
Rose hip honey	100 g	3.53 oz	76.92%
Water	30 g	1.06 oz	23.08%

Combine both ingredients well. Reserve in the refrigerator in an airtight container. Discard after 2 months.

ROSE PETAL CAKE

YIELD: 516 G/1 LB 2.08 OZ

INGREDIENT	METRIC	U.S.	%
Ground dried organic rose petals	10 g	.35 oz	1.94%
Strawberry powder	10 g	.35 oz	1.94%
Beet powder	5 g	.18 oz	.97%
All-purpose flour	125 g	4.41 oz	24.22%
Eggs	220 g	7.76 oz	42.64%
Sugar	125 g	4.41 oz	24.22%
Salt	1 g	.04 oz	.19%
Butter, melted but cool	20 g	.71 oz	3.88%

1. Lightly spray a quarter sheet pan with nonstick oil spray. Line it with a nonstick rubber mat.

2. See the procedure for the Jasmine Tea Cake on page 218. Combine the ground dried organic rose powder, strawberry powder and the beet powder with the all-purpose flour before sifting. Sift together.

3. Once the cake has cooled, refrigerate it. This will help you make a clean cut with almost no crumbs when you cut the cake.

4. Cut the cake into rectangles that measure 5 cm/2 in wide by 15 cm/6 in long by 2 cm/.75 in high. Reserve covered with a damp, clean towel at room temperature during service to keep them moist and tender. If you keep the cakes refrigerated, they will not have as good a texture as they will if kept at room temperature.

NOTE *The beet powder is added exclusively to add color and contributes almost no discernible flavor.*

FROZEN ESPRESSO BOMBE

YIELD: 1.5 KG/2 LB 4.96 OZ

INGREDIENT	METRIC	U.S.	%
Chocolate Soil			
Sugar	50 g	1.76 oz	26.32%
Almond flour	50 g	1.76 oz	26.32%
All-purpose flour	30 g	1.06 oz	15.79%
Cocoa powder	22 g	.78 oz	11.58%
Butter, melted and cooled	35 g	1.23 oz	18.42%
Salt	3 g	.11 oz	1.58%
Espresso Bombe			
Egg yolks	160 g	5.64 oz	15.24%
Sugar 1	105 g	3.7 oz	10%
Heavy cream 1	70 g	2.47 oz	6.67%
Instant coffee	10 g	.35 oz	.95%
Gelatin sheets, silver, bloomed in cold water, excess water squeezed off	5 g	.18 oz	.48%
Heavy cream 2	500 g	1 lb 1.6 oz	47.62%
Sugar 2	100 g	3.53 oz	9.52%
Chocolate Soil	100 g	3.53 oz	9.52%

1. **For the chocolate soil:** Preheat a convection oven to 160°C/325°F.

2. Line a sheet pan with parchment paper.

3. Combine all of the ingredients in a bowl to obtain a homogenous mass.

4. Spread out evenly on the prepared sheet pan. Some of the mixture will accumulate in clusters, but that is the intention.

5. Bake until aromatic and toasted, about 8 minutes. Cool at room temperature. Reserve in an airtight container at room temperature. Discard after 2 weeks.

6. **For the espresso bombe:** Line 10 molds that measure 2.5 cm/1 in wide by 7.5 cm/3 in long by 2.5 cm/1 in high with acetate. Place them on a flat sheet pan lined with a nonstick rubber mat.

7. Combine the egg yolks with the first amount of sugar over a hot water bath. Stirring with a whisk, bring the yolks up to 57°C/135°F. Transfer to the bowl of an electric mixer fitted with a whip attachment and whip until the yolks have quadrupled in volume.

8. Meanwhile, combine the first amount of cream with the instant coffee and the gelatin in a bowl. Stir over a hot water bath to dissolve the gelatin and the coffee. Do not let this mixture get too hot; it should be just hot enough to melt the gelatin and dissolve the coffee.

9. Meanwhile, whip the second amount of cream with the second amount of sugar to medium-soft peaks.

10. Whisk the cream-coffee-gelatin mixture into the pâte à bombe (egg yolk mixture).

11. Fold one-quarter of the whipped cream into this mixture to soften it, then fold in half of the whipped cream. When that is incorporated, fold in the remaining whipped cream. Finally, fold in the chocolate soil.

12. Transfer the bombe mixture to a piping bag and pipe into the prepared molds. Even out the top with an offset spatula and freeze.

13. Once they are frozen, remove them from their molds and take off the acetate. Reserve covered in an airtight container in the freezer; discard after 3 weeks.

DARK CHOCOLATE SPRAY

YIELD: 400 G/14.11 OZ

INGREDIENT	METRIC	U.S.	%
Dark chocolate	200 g	7.05 oz	50%
Cocoa butter	200 g	7.05 oz	50%

1. Combine both ingredients in a bowl and melt completely over a hot water bath.

2. Set up a spray station, a surface that should be covered with plastic to keep the shop clean where you can spray the bombes with the dark chocolate spray.

3. Fill a compressor canister with the dark chocolate spray and spray the bombes with an even coating of spray. Keep the compressor gun at least 60 cm/24 in from the bombes to obtain a velvety smooth look.

4. Reserve them frozen during service, preferably covered so that they do not get any frost on their surface. Discard after 2 days.

LEMON CURD

YIELD: 1.02 KG/2 LB 4 OZ

INGREDIENT	METRIC	U.S.	%
Lemon juice	160 g	5.64 oz	15.65%
Sugar	240 g	8.47 oz	23.47%
Eggs	160 g	5.64 oz	15.65%
Butter	450 g	15.87 oz	44.01%
Gelatin sheets, silver, bloomed in cold water, excess water squeezed off	12 g	.44 oz	1.22%

1. Line 10 PVC tubes measuring 15 cm/6 in long by 1.25 cm/.5 in diameter with acetate. The acetate should be slightly longer than the tube so that it can easily be pulled out.

2. To make the lemon curd, see the method for the Milk Chocolate and Lime Curd on page 134. Add the bloomed gelatin at the end.

3. Let the curd set in the freezer for about 2 hours, until hardened, and then pull it out of the PVC tubes. Remove the acetate and trim both ends with a sharp knife to make an even tube that is 15 cm/6 in long. Transfer the curd tubes to a half sheet pan lined with a nonstick rubber mat. Cover the tubes with a moist and clean heavy-duty paper towel. Reserve refrigerated. Discard after 2 days.

ESPRESSO PASTE

YIELD: 120 G/4.23 OZ

INGREDIENT	METRIC	U.S.	%
Instant coffee	100 g	3.53 oz	83.33%
Water	20 g	.71 oz	16.67%

1. Combine both ingredients and mix until a paste is formed; the consistency may need to be adjusted by either adding more water or more coffee.

2. Reserve well covered in an airtight container at room temperature. This paste will last for at least 1 week or more if kept well covered. If it starts to dry out, add more water.

ALMOND GENOA BREAD

YIELD: 798 G/1 LB 12 OZ

INGREDIENT	METRIC	U.S.	%
Almond paste	298 g	10.5 oz	37.3%
Almond praline paste	74 g	2.62 oz	9.32%
Eggs	233 g	8.2 oz	29.14%
Invert sugar	33 g	1.15 oz	4.08%
Salt	3 g	.1 oz	.35%
All-purpose flour	56 g	1.97 oz	6.99%
Butter	102 g	3.61 oz	12.82%

1. Preheat a convection oven to 160°C/325°F.

2. Lightly spray the border of a quarter sheet pan with nonstick oil spray. Line it with a nonstick rubber mat.

3. Combine the almond paste with the almond praline paste in a mixer bowl fitted with the paddle attachment to obtain a homogenous mixture.

4. Add the eggs one at a time. Stop the mixer, drop the bowl, and scrape it after each egg has been incorporated. If making larger batches, add eggs in a total of 4 additions; it is not necessary to do one egg at a time.

5. Add all of the invert sugar and mix until well combined. Add the salt and the flour on low speed, pulsing the mixer so as not to make a mess. Mix until just combined.

6. Add the butter and mix until just combined. Spread evenly on the prepared sheet pan.

7. Bake until it springs back when it is gently pushed with the fingertips at the center of the pan, 12 to 15 minutes.

8. Cool the cake at room temperature. Once it has cooled, refrigerate it. It cuts cleaner when it is cold.

9. When it is cold, remove the cake from the pan and cut it into rectangles that measure 2.5 cm/1 in wide by 9 cm/3.5 in long by 2 cm/.6 in high.

10. Reserve in an airtight container in refrigeration. Discard after 2 days.

NOTE *This recipe is based on Sébastien Canonne's recipe; there are many variations on the recipe, but I find this to be one of the best. Its original French name is "pain de gênes."*

CARAMEL-POACHED SECKEL PEAR

YIELD: 2.89 KG/6 LB 4.48 OZ

INGREDIENT	METRIC	U.S.	%
Sugar	2 kg	4 lb 6.4 oz	70.18%
Water	350 g	12.35 oz	12.28%
Pear cider	500 g	1 lb 1.6 oz	17.54%
Seckel pears, similar in size, peeled, cored with a parisienne scoop, stems trimmed off	11	11	

1. Combine the sugar and the water in a 3.78-L/4-qt sauce pot. Cook over high heat until the sugar turns amber brown, 180°C/360°F. Meanwhile, bring the pear cider to a simmer.

2. When the sugar reaches the desired temperature, slowly stir in the hot pear cider using a whisk.

3. Turn the heat down to medium. Add the pears and cover them with a clean towel to help keep them completely submerged and thus cook them evenly. Seckel pears are usually hard, even when ripe. Therefore, poaching time may be up to 10 minutes. Always check the extra pear, which is for poking and probing to check for doneness so as to not damage those that will be used for service. The pear should be tender but not falling apart. You should be able to easily slide a paring knife into it.

4. Once the pears have cooked through, remove them from the liquid with a spoon and transfer them to a sheet pan and cool in the refrigerator. Once they are cool, transfer them to an airtight container and reserve refrigerated. Discard after 2 days.

5. Reserve the **hot caramel and pear stock** for service, keeping the liquid hot on medium-low heat. The pot should be covered to prevent evaporation. This liquid can be used about four or five times to poach pears, improving its flavor each time, but after a while it will become too liquid and its caramel color will dissipate.

PEAR ICE CREAM

YIELD: 1 KG/2 LB 3.2 OZ

INGREDIENT	METRIC	U.S.	%
Milk	460 g	1 lb .16 oz	46%
Heavy cream	96 g	3.39 oz	9.6%
Sugar	176 g	6.21 oz	17.6%
Egg yolks	70 g	2.47 oz	7%
Williams pear purée	198 g	6.98 oz	19.8%

1. To make the base, see the stirred custard method on page 8. The pear purée is stirred in once the base is made and has cooled down.

2. Let the base age for at least 4 hours before you churn it.

3. Churn the base and reserve frozen for service. After service, if you have any left, you can re-melt it and churn it once more. Discard any left over after the second churn.

CHOCOLATE VEIL

YIELD: 454 G/1 LB

INGREDIENT	METRIC	U.S.	%
Cocoa Nib Stock			
Water	600 g	1 lb 5.12 oz	66.67%
Cocoa nibs	300 g	10.58 oz	33.33%
Liquid Cocoa Base			
Cocoa Nib Stock	500 g	1 lb 1.64 oz	78.13%
Cocoa powder	50 g	1.76 oz	7.81%
Sugar	90 g	3.17 oz	14.06%
Chocolate Veil			
Liquid Cocoa Base	450 g	15.87 oz	99.08%
Gellan gum, low acyl	4 g	.15 oz	.92%

1. **For the cocoa nib stock:** Bring the water to a boil and pour it onto the cocoa nibs. Cover with plastic wrap and let the nibs steep for 20 minutes.

2. Strain the nibs out using a fine-mesh sieve and then strain the liquid through cheesecloth.

3. Using an ice water bath, cool the liquid down to make the liquid cocoa base.

4. **For the liquid cocoa base:** Combine the cocoa nib stock, cocoa powder, and sugar and mix well using a handheld blender. Pass through a fine-mesh sieve.

5. **For the chocolate veil:** Have 3 flat, square plastic trays measuring 30cm/12 x 30cm/12 in available; there will be 4 orders that come out of each tray. Fill each tray with hot water; the intention is to keep the tray hot so when the chocolate veil comes in contact with the tray, it will not set too quickly. Have a bowl close by to empty the water out when needed.

6. Pour the cold liquid cocoa base into a small sauce pot and whisk in the gellan gum.

7. Bring it to a boil and let it boil for 5 seconds. Skim the surface of any scum.

8. Empty the first tray of its hot water and dry it quickly. Pour one-third of the cocoa liquid into the tray and move it around to distribute the liquid in a thin, even layer.

9. Do the same with the remaining trays and chocolate mixture. Allow the gel to set at room temperature, and then transfer it to a refrigerator.

10. Trim the borders away using a ruler and a paring knife (about 5 mm/.25 in from the rim of the tray). Cut out 4 squares from each tray measuring 12.5 cm/5 in by 2.5 cm/5 in; you will have 12 squares, which is 2 more than you need. Keep the trays covered with plastic wrap during service, making sure the plastic does not come in contact with the veil. Discard after 2 days.

CHOCOLATE DÉCOR CURVED TRIANGLE

YIELD: 300 G/10.58 OZ

INGREDIENT	METRIC	U.S.
Dark chocolate, tempered	300 g	10.58 oz

1. Line a PVC tube measuring 10 cm/4 in long by 10 cm/4 in diameter with parchment paper.

2. Spread the tempered chocolate on a 10-cm/4-in square sheet of acetate in a thin, even layer using an offset spatula.

3. Once it is partially crystallized, cut out isosceles triangles that are 1 cm/.4 in wide at the base.

4. Wrap the acetate around the prepared PVC tube to fully crystallize.

5. Once it has completely crystallized, reserve in a cool, dry place, preferably enclosed.

BLOOD ORANGE SORBET BASE

YIELD: 1 KG/2 LB 3.2 OZ

INGREDIENT	METRIC	U.S.	%
Blood orange juice	680 g	1 lb 7.98 oz	68%
Sorbet Syrup (page 53)	320 g	11.29 oz	32%

1. Combine both ingredients in a bowl using a whisk.

2. Reserve refrigerated until ready to churn.

RICE MILK SORBET BASE

YIELD: 1 KG/2 LB 3.44 OZ

INGREDIENT	METRIC	U.S.	%
Ground cinnamon	5 g	.18 oz	.5%
Rice milk	720 g	1 lb 9.28 oz	71.64%
Sorbet Syrup (page 53)	280 g	9.88 oz	27.86%

1. Toast the cinnamon in a sauté pan over medium heat until aromatic.

2. Combine with the rice milk and sorbet syrup in a bowl. Use whisk to stir until you obtain a homogenous mix.

3. Reserve refrigerated until ready to churn.

PISTACHIO ICE CREAM BASE

YIELD: 1.1 KG/2 LB 6.8 OZ

INGREDIENT	METRIC	U.S.	%
Milk	683 g	1 lb 8 oz	62.09%
Milk powder	64 g	2.26 oz	5.82%
Sugar	170 g	6 oz	15.45%
Ice cream stabilizer	3 g	.11 oz	.27%
Egg yolks	80 g	2.82 oz	7.27%
Pistachio paste	100 g	3.53 oz	9.09%

1. Follow the modern ice cream method on page 50. Add the pistachio paste once the ice cream has cooled down completely. Pass it through a fine-mesh sieve again.

2. Age the ice cream base for at least 4 hours before it is churned.

NOTE *Natural pistachio ice cream is a dull, muted green. Bright green pistachio ice cream has artificial food coloring added.*

SAFFRON ICE CREAM BASE

YIELD: 1 KG/2 LB 3.2 OZ

INGREDIENT	METRIC	U.S.	%
Milk	640 g	1 lb 6.56 oz	64%
Heavy cream	85 g	3 oz	8.5%
Saffron	2 g	.07 oz	.2%
Powdered milk	40 g	1.41 oz	4%
Sugar	160 g	5.64 oz	16%
Ice cream stabilizer	3 g	.11 oz	.3%
Egg yolks	70 g	2.47 oz	7%

1. Follow the modern ice cream method on page 50. Add the saffron at the beginning of the recipe along with the milk and heavy cream. It will infuse its flavor into the base as it cooks. It will be removed when the base is passed through a fine-mesh sieve.

2. Cool the ice cream down in an ice water bath. Let the base age for at least 4 hours before churning it.

    NOTE *It is not necessary to use the very high-end, highest-quality saffron, since it is prohibitively expensive and there are more economical alternatives. Taste the base and make any adjustments if necessary by adding more saffron (or less the next time). Again, it all depends on the quality of what you are using. This particular recipe works well with medium-quality saffron.*

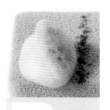

PUMPKIN SEED AND MILK CHOCOLATE BAR

YIELD: 700 G/1 LB 8.64 OZ

INGREDIENT	METRIC	U.S.	%
Pumpkin seed paste (see Resources, page 520)	350 g	12.35 oz	50%
Milk chocolate, tempered	350 g	12.35 oz	50%
Milk chocolate, melted	50 g	1.76 oz	
Canola oil	10 g	.35 oz	

1. Place a nonstick rubber mat on a marble surface. Place a square frame measuring 30 cm/12 in by 30 cm/12 in by 5 mm/.25 in deep on top of the rubber mat.

2. Combine the pumpkin seed paste and the tempered milk chocolate in a bowl using a rubber spatula.

3. Pour the mixture into the frame and spread it evenly.

4. Let it set at room temperature.

5. Once it has set, mix the melted milk chocolate with the oil in a small bowl. Dip a small paint roller (the kind with a sponge roller) into the mixture, and paint it onto the bar to coat the entire surface in an even layer. This will be used as the base of the bar (also known as the *foot*).

6. Flip the bar over and cut out 10 squares using a 7.5-cm/3-in square cutter.

7. Reserve at room temperature in an airtight container in a cool, dry place. Do not refrigerate the chocolate; it will get too hard and become difficult to eat with a fork. Discard after 1 month.

BROWNED BUTTER AND CRANBERRY SHORTBREAD

YIELD: 690 G/1 LB 8.32 OZ

INGREDIENT	METRIC	U.S.	%
Milk solids	30 g	1.06 oz	4.35%
Butter, soft	210 g	7.41 oz	30.43%
Sugar	105 g	3.7 oz	15.22%
All-purpose flour	245 g	8.64 oz	35.51%
Rice flour	35 g	1.23 oz	5.07%
Salt	5 g	.18 oz	.72%
Butter, melted	60 g	2.12 oz	8.7%
Dried cranberries, finely chopped	100 g	3.52 oz	

1. Toast the milk solids in a sauté pan over medium heat, stirring with a wooden spoon to obtain an even browning. Once they are toasted (aromatic and brown), let them cool at room temperature and grind them to a fine powder.

2. Put the soft butter and sugar in the bowl of an electric mixer fitted with a paddle attachment. Mix them on medium speed until they are evenly mixed, 3 to 5 minutes.

3. Add the toasted milk solid powder, all-purpose flour, rice flour, and salt. Mix until they are just incorporated.

4. Spread the batter into an even, 5-mm/.25-in-thick layer on a sheet of parchment paper using a rolling pin. Transfer it to a sheet pan and freeze it until it hardens.

5. Meanwhile, preheat a convection oven to 160°C/325°F.

6. Once the dough is frozen, dock it all over using a fork.

7. Bake it until the surface is golden brown all over, 10 to 15 minutes.

8. Cool at room temperature. Once it is cool, break it into small pieces and grind it into fine crumbs using a Robot Coupe.

9. Add the melted butter while it is mixing in the Robot Coupe.

10. Take the dough out of the cup and mix in the cranberries by hand.

11. Put a half nonstick rubber mat on a flat surface such as a marble table and place a 5-mm/.25-in-thick frame on top of the rubber mat. Put the mixed dough into the frame. Flatten it as much as possible with your hands, then place another half rubber mat on top of the dough and even it out using a rolling pin.

12. Transfer the dough onto a flat sheet pan and freeze. Once it has hardened, cut the dough into 7.5-cm/3-in squares. Reserve in the refrigerator. These squares will be the base of the pumpkin mousse. If there are more than 10 squares, reserve them for future use. Any trimmings can be reshaped and used again.

PUMPKIN MOUSSE SQUARE

YIELD: 2 KG/4 LB 6.4 OZ

INGREDIENT	METRIC	U.S.	%
Roasted Pumpkin			
Sugar pie pumpkin	2 kg	4 lb 6.4 oz	
Pumpkin Mousse			
Heavy cream	640 g	1 lb 6.56 oz	32%
Sugar 1	180 g	6.35 oz	9%
Egg yolks	360 g	12.7 oz	18%
Sugar 2	240 g	8.47 oz	12%
Pumpkin purée	564 g	1 lb 3.88 oz	28.2%
Gelatin sheets, silver, bloomed in cold water, excess water squeezed off	16 g	.56 oz	.8%

1. **For the roasted pumpkin:** Preheat a convection oven to 160°C/325°F.

2. Trim the stem off the top of the pumpkin. Cut it into quarters and remove the seeds.

3. Place the quarters on a sheet pan, flesh facing up.

4. Bake until the flesh is tender, about 20 minutes. It should yield to pressure easily when it is properly cooked.

5. Let it cool at room temperature. Scoop the flesh off of the skin and purée it in a blender until completely smooth. Discard the skin.

6. Weigh the necessary amount for the mousse and keep it at room temperature. This is important, since keeping it cold will have a negative effect on the gelatin when mixing the mousse ingredients together. The remaining amount can be frozen for further use.

7. **For the pumpkin mousse:** Lightly spray a sheet of Plexiglas or a very flat sheet pan with a fine mist of nonstick oil spray. Spread it evenly using a paper towel. Line the surface with a sheet of acetate and smooth it out with your hands using a clean paper towel.

8. Place 10 square molds onto the acetate-lined surface. These squares measure 9 cm/3.5 in by 9 cm/3.5 in long by 1.25 cm/.5 in deep; the corners are curved with a radius of 1.25 cm/.5 in.

9. Place this setup in a freezer to get the molds cold.

10. Whip the heavy cream with the first amount of sugar to medium-soft peaks. Reserve refrigerated.

11. Combine the egg yolks with the second amount of sugar in a bowl and stir constantly with a whisk over a hot water bath until they reach 57°C/135°F. Transfer to a mixer bowl and whip on high speed until it has quadrupled in volume and has cooled to room temperature.

12. Meanwhile, combine one-quarter of the purée with the gelatin in a bowl; place the bowl over a hot water bath and stir to dissolve the gelatin.

13. Once melted, combine this mix with the remaining pumpkin purée.

14. Mix the pumpkin purée with the pâte à bombe (egg yolk and sugar mixture) using a whisk.

15. Stir in one-quarter of the whipped cream using a whisk, then fold in half of the remaining whipped cream using a rubber spatula, and then fold in the remaining whipped cream until you obtain a smooth, homogenous mousse.

16. Transfer the mousse to a piping bag. Take the molds out of the freezer and have the shortbread bases available.

17. Pipe the mousse into the molds, starting with the corners. Keep the tip of the piping bag inside the mousse as you pipe to prevent air pockets from forming. Fill the molds about four-fifths of the way to the top. Place a shortbread square on top of the mousse and press down gently. The shortbread should be slightly higher than the border of the mold. This will help with moving the mousse; if it is completely flat it will certainly be damaged by handling. If there are empty gaps around

the shortbread, fill them with more mousse. Even out the surface with an offset spatula. Cover the mousse with plastic and reserve in the freezer to harden.

18. Once they have hardened, unmold them. Line a full sheet pan with a nonstick rubber mat. Place a frozen mousse square on a spinning cake stand; gently and slowly spin it as you warm up the mold with a torch. Keep the torch a few inches away from the mold and make sure it is directly on the mold and not touching the mousse; otherwise it might melt. Gently slide the mold off the mousse and transfer the mousse to the prepared sheet pan.

19. Repeat with the remaining molds; make sure to space them evenly on the sheet pan. Return the molds to the freezer to harden again.

20. Meanwhile, make the pumpkin seed velvet spray and then spray the mousse.

PUMPKIN SEED VELVET SPRAY

YIELD: 370 G/13.05 OZ

INGREDIENT	METRIC	U.S.	%
Cocoa butter	260 g	9.17 oz	70.27%
Pumpkin seed oil	110 g	3.88 oz	29.73%

1. Combine both ingredients in a small bowl and melt them over a hot water bath. Stir to obtain an even mixture.

2. Set up a spray station, a surface that should be covered with plastic to keep the shop clean where you can spray the mousse.

3. Fill a compressor canister with the pumpkin seed velvet spray and spray the mousse with an even coating of spray. Keep the compressor gun at least 60 cm/24 in from the mousse to obtain a velvety smooth look.

4. Carefully transfer the finished mousse to a clean sheet pan lined with a nonstick rubber mat. Reserve in the refrigerator during service. Discard after 2 days.

CRANBERRY JUICE FROTH

YIELD: 1.07 KG/2 LB 5.76 OZ

INGREDIENT	METRIC	U.S.	%
Frozen cranberries	700 g	1 lb 8.64 oz	65.38%
Water	150 g	5.29 oz	14.01%
Cinnamon sticks, toasted until aromatic	10 g	.35 oz	.93%
Vanilla pods, Tahitian, split and seeds scraped	2	2	
Sugar	200 g	7.05 oz	18.68%
Egg white powder	10 g	.35 oz	.93%
Xanthan gum	1 g	.02 oz	.06%

1. Combine the frozen cranberries with the water, cinnamon, and vanilla pods and seeds in a sauce pot. Bring to a boil. Crush the cranberries as they are cooking to release the moisture in them.

2. Once all of the cranberries have burst and the liquid has boiled for about 5 minutes, pass the liquid through a fine-mesh sieve.

3. Stir in the sugar until it has dissolved. Adjust the sweetness if necessary. There should be about 600 g/1 lb 5.12 oz of cranberry juice.

4. Using a handheld blender, blend the egg white powder in, and then the xanthan gum. Using an immersion blender, mix for about 5 minutes in a deep stainless-steel cylinder, since it will foam and increase in volume as it is mixed.

5. Reserve in the refrigerator for 2 hours before service. The froth will accumulate on the top; this is what you will be spooning onto the mousse during service.

SALTED CARAMEL

YIELD: 1 KG/2 LB 3.2 OZ

INGREDIENT	METRIC	U.S.	%
Glucose syrup	200 g	7.05 oz	20%
Sugar	400 g	14.11 oz	40%
Heavy cream	250 g	8.82 oz	25%
Butter	135 g	4.76 oz	13.5%
Fleur de sel	15 g	.53 oz	1.5%

1. Combine the glucose, sugar, and enough water (about one-quarter of the amount of sugar) in a saucepot to obtain a mixture with the consistency of wet sand.

2. Cook over high heat until it turns a medium amber color.

3. Meanwhile, combine the heavy cream, butter, and salt in another sauce pot and bring to a simmer.

4. When the sugar reaches the desired color, slowly whisk in the hot cream mixture.

5. Let it cool at room temperature. Reserve in an airtight container at room temperature for up to 2 months or more.

BLACK CHOCOLATE TILE

YIELD: 402 G/14.18 OZ

INGREDIENT	METRIC	U.S.	%
Dark chocolate, tempered	400 g	14.11 oz	95.24%
Black cocoa butter, tempered	20 g	.71 oz	4.76%

1. Combine both items in a bowl until evenly mixed.

2. Spread an even, thin layer of tempered chocolate over a crocodile skin–textured sheet of acetate (see Resources, page 520) using an offset spatula.

3. Once it has semi-set, cut the chocolate into rectangles measuring 5 cm/2 in wide by 11.5 cm/4 in long using a ruler and the back of a paring knife.

4. Flip the acetate sheet over onto a flat sheet pan. Place a heavy, flat weight over it, such as a cutting board, so that it sets flat.

5. Once the chocolate has set, store it in a cool, dry area, preferably enclosed. It will keep for more than 1 year if well cared for.

CRISPY MILK

YIELD: 1.2 KG/2 LB 10.24 OZ

INGREDIENT	METRIC	U.S.	%
Whole milk	1 kg	2 lb 3.2 oz	83.33%
Glucose syrup	200 g	7.05 oz	16.67%

1. Lightly spray a full-size hotel pan with nonstick oil spray. Line it with a sheet of parchment paper. If your dehydrator is too small, use 2 half sheet pans.

2. Turn a dehydrator on to 50°C/120°F.

3. Combine both ingredients in a deep pot, much larger than what you need for the ingredients alone. It should be tall enough to contain the liquid when it comes to a rolling boil and should preferably not be too wide. Put the pot over medium-low to medium heat.

4. Using a handheld mixer, whip the mixture as it is warming up. It is important to get to the bottom of the pot and to make sure the mixture slowly rises in temperature. This procedure may take up to 30 minutes.

5. When the milk mixture just starts to come to a boil, take the pot off the heat. Spoon the foam onto the prepared hotel pan. There will be some unfoamed milk at the bottom of the pot; do not use it.

6. Put the hotel pan(s) in the dehydrator. Let the foam dry for at least 12 hours.

7. Remove the crispy foam from the dehydrator and the hotel pan and cut it into rectangles that measure 5 cm/2 in wide by 10 cm/4 in long. Try to cut it using a serrated knife. It may not cut into a very even shape because it is very brittle, which is not a problem; it can be semi-organically shaped.

8. Reserve the pieces in the dehydrator during service. After service, if there are any left over, transfer them to an airtight container with silica gel packs. They will keep indefinitely if stored under these conditions.

NOTE *You may substitute a milk frother for the handheld blender in the whipping step; it produces very consistent results, but the disadvantage is that it can only froth 120 g/4.23 oz at a time.*

BAGUETTE ICE CREAM

YIELD: 1 KG/2 LB 3.2 OZ

INGREDIENT	METRIC	U.S.	%
Baguette Milk			
Milk	750 g	1 lb 10.4 oz	75%
Baguette, sliced, toasted dark	250 g	8.82 oz	25%
Baguette Ice Cream Base			
Baguette Milk	735 g	1 lb 9.92 oz	73.46%
Yeast, instant dry	1 g	.04 oz	.1%
Milk powder	30 g	1.06 oz	3%
Sugar	105 g	3.7 oz	10.49%
Ice cream stabilizer	4 g	.13 oz	.36%
Glucose powder	40 g	1.41 oz	4%
Malt syrup	16 g	.56 oz	1.6%
Egg yolks	70 g	2.47 oz	7%

1. **For the baguette milk:** Bring the milk to a simmer in a sauce pot while the baguette is toasting. Add the hot toasted baguette to the milk and let it soak in the milk until soft.

2. Using a handheld blender, purée as smooth as possible. Cool this liquid in an ice water bath. Proceed with the ice cream base.

3. **For the baguette ice cream base:** Follow the modern ice cream method on page 50. Let the base age for 4 hours before churning. Add the yeast after the milk.

4. Once churned, reserve well covered in a freezer at −10°C/14°F during service. After service, you may melt the base and re-churn it a second time, but you should not churn it again after that.

CARAMELIZED WHITE CHOCOLATE SPIRAL

YIELD: 10 TO 12 SPIRALS

INGREDIENT	METRIC	U.S.
Caramelized white chocolate, melted (page 316)	300 g	10.58 oz

1. One hour before you are going to make the spirals, freeze a marble slab about the size of a half sheet pan.

2. When the slab is frozen cold and the caramelized white chocolate is melted and in a piping bag, make the spirals one at a time. Drizzle a thin line from top to bottom of the marble horizontally, enough to be about 5 cm/ 2 in wide.

3. Before the chocolate sets, roll it up from the bottom of the marble to the top. Place the finished spiral on a sheet pan lined with parchment paper.

4. Once all of the spirals are made, keep them in a freezer. Melt down again after 2 months or when they break.

NOTE *The chocolate does not need to be tempered to make these spirals; it only needs to be fluid.*

ENCAPSULATED HUCKLEBERRY COMPOTE

YIELD: 751 G/1 LB 10.4 OZ

INGREDIENT	METRIC	U.S.	%
Huckleberry Compote			
Huckleberries	500 g	1 lb 1.6 oz	66.58%
Sugar	150 g	5.29 oz	19.97%
Water	100 g	3.53 oz	13.32%
Salt	1 g	.04 oz	.13%
Encapsulation			
Water	625 g	1 lb 5.92 oz	89.29%
Sugar	50 g	1.76 oz	7.14%
Genutine 400-C (60% kappa carrageenan plus 40% locust bean gum; see Note)	25 g	.88 oz	3.57%
Simple syrup, at 50° Brix	500 g	1 lb 1.6 oz	

1. **For the huckleberry compote:** Combine the huckleberries, sugar, water, and salt in a small sauce pot and bring to a quick boil. Turn off the heat and let the mixture cool to room temperature. Transfer half of the compote to a blender cup and blend until smooth. Reserve the other half in the refrigerator without straining. Discard after 5 days.

2. Pass the puréed liquid through a fine-mesh sieve. Using a funnel gun, portion the puréed liquid into 20-g/.7-oz dome silicone molds and freeze. Once they have hardened, push them out of the molds and reserve them in the freezer. Keep well covered.

3. **For the encapsulation:** Combine the water, sugar, and Genutine 400-C in a sauce pot and bring to a boil.

4. Wait for the liquid to cool to 80°C/175°F.

5. Using a scribe or long needle, stab a frozen huckleberry compote dome at its base/flat end, and dip it in the warm encapsulating bath.

6. Carefully pull it out and dip the encapsulated compote in the simple syrup, gently pushing it off the scribe or needle with the tip of your finger.

7. Repeat with the other domes. Reserve the encapsulated compote in the liquid compote in the refrigerator. Discard after 2 days.

    NOTE *Genutine 400-C is a commercial brand name (see Resources, page 520); if you cannot find it, simply combine 60 percent kappa carrageenan and 40 percent locust bean gum.*

MEXICAN VANILLA CREAM

YIELD: 1.49 KG/3 LB 4.64 OZ

INGREDIENT	METRIC	U.S.	%
Cornstarch	80 g	2.82 oz	5.35%
Milk 1, at room temperature	80 g	2.82 oz	5.35%
Egg yolks, at room temperature	200 g	7.05 oz	13.38%
Sugar	200 g	7.05 oz	13.38%
Milk 2	920 g	2 lb .32 oz	61.54%
Vanilla paste	15 g	.53 oz	1%

NOTES *While this method produces a more superior pastry cream than the traditional method, it does have a flaw. There is an enzyme in egg yolks that breaks down the cornstarch if it is not boiled out as in the traditional pastry cream method, and so after 2 days this pastry cream has a very unsightly appearance and texture.*

This recipe does not work if you choose to make it in smaller quantities. It does, however, work very well if you make larger quantities.

1. Mix the cornstarch with the first amount of milk to form a paste. Add the egg yolks and mix until smooth.

2. Pass the mixture through a fine-mesh sieve. Make sure that the bowl it is in is large enough to hold all of the ingredients, including the second amount of milk.

3. Boil the sugar with the second amount of milk and the vanilla paste. This is the most crucial step; make sure you have a pot that is tall enough so that when the milk comes to a rolling boil, it won't spill over. The rolling boil is needed so that the milk reaches a high enough temperature that when it is poured over the milk-cornstarch-yolk mixture, the yolk and the cornstarch proteins will coagulate. Let the milk mixture boil for about 10 seconds.

4. In one motion, pour the sugar-milk mixture into the milk-cornstarch-yolk mixture. Ideally this is done with two people, where one pours the boiled milk and the other whisks as quickly as possible. It is crucial that the milk be poured in one motion in order for this method to work; if you pour it too slowly, it will not coagulate the egg yolk protein and the starch protein will not gelatinize. Stir vigorously while and after the milk is poured. Wait for it to thicken (it will take a few seconds).

5. Cover the pastry cream with plastic wrap and cool over an ice water bath.

6. Cover the cream with plastic wrap directly on its surface and store in an airtight container in the refrigerator. Discard after 2 days.

LEMON JOCONDE CRUMBS

YIELD: 859 G/1 LB 13.92 OZ

INGREDIENT	METRIC	U.S.	%
Confectioners' sugar	170 g	6 oz	19.79%
Almond flour	170 g	6 oz	19.79%
All-purpose flour	105 g	3.7 oz	12.22%
Lemon zest	3 g	.11 oz	.35%
Eggs, at room temperature	210 g	7.41 oz	24.45%
Natural yellow food coloring (see Note)	1 g	.04 oz	.12%
Egg whites	140 g	4.94 oz	16.3%
Superfine or bakers' sugar	30 g	1.06 oz	3.49%
Butter, melted but cool	30 g	1.06 oz	3.49%

1. Preheat a convection oven to 135°C/275°F; if possible, turn the fan speed down to low.

2. Lightly grease the interior border of a half sheet pan with nonstick oil spray. Line the sheet pan with a nonstick rubber mat.

3. Sift the confectioners' sugar, almond flour, and all-purpose flour together and place in an electric mixer bowl.

4. Add the lemon zest to the bowl and mix on low speed using a paddle attachment.

5. Add the eggs slowly and incorporate completely. Add the food coloring and mix until it is completely combined. Take the bowl off the mixer.

6. Whip the egg whites with an electric mixer on high speed. When they have doubled in volume, slowly pour in the sugar. Whip until the whites have whipped to stiff peaks. Fold the whites into the flour mixture in 2 additions.

7. Fold in the melted butter.

8. Spread the batter in an even layer on the prepared sheet pan.

9. Bake the Joconde until done but without any color, about 8 minutes. This is why the cake is baked at such a low temperature on low fan speed, so that it bakes through without gaining any color.

10. Cool the cake to room temperature. Place it in a dehydrator set to 50°C/120°F or an oven set as low as it can go. Alternatively, you may leave it in the oven overnight with the heat of the pilot alone to fully dehydrate it.

11. Once it is dry, break it into small pieces and grind it into crumbs in a Robot Coupe.

12. Reserve in an airtight container at room temperature in a cool, dry place. Discard after 2 weeks.

NOTE *When possible, use natural food colorings (see Resources, page 520). Some color, used intelligently and sparingly, can only make a dessert look more appealing. Theories that intensity of color can determine flavor perception back this idea up.*

LEMON STREUSEL

YIELD: 1 KG/2 LB 3.36 OZ

INGREDIENT	METRIC	U.S.	%
Butter	330 g	11.64 oz	32.9%
Pastry flour	330 g	11.64 oz	32.9%
Sugar	330 g	11.64 oz	32.9%
Lemon zest	3 g	.11 oz	.3%
Salt	10 g	.35 oz	1%

Follow the method for cinnamon streusel on page 314.

CHOCOLATE SHELL TUBES

YIELD: 570 G/1 LB 4 OZ

INGREDIENT	METRIC	U.S.	%
Bergamot-Infused White Chocolate			
White chocolate coins	1 kg	2 lb 3.2 oz	83.33%
Bergamot orange peel	200 g	7.05 oz	16.67%
Chocolate Shell Tubes			
Bergamot-Infused White Chocolate	500 g	17.64	87.72%
Natural yellow cocoa butter	50 g	1.76	8.77%
Natural green cocoa butter	20 g	.71	3.51%

1. **For the infused chocolate:** Turn a circulating water bath on to 35°C/95°F.

2. Make sure the bergamot peel has no pith attached.

3. Place the chocolate and the peel in a vacuum-seal bag and vacuum seal it. Place the bag in the hot water bath and let it infuse for 2 hours.

4. Remove the melted chocolate first from the bath, and then from the bag, and pour it onto a sheet pan to cool and set. Remove the peel pieces.

5. Once the chocolate has set, chop and reserve it in an airtight container at room temperature. It will keep and be aromatic for up to 1 year.

6. **For the chocolate shell tubes:** Cut out 10 sheets of textured acetate 12 cm/3.75 in wide by 12.5 cm/5 in long (see Resources, page 520). Have 10 PVC tubes measuring 12.5 cm/5 in long by 5 cm/2 in diameter ready for use.

7. Melt the chocolate and cocoa butters together and then temper them (see method on pages 27–28).

8. Spread an even layer of chocolate on the textured acetate rectangles using an offset spatula. Gently roll the acetate into a tube shape and slide it into the PVC tubes to set. Reserve in a cool, dry area for up to 1 year.

NOTE *Bergamot is in season during the month of January only. If you do not have access to bergamot, you may choose to infuse the chocolate with Earl Grey tea instead. If so, replace the amount of bergamot peel with 50 g/1.76 oz of tea.*

YELLOW CHOCOLATE PLAQUES

YIELD: 285 G/ 10.05 OZ

INGREDIENT	METRIC	U.S.	%
Bergamot-Infused White Chocolate (page 238)	250 g	8.82 oz	87.72%
Yellow cocoa butter, natural	35 g	1.23 oz	12.28%

1. Place a half sheet of textured acetate (see Resources, page 520) on a flat surface.

2. Combine both ingredients and temper together.

3. Spread the tempered chocolate onto the prepared acetate into a thin, even layer using an offset spatula. Once it has set halfway but is still pliable, cut it into 6-cm/2.25-in squares using a ruler and the back of a paring knife.

4. Turn the acetate over onto a flat surface and place a flat weight on top of the acetate so that it sets flat; otherwise the chocolate will bow.

5. Once the chocolate is fully set, place it in a cool, dry area, preferably covered. It will remain aromatic for up to 1 year.

CHOCOLATE LETTER "B"

YIELD: 250 G/8.82 OZ

INGREDIENT	METRIC	U.S.	%
Bergamot-Infused Dark Chocolate, tempered	250 g	8.82 oz	100%

1. Make the infused chocolate using the same procedure as the Bergamot-Infused White Chocolate on page 238, substituting dark chocolate for the white chocolate.

2. Using a piping bag, pipe the chocolate into a letter "B" polycarbonate chocolate mold (see Resources, page 520). You will need at least 10 molds for this yield.

3. Let the chocolate set, and then turn the mold over to release it. Reserve the chocolate in a cool, dry place, preferably covered. It will remain aromatic for up to 1 year.

BERGAMOT SORBET

YIELD: 1 KG/2 LB 3.2 OZ

INGREDIENT	METRIC	U.S.	%
Bergamot juice	340 g	11.99 oz	34%
Simple syrup, at 50° Brix	660 g	1 lb 7.28 oz	66%

1. Line 10 PVC tubes that measuring 12.5 cm/5 in long by 2 cm/.75 in diameter with acetate; make sure the acetate is a little longer than the length of the PVC tube so that it is easier to pull the acetate out of the tube. Reserve the lined tubes on a half sheet pan in the freezer.

2. Combine both ingredients. Churn in an ice cream machine and pour into a piping bag.

3. Pipe the sorbet into the prepared tubes and freeze them until the sorbet has hardened.

4. Once they have hardened, pull them out of the PVC tubes and reserve them frozen with the acetate still on. Re-melt and re-churn after 5 days in the freezer.

FROZEN EARL GREY FOAM

YIELD: 1 KG/2 LB 3.2 OZ

INGREDIENT	METRIC	U.S.	%
Earl Grey tea	660 g	1 lb 7.28 oz	65.93%
Egg white powder	36 g	1.27 oz	3.6%
Sugar	150 g	5.29 oz	14.99%
Water	150 g	5.29 oz	14.99%
Gelatin sheets, silver, bloomed in cold water, excess water squeezed off	5 g	.18 oz	.5%
Earl Grey Génoise cubes (page 218)	10	10	
Bergamot Sorbet Tubes (page 239)	10	10	
Chocolate Shell Tubes (page 238)	10	10	

1. Place the chocolate shell tubes on a flat sheet pan lined with a nonstick rubber mat in a standing position in a freezer; they should still be inside the PVC tubes for stability.

2. Remove the acetate from the bergamot sorbet tubes; trim the ends if necessary so that they are 12.5 cm/5 in long.

3. Combine the Earl Grey tea with the egg white powder in the bowl of an electric mixer fitted with a whip attachment and mix on low speed.

4. Meanwhile, make a syrup with the sugar and the water by combining them in a small sauce pot and bringing them to a boil. Turn off the heat and make sure that all of the sugar has dissolved. Add the gelatin and stir until it has dissolved. Let it cool to room temperature.

5. Add this syrup to the tea and egg white powder mixture when it has reached half its maximum volume (it will have tripled in volume when it is at half the maximum volume). Pour the liquid down the side of the bowl as the mixer whips.

6. Continue to whip on high speed until the mixture reaches full volume. It will have increased in volume six times from its original volume.

7. Transfer the mixture into a piping bag and pipe it into the chocolate shell tubes to fill three-quarters of the way up.

8. Insert a frozen bergamot sorbet tube into the center of each chocolate shell tube, going through the foam.

9. Insert a rectangle of Earl Grey génoise next to the sorbet.

10. Even out the foam at the top of the shell tube with an offset spatula.

11. Return to the freezer to harden. Reserve frozen during service, keeping the exposed surface covered. Discard after 4 days.

VIETNAMESE ICE CREAM

YIELD: 1 KG/2 LB 3.2 OZ

INGREDIENT	METRIC	U.S.	%
Milk	470 g	1 lb .48 oz	47%
Heavy cream	250 g	8.82 oz	25%
Milk powder	45 g	1.59 oz	4.5%
Sugar	155 g	5.47 oz	15.5%
Ice cream stabilizer	3 g	.11 oz	.3%
Egg yolks	70 g	2.47 oz	7%
Vietnamese instant coffee (see Resources, page 520)	7 g	.25 oz	.7%

1. Make the base following the modern ice cream method on page 50. The instant coffee is added just after the yolks.

2. Once the base has cooled, let it age for at least 4 hours before churning.

3. Meanwhile, put a sheet of flexible silicone half-domes that measure 5 cm/2 in base diameter by 4 cm/1.5 in high on a sheet pan and then freeze.

4. Churn the base and pour it into a piping bag. Pipe the churned ice cream into the prepared molds and even out the top with an offset spatula. Reserve frozen, keeping the exposed surface well covered to prevent freezer damage.

5. You may melt these domes down if they are frozen for more than 5 days and then re-churn them.

WARM JASMINE RICE PUDDING

YIELD: 1.31 KG/2 LB 14.08 OZ

INGREDIENT	METRIC	U.S.	%
Heavy cream	1.15 kg	2 lb 8.48 oz	87.79%
Jasmine rice	50 g	1.76 oz	3.82%
Sugar	110 g	3.88 oz	8.4%

1. Combine all of the ingredients in the Thermomix (see Note).

2. Set to speed 3 and cook for 1 ½ hours at 90°C/195°F, or until thickened. The jasmine rice should be completely cooked and puréed into the cream; the rice is the thickener for this pudding.

3. Transfer to an insulated thermal container for service; use a high-quality container in order to keep the contents hot for the longest period of time. If possible, split the liquid into 2 thermal containers in order to preserve the temperature for the longest period of time. Keep tightly closed. Discard after service.

NOTE *This is a very interesting recipe. It requires a very small amount of jasmine rice that is combined with heavy cream and then slowly cooked and stirred until it is thickened to a consistency much like that of a pudding. It takes a long time and patience, and the use of a specific machine known as the Thermomix. This is a blender that is equipped with a heating element, so that you can stir and cook ingredients simultaneously (see Resources, page 520). This recipe is inspired by a method developed by Claudio Cracco, chef and owner of Cracco restaurant in Milan, Italy.*

COFFEE JELLY TUBE

YIELD: 258 G/9.1 OZ

INGREDIENT	METRIC	U.S.	%
Water	220 g	7.76 oz	85.27%
Instant Vietnamese coffee (see Resources, page 520)	4 g	.14 oz	1.55%
Superfine sugar	30 g	1.06 oz	11.63%
Agaroid RS-507 (see Resources, page 520)	4 g	.14 oz	1.55%

Combine the water, coffee, and sugar in a small sauce pot and stir to dissolve the sugar and the instant coffee. To make the jelly, follow the method for the strawberry jelly tube on page 220.

PANDAN LEAF–INFUSED CARAMELIZED CREAM TUBE

YIELD: 774 G/1 LB 11.2 OZ

INGREDIENT	METRIC	U.S.	%
Pandan-Infused Heavy Cream			
Pandan leaves (see Resources, page 520)	200 g	7.05 oz	21.05%
Heavy cream	750 g	1 lb 10.4 oz	78.95%
Pandan Leaf Caramelized Cream			
Pandan-Infused Heavy Cream	690 g	1 lb 8.32 oz	89.1%
Sugar	80 g	2.82 oz	10.33%
Agar-agar	3 g	0.1 oz	.36%
Locust bean gum	2 g	.06 oz	.21%

1. **For the pandan-infused heavy cream:** Chop the pandan leaves coarsely and combine with the heavy cream in a small sauce pot.

2. Bring to a simmer over medium-high heat. Take the pot off the heat and let the leaves steep for about 5 minutes. If the cream boils or if the leaves are steeped for too long, the cream will taste like fish.

3. Strain the liquid and use immediately or keep hot. Measure the amount for the caramelized cream. If not using immediately, cool in an ice water bath and reserve refrigerated for up to 5 days.

4. **For the pandan leaf caramelized cream:** Place 10 oval tubes measuring 7.5 cm/3 in long by 4 cm/1.5 in diameter over a flat sheet pan lined with a 3-mm/.12-in-thick sheet of rolling fondant. The dimensions of the fondant should be a 15.25-cm/6-in square; roll it out by hand or use a sheeter. This will ensure that the liquid does not seep through the tubes as long as the tubes are pushed slightly into the fondant. It also helps keep the tubes in place. The tubes do not need to be lined because once the cream sets, it can be gently pushed out without it sticking to the tube.

BLACK SESAME GENOA BREAD

YIELD: 858 G/1 LB 14.24 OZ

5. Combine the pandan-infused heavy cream and the sugar in a small sauce pot. Using a handheld blender, shear in the agar and locust bean gum (pour it in slowly). Switch to a whisk at this point because the continued use of the blender will introduce too many bubbles.

6. Bring the liquid to a boil while stirring. Let it boil for 5 seconds, then turn off the heat.

7. Pour the cream into the prepared tubes and refrigerate.

8. Once the cream has set, it can gently be pushed out of the tubes from the bottom of the mold. Discard after 3 days.

NOTE *Pandan leaves are from Southeast Asia and are used in that region's cooking, for both savory and sweet preparations. For export, this leaf it has to be frozen or it will spoil.*

INGREDIENT	METRIC	U.S.	%
Salt	3 g	.11 oz	.35%
All-purpose flour	60 g	2.12 oz	6.99%
Almond paste	320 g	11.29 oz	37.3%
Black sesame paste	80 g	2.82 oz	9.32%
Eggs	250 g	8.82 oz	29.14%
Invert sugar	35 g	1.23 oz	4.08%
Butter, melted but cool	110 g	3.88 oz	12.82%

1. Spray the interior border of a half sheet pan with non-stick oil spray. Line it with a nonstick rubber mat.

2. Preheat a convection oven to 160°C/325°F.

3. Sift the salt with the flour. Mix the almond paste with the black sesame paste in the bowl of an electric mixer fitted with a paddle attachment until a homogenous mass is obtained.

4. Add the eggs slowly and mix until they are completely combined. Scrape the bowl and mix well for a few more seconds. Add the invert sugar and mix completely.

5. Stop the mixer and add the flour mixture. Pulse the mixer until it is just incorporated. Scrape the bowl and mix for a few more seconds. Pour in the melted butter and mix until fully incorporated.

6. Pour the batter onto the prepared sheet pan and spread it out evenly. Bake until done, 8 to 10 minutes, or when the cake springs back when gentle pressure is applied with your fingertips.

7. Cool to room temperature, and then transfer to the refrigerator for at least 1 hour before cutting. It cuts better when it is chilled. Cut the bread into rectangles that measure 5 cm/2 in wide by 7.5 cm/3 in long by 5 mm/.25 in thick.

8. Reserve in an airtight container at room temperature during service. Discard any left over after service.

NOTE *This recipe is adapted from Michael Laiskonis, pastry chef at Le Bernardin in New York City.*

HIBISCUS GLAZE

YIELD: 450 G/15.87 OZ

INGREDIENT	METRIC	U.S.	%
Hisbiscus Infusion			
Dried hibiscus leaves	50 g	1.76 oz	11.11%
Water, at 95°C/205°F	400 g	14.11 oz	88.89%
Glaze			
Hibiscus Infusion	230 g	8.11 oz	73.02%
Sugar	60 g	2.12 oz	19.05%
Clear glaze (mirror glaze; see Resources, page 520)	25 g	.88 oz	7.94%

1. **For the hibiscus infusion:** Combine the hibiscus leaves and the water and let the hibiscus infuse the water for 10 minutes. Strain the liquid.

2. **For the glaze:** Combine the infusion with the sugar in a small sauce pot and bring the liquid to a boil. Reduce the mixture to one-third of its original weight (about 75 g/2.5 oz).

3. Let the liquid cool to room temperature.

4. Stir in the clear glaze. Reserve at room temperature in an airtight container. This glaze will keep indefinitely due to its high sugar content and low moisture content.

POWDERED POPCORN

YIELD: 300 G/10.58 OZ

INGREDIENT	METRIC	U.S.
Popcorn (popped, seasoned with salt)	300 g	10.58 oz

1. Grind the popcorn in a Robot Coupe as finely as possible. Pass through a drum sieve.

2. Reserve the powder in an airtight container. Discard after service.

VELVET COATED WORMWOOD ICE CREAM

YIELD: 1.02 KG/2 LB 3.84 OZ

INGREDIENT	METRIC	U.S.	%
Wormwood Ice Cream Base			
Milk	640 g	1 lb 6.56 oz	62.78%
Heavy cream	85 g	2.98 oz	8.29%
Powdered milk	42 g	1.48 oz	4.12%
Sugar	160 g	5.64 oz	15.69%
Ice cream stabilizer	3 g	.11 oz	.29%
Egg yolks	70 g	2.47 oz	6.86%
Wormwood schnapps essence	20 g	.71 oz	1.96%
72 Percent Chocolate Cake Crumbs (page 246)	350 g	12.34 oz	
Chocolate Spray			
72% dark chocolate coins	200 g	7.05 oz	45.45%
Cocoa butter	200 g	7.05 oz	45.45%
Onyx black food coloring	40 g	1.41 oz	9.09%

1. **For the ice cream base:** Follow the modern ice cream method on page 50. Add the wormwood essence once the base has cooled down completely.

2. Let the base age for at least 4 hours before churning.

3. Meanwhile, cut out 10 acetate rectangles measuring 11.25 cm/4.5 in wide by 12.5 cm/5 in long. They will line oval molds measuring 1.25/.5 in wide by 5 cm / 2.5 in long by 12.5 cm/5 in deep. Freeze the molds on a half sheet pan lined with a nonstick rubber mat.

4. Churn the ice cream, fold in the cake crumbs, and then pipe it into the frozen molds. Freeze to harden. Once they are hardened, they can be pushed out of the mold and sprayed.

5. **For the spray:** Combine the chocolate coins, cocoa butter, and food coloring in a bowl and melt them over a hot water bath.

6. Set up a spray station, a surface that should be covered with plastic to keep the shop clean where you can spray the ice cream.

7. Fill a compressor canister with the chocolate spray and spray the ice cream with an even coating of spray. Keep the compressor gun at least 60 cm/24 in from the ice cream to obtain a velvety smooth look.

8. Return the sprayed ice creams to the freezer and keep them covered there during service; try to prevent whatever you use to cover them, such as plastic wrap, from coming in direct contact with them, since the spray will easily come off.

9. Discard after 3 days. Keep them well protected in the freezer so they do not get freezer burned or get frosted.

72 PERCENT CHOCOLATE CAKE

YIELD: 590 G/1 LB 4.8 OZ

INGREDIENT	METRIC	U.S.	%
Eggs, at room temperature	175 g	6.17 oz	29.66%
Invert sugar	45 g	1.59 oz	7.63%
Sugar	75 g	2.65 oz	12.71%
Almond flour	45 g	1.59 oz	7.63%
All-purpose flour	75 g	2.65 oz	12.71%
Baking powder	5 g	.18 oz	.85%
Cocoa powder	15 g	.53 oz	2.54%
Heavy cream, at room temperature	75 g	2.65 oz	12.71%
Butter, melted but cool	50 g	1.76 oz	8.47%
72% chocolate coins, melted	30 g	1.06 oz	5.08%

1. Preheat a convection oven to 160°C/325°F.

2. Lightly grease the interior border of a half sheet pan with nonstick oil spray. Line it with a nonstick rubber mat.

3. Combine the eggs, invert sugar, and sugar in a bowl and mix well using a whisk.

4. Sift the almond flour, all-purpose flour, baking powder, and cocoa powder together; add to the egg-sugar mixture, stirring with a whisk.

5. Pour in the heavy cream and the butter and stir with the whisk to fully incorporate. Stir in the melted chocolate.

6. Pour onto the prepared sheet pan and spread it out evenly using an offset spatula.

7. Bake until just done, 7 to 10 minutes, or until the cake springs back when gentle pressure is applied with your fingertips at the center of the cake. Cool at room temperature.

8. Transfer the cake to a dehydrator to dry completely.

9. Grind in a Robot Coupe to obtain crumbs.

10. Reserve the crumbs frozen. They will fold into the ice cream better and not melt it if frozen.

QUARK CHOCOLATE TILE

YIELD: 400 G/14.11 OZ

INGREDIENT	METRIC	U.S.	%
Quark Chocolate			
Superfine sugar or bakers' sugar	1.56 kg	3 lb 6.88 oz	38.81%
Cocoa butter	1.64 kg	3 lb 9.76 oz	40.8%
Quark powder (see Resources, page 520)	800 g	1 lb 12.16 oz	19.9%
Lecithin powder	20 g	.71 oz	.5%
Chocolate Tiles			
Quark chocolate, tempered	400 g	14.11 oz	99.5%
Gold luster dust	2 g	.07 oz	.5%

1. **For the quark chocolate:** Grind the sugar in a coffee grinder.

2. Melt the cocoa butter to 45°C/110°F, place it inside the mélangeur (see Resources, page 520), and turn it on.

3. As soon as the mélangeur starts moving, start adding the sugar in 4 additions, and then add the quark powder in 4 additions.

4. Let the mélangeur run for at least 12 hours and up to 18 hours.

5. Add the lecithin powder toward the end of the process and let it grind for about 2 more hours.

6. Transfer the chocolate to a sheet pan lined with parchment paper and let it cool until set.

7. **For the tiles:** Temper the quark chocolate and spread it over a textured acetate sheet in a thin, even layer using an offset spatula.

8. Once the chocolate is semi-set, cut out rectangles measuring 3.75 cm/1.5 in wide by 5 cm/2 in long using a ruler and a paring knife.

9. Flip the acetate over and place a weight on top of the acetate, such as a flat, heavy cutting board or slab of

marble, to keep it flat so that the chocolate sets flat and does not bow.

10. Once the chocolate sets, carefully lift the acetate sheet. Brush each rectangle with the gold luster dust.

11. Reserve in a cool, dry area, preferably covered. Discard after 1 year.

NOTE *If you cannot find quark powder, use yogurt powder. This method is used also to make regular white chocolate.*

FRIED MINT LEAF

YIELD: 10 MINT LEAVES

INGREDIENT	METRIC	U.S.
Canola oil	200 g	7.05 oz
Mint leaves, large	10	10

1. Bring the canola oil up to 175°C/350°F in a 960-mL/1-qt sauce pot.

2. Fry 1 leaf at a time. They will fry quickly and turn bright green. They are done when they cease to produce bubbles. Remove from the oil and place on a paper towel to absorb the oil.

3. Reserve at room temperature, uncovered, during service. Discard after service.

LILAC ICE CREAM

YIELD: 1.54 KG/3 LB 6. 4 OZ

INGREDIENT	METRIC	U.S.	%
Milk	947 g	2 lb 1.28 oz	61.32%
Candied lilac flowers	135 g	4.76 oz	8.75%
Heavy cream	153 g	5.4 oz	9.91%
Sugar	150 g	5.29 oz	9.72%
Egg yolks	120 g	4.23 oz	7.77%
Milk powder	32 g	1.11 oz	2.04%
Ice cream stabilizer	8 g	.26 oz	.49%

1. Bring the milk to a boil in a sauce pot with the candied lilac flowers. Turn off the heat and let the flowers steep for 10 minutes.

2. Using a handheld blender, blend the flowers into the milk, and then pass the liquid through a fine-mesh sieve. Cool to room temperature and then proceed with the modern ice cream method on page 50.

3. Let the base age for 4 hours before churning.

4. Place 10 square molds measuring 8.75 cm/3.5 in by 8.75 cm/3.5 in by 1.25 cm/.5 in deep on a half sheet pan lined with a nonstick rubber mat. Line each mold with a strip of acetate that fits evenly inside it.

5. Churn the ice cream base and transfer it to a piping bag. Pipe the ice cream into the molds. Even out the top of each mold with an offset spatula.

6. Place the molds in the freezer to harden completely.

7. Once they are hardened, they can be unmolded and sprayed. To unmold them, simply push them out of the mold and remove the acetate strip.

PINK VELVET SPRAY

YIELD: 410 G/14.46 OZ

INGREDIENT	METRIC	U.S.	%
Cocoa butter	200 g	7.05 oz	48.78%
White chocolate coins	200 g	7.05 oz	48.78%
Natural red cocoa butter	10 g	.35 oz	2.44%

1. Combine all of the ingredients in a bowl and melt over a hot water bath. Add more red cocoa butter, if necessary, to achieve a light pink color.

2. Strain through a fine-mesh sieve.

3. Set up a spray station, a surface that should be covered with plastic to keep the shop clean where you can spray the ice cream.

4. Fill a compressor canister with the pink velvet spray and spray the ice cream with an even coating of spray. Keep the compressor gun at least 60 cm/24 in from the ice cream to obtain a velvety smooth look. Reserve frozen for service.

5. Cover after service. Make sure they are in an airtight container, not wrapped, since the plastic can damage the velvet look.

   NOTE *For green velvet spray, substitute natural green cocoa butter for the natural red cocoa butter. For red velvet spray, increase the amount of red cocoa butter used to color the spray.*

MINT POUND CAKE

YIELD: 1.73 KG/3 LB 12.96 OZ

INGREDIENT	METRIC	U.S.	%
All-purpose flour	435 g	15.34 oz	25.14%
Salt	6 g	.21 oz	.35%
Baking powder	9 g	.32 oz	.52%
Sugar	470 g	1 lb .58 oz	27.17%
Eggs	175 g	6.17 oz	10.12%
Natural green mint paste; no coloring	60 g	2.12 oz	3.47%
Canola oil	235 g	8.29 oz	13.58%
Milk	340 g	11.99 oz	19.65%
Green Velvet Spray			
Cocoa butter	200 g	7.05 oz	44.44%
White chocolate	200g	7.05 oz	44.44%
Carnival green cocoa butter	50 g	1.76 oz	11.11%

1. Lightly grease the interior border of a half sheet pan with nonstick oil spray. Line it with a nonstick rubber mat.

2. Preheat a convection oven to 160°C/325°F.

3. Sift the flour, salt, and baking powder together.

4. In the bowl of an electric mixer fitted with a paddle attachment, whip the sugar, eggs, and green mint paste with an electric mixer until it is a homogenous mass and has quadrupled in volume (ribbon stage). Slowly pour in the canola oil to make an emulsion by pouring it down the side of the bowl as it mixes.

5. Alternate adding the sifted dry ingredients with the milk to the mixer bowl.

6. Pour the batter into the prepared pan and bake it until done, 12 to 18 minutes or until the cake springs back when gentle pressure is applied with your fingertips at the center of the pound cake.

7. Cool to room temperature, and then chill in the refrigerator; it cuts better when it is cold.

8. Cut the cake using a 6.25-cm/2.5-in diameter doughnut cutter. Freeze the rings on a flat sheet pan lined with a nonstick rubber mat.

9. **For the green velvet spray:** Combine all of the ingredients in a bowl and melt over a hot water bath.

10. Set up a spray station, a surface that should be covered with plastic to keep the shop clean where you can spray the cake.

11. Fill a compressor canister with the green velvet spray and spray the cakes with an even coating of spray. Keep the compressor gun at least 60 cm/24 in from the cake to obtain a velvety smooth look. Reserve in the refrigerator during service. Discard after 2 days.

RHUBARB AND ELDERFLOWER GELÉE

YIELD: 310 G/10.93 OZ

INGREDIENT	METRIC	U.S.	
Poached Rhubarb			
Rhubarb stalks	2		
	2		
Grenadine	600 g	1 lb 5.12 oz	
Gelée			
Poached rhubarb rectangles	10	10	
Elderflower syrup	150 g	5.29 oz	48.39%
Water	150 g	5.29 oz	48.39%
Gelatin sheets, silver, bloomed in cold water, excess water squeezed off	10 g	.35 oz	3.23%

1. **For the poached rhubarb:** Cut the rhubarb into rectangles measuring 3 mm/.12 in wide by 17.5 cm/7 in long by 3 mm/.12 in high. Reserve in a quarter hotel pan.

2. Bring the grenadine to a boil and pour it over the rhubarb.

3. Quickly wrap the pan and let the rhubarb poach in the liquid. Leave it in the refrigerator overnight.

4. The following day, make the gelée, or reserve the rhubarb in the liquid for up to 2 weeks in the refrigerator.

5. Lightly spray a very flat sheet pan with nonstick oil spray; spread it out evenly with a paper towel. Place a sheet of acetate over the sprayed surface and smooth it out with a clean paper towel to eliminate any air pockets.

6. Place a stainless-steel rectangular frame measuring 8.75 cm/3.5 in wide by 17.5 cm/7 in long by 1.25 cm/.5 in deep on top of the acetate-lined sheet pan. Seal the exterior border base with rolling fondant (it works like caulk to prevent the liquid from seeping out of the frame).

MINI VIOLET MACARONS

YIELD: 485 G/1 LB 1.11 OZ

7. Take the rhubarb out of the poaching liquid and pat it dry.

8. Line up the rhubarb rectangles horizontally inside the prepared frame, spacing them out evenly and ensuring that they are straight.

9. Make the gelée by combining the elderflower syrup, water, and gelatin sheets in a bowl and placing them over a hot water bath, stirring gently to melt them together.

10. Let the gelée cool to about 27°C/80°F, and then gently and slowly pour it into the frame. Fill it up as much as possible.

11. Transfer the gelée setup to the refrigerator to set. Once it has set, pass the tip of a paring knife around the inside of the frame and take it off.

12. Dip a long, thin slicing knife into a bain-marie filled with hot water and dry it with a paper towel. Cut out 1-cm/.4-in-wide rectangles across the rhubarb. Cut across the 8.75-cm/3.5-in width of the gelée to obtain gelée-and-rhubarb rectangles measuring 1 cm/.4 in wide by 8.75 cm/3.5 in long by 1.25 cm/.5 in deep.

13. Reserve the rectangles in an airtight container in the refrigerator. Discard after 2 days.

INGREDIENT	METRIC	U.S.	%
Egg whites	100 g	3.53 oz	20.62%
Powdered egg whites	5 g	.18 oz	1.03%
Sugar	30 g	1.06 oz	6.19%
Almond flour	125 g	4.41 oz	25.77%
Confectioners' sugar	225 g	7.94 oz	46.39%
Purple food coloring	as needed	as needed	

1. Combine the egg whites with the powdered egg whites by stirring in the powdered egg whites in a slow cascading motion with a whisk.

2. Grind the sugar in a coffee grinder until very fine.

3. Combine the almond flour with the confectioners' sugar and then mix in a Robot Coupe for 30 seconds; pass through a drum sieve.

4. Whip the egg whites on high speed; when they have reached medium peaks, sprinkle in the ground sugar, and then whip to stiff peaks. Add a few drops of purple food coloring.

5. Fold the meringue into the flour mixture until smooth; do not overmix (it will become very loose).

6. Pour into a piping bag fitted with a #2 tip.

7. Pipe the macarons onto a sheet pan lined with a non-stick rubber mat, leaving at least a 2.5-cm/1-in space between each. The diameter of the macaron should be about 5 mm/.2 in. Let them air-dry for 15 minutes.

8. Meanwhile, turn a convection oven on to 149°C/300°F and set to fan speed 2. Bake the macarons for 7 minutes, then turn off the oven and let the macarons dry for 3 more minutes

9. Cool at room temperature. Fill with the violet ganache. Reserve frozen for up to three months or refrigerated for up to ten days.

VIOLET GANACHE

YIELD: 210 G/7.41 OZ

BUTTERNUT SQUASH AND CINNAMON ICE CREAM

YIELD: 1.05 KG/2 LB 5.12 OZ

INGREDIENT	METRIC	U.S.	%
Heavy cream	50 g	1.76 oz	23.81%
Candied violet petals, ground in a coffee grinder	35 g	1.23 oz	16.67%
White chocolate, melted and cooled	125 g	4.41 oz	59.52%

1. Bring the heavy cream to a boil in a sauce pot. Add the candied violet petal powder.

2. Stir in the melted white chocolate.

3. Let the mixture cool to room temperature before piping it into the macarons.

4. Pipe about 2 g/.07 oz onto the flat side half of the macarons, then top each macaron with another macaron, sandwiching the filling. Reserve the filled macarons refrigerated in an airtight container.

INGREDIENT	METRIC	U.S.	%
Milk	460 g	1 lb .23 oz	43.64%
Indonesian cinnamon sticks	40 g	1.41 oz	3.8%
Heavy cream	96 g	3.39 oz	9.11%
Sugar	176 g	6.21 oz	16.7%
Egg yolks	80 g	2.82 oz	7.59%
Ice cream stabilizer	2 g	.07 oz	.19%
Butternut squash purée	200 g	7.05 oz	18.98%

1. Combine the milk and cinnamon sticks in a pot and bring to a simmer. Turn off the heat and cover the pot. Let the cinnamon steep for 30 minutes.

2. Strain the milk and let it cool in an ice water bath.

3. Proceed with the modern ice cream method on page 50; the butternut squash purée is added once the base is completely cooled down.

4. Let the base age for at least 4 hours before churning.

5. Place 10 rectangular stainless-steel molds measuring 2.5 cm/1 in wide by 6.25 cm/2.5 in long by 7.5 cm/3 in deep on a flat half sheet pan lined with a nonstick rubber mat. Place this setup in a freezer.

6. Churn the ice cream base and pour into a piping bag.

7. Pipe into the frozen rectangle molds and even out the top with an offset spatula. Freeze to harden.

8. To unmold, gently warm the frames with a torch. Lift the frame up and lay the ice cream on its side. Return the ice cream to the freezer to harden.

ORANGE VELVET SPRAY

YIELD: 430 G/15.17 OZ

INGREDIENT	METRIC	U.S.	%
Cocoa butter	200 g	7.05 oz	46.51%
White chocolate	200 g	7.05 oz	46.51%
Natural orange cocoa butter	30 g	1.06 oz	6.98%

1. Melt all of the ingredients together in a bowl over a hot water bath.

2. Set up a spray station, a surface that should be covered with plastic to keep the shop clean where you can spray the ice cream.

3. Fill a compressor canister with the orange velvet spray and spray the ice cream with an even coating of spray. Keep the compressor gun at least 60 cm/24 in from the ice cream to obtain a velvety smooth look. Carefully flip them over and spray the other side.

4. Reserve frozen during service. Keep covered while frozen to prevent frost accumulation on the surface. Discard after 2 days.

TRUE RED VELVET CAKE

YIELD: 1.36 KG/3 LB

INGREDIENT	METRIC	U.S.	%
Cocoa powder, natural (not Dutch process)	30 g	1.06 oz	2.2%
All-purpose flour	330 g	11.64 oz	24.23%
Vanilla powder	5 g	.18 oz	.37%
Salt	3 g	.11 oz	.22%
Butter, at 21°C/70°F	225 g	7.94 oz	16.52%
Superfine or bakers' sugar	400 g	14.11 oz	29.37%
Eggs, at 21°C/70°F	100 g	3.53 oz	7.34%
Buttermilk, at 21°C/70°F	245 g	8.64 oz	17.99%
Baking soda	9 g	.32 oz	.66%
White vinegar	15 g	.53 oz	1.1%

1. Sift the cocoa powder, flour, vanilla powder, and salt together.

2. Lightly spray the interior border of a full sheet pan with nonstick oil spray. Line it with a nonstick rubber mat.

3. Preheat a convection oven to 160°C/325°F.

4. Cream the butter and sugar in an electric mixer fitted with the paddle attachment on medium speed until it is light and fluffy, about 4 minutes. Add the eggs in 2 additions, scraping the sides of the bowl and the paddle between each addition. If making larger amounts, add the eggs in more additions.

5. Add half of the sifted dry ingredients and mix for a few seconds, until incorporated. Add half of the buttermilk and mix for a few seconds, until incorporated. Repeat with the other half of the dry ingredients and the remaining half of the buttermilk.

6. Once the mixture has achieved a homogenous mass, combine the baking soda with the vinegar and immediately mix it into the batter. Pulse the mixer a few times to incorporate all of the ingredients.

7. Pour the batter onto the prepared sheet pan and spread it out evenly.

8. Bake until the exterior of the cake turns a deep brown-red, 10 to 15 minutes.

9. Let the cake cool to room temperature. Once it has cooled, place it in the refrigerator to cool completely.

10. Cut out 10 rectangles measuring 3.75 cm/1.5 in wide by 7.5 cm/3 in long by 2 mm/.08 in high. Reserve the cakes in an airtight container in the refrigerator during service. Discard after service.

NOTE *This recipe makes more pieces than you need, but it is better to make the cake in this quantity than in smaller amounts since it mixes and bakes a lot better with this amount. You can always reserve the rest of the cake in the freezer for future services.*

BLACK CURRANT "PAPER"

YIELD: 303 G/10.69 OZ

INGREDIENT	METRIC	U.S.	%
Black currant fruit purée	250 g	8.82 oz	82.51%
Sugar	50 g	1.76 oz	16.5%
Methocel A7C	3 g	.11 oz	.99%

1. Cut a sheet of acetate into 10 rectangles measuring 5 cm/2 in wide by 7.5 cm/3 in long.

2. Turn a dehydrator on to 65°C/149°F.

3. Pour the fruit purée into a blender cup and turn it on medium speed. Add the sugar and blend for a few seconds.

4. Pour in the Methocel A7C as the blender is mixing. Shear for 45 seconds.

5. Spread the purée onto the prepared acetate rectangles in a thin, even layer using a small offset spatula. Transfer to the dehydrator and let it dry for at least 4 hours or until it is completely dried.

6. Reserve in the dehydrator during service to ensure that it will be crisp.

SILVER HONEY SAUCE

YIELD: 13 G/.46 OZ

INGREDIENT	METRIC	U.S.	%
Silver powder	1 g	.04 oz	7.69%
Honey	12 g	.42 oz	92.31%

Combine both ingredients. Reserve in an airtight container. This sauce may keep indefinitely because honey has a very long shelf life.

INDONESIAN CINNAMON BUBBLES

YIELD: 1.17 KG/2 LB 9.28 OZ

INGREDIENT	METRIC	U.S.	%
Water	1 kg	2 lb 3.2 oz	85.37%
Indonesian cinnamon sticks, toasted	200 g	7.05 oz	
Sugar	150 g	5.29 oz	12.81%
Salt	.2 g	.01 oz	.02%
Egg white powder	20 g	.71 oz	1.71%
Xanthan gum	1 g	.04 oz	.1%

1. Bring the water to a boil in a small pot. Add the toasted cinnamon and turn off the heat. Ideally, the cinnamon should still be hot from toasting for the best flavor infusion. Cover the pot with plastic wrap and let the cinnamon steep for 10 minutes.

2. Strain the liquid and cool it over an ice water bath. Discard the cinnamon.

3. Mix the infused water, sugar, salt, egg white powder, and xanthan gum in a blender on medium speed for 5 minutes.

4. Chill for 2 hours before service. Discard the bubbles after service.

TOASTED MILK PANNA COTTA

YIELD: 618 G/1 LB 5.8 OZ

INGREDIENT	METRIC	U.S.	%
Milk solids	175 g	6.17 oz	28.32%
Heavy cream	375 g	13.23 oz	60.68%
Sugar	60 g	2.12 oz	9.71%
Gelatin sheets, silver, bloomed in cold water, excess water squeezed off	8 g	.28 oz	1.29%
Caramelized milk chocolate spray (page 255)	400 g	14.11 oz	

1. Spread the milk solids over a sheet pan lined with parchment paper.

2. Toast until browned in a 160°C/320°F oven, 7 to 10 minutes; move the milk solids around with an offset spatula every few minutes to ensure even toasting.

3. Cool to room temperature.

4. Have 10 silicone ring molds measuring 10 cm/4 in external diameter by 2.5 cm/1 in internal diameter by 5 mm/.2 in deep (see Resources, page 520) set on a sheet pan on hand.

5. Combine the milk solids, heavy cream, and sugar in a small sauce pot and bring to a boil over high heat. Turn off the heat. Use a handheld blender to ensure that the milk solids have dissolved completely into the cream.

6. Stir in the gelatin and mix until it has dissolved completely. Pour into the silicone ring molds. Set in a freezer.

7. Once frozen, you can unmold them onto a half sheet pan lined with a nonstick rubber mat. Reserve frozen.

8. Meanwhile, set up a spray station, a surface that should be covered with plastic to keep the shop clean where you can spray the panna cotta.

9. Melt the caramelized milk chocolate velvet spray. Fill a compressor canister and spray the panna cotta with an even coating of spray. Keep the compressor gun at least 60 cm/24 in from the panna cotta to obtain a velvety smooth look. Reserve frozen. If you do not keep them frozen, it will be impossible to transfer them to the serving plate without them losing their shape.

CARAMELIZED MILK CHOCOLATE VELVET SPRAY

YIELD: 400 G/14.11 OZ

INGREDIENT	METRIC	U.S.	%
Milk chocolate	200 g	7.05 oz	50%
Cocoa butter	200 g	7.05 oz	50%

1. Preheat a convection oven to 120°C/250°F.

2. Place the chocolate in a hotel pan in the warm oven.

3. Leave the chocolate in the oven for 2 hours, stirring it every 30 minutes.

4. Transfer the chocolate to a mélangeur to refine the chocolate (it gets somewhat grainy during the caramelization process). Add the melted cocoa butter and refine the chocolate for 3 hours.

5. While fluid, it can be used to spray the panna cotta; otherwise, reserve in a cool, dry place in an airtight container for up to 1 year.

CROISSANT CROUTON

YIELD: 400 G/14.11 OZ

INGREDIENT	METRIC	U.S.	%
Croissants	3 to 5, depending on the size	3 to 5, depending on the size	
Clarified butter, melted	100 g	3.53 oz	25%
Honey, warm	300 g	10.58 oz	75%

1. Slice the croissants 2 cm/.75 in thick with a serrated knife; only use the largest part of the croissant.

2. Preheat a convection oven to 160°C/325°F.

3. Brush the croissant slices with about 5 g/.17 oz clarified butter per side, and then brush each side with about 15 g/.5 oz of the warm honey. Place them on a sheet pan lined with a nonstick rubber mat.

4. Bake until golden, about 5 minutes, then flip them over, and bake for 5 more minutes or until golden brown.

5. Let the croissant slices cool to room temperature. Store in an airtight container at room temperature for service. Use for up to 2 days if they are still crisp the day after they are made.

NOTE *Source the fresh croissants from a reputable baker, not bagged from a supermarket. A quality croissant makes all the difference.*

DEVIL'S FOOD CAKE SOUP

YIELD: 1.01 KG/2 LB 3.52 OZ

INGREDIENT	METRIC	U.S.	%
Sugar	280 g	9.88 oz	27.7%
All-purpose flour	160 g	5.64 oz	15.83%
Cocoa powder	75 g	2.65 oz	7.42%
Baking soda	3 g	.11 oz	.3%
Baking powder	2 g	.07 oz	.2%
Salt	1 g	.04 oz	.1%
Eggs, at 21°C/70°F	100 g	3.53 oz	9.89%
Egg yolks, at 21°C/70°F	40 g	1.41 oz	3.96%
Butter, melted but cool	40 g	1.41 oz	3.96%
Buttermilk, at 21°C/70°F	160 g	5.64 oz	15.83%
Fresh brewed coffee, at 21°C/70°F	150 g	5.29 oz	14.84%
Water	350 g	12.34 oz	
Corn syrup	100 g	3.52 oz	

1. Line a half sheet pan with a nonstick rubber mat; spray the interior border with a light mist of nonstick oil spray.

2. Preheat a convection oven to 160°C/325°F.

3. Sift all of the dry ingredients onto a sheet of parchment paper.

4. Place the eggs and the egg yolks in a bowl large enough to hold all of the ingredients in the recipe, and then slowly whisk in the melted butter. Slowly whisk in the buttermilk and, finally, the coffee.

5. Whisk the dry ingredients into the emulsified liquid, whisking constantly until a homogenous mass is obtained.

6. Pour the batter onto the prepared sheet pan and spread it out evenly using an offset spatula.

7. Bake for 10 minutes, rotate the sheet pan, and bake for 7 to 9 more minutes or until the center of the cake springs back when gentle pressure is applied with the fingertips.

8. Let the cake cool to room temperature. Once it has cooled, break it into small pieces and put the pieces in a blender cup, along with the water and corn syrup. Blend on high speed until puréed. Adjust the consistency if necessary. It needs to be soup-like, not very loose but not very thick either; it will thicken as it sits, so you may need to add some water and stir it in during service.

9. Reserve at room temperature. Discard after 2 days. Do not refrigerate; refrigerating will slow down the softening of the frozen panna cotta when you assemble the dessert.

GOLDEN CARAMELIZED MILK CHOCOLATE DÉCOR

YIELD: 600 G/1 LB 5.16 OZ

INGREDIENT	METRIC	U.S.	%
Milk chocolate	400 g	14.11 oz	66.67%
Cocoa powder	200 g	7.05 oz	33.33%
Gold luster dust	as needed	as needed	

1. See the procedure for the caramelized milk chocolate on page 316.

2. Place 2 PVC tubes measuring 50 cm/20 in long by 5 cm/2 in diameter on a flat surface, parallel to each other, 10 cm/4 in apart; secure them to the work surface with tape. Cover the tubes with parchment paper.

3. Temper the milk chocolate and then stir in the cocoa powder. Place inside a piping bag fitted with a #2 plain piping tip.

4. Pipe irregular strands onto the PVC tube setup, going from one PVC tube across to the other; try to obtain sets of 3 to 4 strands of the chocolate-cocoa mixture. Make at least 10 sets (1 per dessert order).

5. Let them harden at room temperature.

6. Once they have hardened, dampen a cloth towel with warm water and rub the surface of each piece to smooth it out by rubbing it with the towel. Dip the cloth in warm water and wring it out between rubbing each piece of décor so that the warm water can help with smoothing out the surface of the chocolate.

7. Once all of the pieces are smooth, brush them with edible gold luster dust, taking care to remove any excess.

8. Reserve in a cool, dry area, preferably enclosed. Discard after 6 months.

SALTED PEANUT ICE CREAM BAR

YIELD: 1.01 KG/2 LB 3.52 OZ

INGREDIENT	METRIC	U.S.	%
Salted Peanut Butter			
Peanuts, toasted and warm	1 kg	2 lb 3.17 oz	99.01%
Fleur de sel	10 g	.35 oz	.99%
Salted Peanut Butter Ice Cream			
Milk	683 g	1 lb 8 oz	62.09%
Milk powder	64 g	2.26 oz	5.82%
Sugar	170 g	6 oz	15.45%
Ice cream stabilizer	3 g	.11 oz	.27%
Egg yolks	80 g	2.82 oz	7.27%
Salted Peanut Butter	100 g	3.53 oz	9.09%

1. **For the salted peanut butter:** Grind the peanuts with the salt in a Robot Coupe while the peanuts are still warm until completely smooth.

2. **For the salted peanut butter ice cream:** Follow the method for pistachio ice cream on page 227.

3. Age the base for least 4 hours before churning.

4. Place 10 rectangular stainless-steel molds measuring 2 cm/.75 in wide by 15 cm/6 in long by 2 cm/.75 in deep on top of a flat half sheet pan lined with a nonstick rubber mat in the freezer.

5. Churn the ice cream and pour it into a piping bag.

6. Pipe the ice cream into the frozen molds. Even out the top with an offset spatula.

7. Return the filled molds to the freezer to harden the ice cream.

8. Once the ice cream is hard, take the steel molds off by gently applying heat with a torch, trying to not get too close to the ice cream but focusing on the mold.

9. Take the mold off and return the ice cream rectangles to the freezer to harden. Once they have hardened again, keep them covered to prevent frost from accumulating on their surface.

10. After 2 days, melt the ice cream rectangles down and re-churn once more.

NOTE *The recipe for salted peanut butter yields much more than you need, but making smaller batches does not work well for grinding in a Robot Coupe. You will need some to make the Virginia peanut Genoa bread. The remainder can be used for other batches or purposes.*

TOASTED VIRGINIA PEANUT GENOA BREAD

YIELD: 980 G/2 LB 2.56 OZ

INGREDIENT	METRIC	U.S.	%
Almond paste	320 g	11.29 oz	32.65%
Salted Peanut Butter (page 258)	80 g	2.82 oz	8.16%
Eggs	250 g	8.82 oz	25.51%
Invert sugar	35 g	1.23 oz	3.57%
All-purpose flour	60 g	2.12 oz	6.12%
Butter, melted but cool	110 g	3.88 oz	11.22%
Virginia peanuts, toasted and coarsely chopped	125 g	4.41 oz	12.76%

1. Follow the method for the black sesame Genoa bread on page 243. Add the Virginia peanuts at the end of the mixing process.

2. Once the cake has cooled, cut it into rectangles measuring 2 cm/.75 in wide by 15 cm/6 in long by 5 mm/.25 in high.

3. Reserve in the refrigerator in an airtight container. Discard after 3 days.

RAISIN JELLY VEIL

YIELD: 454 G/1 LB

INGREDIENT	METRIC	U.S.	%
Raisin Stock			
Cola	1 kg	2 lb 3.27 oz	58.82%
Raisins	700 g	1 lb 8.69 oz	41.18%
Raisin Jelly Veil			
Raisin Stock	400 g	14.11 oz	88.07%
Sugar	50 g	1.76 oz	11.01%
Gellan gum	4 g	.15 oz	.92%

1. **For the raisin stock:** Combine the cola and raisins in a sauce pot and bring to a boil. Turn off the heat and cover the pot with plastic wrap. Steep for 30 minutes.

2. Strain the liquid through a fine-mesh sieve, pushing as much liquid out as possible.

3. Cool the liquid over an ice water bath. There should be about 500 g/1 lb 1.64 oz of the mixture left after steeping.

4. **For the raisin jelly veil:** Follow the method for the Chocolate Veil on page 226. The sugar is combined with the raisin stock in the sauce pot.

5. Once the gel has set, cut it into rectangles measuring 10 cm/4 in wide by 15 cm/6 in long.

6. Reserve the rectangles on the tray on which they were made. Keep covered during service. Discard after 3 days.

PEANUT BRITTLE

YIELD: 801 G/1 LB 12.16 OZ

INGREDIENT	METRIC	U.S.	%
Roasted and salted peanuts	290 g	10.23 oz	36.2%
Sugar	237 g	8.36 oz	29.59%
Corn syrup	257 g	9.07 oz	32.08%
Baking soda	17 g	.6 oz	2.12%

1. Combine the peanuts, sugar, and corn syrup in a 3.78-L/4-qt sauce pot.

2. Cook over medium-high heat while stirring with a heat-resistant spoon until the sugar begins to caramelize. Take the pot off the heat and stir in the baking soda.

3. Pour onto a greased marble surface or a sheet pan lined with a nonstick baking mat.

4. Let the brittle cool and then break it into bite-size pieces.

5. Reserve in a dehydrator set to 45°C/115°F during service. Brittle is very susceptible to moisture and will become tacky at the slightest increase in ambient humidity. Stored in an airtight container with silica gel in a cool, dry place, it can keep for a few months.

Ch 4

DESSERT BUFFETS

While the term *buffet* may or may not have a negative connotation because of its association with the "all-you-can-eat" establishment, there simply is no other term for this style of service. What does this style of service entail? It is food that is placed on display for the customers to help themselves at their discretion.

The food will often be completely finished and ready to eat; on some occasions there are "action stations," in which a cook (or chef) will put the finishing touches on a product, finish cooking an item, cut an item to order, or completely cook an item in front of the customer. A classic example of an action station is the omelet station. Having said that, it is important to remark that this style of service is mostly used in hotels, on cruises, and at banquet/catering halls, and to a much lesser degree in some types of restaurants.

Now, there is the wrong way to do a buffet, but there is also the right way: a way to make it a great and visually stunning piece. When focusing on desserts, there are a few points to keep in mind to understand what makes that difference:

■ There is no menu. Simply put, the customer chooses food based on what he or she sees. Of course, each item should have a sign in front of it describing what it is, but the visual impact comes first. For this reason alone, color and shape variety are important considerations, as well as placement on the table. How will you place the desserts on the table? Brown food next to brown food, or will you alternate colors? In some instances it is important to give the display a sense of movement; for example, using risers to place the trays that hold your desserts at different heights. Having those trays point in different directions will also give a sense of flow to the food. On the other hand, perfectly lined-up trays can also look great; it all depends on the visual effect you are going for. I personally prefer symmetry and clean, straight lines. Many decorative elements can be used; special lighting, linens, flowers, herbs, and serving utensils can all contribute to enhancing the look of your buffet.

■ In most cases, these desserts will not be finished *à la minute*. They will typically be completely finished and ready to be taken away by your customers. Keep in mind that these desserts will be sitting at room temperature; therefore you must make sure that they are not out for more than 4 hours at a time, since this may cause your desserts to start going bad and possibly make your customers ill, and that is never a good idea. However, you can add textural elements to these desserts like tuiles, pulled sugar, or lace cookies, since they will not be sitting in a moist, refrigerated area. These are all items that you cannot use in a refrigerated display but that are fine to use for desserts sitting in the open air since there is nothing to damage their texture, unless you happen to be in a humid area.

■ Speaking of open air, if your desserts are being displayed outdoors, you may want to consider covering your desserts to prevent vermin (flying insects and ants mostly) from coming in contact with them.

- The larger challenge with these desserts is this: The dessert needs to be shelf stable for up to 4 hours without losing its integrity. For most desserts this will be no problem as long as the room where they are sitting is properly air-conditioned. In fact, tempered desserts always taste better than those just out of the refrigerator. The mouth feel is smoother and the flavors are more pronounced.

- Another consideration is the vessel for these desserts. There are many options as far as materials go. The most common option is cardboard bases, which are available in a variety of shapes and sizes; there are alternatives to cardboard with materials that are reusable, recyclable, and even biodegradable, such as plastic, glass, bamboo, stainless steel, food-grade aluminum, and wood. As a matter of fact, since these desserts are meant to be consumed *in situ* (not "to go"), it is a reasonable idea not to use single-use bases, since reusable vessels can be washed and used again. On the other hand, be prepared for a lot of these vessels to disappear; they will frequently break or accidentally be thrown out.

- You should not only have a sign in front of each dessert, but should also have a member of your staff (or yourself) available to answer guests' questions and to simply be present; otherwise it looks like an abandoned table with food on it. This same person can also be responsible for replenishing desserts during service and making sure the display is not a mess. Customers will grab desserts, put them back, and move trays around. It is very similar to a retail environment, which can become very frustrating for the vendor but there really is nothing you can do to stop it; all you can do is put things back in place. On the other hand, you may want to have an action station, in which a dessert is finished or portioned for the guest. Some examples of this include cotton candy and crêpes. Even desserts that are classically considered tableside fare, such as cherries jubilee and bananas Foster, can be part of the dessert buffet. In this case, you will need to have a person working this section, and he or she can be responsible for all replenishing of trays and keeping the display neat.

- Portion size is also relevant. Consider that these desserts are generally built as a single piece with most of the components assembled and built together, as opposed to a plated dessert, where the components are made separately and will all come together at the last moment when the plate is being assembled to be sent out to the dining room. Keep in mind that buffet desserts must be "user-friendly"; they should be easy to pick up from their display tray and they should be easy to cut through with a fork, not complicated and cumbersome. When the fork or spoon goes through the dessert, it should do so with ease and without the dessert falling apart, which would make it a chore to eat instead of the pleasurable experi-ence it should always be. This is not to say that the dessert needs to be completely soft; it means that all of the components of the dessert should effortlessly yield to pressure, and this is possible even with solid components. The size can vary, but anywhere between 120 g/4.23 oz and 180 g/6.35 oz total weight is recommended (it can go up or down slightly).

- Finally, these desserts need to be coated or covered because, for the most part, desserts that are not coated tend to develop a skin on their surface and therefore will get a dried-out look. Glazes work well but velvet spray is even better, since velvet spray can also contribute to the texture of the dessert. Keeping desserts in an enclosed environment such as a box, jar, or container will also keep them fresher for longer. Now, not all desserts can be contained, but some can. This will also enhance the display and variety of your desserts. If you have any of these desserts left over after they have been displayed for 4 hours, discard them. Do not save them for another day.

BREAKFAST BAR: CRISPY WAFER AND MILK CHOCOLATE BASE | "FRENCH TOAST"

YIELD: 10 SERVINGS

WHY THESE FLAVORS WORK

The crispy base is made with feuilletine, which is essentially a thin wafer broken into small pieces. This emulates breakfast cereal without having a processed cereal taste; in fact, it is more of a textural component than a flavor per se. This base is made with milk chocolate as a binder and cinnamon, and it stays crisp for long periods of time. The brioche is also a textural component, but its reason for being is so that it is similar to French toast in texture, without the custard base. The brioche is soaked in a light and very fluid ganache, which gives the impression that it is soaked like a slice of French toast. The ganache is flavored with rum, cinnamon, and vanilla. All of these flavors are used in breakfast items; although you wouldn't necessarily have cereal followed by French toast, the dessert brings together flavors that are associated with breakfast, and it has a good textural balance as well. The milk chocolate is another textural component that binds well with the other flavors without dimming them; a darker chocolate would hide the important flavor notes of the dessert.

COMPONENTS

Crispy Wafer Morsels and Milk Chocolate Base (page 301)

"French Toast" in Milk Chocolate Shell (page 300)

Caramelized Milk Chocolate Velvet Spray (page 255)

Maple Gold Drop (page 301)

ASSEMBLY PROCEDURE

1. Place a square of crispy wafer morsels on top of the brioche. Let this set up in the refrigerator.

2. Turn the French toast bars out of their mold and onto a sheet pan lined with a nonstick rubber mat. Reserve in a freezer for about 30 minutes.

3. Meanwhile, melt the milk chocolate spray and set up a spray station, a surface that should be covered with plastic to keep the shop clean where you can spray the French toast.

4. Fill a compressor canister and spray the French toast with an even coating of spray. Keep the compressor gun at least 60 cm/24 in from the French toast to obtain a velvety smooth look.

5. Transfer the bars to a base for display.

6. Apply a single drop of maple gold on the front left corner of the bar using an eye dropper. Display.

MEYER LEMON CREAM | WILD BLUEBERRY COMPOTE | CHOCOLATE SOIL | LAVENDER-SCENTED BOX

YIELD: 10 SERVINGS

WHY THESE FLAVORS WORK

Meyer lemons and blueberries are a classic combination. They work well together because the citrus notes and acidity of the lemon enhance the flavor of the blueberries. It is similar to the combination of lemon and huckleberries. The chocolate acts as a third frontal flavor, but it is also there for texture. The micro basil is sweet and is often used for dessert applications. It has grassy notes that act as background flavors that simply serve to strengthen the frontal flavors.

COMPONENTS

Meyer Lemon Cream (page 302)

Wild Blueberry Compote (page 301)

Green Velvet Spray (page 302)

Chocolate Soil (page 302)

Micro basil

Fresh lavender

ASSEMBLY PROCEDURE

1. Lightly coat the special plastic molds with a light mist of "de-mold spray" (see page 521 for resources for the molds and the spray). These molds are made of thin polycarbonate and come in a variety of shapes; this particular shape is made to look like a small hill. The molds can be reused if maintained properly. Place them all on a sheet pan.

2. Fill the molds three-quarters of the way with the Meyer lemon cream. Insert a frozen blueberry compote inclusion into the cream. Even out the top of the mold with an offset spatula so that it is flat. Freeze to harden.

3. Unmold the cream by dipping the mold in slightly warm water. Turn the mold over onto a sheet pan lined with a nonstick rubber mat and gently push down on the mold. It should release easily like ice from an ice tray; if it doesn't, then the water may have been too cold or the mold should have spent some more time in the warm water. Return the frozen unmolded Meyer lemon creams to the freezer to harden completely.

4. Set up a spray station, a surface that should be covered with plastic to keep the shop clean where you can spray the lemon creams.

5. Fill a compressor canister and spray the lemon creams with an even coating of the green velvet spray. Keep the compressor gun at least 60 cm/24 in from the lemon creams to obtain a velvety smooth look.

6. Place each sprayed frozen cream inside the serving box it will be displayed in.

7. Surround the cream with 60 g/2.11 oz of chocolate soil.

8. Put 2 of the micro basil leaves on the dessert (one on the actual dessert, one in the soil).

9. Using the Volcano Vaporizer, scent the boxes with lavender. You need a total of 30 g/1.06 oz of lavender.

10. Reserve in the refrigerator until ready to display.

64% DARK CHOCOLATE MOUSSE | CRÈME FRAÎCHE | LUXARDO CHERRIES | CHOCOLATE BLACKOUT CAKE

YIELD: 10 SERVINGS

WHY THESE FLAVORS WORK

This dessert is inspired by the Black Forest cake, a classic cake that combines the flavors of chocolate, cherries, and cream. Cherries and chocolate play off each other well, with the intense cherry notes enhanced by the dark chocolate. The cream component is a basic background flavor that helps smooth other flavors out.

COMPONENTS

Chocolate Blackout Cake with Luxardo Cherries and Crème Fraîche (page 303)
Dark Chocolate Mousse (page 304)
Shiny Chocolate Glaze (page 304)
Golden Chocolate Plaque (page 305)

ASSEMBLY PROCEDURE

1. Line a flat half sheet pan with a nonstick rubber mat and place 10 square molds measuring 9 cm/3.5 in square by 2.5 cm/1 in deep on the mat. Line the inside of each mold with a strip of acetate.

2. Cut out ten 7.50-cm/3-in squares of the chocolate blackout cake with Luxardo cherries and crème fraîche using a square cutter. Reserve frozen.

3. Pipe enough dark chocolate mousse into each mold to fill it one-third of the way.

4. Place the cut-out cakes on top of the mousse and push them in, crème fraîche side first. The mousse should push out the sides of the cake to the top of the mold. If it does not, then pipe more mousse in. Even out the mousse on the top of the mold using an offset spatula. Freeze this setup.

5. Once it is frozen, take the frames off, as well as the acetate strips. Transfer to a wire rack with 7.5 cm/3 in space between them and reserve frozen.

6. Meanwhile, bring the shiny glaze up to about 40°C/105°F by placing it in a bowl over a hot water bath.

7. Take the chocolate mousse squares out of the freezer. Pour an even coat of shiny glaze over the entire surface of the mousse, letting it drip over. Before the glaze sets, push each mousse forward on the wire rack about 7.5 cm/3 in; this helps prevent "feet" from forming at its base.

8. Transfer the glazed mousse to their display bases.

9. Apply the gold chocolate plaque. Reserve refrigerated until ready to display.

PEANUT BUTTER AND MASCARPONE CREAM | PEANUT PRALINE | RELIANT GRAPE JELLY

YIELD: 10 SERVINGS

WHY THESE FLAVORS WORK

Peanut butter has toasted peanut flavors but also a smooth mouth feel that is hard to replicate. The grape jelly, usually made with Concord grapes, adds a sweetness and mild sourness that smoothes out the fattiness from the peanut butter. This dessert uses Reliant grapes, which are lighter in color than Concord grapes and have a more pronounced grape flavor. The peanut praline adds a much-needed crunch to an otherwise soft dessert.

COMPONENTS

Peanut Butter and Mascarpone Cream (page 306)

Peanut Praline (page 306)

Peanut Butter Velvet Spray (page 306)

Reliant Grape Jelly (page 305)

Peanut Brittle (page 259)

ASSEMBLY PROCEDURE

1. Line 10 molds measuring 2.5 cm/1 in wide by 6.25 cm/2.5 in long by 5 cm/2 in deep with a strip of acetate. Place them on a flat sheet pan lined with a nonstick rubber mat.

2. Pipe enough of the peanut butter and mascarpone cream into each mold to fill it 3 cm/1.25 in high. Let it set in the refrigerator for 20 minutes. Place a rectangle of peanut praline at the center of the cream and push it through without letting it go all the way to the bottom of the dessert. Even out the top of the mold using an offset spatula. Freeze to harden.

3. Meanwhile, make (or melt if it is already made) the peanut velvet spray; keep the spray warm. Set up a spray station, a surface that should be covered with plastic to keep the shop clean where you can spray the peanut butter cream.

4. Unmold the frozen peanut butter cream onto a sheet pan lined with a nonstick rubber mat; return to the freezer to harden. Fill a compressor canister and spray the creams with an even coating of peanut butter spray. Keep the compressor gun at least 60 cm/24 in from the creams to obtain a velvety smooth look.

5. Transfer the creams to their display bases to thaw. Meanwhile, apply the frozen grape jelly to the top of the dessert and allow it to thaw as well. Once both items are thawed, keep them refrigerated until ready to display.

6. Once they are ready to be displayed, place a piece of peanut praline over the top of the dessert.

WHITE MISO "POT DE CRÈME" | GREEN TEA GÉNOISE CRUMBS | KUMQUAT MARMALADE | KUMQUAT JELLY

YIELD: 10 SERVINGS

WHY THESE FLAVORS WORK

In very general terms, flavors from a particular area may go well together, with the emphasis on "may." In this case, these are Asian ingredients that happen to get along well. White miso, more a taste (umami) than a flavor (caramel-like), helps really round out all of the flavors in this dessert. The green tea is the subtlest flavor, with grassy, herbal notes, and the kumquat is the foremost frontal flavor, adding citrus sweetness to the dessert.

COMPONENTS

Kumquat Marmalade (page 307)

White Miso "Pot de Crème" (page 307)

Green Tea Génoise Crumbs (page 308)

Kumquat Jelly Disk (page 308)

Silver leaf (see Resources, page 520)

ASSEMBLY PROCEDURE

1. Spoon 30 g/1.06 oz of kumquat marmalade inside a cup or bowl.

2. Make the white miso "pot de crème" and pour about 75 g/2.5 oz of it on top of the marmalade. Let it set in the refrigerator. The top layer may form a skin; therefore it should be coated with the green tea génoise crumbs as soon as possible.

3. Spoon 15 g/.5 oz of green tea génoise crumbs over the pot de crème and even it out so that there is a straight layer of crumbs.

4. Place a kumquat jelly disk over the crumbs.

5. Place a small piece of silver leaf over the disk. Reserve refrigerated or display.

NOTE

You will need about a half a sheet of silver leaf for all 10 desserts.

REINE-DES-PRÉS CREMA CATALANA

YIELD: 10 SERVINGS

WHY THESE FLAVORS WORK	Reine-des-prés is a flower that is in the *Rosaceae* (rose) family and is used to flavor pastry products. As a flower, it has a floral aroma; it sounds redundant but there is no other way to describe its flavor. A classic *crema catalana* is a custard that is flavored with cinnamon, lemon, and orange. In this case, it will be flavored with reine-des-prés (see Resources, page 520).
COMPONENTS	**Turbinado sugar** **Reine-des-Prés Crema Catalana** (page 309)
ASSEMBLY PROCEDURE	1. Sprinkle an even layer of turbinado sugar over the surface of the portioned pastry cream. 2. Caramelize it to order using an electric iron; this should be done as part of an "action station," where things are done to order. You cannot caramelize the sugar too far ahead of time, since this will dissolve the sugar and take its crispness away.

PINK GUAVA CREAM | VANILLA CHIFFON CAKE | WHITE CHOCOLATE–COVERED PUFFED RICE

YIELD: 10 SERVINGS

WHY THESE FLAVORS WORK

The main flavor here is that of the pink guava, which is very intense and clearly identifiable. The vanilla and white chocolate simply round it out and temper it while the puffed rice is a textural component.

COMPONENTS

Vanilla Chiffon Cake Disks (page 310)
Pink Guava Cream (page 309)
Red Velvet Spray (page 248)

ASSEMBLY PROCEDURE

1. Have 10 chiffon cake disks available.

2. Lightly spray a coat of "de-mold spray" into 20 of the special pillow-shaped molds (see page 520 for resources on the de-mold spray and the molds). Put them on a sheet pan. You will need 1 molds per piece (a top piece and a bottom piece).

3. Fill the molds two-thirds full with the guava cream. Place a vanilla chiffon disk on top of the cream and push it down so that the cream comes up the sides of the cake. Attach both pieces together (top and bottom); the excess cream on top will adhere both pieces together.

4. Place the molds in a freezer to harden. Meanwhile, put a sheet pan lined with a nonstick rubber mat in a freezer.

5. Once the creams have hardened, push them out of the molds. If they do not come out cleanly, they weren't hard enough. You may need to dip them in tepid water to loosen them up slightly.

6. Place them on the frozen prepared sheet pan as you take them out of the molds and keep them frozen.

7. Set up a spray station, a surface that should be covered with plastic to keep the shop clean where you can spray the cream.

8. Fill a compressor canister and spray the creams with an even coating of red velvet spray. Keep the compressor gun at least 60 cm/24 in from the creams to obtain a velvety smooth look.

9. Transfer the pieces to their serving bases. Allow to thaw in the refrigerator. Present to display and serve or reserve in refrigeration for up to 36 hours.

VANILLA MASCARPONE | STRAWBERRY COMPOTE | CRÈME FRAÎCHE CAKE

YIELD: 10 SERVINGS

WHY THESE FLAVORS WORK	Vanilla is a flavor that goes very well with practically anything, since it is more of a neutral background flavor that works as an enhancer. Strawberries and cream, in this case mascarpone, are a classic flavor composition, since the tartness of a strawberry is offset by the richness of the dairy component. The crème fraîche cake is a textural component more than a flavor.
COMPONENTS	**White and Black Striped Tube** (page 312) **Vanilla Mascarpone Cream** (page 313) **Strawberry Compote Tube** (page 312) **Crème Fraîche Cake** (page 311) **Red Tube Caps** (page 313)
ASSEMBLY PROCEDURE	1. Fill a white and black striped tube halfway full with the vanilla mascarpone cream. 2. Slide a tube of the frozen strawberry compote inside the tube, and then a rectangle of frozen crème fraîche cake directly on top of the compote tube. This should be enough to force the vanilla mascarpone cream up and fill the chocolate tube all the way; if not, simply pipe more vanilla mascarpone cream to fill it. 3. Let the cream set with the tubes in a standing position in the refrigerator. 4. Once set, place the red tube caps on both sides of the openings in the tubes. 5. Reserve in the refrigerator or display.

CARAMEL MOUSSE | CINNAMON STREUSEL | CHOCOLATE GLAZE | RICE MILK VEIL

WHY THESE FLAVORS WORK

The frontal flavors are cinnamon and chocolate and the background, supporting flavors are caramel and rice milk. The particular flavor of cinnamon has often been used in combination with chocolate because chocolate can stand up to it and benefit from it without giving up its own particular flavor. Rice milk and cinnamon are often used together in the rice milk drink horchata. Caramel and dark chocolate have been used together very frequently, and particularly dark chocolate, since caramel and its dairy flavors help tone down some bitterness from the chocolate.

COMPONENTS

Chocolate Base (page 314)

Cinnamon Streusel (page 314)

Caramel Mousse (page 315)

Shiny Chocolate Glaze (page 304)

Rice Milk Veil (page 315)

ASSEMBLY PROCEDURE

1. Place ten 5-cm/2-in diameter stainless-steel or PVC rings on a flat sheet pan lined with a nonstick rubber mat.

2. Pour 20 g/.7 oz of the chocolate base into each of the steel rings and then spoon 30 g/1.06 oz of cinnamon streusel on top of it before it sets. Once set, remove the rings. Reserve in the refrigerator.

3. Place a set of 10 flexible silicone dome molds measuring 7.5 cm/3 in diameter by 5 cm/2 in deep on top of a flat half sheet pan. Pour the caramel mousse into the silicone molds. Do not fill the molds to the top; only fill them about 2.5 cm/1 in high using about 60 g/2.12 oz of mousse. Place a disk of chocolate with the cinnamon streusel on top of the mousse, streusel side down. Let the mousse set in a freezer.

4. Meanwhile, bring the shiny chocolate glaze to 38°C/100°F in a bowl set over a hot water bath.

5. Once the mousse domes are frozen, turn them out of the molds onto a wire rack. Glaze them completely with the chocolate glaze.

6. Transfer the glazed domes to a sheet pan lined with a nonstick rubber mat.

7. When ready to finish, transfer the domes to their intended display bases.

8. Place a rice milk veil rectangle on top of the dome. Using a very sharp, clean, and new razor blade, cut a 2.5-cm/1-in long slit on the veil directly at the center/top of the dome.

9. Display or reserve in the refrigerator.

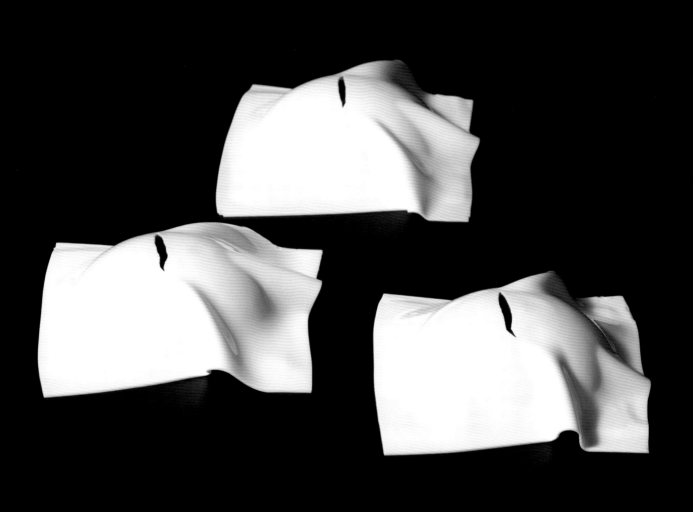

CARAMELIZED WHITE CHOCOLATE MOUSSE | TOASTED BAGUETTE PURÉE | SCOTTISH SHORTBREAD | CARAMELIZED MILK CHOCOLATE LEAF | QUENELLE OF SWEET CRÈME FRAÎCHE

YIELD: 10 SERVINGS

WHY THESE FLAVORS WORK	Most of the items in this dessert have undergone the Maillard reaction. That flavor alone is the common thread of the dessert, even though they all have their own distinct flavors. The crème fraîche adds a note of acidity, but not too much. That acidity helps enhance all the flavors that compose the dessert.
COMPONENTS	**Scottish Shortbread Base** (page 316) **Toasted Baguette Purée Squares** (page 317) **Caramelized White Chocolate Mousse** (page 317) **Caramelized White Chocolate Velvet Spray** (page 255) **Caramelized Milk Chocolate Leaf** (page 318) **Crème fraîche**
ASSEMBLY PROCEDURE	1. Place a thin rectangle of Scottish shortbread inside the presentation dish. 2. Place a frozen square of toasted baguette purée over the Scottish shortbread. Reserve frozen. 3. Make the caramelized white chocolate mousse and pour about 75 g/2.5 oz into the dish, covering the other two components completely. 4. Even out the surface with an offset spatula. Freeze this setup. 5. Set up a spray station, a surface that should be covered with plastic to keep the shop clean where you can spray the mousse. 6. Fill a compressor canister, spray the surface of the mousse, and reserve it in the refrigerator. Keep the compressor gun at least 60 cm/24 in from the mousse to obtain a velvety smooth look. 7. Place a chocolate leaf at the center of the mousse. 8. Whip the crème fraîche to stiff peaks, and then spoon a 45 g/1.5 oz quenelle inside of the décor. You will need a total of 450 g/15.87 oz of crème fraîche for ten desserts. 9. Reserve refrigerated or display.

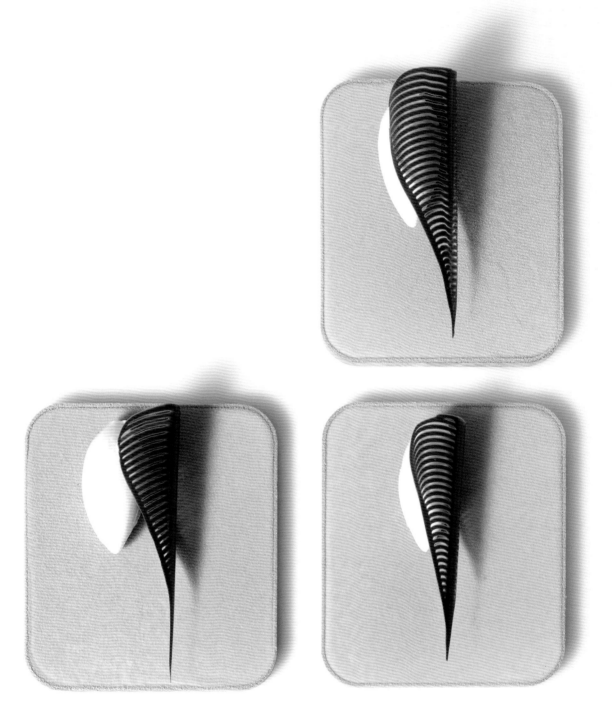

CITRON CREAM | ANGEL FOOD CAKE | BALSAMIC VINEGAR REDUCTION

YIELD: 10 SERVINGS

WHY THESE FLAVORS WORK

The particular flavor of citron is unique and so subtle that it is not necessary to confuse those who eat it with either subtler or more frontal flavors; all that is needed is some acid, in this case reduced and sweetened balsamic vinegar, to enhance the flavor for the citron.

COMPONENTS

Angel Food Cake (page 318)
Citron Cream (page 319)
Pure White Glaze (page 319)
Balsamic Vinegar Reduction (page 320)

ASSEMBLY PROCEDURE

1. Line 10 rectangular molds measuring 5 cm/2 in wide by 10 cm/4 in long by 2.5 cm/1 in high with a strip of acetate. Place them on a flat half sheet pan lined with a nonstick rubber mat.

2. Put a rectangle of angel food cake on the bottom of the mold. Put 10 g/.35 oz of candied citron of top of the cake in an even layer.

3. Pipe the citron cream around and over the angel food cake to the top of the mold. Even it out with an offset spatula and freeze.

4. Bring the pure white glaze to 35°C/95°F; meanwhile, put the frozen citron creams on a wire rack. Place the wire rack on a sheet pan lined with plastic wrap.

5. Pour the glaze over the frozen citron creams to coat them completely. To prevent feet from forming at the bottom of the desserts, slide a small offset spatula under each dessert and slide it 5 cm/2 in in any direction while on the wire rack before the glaze sets completely. This will give it an even-looking base.

6. Transfer the desserts to their display bases.

7. Drizzle a thin, straight line, about 3 g/.1 oz, of the balsamic reduction across the top of the desserts. Wait until they are completely thawed before they are displayed. Thaw in the refrigerator.

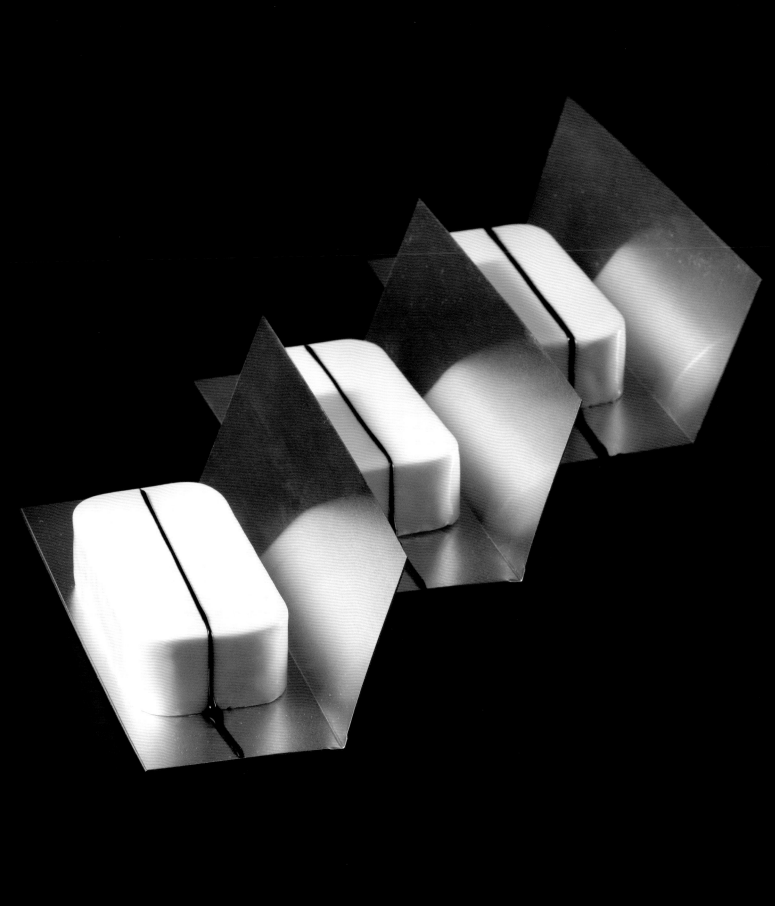

DOUGLAS FIR ICE CREAM

YIELD: 10 SERVINGS

WHY THESE FLAVORS WORK	There isn't really an interaction of flavors in this ice cream, just one flavor that happens to be frontal. It doesn't need much else.
COMPONENTS	**Douglas Fir Ice Cream Base** (page 320)
ASSEMBLY PROCEDURE	1. Freeze 120 g/4.23 oz containers before churning the ice cream base so it does not melt when it comes into contact with the containers.
	2. Churn the ice cream base and pour into a piping bag.
	3. Pipe into the frozen containers. Reserve frozen.
	4. Fill a rectangular display base with crushed dry ice. Place a fine-mesh mat over it. Put the frozen containers over the mat. Refresh the dry ice every hour or so.

ARBORIO RICE PUDDING | PASSION FRUIT CURD

WHY THESE FLAVORS WORK	The rice pudding is sweet and flavored with vanilla bean. This makes it an ideal pairing for something that is somewhat tart and tropical like the passion fruit curd, which has a frontal flavor. The creamy consistency of the pudding and the smooth curd are given texture with the white chocolate plaque, which is there mostly for texture rather than flavor.
COMPONENTS	**Arborio Rice Pudding** (page 321) **Passion Fruit Curd Rings** (page 321) **White and Red Chocolate Plaque** (page 322)
ASSEMBLY PROCEDURE	1. Pour 60g/2 oz to 75 g/2.5 oz of the rice pudding inside the passion fruit curd ring. Even out the top so that it is flat. 2. Remove the mold from around the passion fruit curd and then remove the acetate strip that surrounds the curd. 3. Place a chocolate plaque on top of the rice pudding. Reserve refrigerated or display.

NUTELLA CREAM | BANANA BUTTER | CRISPY HAZELNUT GIANDUJA

YIELD: 10 SERVINGS

WHY THESE FLAVORS WORK

Banana and hazelnut are both frontal flavors that do not cover each other up; they enhance each other. They are both smooth components, highly rich, but the nut flavor of the hazelnut truly pushes and enhances that of the banana; it is similar to the effect of peanut butter and banana together.

COMPONENTS

Nutella Cream (page 323)

Banana Butter Inclusion (page 322)

Crispy Hazelnut Gianduja Base (page 323)

Assorted Colors Velvet Spray (page 323)

ASSEMBLY PROCEDURE

1. Pour the Nutella cream into the large "Lego" mold (see Resources, page 520), filling halfway only while it is most fluid so it can fill all of the nooks and prevent formation of air pockets. Let it set slightly in the refrigerator.

2. Put the frozen banana butter inclusion at the center of the Nutella cream, pushing slightly into the cream. Fill the mold with Nutella cream almost all the way to the top.

3. Place the crispy gianduja base at the top of the mold, pushing in slightly. The cream should come up just to the top of the mold. If it does not, then fill it with more cream. Make sure the base is at the top of the mold.

4. Freeze to harden. Set up a spray station, a surface that should be covered with plastic to keep the shop clean where you can spray the cream. Fill a compressor canister with velvet spray.

5. Once hardened, unmold each piece and spray them in assorted colors of velvet spray, one color at a time with an even coating of spray. Keep the compressor gun at least 60 cm/24 in from the ice cream to obtain a velvety smooth look.

6. Thaw in the refrigerator and then reserve refrigerated or display.

LEMON MERINGUE "TART"

YIELD: 10 SERVINGS

WHY THESE FLAVORS WORK

This dessert is based on the classic lemon meringue pie, except it looks nothing like it. The somewhat acidic and pronounced lemon curd is tamed by the Italian meringue, which does not contribute much flavor (except for some of the toasted meringue flavor on the surface); it contributes more texture. The sablé breton adds texture, being the only solid texture in the dessert, but it also has its own flavor, less pronounced than the lemon curd. This is a very simple dessert but with components that have a great balance of flavor.

COMPONENTS

Sablé Breton (page 324)

Lemon Curd (page 325)

Italian Meringue (page 325)

ASSEMBLY PROCEDURE

1. Assemble 10 Plexiglas bases measuring 2.5 cm/1 in wide by 10 cm/4 in long by 2 cm/.75 in deep internally.

2. Place the sablé breton rectangle inside the base.

3. Pipe about 90 g/3.17 oz of the lemon curd to the top of the sablé. Even out the top with an offset spatula.

4. Pipe the Italian meringue on the surface of the curd using a #4 plain piping tip, covering the curd completely.

5. Toast the top of the meringue with a torch.

6. Reserve in the refrigerator until ready to serve and display. Discard after 24 hours.

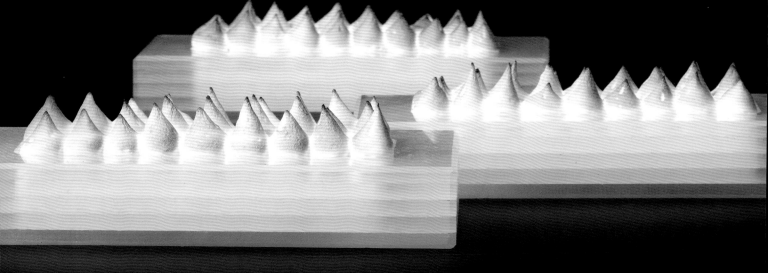

TOASTED PAIN AU LEVAIN | CONFITURE DE LAIT | FLEUR DE SEL

YIELD : ABOUT 40 SERVINGS

WHY THESE FLAVORS WORK	This is one of the simplest and purest forms of flavor combination; they are so different and distinct yet work so well together. The bread has sour notes from the pre-ferment that is used to leaven it, as well as Maillard notes. This is tempered by the sweetness and flavor of the confiture de lait, which is a form of dulce de leche and essentially a milk caramel. The salt accents all of the flavors but also tempers the sweetness of the confiture.
COMPONENTS	**Toasted Pain au Levain** (page 325) **Confiture de Lait** (page 326) **Fleur de sel**
PLATING PROCEDURE	1. Assemble the toasted and sliced pain au levain in a standing position. 2. Spoon 10 g/.35 oz of confiture de lait in front of every slice of pain au levain. You may alternatively spoon it on top of the toasted bread. 3. Sprinkle a pinch of fleur de sel over each of the confiture servings (you will need 8 g/.28 oz total). Serve.

CAFFEINATED NUNS (ESPRESSO RELIGIEUSES)

YIELD: 10 SERVINGS

WHY THESE FLAVORS WORK	Coffee and chocolate work extremely well together since they both share bitter taste notes; they are also very similar in their physical composition and in the way they are treated once harvested (dried, fermented, toasted, ground). Coffee and chocolate have been sharing the same plate for a very long time.
COMPONENTS	**Espresso Pastry Cream** (page 326) **10 small and 10 large Pâte à Choux Puffs** (page 327) **10 large and 10 small Chocolate Glaze Disks** (page 328) **½ sheet gold leaf**
ASSEMBLY PROCEDURE	1. Pipe 50 g/1.75 oz of the espresso pastry cream into each large choux puff and 30 g/1.06 oz into each small choux puff. Reserve chilled until ready to apply the glaze. 2. Place the frozen chocolate glaze disks over the filled choux puffs (large on large and small on small). 3. Once the glaze disks thaw, place the small choux on top of the large choux, centered as best as possible. 4. Put a small piece of gold leaf on top of the small choux puff.
NOTE	Religieuses *is the name that is used for this classic French pastry. It means, loosely translated, "nuns." One would assume that it is a humorous view of nuns, but literally it means "religious."*

COCONUT AVALANCHE

YIELD: 10 SERVINGS

WHY THESE FLAVORS WORK

This dessert is based on a classic candy bar that contains almonds, coconut, and chocolate. In this bar, the almonds are not toasted; they are mostly there for texture and a little flavor. Here, almond praline pearls are used for flavor and crunch. Almond, coconut, and chocolate go well together because even though the almond and the coconut are background flavors, they are strengthened by the chocolate and play off each other well when used in the right amounts.

COMPONENTS

Feuilletine coated in silver luster dust (see Resources, page 520)

Coconut Cream (page 329)

Coconut Dacquoise (page 328)

Coconut milk powder (see Resources, page 520)

Chocolate Stars Coated in Edible Copper Luster Dust (page 329)

ASSEMBLY PROCEDURE

1. Assemble 10 plastic cube containers (see Resources, page 520). Spoon 30 g/1.06 oz of the feuilletine into each container. Make the coconut cream, and pour 50 g/1.75 oz of coconut cream into each container.

2. Place a square of coconut dacquoise on top of the coconut cream. Cover the dacquoise with about 85 g/3 oz additional coconut cream. Use an offset spatula to even out the top.

3. Coat the surface of the coconut cream with an even layer of about 10 g/.35 oz coconut milk powder.

4. Place 1 chocolate star on the surface of the coconut milk powder.

5. Reserve refrigerated until ready to display.

MILK CHOCOLATE SHELL

YIELD: 700 G/1 LB 8.64 OZ

INGREDIENT	METRIC	U.S.	%
Milk chocolate, tempered	700 g	1 lb 8.64 oz	100%

1. Brush the mold (see Resources, page 520) with the tempered chocolate and then fill it. The internal dimensions of the chocolate mold are 9.5 cm/3.75 in by 9.5 cm/3.75 in by 2 cm/.75 in deep. Turn the mold over and let the excess pour out. Follow the procedure for molded chocolates on page 42.

2. Reserve the shells inside the molds in a cool, dry place until needed.

"FRENCH TOAST" MAPLE MASCARPONE CREAM

YIELD: 1.10 KG/2 LB 6.72 OZ

INGREDIENT	METRIC	U.S.	%
Mascarpone	920 g	2 lb .32 oz	83.64%
Maple sugar	170 g	6 oz	15.45%
Gelatin sheets, silver, bloomed in cold water, excess water squeezed out	10 g	.35 oz	.91%
Brioche loaf, sliced .75 cm/.25 in thick, crust removed	10	10	

1. Combine the mascarpone, maple sugar, and gelatin sheets in a bowl and melt gently over a hot water bath.

2. Meanwhile, place the brioche slices in a hotel pan lined with plastic wrap. A normal Pullman brioche loaf slice is about 10 cm /4 in square. You will need to trim each slice to be 8.75 cm/3.5 in square.

3. Pour half of the warm mascarpone cream on top of the brioche slices and allow it to soak in. Refrigerate.

4. Let the remaining cream cool, then pour it into the chocolate shell to fill 5 mm/.2 in. Transfer to the refrigerator to set.

5. Put 1 soaked brioche square inside each chocolate shell; push down to flatten the brioche. Reserve in the refrigerator for up to 1 week. Meanwhile, make the crispy wafer morsels and milk chocolate base.

CRISPY WAFER MORSELS AND MILK CHOCOLATE BASE

YIELD: 470 G/1 LB .58 OZ

INGREDIENT	METRIC	U.S.	%
Milk chocolate	300 g	10.58 oz	63.83%
Canola oil	60 g	2.12 oz	12.77%
Ground cinnamon	10 g	.35 oz	2.13%
Feuilletine (wafer morsels)	100 g	3.53 oz	21.28%

1. Line a flat half sheet pan with a nonstick rubber mat. Place a 3-mm/.1-in frame inside it. Melt the chocolate together with the oil.

2. Add the cinnamon and fold in the feuilletine.

3. Pour into the frame and even it out with an offset spatula. Refrigerate to harden.

4. Once hardened, cut into 8.75-cm/3.5-in squares.

5. Place the squares at the bottom of the chocolate shells.

6. Flip the shells over and unmold.

7. Place the shells on a flat sheet pan lined with a rubber mat and freeze.

8. Once chilled, spray the shells with velvet spray. Once the shells are sprayed, reserve in refrigeration until ready to serve.

WILD BLUEBERRY COMPOTE

YIELD: 302 G/10.67 OZ

INGREDIENT	METRIC	U.S.	%
Blueberries	175 g	6.17 oz	57.85%
Sugar	90 g	3.17 oz	29.75%
Water	35 g	1.23 oz	11.57%
Salt	2 g	.07 oz	.66%

1. Combine all of the ingredients and bring them to a boil. Cook until the liquid is reduced by half, about 10 minutes.

2. Portion the compote into half sphere molds measuring 2.5 cm/1 in diameter by 2.5 cm/1 in deep and freeze. Once frozen, they can be unmolded. Reserve frozen for up to 2 months.

MAPLE GOLD DROP

YIELD: 11 G/.39 OZ

INGREDIENT	METRIC	U.S.	%
Gold powder	1 g	.04 oz	9.09%
Maple syrup	10 g	.35 oz	90.91%

1. Combine both ingredients and stir.

2. Reserve in the refrigerator. This mixture will keep indefinitely if kept refrigerated.

MEYER LEMON CREAM

YIELD: 1.28 KG/2 LB 13.12 OZ

INGREDIENT	METRIC	U.S.	%
Meyer lemon juice	160 g	5.64 oz	12.5%
Sugar	240 g	8.47 oz	18.75%
Eggs	160 g	5.64 oz	12.5%
Butter	200 g	7.05 oz	15.63%
Heavy cream	500 g	17.64 oz	39.06%
Gelatin sheets, silver, bloomed in cold water, excess moisture squeezed out	15 g	.53 oz	1.17%
Meyer lemon zest	5 g	.18 oz	.39%

1. Combine the lemon juice, sugar, and eggs in a bowl and cook over a hot water bath until the mixture reaches 80°C/175°F. After it reaches that temperature, stir for 3 minutes over the hot water bath.

2. Take the bowl off the hot water bath and stir in the butter until it is completely dissolved.

3. Let the curd cool at room temperature.

4. Meanwhile, whip the heavy cream to medium-soft peaks and reserve refrigerated.

5. Add one-quarter of the curd to the bloomed gelatin and melt over a hot water bath. Stir the remaining curd into it.

6. Stir one-quarter of the whipped cream vigorously into the curd with a whisk.

7. Fold half of the remaining whipped cream into the curd with a rubber spatula. Fold in the rest of the whipped cream and the lemon zest.

8. Use the mixture immediately to fill the molds.

GREEN VELVET SPRAY

YIELD: 450 G/15.87 OZ

INGREDIENT	METRIC	U.S.	%
White chocolate	200 g	7.05 oz	44.44%
Cocoa butter	200 g	7.05 oz	44.44%
Natural green food coloring	50 g	1.76 oz	11.11%

1. Combine all of the ingredients in a bowl and melt over a hot water bath.

2. Transfer to an airtight container and reserve at room temperature for up to 1 year.

CHOCOLATE SOIL

YIELD: 760 G/1 LB 10.72 OZ

INGREDIENT	METRIC	U.S.	%
Sugar	200 g	7.05 oz	26.32%
Almond flour	200 g	7.05 oz	26.32%
All-purpose flour	120 g	4.23 oz	15.79%
Cocoa powder	88 g	3.1 oz	11.58%
Butter, melted and cooled	140 g	4.94 oz	18.42%
Salt	12 g	.42 oz	1.58%

Follow the procedure for the chocolate soil on page 432.

CHOCOLATE BLACKOUT CAKE WITH LUXARDO CHERRIES & CRÈME FRAÎCHE

YIELD: 1.99 KG/4 LB 6.24 OZ

INGREDIENT	METRIC	U.S.	%
All-purpose flour	150 g	5.29 oz	7.53%
Cocoa powder	60 g	2.12 oz	3.01%
Salt	5 g	.16 oz	.23%
Baking soda	8 g	.26 oz	.38%
Baking powder	6 g	.21 oz	.3%
Sugar	300 g	10.58 oz	15.05%
Eggs	125 g	4.41 oz	6.27%
Buttermilk	185 g	6.53 oz	9.28%
Cold brewed coffee	170 g	6 oz	8.53%
Butter, melted but cool	85 g	3 oz	4.26%
Luxardo cherries, drained	300 g	10.58 oz	15.05%
Crème fraîche	500 g	1 lb 1.64 oz	25.09%
Sugar	100 g	3.53 oz	5.02%
Dark chocolate, melted	150 g	5.3 oz	

1. Preheat a convection oven to 160°C/325°F.

2. Lightly grease a half sheet pan with nonstick oil spray, and line it with a nonstick rubber mat.

3. Sift the flour, cocoa, salt, baking soda, baking powder, and sugar. Place in a large bowl.

4. Combine the eggs, buttermilk, and coffee in a mixer bowl and whisk together to obtain a homogenous mix.

5. Place the bowl with the dry ingredients on an electric mixer fitted with the paddle attachment. Mix on low speed and slowly pour in the egg mixture.

6. Once the liquid has been completely incorporated, pour in the butter and mix until it has combined completely.

7. Pour the batter into the prepared sheet pan. Sprinkle the cherries on top of the batter in a single, even layer. Bake until the cake springs back when it yields to gentle pressure, 8 to 12 minutes.

8. Let the cake cool at room temperature, and then refrigerate it.

9. Meanwhile, whip the crème fraîche with the sugar until stiff and then spread it on top of the cake in an even layer.

10. Place the cake in a freezer to harden. Using an offset spatula, flip the cake over and spread the melted chocolate over the entire cake base in a thin, even layer. The chocolate will crystallize almost immediately, so work quickly. Flip the cake back over and reserve until needed. The cake will keep for up to 3 days.

DARK CHOCOLATE MOUSSE

YIELD: 1.6 KG/3 LB 8.48 OZ

INGREDIENT	METRIC	U.S.	%
Eggs	325 g	11.46 oz	20.25%
Sugar	135 g	4.76 oz	8.41%
Dark chocolate coins 64%	430 g	15.17 oz	26.79%
Heavy cream	715 g	1 lb 9.12 oz	44.55%

1. Combine the eggs with the sugar in a bowl and bring the mixture up to 60°C/140°F over a hot water bath while stirring constantly.

2. Remove the mixture from the heat and pour it into the bowl of an electric mixer. Whip on high speed until it cools to 35°C/95°F and creates ribbons, about 10 minutes.

3. Meanwhile, melt the chocolate over a hot water bath or in a microwave. Let it cool to 35°C/95°F.

4. Once both the egg mixture and the chocolate are at the right temperature, strain the egg mixture through a sieve over the chocolate and mix with a whisk until you obtain a homogenous mass.

5. Whip the heavy cream to medium peaks.

6. Fold half of the whipped cream into the chocolate mixture. Fold in the remaining whipped cream. Fill a piping bag with the mousse and follow the assembly procedure instructions for finishing the cakes.

SHINY CHOCOLATE GLAZE

YIELD: 2 KG/4 LB 6.4 OZ

INGREDIENT	METRIC	U.S.	%
Sugar	830 g	1 lb 13.28 oz	41.5%
Water	435 g	15.34 oz	21.75%
Cocoa powder	255 g	8.99 oz	12.75%
Crème fraîche	255 g	8.99 oz	12.75%
Dark chocolate coins 55%	185 g	6.53 oz	9.25%
Gelatin sheets, bloomed in cold water, excess water squeezed out	40 g	1.41 oz	2%

1. Bring the sugar, water, cocoa powder, and crème fraîche to a boil while stirring constantly.

2. Once it comes to a boil, stir in the chocolate and mix until dissolved.

3. Squeeze the excess water off the bloomed gelatin, add it to the pot, and stir until dissolved.

4. Pass the mixture through a fine-mesh sieve.

5. Cool over an ice water bath until completely cool, or use it to glaze the mousse cakes when it reaches 38°C/100°F.

6. Once it has cooled, transfer to an airtight container and refrigerate. It will keep for up to 10 days in the refrigerator.

NOTE *It is always necessary to make more glaze than needed, because the entire cake needs to be covered with glaze. As the glaze is poured over the cake, some will pour off, resulting in an even coat. If possible, try to "rescue" some of the dripped off glaze to reuse. If it has cake debris or other foreign but solid matter, pass it through a fine-mesh sieve. If it has liquid matter such as mousse or cream, it cannot be reused with the same results; it will not be as shiny.*

GOLDEN CHOCOLATE PLAQUE

YIELD: 200 G/7.05 OZ

INGREDIENT	METRIC	U.S.
Dark chocolate, tempered	200 g	7.05 oz
Edible lacquer spray	as needed	as needed
Gold leaf sheets	2	2

1. See the method for making chocolate tiles on page 233. Cut the chocolate into rectangles that measure 2.5 cm/1 in wide by 5 cm/2 in long.

2. Apply a light coat of edible lacquer spray on the surface of the rectangles, then affix a piece of gold leaf to cover the entire surface.

3. Reserve in a cool, dry area, preferably enclosed. Discard after 1 year.

RELIANT GRAPE JELLY

YIELD: 412 G/14.53 OZ

INGREDIENT	METRIC	U.S.	%
Calcium Solution			
Calcium lactate	2.2 g	.07 oz	1.8%
Water	120 g	4.23 oz	98.2%
Jelly			
Calcium Solution	4 g	.14 oz	.97%
Sugar 1	50 g	1.76 oz	12.14%
Reliant grape juice	350 g	12.35 oz	84.95%
Pectin (see Note)	4 g	.14 oz	.97%
Sugar 2	4 g	.14 oz	.97%

1. **For the calcium solution:** Combine both ingredients. Reserve refrigerated.

2. **For the jelly:** Bring the calcium solution, the first amount of sugar, and the Reliant grape juice to a boil in a small sauce pot.

3. Meanwhile, mix the pectin well with the second amount of sugar.

4. Shear the pectin-sugar mixture into the grape juice mixture with a handheld blender.

5. Return to a boil for 1 minute.

6. Pour into silicone oval molds (see Resources, page 520).

7. Cool in refrigeration and then freeze.

8. Once they are frozen, they can be unmolded and reserved frozen in an airtight container or well wrapped. Discard after 1 month.

NOTES *This recipe uses universal pectin, or pectin NH 95, which requires calcium rather than an acid to gel; this pectin is also thermo-reversible).*

When preparing the calcium solution, you are making much more than you need because it is not efficient to make less than this. You can always reserve the remaining solution in the refrigerator for later use. Discard after 2 months.

PEANUT PRALINE

YIELD: 1.07 KG/2 LB 5.6 OZ

INGREDIENT	METRIC	U.S.	%
Sugar	450 g	15.87 oz	42.06%
Salted peanuts	500 g	1 lb 1.64 oz	46.73%
Cocoa butter, melted	120 g	4.23 oz	11.21%

1. Line a flat half sheet pan with a nonstick rubber mat. Place a 5-mm/.2-in deep frame inside the sheet pan.

2. Make a dry caramel with the sugar; cook to a medium-dark amber. You will not be able to get an accurate reading from a thermometer since it is such a small amount. It is better to go by color, but if you go by the temperature, cook the sugar to 180°C/360°F. Stir in the peanuts until they are completely coated with sugar.

3. Pour out onto a nonstick rubber mat and spread out evenly to cool.

4. When the praline is cool, break it into pieces and grind it in a Robot Coupe until there are small chunks of peanut.

5. Pour in the melted cocoa butter and continue grinding for a few more seconds, until you obtain a homogenous mass.

6. Pour the mixture into the prepared frame and even it out with an offset spatula. Let it set in the refrigerator.

7. Once hardened, flip the praline over onto a cutting board and remove the nonstick rubber mat and the frame.

8. Cut out rectangles measuring 2.5 cm/1 in wide by 5 cm/2 in long.

9. Reserve in the refrigerator. Discard after 2 weeks.

> **VARIATION** *For hazelnut praline, replace the peanuts with toasted, blanched Piemontese hazelnuts. Do not grind it too much, as chunks of hazelnut are desirable. Cut the praline into 6.25-cm/2.5-in squares. Reserve frozen.*

PEANUT BUTTER AND MASCARPONE CREAM

YIELD: 1.5 KG/3 LB 4.96 OZ

INGREDIENT	METRIC	U.S.	%
Mascarpone, soft	680 g	1 lb 7.84 oz	45.21%
Peanut butter	230 g	8.11 oz	15.29%
Superfine sugar	230 g	8.11 oz	15.29%
Heavy cream	350 g	12.35 oz	23.27%
Gelatin sheets, silver, bloomed in cold water, excess water squeezed out	14 g	.49 oz	.93%

1. Combine the mascarpone, peanut butter, sugar, and heavy cream in a bowl and mix over a warm water bath until homogenous.

2. Remove one-quarter of the mixture and heat it up with the bloomed gelatin in a separate bowl over a hot water bath.

3. Return the warmed peanut butter–gelatin portion to the original mixture and stir until homogenous using a whisk.

4. Pour into the prepared molds or cool in an ice water bath, and then refrigerate. This cream can be refrigerated and melted down again for further use. Discard after 10 days.

PEANUT BUTTER VELVET SPRAY

YIELD: 500 G/1 LB 1.64 OZ

INGREDIENT	METRIC	U.S.	%
Peanut butter, smooth	100 g	3.53 oz	20%
White chocolate	100 g	3.53 oz	20%
Cocoa butter	300 g	10.58 oz	60%

1. Combine all of the ingredients in a small bowl and melt over a hot water bath.

2. Pass through a fine-mesh sieve and fill a spray gun canister if using immediately (to spray the peanut butter cream), or reserve in an airtight container for up to 3 months.

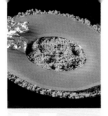

KUMQUAT MARMALADE

YIELD: 1.5 KG/3 LB 4.8 OZ

INGREDIENT	METRIC	U.S.	%
Kumquats, halved, seeded, blanched	750 g	1 lb 10.4 oz	50%
Sugar	750 g	1 lb 10.4 oz	50%

1. Blanch the kumquats in boiling water; drain.

2. Combine the kumquats with the sugar in a sauce pot and cook over medium heat until the rind of the kumquats is translucent or the mixture reaches 69° Brix.

3. Let the mixture cool slightly, and then purée slightly in a Robot Coupe. It shouldn't be completely smooth; it should be chunky.

4. Cool over an ice water bath and refrigerate or portion into the desired bowls. Discard after 2 months.

WHITE MISO "POT DE CRÈME"

YIELD: 854 G/1 LB 14.08 OZ

INGREDIENT	METRIC	U.S.	%
Heavy cream	700 g	1 lb 8.64 oz	81.97%
Sugar	120 g	4.23 oz	14.05%
White miso paste	30 g	1.06 oz	3.51%
Universal pectin	4 g	.14 oz	.47%

1. Have the bowls with the kumquat marmalade ready (or the cup or bowl to be used to hold the cream).

2. Combine the heavy cream, sugar, and miso paste and bring to a boil, stirring to dissolve the miso paste. Alternatively, a handheld blender will do a better job of dissolving the paste completely.

3. Pass the mixture through a fine-mesh sieve. Return to a boil and, once it boils, use a handheld immersion blender to shear in the pectin (pour it in slowly).

4. Cook at a low boil over medium heat for 1 minute while stirring.

5. Pour into the prepared bowls using a funnel. Refrigerate to cool the cream.

NOTES *The dessert should be used the day it is made. You can make the pot de crème ahead of time and store it in the refrigerator, melting it down each time you need to portion it.*

The term pot de crème *is used very loosely here, since this is not a pot de crème in the strict sense of the term. It contains no eggs and is not baked, but the final texture is incredibly custard-like and very reminiscent of its namesake.*

GREEN TEA GÉNOISE CRUMBS

YIELD: 1.05 KG/2 LB 3.36 OZ

INGREDIENT	METRIC	U.S.	%
Cake flour	95 g	3.35 oz	9.45%
Matcha (green tea powder)	25 g	.88 oz	2.49%
White chocolate, melted	235 g	8.29 oz	23.38%
Butter, soft	190 g	6.7 oz	18.91%
Egg yolks	120 g	4.23 oz	11.94%
Invert sugar	40 g	1.41 oz	3.98%
Egg whites	200 g	7.05 oz	19.9%
Sugar	100 g	3.53 oz	9.95%

1. Lightly spray the interior frame of a half sheet pan with a coat of nonstick oil spray. Line the sheet pan with a nonstick rubber mat.

2. Preheat a convection oven to 160°C/325°F.

3. Sift the cake flour with the matcha powder. Stir the chocolate and butter together in a bowl, and then stir in the egg yolks and invert sugar.

4. Whip the egg whites on high speed, adding the sugar slowly when they have reached half their volume. Whip to medium-soft peaks.

5. Fold the flour-matcha mixture into the whipped whites, then fold in the white chocolate mixture.

6. Pour the mixture into the prepared pan and even it out using an offset spatula.

7. Bake until the cake springs back at the center of the sponge when gently pressed, 9 to 12 minutes.

8. Let it cool to room temperature.

9. Place the sponge cake in a dehydrator set to 50°C/120°F. Let it dry out overnight.

10. Grind the cake into crumbs using a Robot Coupe.

11. Reserve in an airtight container in the freezer for up to 1 month, or pour it onto the white miso "pot de crème" bowls.

    NOTE *This recipe was adapted from Oriol Balaguer.*

KUMQUAT JELLY DISK

YIELD: 267 G/9.42 OZ

INGREDIENT	METRIC	U.S.	%
Kumquat purée	150 g	5.29 oz	56.22%
Water	75 g	2.65 oz	28.11%
Sugar	40 g	1.41 oz	14.99%
Gellan gum, low acyl	2 g	.06 oz	.67%

1. Assemble 10 silicone ring molds that measure 7.5 cm/3 in external diameter by 2.5 cm/1 in internal diameter by 2 mm/.08 in deep (see Resources, page 520).

2. Combine all of the ingredients in a small sauce pot. Bring to a boil over high heat while stirring constantly. Turn off the heat.

3. Using a funnel gun, portion the jelly into the molds. Let set in refrigeration. They can remain in the molds, refrigerated, until they are needed. Discard after 3 days.

REINE-DES-PRÉS CREMA CATALANA

YIELD : 1.4 KG/3 LB 4.16 OZ

INGREDIENT	METRIC	U.S.	%
Milk 1	1.2 kg	2 lb 10.24 oz	82.76%
Reine-des-prés	250 g	8.82 oz	17.24%
Cornstarch	80 g	2.82 oz	5.41%
Milk 2, at room temperature	80 g	2.82 oz	5.41%
Egg yolks, at room temperature	200 g	7.05 oz	13.51%
Sugar	200 g	7.05 oz	13.51%
Milk 3	920 g	32.45 oz	62.16%

1. Bring the first amount of milk to a simmer and stir in the reine-des-prés. Turn off the heat and cover the milk with plastic wrap.

2. Let the mixture steep for 20 minutes, then pass the milk through a fine-mesh sieve.

3. Cool it over an ice water bath, and then measure out the amount needed for the recipe (1 kg/2 lb 3.2 oz).

4. Set the bowls intended for the pastry cream aside on a flat sheet pan; each bowl should hold about 290 g/ 10.3 oz.

5. Follow the method for pastry cream on page 6.

6. Pour 290 g/10.3 oz of the pastry cream into each the bowls; tap the bowls down so that the pastry cream evens out on the surface of the bowl.

7. Reserve refrigerated; once the pastry cream has cooled, keep the bowls covered.

8. Take the bowls out of the refrigerator once you are ready to display them. Keep them uncovered during presentation.

   NOTE *This recipe presents itself like an exercise in simplicity, but it is not simple to make by any means. Making this pastry cream may take you a few tries.*

PINK GUAVA CREAM

YIELD: 940 G/2 LB 1.12 OZ

INGREDIENT	METRIC	U.S.	%
Pink guava purée	500 g	1 lb 1.64 oz	53.19%
Sugar 1	50 g	1.76 oz	5.32%
Egg whites	25 g	.88 oz	2.66%
Heavy cream	275 g	9.7 oz	29.26%
Sugar 2	75 g	2.65 oz	7.98%
Heavy cream stabilizer	4 g	.14 oz	.43%
Gelatin sheets, silver, bloomed in cold water, excess water squeezed out	11 g	.39 oz	1.17%
White chocolate–covered puffed rice	150 g	5.29 oz	

1. Lightly spray a coat of "de-mold spray" into the molds (see page 520 for resources for the de-mold spray and the molds).

2. Warm the cold guava purée to 15°C/60°F over a warm water bath. Reserve at room temperature.

3. Make an Italian meringue by combining the first amount of sugar with one-quarter of its weight in water in a small sauce pot. Cook the sugar to 118°C/244°F. Meanwhile, whip the egg whites to stiff peaks.

4. Once the sugar has reached the correct temperature and the egg whites have reached stiff peaks, pour the sugar into the egg whites as they whip on medium-high speed. Continue to whip until the meringue cools to room temperature.

5. Combine the heavy cream, second amount of sugar, and the heavy cream stabilizer in an electric mixer bowl on medium-high speed and whip until it reaches medium-soft peaks. Reserve refrigerated.

6. Place 10 percent of the tempered guava purée and the bloomed gelatin in a small bowl. Place the bowl over a hot water bath and stir until the gelatin dissolves. Pour this mixture into the larger amount of guava purée.

7. Fold in the Italian meringue in 2 additions. Fold in the whipped heavy cream in 2 additions. Fold in the white chocolate–coated puffed rice.

8. Pour the guava cream into a piping bag. Follow the instructions for assembling the cakes on page 276.

VANILLA CHIFFON CAKE DISKS

YIELD: 1.26 KG/2 LB 11.2 OZ

INGREDIENT	METRIC	U.S.	%
Cake flour	300 g	10.58 oz	24.47%
Sugar	260 g	9.17 oz	21.21%
Baking powder	12 g	.42 oz	.98%
Salt	5 g	.18 oz	.41%
Vanilla paste	7 g	.25 oz	.57%
Egg yolks	190 g	6.7 oz	15.5%
Canola oil	30 g	1.06 oz	2.45%
Water	145 g	5.11 oz	11.83%
Egg whites	190 g	6.7 oz	15.5%
Sugar	75 g	2.65 oz	6.12%
Lemon juice	12 g	.42 oz	.98%
White chocolate, melted	200 g	7.05 oz	

1. Lightly grease the interior border of a half sheet pan with nonstick oil spray.

2. Line the sheet pan with a nonstick rubber mat.

3. Preheat a convection oven to 160°C/325°F.

4. Combine the cake flour, sugar, baking powder, and salt and sift into the bowl of an electric mixer.

5. Combine the vanilla paste, egg yolks, oil, and water and slowly add the mixture to the dry ingredients.

6. Whip the egg whites, sugar, and lemon juice to medium peaks and fold into the above mixture.

7. Spread the batter onto the prepared sheet pan. Bake until light golden brown, 8 to 10 minutes. Cool at room temperature.

8. Freeze the cake. Once frozen, turn the cake out onto a sheet pan lined with parchment paper. Spread the melted white chocolate all over the base in a thin, even coat. Work quickly because the chocolate will set soon after it is applied to the cake.

9. Turn the cake over and cut out disks using a 3-cm/1.25-in ring cutter.

10. Reserve the cakes in an airtight container in the freezer. Discard after 2 weeks.

CRÈME FRAÎCHE CAKE

YIELD: 1 KG/2 LB 3.2 OZ

INGREDIENT	METRIC	U.S.	%
Butter, at 21°C/70°F	185 g	6.53 oz	18.5%
Sugar	165 g	5.82 oz	16.5%
Vanilla paste	4 g	.12 oz	.35%
Eggs, at 26°C/80°F	125 g	4.41 oz	12.5%
All-purpose flour	175 g	6.17 oz	17.5%
Baking powder	14 g	.49 oz	1.4%
Salt	3 g	.09 oz	.25%
Crème fraîche	330 g	11.64 oz	33%

1. Preheat a convection oven to 160°C/325°F.

2. Lightly grease the border of a half sheet pan with nonstick oil spray. Line the sheet pan with a nonstick rubber mat.

3. Follow the creaming method on page 4. The vanilla paste is added with the eggs. The crème fraîche is added at the end and is quickly mixed just to incorporate.

4. Spread the batter in the prepared sheet pan in an even layer using an offset spatula.

5. Bake until light golden brown around the border, 8 to 12 minutes.

6. Let it cool at room temperature. Once cool, refrigerate it for 2 hours; it cuts much better when it is cold.

7. Cut into rectangles measuring 6 mm/.25 in wide by 11.25 cm/4.5 in long by 6 mm/.25 in thick. Reserve covered in the freezer.

dessert wines and liquors

Typically these items are listed on the same menu as the dessert menu so that you can order a dessert and pair it with a wine or liquor or liqueur. This is the way restaurant can up-sell (increase check averages), exceeding what money might be made from coffee or tea. Technically, though, dessert wines and liquors should be served at the very end of the meal, once all the dessert plates have been cleared and mignardises have been placed on the table, when everyone is completely (or overly) sated. Most dessert wines are sweet, but many types of liquor are not. They all have a higher alcohol content than regular wine and beer and are therefore served in smaller portions. Personally I am not an advocate of pairing a dessert with a dessert-type wine or even a liquor. I feel that this is overkill and that the sweetness and alcohol content will most definitely mask the flavors of the actual dessert. It is not like drinking wine with food, where the wine enhances the meal and they both play off of each other; it is more of a one-sided relationship that leans away from the dessert. Having said that, I suggest that these items can in fact be ordered at the same time as dessert but served with mignardises. This may conflict with coffee and tea service, but you will find that customers will hardly ever have coffee and a dessert wine as well; it is mostly one or the other.

STRAWBERRY COMPOTE TUBE

YIELD: 871 G/1 LB 14.72 OZ

INGREDIENT	METRIC	U.S.	%
Fresh strawberries, stemmed and hulled	600 g	1 lb 5.12 oz	68.89%
Sugar	240 g	8.47 oz	27.55%
Vanilla paste	6 g	.21 oz	.69%
Gelatin, sheets, silver, bloomed in cold water, excess water squeezed out	25 g	.88 oz	2.87%

1. Roll a sheet of acetate horizontally to form a tube that is 1.25 cm/.5 in diameter. A sheet of acetate is usually about 34 cm/13.5 in wide by 54 cm/21.5 in long. Make 4 tubes in total; tape each roll so it does not unravel and then secure one end of each tube with a clamp. Each tube will yield 3 compote tubes; you will need only 1 strawberry compote tube from the fourth acetate tube for this recipe's yield of 10 orders. Save the remaining 2 tubes for future use.

2. Combine the strawberries, sugar, and vanilla paste in a 1.92-L/2-qt sauce pot.

3. Bring to a boil and cook until the strawberries are tender, 6 to 8 minutes.

4. Purée the mixture using a handheld immersion blender. Stir in the bloomed gelatin to dissolve it.

5. Let it cool enough so you can handle it. Pour it into a piping bag, then pipe the compote into the prepared tubes. Close the open end of each tube with another clamp. Freeze to harden.

6. Once they have hardened, cut an end off of each tube using a knife and cutting board, then measure 10-cm/4-in-long pieces from each tube and slice them the same way.

7. Reserve frozen with the acetate still around them. Take the acetate off just before assembling the desserts.

WHITE AND BLACK STRIPED TUBE

YIELD: 460 G/1 LB .23 OZ

INGREDIENT	METRIC	U.S.	%
Tempered white chocolate	400 g	14.11 oz	86.96%
Black cocoa butter	60 g	2.12 oz	13.04%

1. Cut out 10 rectangles of acetate measuring 7 cm/2.75 in wide by 13.75 cm/5.5 in long.

2. Line the exterior surface of 10 PVC tubes measuring 15 cm/6 in long by 2.5 cm/1 in diameter (external diameter, not internal) with parchment paper; tape the ends so they do not unravel. Cut out 10 rectangles of parchment paper measuring 10 cm/4 in wide by 15 cm/6 in long. Keep on hand.

3. Pour a small amount of chocolate over the surface of an acetate rectangle and even it out with an offset spatula. Using a chocolate comb, scrape through the chocolate to form channels; go from one side to the other in a straight line, making sure to comb the entire surface of the acetate. You can use a caramel bar (heavy stainless-steel bar) to give the comb support while you scrape the chocolate to ensure you get straight lines. You should now have white stripes on your acetate. Lift the acetate off the surface and place it on a clean surface. Scrape the chocolate off the work table and repeat this with all the acetate rectangles.

4. Melt the black cocoa butter and brush it onto the acetate rectangles to fill in the empty channels with the black cocoa butter. Let it set completely.

5. Pour the remaining tempered white chocolate over each rectangle and even it out using an offset spatula. Lift it up from the work surface when it is still liquid and wrap it around the prepared PVC tubes. Wrap the tubes with the other rectangles of parchment paper and tape them shut; this is to keep the tubes from unraveling and to maintain a tubular shape. Pull the chocolate tubes out of the PVC tubes and refrigerate for about 5 minutes to set.

6. Once the chocolate is completely crystallized, you may leave it on the parchment paper tube to store in a cool, dry area, or you may then remove the paper and fill them with the other components.

RED TUBE CAPS

YIELD: 250 G/8.82 OZ

INGREDIENT	METRIC	U.S.	%
White chocolate	200 g	7.05 oz	80%
Red cocoa butter	50 g	1.76 oz	20%

1. Melt the white chocolate and the red cocoa butter together in a bowl over a hot water bath.

2. Temper the mixture.

3. Spread it over a sheet of acetate in an even layer using an offset spatula.

4. When it is semi-crystallized, cut out rectangles measuring 2.5 cm/1 in by 3 cm/1.25 in using a ruler and the back of a paring knife.

5. Flip the sheet over onto a flat sheet pan lined with parchment paper, with the chocolate facing the sheet pan, and place a flat weight over it so that it sets flat and does not bow.

6. Reserve in a cool, dry area, preferably enclosed. The squares will keep for up to 1 year if stored properly.

VANILLA MASCARPONE CREAM

YIELD: 1.2 KG/2 LB 10.24 OZ

INGREDIENT	METRIC	U.S.	%
Mascarpone	1 kg	2 lb 3.2 oz	83.33%
Vanilla paste	30 g	1.06 oz	2.5%
Sugar	160 g	5.64 oz	13.33%
Gelatin sheets, silver, bloomed in cold water, excess water squeezed out	10 g	.35 oz	.83%

1. Combine the mascarpone, vanilla paste, and sugar in a bowl and soften over a hot water bath until pourable, about 30°C/86°F.

2. Melt the bloomed gelatin in the microwave and then stir it into the mascarpone mixture quickly, using a whisk.

3. Pour it into a piping bag and assemble the desserts.

CINNAMON STREUSEL

YIELD: 330 G/11.64 OZ

INGREDIENT	METRIC	U.S.	%
Butter	80 g	2.82 oz	24.24%
Sugar	80 g	2.82 oz	24.24%
Pastry flour	165 g	5.82 oz	50%
Ground cinnamon	4 g	.14 oz	1.21%
Salt	1 g	.04 oz	.3%

1. Preheat a convection oven to 160°C/325°F.

2. In the bowl of an electric mixer fitted with the paddle attachment, paddle the butter with the sugar for about 2 minutes simply to soften the butter. Meanwhile, sift the flour, cinnamon, and salt together.

3. Stop the mixer and add all of the dry ingredients at once. Pulse the mixer to incorporate the dry ingredients. Do not overmix; just mix enough to fully incorporate the ingredients together.

4. Pass the dough through a wire rack onto a sheet pan lined with parchment paper to make small morsels of streusel.

5. Bake the streusel until golden brown, about 10 minutes.

6. Cool to room temperature.

7. Once cool, reserve in a cool, dry area in an airtight container. Discard after 10 days.

CHOCOLATE BASE

YIELD: 220 G/7.76 OZ

INGREDIENT	METRIC	U.S.	%
Dark chocolate, melted	200 g	7.05 oz	90.91%
Canola oil	20 g	.71 oz	9.09%

1. Combine both ingredients and portion while fluid (see Assembly Procedure on page 280).

2. Reserve in an airtight container at room temperature for up to 6 months.

CARAMEL MOUSSE

YIELD: 757 G/1 LB 10.56 OZ

INGREDIENT	METRIC	U.S.	%
Heavy cream 1	110 g	3.88 oz	14.53%
Sugar	140 g	4.94 oz	18.49%
Butter	45 g	1.59 oz	5.94%
Eggs	95 g	3.35 oz	12.55%
Gelatin sheets, silver, bloomed in cold water, excess water squeezed off	7 g	.25 oz	.92%
Heavy cream 2	360 g	12.7 oz	47.56%

1. Warm up the first amount of heavy cream in the microwave until it is hot.

2. Cook the sugar over high heat in a small sauce pot, stirring constantly until it turns to medium amber, 170°C/338°F. Stir in the butter completely, then stir in the warm heavy cream. Remove the caramel from the heat.

3. Place the eggs over a hot water bath and warm them to 60°C/140°F while stirring constantly. Transfer them to the bowl of an electric mixer fitted with the whip attachment. Whip until they have cooled to room temperature. When the eggs have cooled and are still whipping, stream in the hot caramel. Add the gelatin and whip until the gelatin dissolves and the mixture has cooled to 21°C/70°F.

4. Whip the second amount of heavy cream in an electric mixer to medium peaks. Fold the whipped cream into the caramel base in 2 additions.

5. Pour into the prepared mold (see Assembly Procedure on page 280).

RICE MILK VEIL

YIELD: 402 G/14.21 OZ

INGREDIENT	METRIC	U.S.	%
Rice milk	300 g	10.58 oz	74.48%
Sugar	100 g	3.53 oz	24.83%
Gellan gum, low acyl	3 g	.1 oz	.7%

1. Combine all of the ingredients in a small sauce pot and bring to a boil while gently whisking.

2. Follow the instructions for the raisin jelly veil on page 259.

3. Cut the veil while on the tray into rectangles measuring 10 cm/4 in wide by 12.5 cm/5 in long, using a ruler and the back of a paring knife.

4. Reserve refrigerated and covered until use. Discard after 2 days.

SCOTTISH SHORTBREAD BASE

YIELD: 600 G/1 LB 5.16 OZ

INGREDIENT	METRIC	U.S.	%
All-purpose flour	245 g	8.64 oz	40.83%
Rice flour	35 g	1.23 oz	5.83%
Salt	5 g	0.18 oz	0.83%
Butter, soft	210 g	7.41 oz	35.00%
Sugar	105 g	3.70 oz	17.50%

1. Sift the all-purpose flour, rice flour, and the salt together.

2. In a mixer bowl fitted with a paddle attachment, cream the butter with the sugar until light and smooth on medium speed.

3. Turn the mixer off and add the dry ingredients to the creamed butter and sugar mixture. Pulse the mixer on and off until all of the dry ingredients are completely incorporated.

4. Make a flat block of dough with your hands and wrap it in plastic. Refrigerate until firm for about 1 hour.

5. Sheet out the dough using a sheeter or a rolling pin until it is about 2 mm/.08 in thick.

6. Freeze the dough. Meanwhile preheat a convection oven to 160°C/320°F.

7. Cut out the dough into squares that measure 7.5 cm/ 3 in x 7.5 cm/3 in. using a square cutter. Score each piece with a fork in four separate areas of the cookie.

8. Bake the dough until light golden brown around the border, about 6 minutes.

9. Cool off at room temperature. Reserve well covered in an airtight container in a cool dry place until you are ready to use it. Discard after 2 days or freeze it for up to 1 month.

CARAMELIZED WHITE CHOCOLATE AND CARAMELIZED MILK CHOCOLATE

YIELD: 2.5 KG/5 LB 8.03 OZ

INGREDIENT	METRIC	U.S.	%
White chocolate coins	2 kg	4 lb 6.4 oz	66.23%
Milk chocolate	500 g	1 lb 1.63 oz	
Cocoa butter, melted	250 g	8.82 oz	

1. Preheat a convection oven to 115°C/240°F.

2. Put the white chocolate coins in a hotel pan and the milk chocolate in a separate half hotel pan and place in the oven.

3. Every 30 minutes, stir both mixtures with a wooden spoon. It will take about 2 hours for the chocolate to caramelize and take on a medium-brown hue.

4. Pour the hot white chocolate into a bowl and stir in 200 g/7.05 oz of cocoa butter into it. Pour the milk chocolate into another bowl, and add 50 g/1.76 oz of cocoa butter to it. The cocoa butter helps improve the fluidity of the chocolate, since caramelizing it thickens it too much.

5. Pour the chocolates into separate sheet pans lined with parchment paper to cool.

6. Once it is set, it can be melted and then tempered if necessary. Discard after 1 year.

NOTE *You will need to make this for the mousse, the velvet spray, and the leaf décor.*

TOASTED BAGUETTE PURÉE SQUARES

YIELD: 453 G/15.98 OZ

INGREDIENT	METRIC	U.S.	%
Baguette, sliced thin	300 g	10.58 oz	66.23%
Sugar	50 g	1.76 oz	11.04%
Water	100 g	3.53 oz	22.08%
Xanthan gum	3 g	.11 oz	.66%

1. Preheat a convection oven to 160°C/325°F.

2. Place the baguette slices on a sheet pan lined with parchment paper and toast in the oven until dark brown, 8 to 12 minutes.

3. Cool the baguette slices.

4. Meanwhile, line a half sheet pan with a nonstick rubber mat and place a 3-mm/.12-in-deep frame on top of the mat. Freeze this setup.

5. Place the baguette in a blender with the sugar and the water. Purée until smooth and uniform. Add the xanthan gum and shear for about 1 minute.

6. Pour this mixture into the frozen prepared frame.

7. Freeze to harden. Once it has hardened, remove the frame from the pan and flip the frame over. Peel off the nonstick rubber mat. Cut out ten 7.5-cm/3-in squares. Reserve frozen, well covered, until ready to assemble.

CARAMELIZED WHITE CHOCOLATE MOUSSE

YIELD: 1.03 KG/2 LB 4.24OZ

INGREDIENT	METRIC	U.S.	%
Eggs	200 g	7.05 oz	19.46%
Sugar	70 g	2.47 oz	6.81%
Caramelized White Chocolate (page 316)	350 g	12.35 oz	34.06%
Heavy cream	400 g	14.11 oz	38.93%
Gelatin sheets, silver, bloomed in cold water, excess water squeezed out	8 g	.26 oz	.73%

1. Have the containers for the mousse readily available in a freezer.

2. Combine the eggs and sugar over a hot water bath and bring to 60°C/140°F, whisking constantly. Strain through a fine-mesh sieve into a bowl to remove any lumps.

3. Melt the caramelized chocolate over a hot water bath and add to the egg mixture. Stir well with a whisk.

4. Let the mixture cool to about 30°C/86°F.

5. Meanwhile, whip the cream to medium peaks, and then refrigerate.

6. Melt the gelatin in the microwave and stir it quickly into the chocolate-egg mixture.

7. Fold in the whipped cream in 2 additions. Immediately pour the mousse into the prepared containers.

CARAMELIZED MILK CHOCOLATE LEAF

YIELD: 300 G/10.58 OZ

INGREDIENT	METRIC	U.S.
Caramelized Milk Chocolate (page 316), tempered	300 g	10.58 oz

1. Cut out ten 12.5-cm/5-in squares of parchment paper. Have 10 small pieces of tape available.

2. Pipe a strip of chocolate measuring 2.5 cm/1 in wide by 10 cm/4 in long across the center of each parchment paper square.

3. Place a chocolate comb at the center of the slug, and rotate it from the center to the left. Return the comb to the center of the slug, and rotate it toward the right.

4. With a gloved hand, run a finger on both sides of the combed chocolate stripes to form a leaf.

5. When the chocolate has semi-crystallized, bring two ends together and tape them so they stay in place.

6. Let the chocolate set completely on the parchment paper. Take it off of the paper and remove the tape when ready to use.

ANGEL FOOD CAKE

YIELD: 1.5 KG/3 LB 4.8 OZ

INGREDIENT	METRIC	U.S.	%
Salt	4 g	.14 oz	.27%
Pastry flour	235 g	8.29 oz	15.66%
Sugar	315 g	11.11 oz	20.99%
Egg whites	630 g	1 lb 6.08 oz	41.99%
Cream of tartar	2 g	.05 oz	.1%
Superfine or bakers' sugar	315 g	11.11 oz	20.99%

1. Preheat a convection oven to 160°C/325°F.

2. Line a half sheet pan with a nonstick rubber mat. Do not coat the border with nonstick oil spray; the angel food cake needs something to hold onto while it bakes. It will collapse when it comes out of the oven if the border is greased.

3. Sift the salt, pastry flour, and sugar together.

4. In an electric mixer fitted with the whip attachment whip the egg whites with the cream of tartar on high speed. Once they reach medium volume (quadrupled in volume), pour in the sugar slowly and steadily.

5. Fold the dry ingredients into the meringue gently. Pour the batter into the prepared pan and bake until done, 8 to 12 minutes; it should spring back at the center of the sheet pan when gentle pressure is applied with the fingertips.

6. Cool at room temperature and then freeze it.

7. Once hardened, pass a small offset spatula around the border of the cake where it comes in contact with the sheet pan to detach it. Flip the cake onto a cutting board and peel off the nonstick rubber mat. Cut out rectangles measuring 3.75 cm/1.5 in wide by 8.75 cm/3.5 in long from the cake.

8. Reserve frozen in an airtight container until needed. Discard after 2 weeks.

CITRON CREAM

YIELD: 961 G/2 LB 1.76 OZ

INGREDIENT	METRIC	U.S.	%
Heavy cream	600 g	1 lb 5.12 oz	62.43%
Sugar	150 g	5.29 oz	15.61%
Citron zest	10 g	.35 oz	1.04%
Egg yolks	190 g	6.7 oz	19.77%
Gelatin sheets, silver, bloomed in cold water, excess water squeezed off	11 g	.39 oz	1.14%

1. Make a crème anglaise with the heavy cream, sugar, citron zest, and egg yolks using the method for crème anglaise on page 8. Zest the citron directly into the pot where you will be making the crème anglaise base to obtain the strongest possible flavor.

2. Once the crème anglaise is cooked, pass it through a fine-mesh sieve and cool it over an ice water bath.

3. Place one-fifth of the crème anglaise in a small bowl and add the bloomed gelatin to it. Melt the gelatin over a hot water bath while stirring with a whisk.

4. Meanwhile, whip the remaining crème anglaise in the bowl of an electric mixer fitted with the whip attachment until it is medium stiff.

5. Transfer the gelatin mixture to a larger bowl and fold half of the whipped crème anglaise into it; stir until it is evenly mixed. Fold in the remaining half of the whipped crème anglaise; pipe into the prepared molds immediately.

PURE WHITE GLAZE

YIELD: 1.2 KG/2 LB 10.4 OZ

INGREDIENT	METRIC	U.S.	%
Milk	250 g	8.82 oz	20.79%
Glucose	80 g	2.82 oz	6.65%
Gelatin sheets, silver, bloomed in cold water, excess water squeezed out	13 g	.44 oz	1.04%
White chocolate coins	600 g	1 lb 5.12 oz	49.9%
Titanium dioxide (white food coloring powder), sifted	10 g	.35 oz	.83%
Neutral mirror glaze or clear glaze (see Resources, page 520)	250 g	8.82 oz	20.79%

1. Bring the milk and glucose to a boil in a sauce pot. Take off the heat and stir in the bloomed gelatin until dissolved.

2. Pour over the white chocolate and titanium dioxide. Pour in the mirror glaze and mix well with a handheld immersion blender. Pass the mixture through a fine-mesh sieve.

3. Reserve in an airtight container and refrigerate until needed, or wait for it too cool to 35°C/95°F to glaze the desserts. Discard after 7 days.

BALSAMIC VINEGAR REDUCTION

YIELD: 600 G/1 LB 5.12 OZ

INGREDIENT	METRIC	U.S.	%
Balsamic vinegar	400 g	14.11 oz	66.67%
Sugar	200 g	7.05 oz	33.33%

1. Combine both ingredients in a sauce pot and cook over high heat. Bring to a boil, and then reduce the heat to medium and cook until it has reduced to about one-quarter of its original volume. It should look thickened and shiny.

2. Cool to room temperature and reserve in an airtight container. The reduction may keep indefinitely if stored in these conditions.

DOUGLAS FIR ICE CREAM BASE

YIELD: 1.67 KG/3 LB 10.88 OZ

INGREDIENT	METRIC	U.S.	%
Douglas Fir Milk			
Douglas fir branches	400 g	14.11 oz	22.22%
Milk	1.4 kg	3 lb 1.28 oz	77.78%
Ice Cream Base			
Douglas Fir Milk	1.07 kg	2 lb 5.6 oz	64.07%
Heavy cream	140 g	4.94 oz	8.38%
Powdered milk	70 g	2.47 oz	4.19%
Sugar	270 g	9.52 oz	16.17%
Ice cream stabilizer	5 g	.18 oz	.3%
Egg yolks	115 g	4.06 oz	6.89%

1. **For the Douglas Fir milk:** Rinse the branches under hot water to remove any undesirable elements.

2. Chop the branches coarsely.

3. Bring the milk to a simmer and then stir in the chopped branches. Turn off the heat and cover the pot with plastic wrap. Let steep for about 30 minutes or until the milk is fully infused with the Douglas fir.

4. Strain the milk through a fine-mesh sieve. Cool over an ice water bath.

5. Weigh out the necessary amount for the ice cream base.

6. **For the ice cream base:** Follow the procedure for the modern ice cream method on page 50.

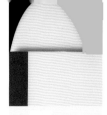

ARBORIO RICE PUDDING

YIELD: 1.75 KG/3 LB 13.6 OZ

INGREDIENT	METRIC	U.S.	%
Water	505 g	1 lb 1.81 oz	28.86%
Arborio rice	225 g	7.94 oz	12.86%
Milk	605 g	1 lb 5.28 oz	34.57%
Sugar	180 g	6.35 oz	10.29%
Salt	3 g	.09 oz	.14%
Vanilla paste	5 g	.18 oz	.29%
Eggs	75 g	2.65 oz	4.29%
Heavy cream	130 g	4.59 oz	7.43%
Butter	23 g	.79 oz	1.29%

1. Bring the water to a boil in a 3.78-L/4-qt sauce pot. Add the rice and stir.

2. Reduce the heat to low and cover with plastic wrap. Simmer for about 20 minutes or until the rice is fully cooked; do not overcook.

3. In another saucepan, combine the cooked rice, milk, sugar, salt, and vanilla paste.

4. Cook over medium heat until thick and creamy, about 20 minutes, stirring constantly.

5. Remove from the heat. Whisk the eggs and cream together and then temper the hot rice mixture into the egg mixture. Return the mixture to medium heat and cook for 2 minutes more. It should look like a thick crème anglaise.

6. Remove the pot from the heat and stir in the butter.

7. Pour the rice pudding into a hotel pan and then cool over an ice water bath, covered with plastic wrap directly on the surface of the rice pudding.

8. Cool completely before pouring into the passion fruit curd ring. Discard leftover rice pudding the day after it is made.

PASSION FRUIT CURD RINGS

YIELD: 1 KG/2 LB 3.2 OZ

INGREDIENT	METRIC	U.S.	%
Passion fruit purée (see Note)	175 g	6.17 oz	17.47%
Lemon juice	20 g	.71 oz	2%
Sugar	225 g	7.94 oz	22.47%
Salt	1 g	.02 oz	.05%
Egg yolks	235 g	8.29 oz	23.46%
Butter, diced	330 g	11.64 oz	32.95%
Gelatin sheets, silver, bloomed in cold water, excess water squeezed off	16 g	.56 oz	1.6%

1. Place 10 oval rings measuring 5 cm/2 in wide by 10 cm/4 in long by 1.25 cm/.5 in deep on a flat sheet pan lined with a nonstick rubber mat.

2. Line a half sheet pan with a nonstick rubber mat and put a 3-mm/.1-in Plexiglas frame on top of it.

3. Prepare the curd using the method for lemon curd on page 223. Pour into the prepared frame, even it out so that it is flat, and then cover it with a sheet of acetate. Let set in the freezer.

4. Once hardened, flip the curd onto a cutting board. Peel off the nonstick rubber mat and remove the Plexiglas frame.

5. Using a ruler and a knife, cut out 1.25-cm/.5-in-wide strips vertically, cutting through the acetate sheet. You will have about 25 strips, but you will only need 10 (1 per order). Take each one of the strips and, when it has softened slightly, line the inside of each prepared oval ring. Trim the ends if necessary so that the ends of each curd strip do not overlap.

6. Reserve covered and refrigerated until ready to pour in the rice pudding.

NOTE *If the passion fruit purée is concentrated, use half passion fruit purée and half orange juice.*

WHITE AND RED CHOCOLATE PLAQUE

YIELD: 450 G/15.87 OZ

INGREDIENT	METRIC	U.S.	%
Red cocoa butter transfer sheet (natural, see Resources, page 520)	50 g	1.76 oz	11.11%
White chocolate	400 g	14.11 oz	88.89%

1. Cut a red-colored cocoa butter transfer sheet into ten 2-cm/.8-in-wide strips.

2. Place the strips on an acetate sheet large enough to hold all of the strips, cocoa butter side facing up.

3. Temper the white chocolate.

4. Spread the white chocolate over the surface of each acetate rectangle, spreading it evenly into a thin layer with an offset spatula.

5. When the chocolate has semi-crystallized, cut out 10 rectangles that measuring 6.5 cm/2.6 in wide by 10 cm/4 in long using a ruler and the back of a paring knife, making sure to keep a red band of the transfer sheet on one of the long sides of the rectangle.

6. Flip the acetates over onto a flat surface lined with parchment paper. Place a flat, heavy weight over them to help the chocolate set flat and not bow.

7. Keep in a cool, dry area, preferably enclosed. Discard after 1 year.

BANANA BUTTER INCLUSION

YIELD: 1.02 KG/2 LB 4.16 OZ

INGREDIENT	METRIC	U.S.	%
Bananas, very ripe	900 g	1 lb 15.68 oz	87.8%
Butter	100 g	3.53 oz	9.76%
Ground cinnamon	5 g	.18 oz	.49%
Tahitian vanilla powder	20 g	.71 oz	1.95%

1. Combine all of the ingredients in a 2.83-L/3-qt sauce pot. Cook over medium-high heat until the bananas have completely broken down. Purée this mixture using a handheld immersion blender.

2. Put the banana butter into a piping bag and pour it into 10 silicone spherical molds with a diameter measuring 4 cm/1.5 in.

3. Freeze the banana butter until hardened. Once hardened, the spheres can be pushed out of the molds and kept frozen in an airtight container. Discard after 2 months.

CRISPY HAZELNUT GIANDUJA

YIELD: 660 G/ 1 LB 7.28 OZ

INGREDIENT	METRIC	U.S.	%
Gianduja	500 g	1 lb 1.76 oz	75.76%
Caramelized sugar	100 g	3.53 oz	15.15%
Canola oil	60 g	2.12 oz	9.09%

1. Line a flat half sheet pan with a nonstick rubber mat. Place a 5 mm-/.2-in-thick frame over the nonstick mat (it should fit inside the sheet pan). Chop the gianduja finely and put into the bowl of an electric mixer fitted with the paddle attachment. Turn on the lowest speed.

2. Make a dry caramel with the sugar in a small sauce pot over high heat.

3. Stream the caramel into the gianduja in the mixer bowl slowly and increase the speed to medium. Stream in oil.

4. Allow to cool to room temperature before spreading into the frame.

5. Spread into the frame to create and evenly thick base.

6. Allow to harden in the refrigerator. Once hardened, cut out into 5 cm/2 in x 5 cm/2 in squares. Reserve well covered in an airtight container in refrigeration. Discard after 4 days or freeze for up to 1 month.

NUTELLA CREAM

YIELD: 1.19 KG/2 LB 9.92 OZ

INGREDIENT	METRIC	U.S.	%
Mascarpone, soft	600 g	1 lb 5.12 oz	50.31%
Nutella	200 g	7.05 oz	16.77%
Superfine sugar	80 y	2.82 uz	6.71%
Heavy cream	300 g	10.58 oz	25.16%
Gelatin sheets, silver, bloomed in cold water, excess water squeezed off	13 g	.44 oz	1.05%

Follow the method and procedure for Peanut Butter and Mascarpone Cream on page 306.

ASSORTED COLORS VELVET SPRAY

YIELD: 225 G/7.88 OZ

INGREDIENT	METRIC	U.S.	%
White chocolate	100 g	3.5 oz	44.44%
Cocoa butter	100 g	3.5 oz	44.44%
Naturally colored cocoa butter (red, blue, yellow, green, white, and/or black)	25 g	.88 oz	11.11%

1. Prepare each color separately. Combine white chocolate, cocoa butter, and colored cocoa butter in a bowl and melt over a hot water bath. You will need to make 225 g/7.88 oz for each color you want to use.

2. Once melted you can spray the frozen desserts with a spray paint gun or reserve in an airtight container in a cool, dry place.

SABLÉ BRETON

YIELD: 998 G/2 LB 3.2 OZ

INGREDIENT	METRIC	U.S.	%
Almond flour	30 g	1.06 oz	3.01%
All-purpose flour	130 g	4.59 oz	13.03%
Cake flour	300 g	10.58 oz	30.06%
Butter	210 g	7.41 oz	21.04%
Salt	3 g	.11 oz	.3%
6X confectioners' sugar	160 g	5.64 oz	16.03%
Eggs	90 g	3.17 oz	9.02%
Butter, melted but cool	75 g	2.65 oz	7.52%

1. Sift the almond, all-purpose, and cake flours together.

2. In the bowl of an electric mixer fitted with the paddle attachment, paddle the butter, salt, and sugar on medium speed until you obtain a homogenous mix, about 2 minutes.

3. Add the eggs in 2 additions (more if you are making a larger recipe) with the machine on medium speed, waiting for each addition to incorporate before adding the next.

4. Stop the mixer, add the sifted dry ingredients, and mix on low speed until you obtain a homogenous mix. Do not overmix.

5. Shape the dough into a thin square, wrap it with plastic wrap, and chill it for at least 1 hour.

6. Meanwhile, preheat a convection oven to 160°C/ 320°F.

7. Sheet the dough to 3 mm/.1 in thick on a sheeter or by hand.

8. Freeze to harden for a few minutes.

9. Bake until golden brown (docking is not necessary), 7 to 9 minutes.

10. Cool at room temperature.

11. Once cool, grind to even crumbs using a robot coupe. Add the melted butter and mix to combine evenly.

12. Extend the dough onto a nonstick rubber mat to a thickness of 5 mm/.2 in.

13. Chill in the refrigerator to harden. Once firm, cut out rectangles (in this case, to fit inside the Plexiglas base). Reserve well covered in the refrigerator for up to 1 week, or freeze for up to 2 months.

LEMON CURD

YIELD: 1.01 KG/2 LB 3.63 OZ

INGREDIENT	METRIC	U.S.	%
Lemon juice	160 g	5.64 oz	15.84%
Sugar	240 g	8.47 oz	23.76%
Eggs	160 g	5.64 oz	15.84%
Butter, cubed	450 g	15.87 oz	44.55%

1. Combine the lemon juice, sugar, and eggs in a bowl and cook over a hot water bath until thickened, while whisking constantly.

2. Take the bowl off the heat and add the butter, mixing it in with a handheld immersion blender.

3. Cool at room temperature, keeping the bowl covered with plastic wrap.

4. Once cool, reserve in the refrigerator until ready to use. Discard after 1 week.

ITALIAN MERINGUE

YIELD: 630 G/1 LB 6.22 OZ

INGREDIENT	METRIC	U.S.	%
Sugar	360 g	12.7 oz	57.14%
Water	90 g	3.17 oz	14.29%
Egg whites	180 g	6.35 oz	28.57%

Follow the procedure for Italian meringue on page 13.

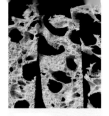

TOASTED PAIN AU LEVAIN

YIELD: 1 KG/2 LB 3.27 OZ

INGREDIENT	METRIC	U.S.
Pain au levain loaf, bâtard shaped	1 kg	2 lb 3.2 oz

1. Chill the bread in the refrigerator for about 3 hours; this helps make the bread firm so that it can be thinly sliced without damaging it.

2. Preheat a convection oven to 160°C/320°F.

3. Line a full-size sheet pan with a nonstick rubber mat.

4. Slice the bread to 3 mm/.12 in thick using an electric slicer.

5. Cut the bread into evenly shaped rectangles using a chef's knife and a ruler; they don't have to be perfect, but they should be proportionately even. It's fine to leave the crust on some pieces.

6. Toast the bread in the convection oven until it is golden brown, 8 to 12 minutes.

7. Cool at room temperature. Reserve in an airtight container at room temperature. Discard after 24 hours.

NOTE *Pain au levain is a bread that is leavened naturally with wild, not commercial, yeast.*

CONFITURE DE LAIT

YIELD: 1.35 KG/2 LB 15.62 OZ

INGREDIENT	METRIC	U.S.	%
Milk	2 kg	4 lb 6.55 oz	66.67%
Sugar	1 kg	2 lb 3.27 oz	33.33%

1. Bring both ingredients to a boil in a large sauce pot over high heat, and then lower to a simmer. Cook until it thickens like a caramel sauce; this will take 3 to 4 hours.

2. Reserve in an airtight container at room temperature. Discard after 1 month.

ESPRESSO PASTRY CREAM

YIELD: 1.49 KG/3.28 LB

INGREDIENT	METRIC	U.S.	%
Milk 1, at room temperature	80 g	2.82 oz	5.37%
Instant coffee crystals	10 g	.35 oz	.67%
Sugar	200 g	7.05 oz	13.42%
Cornstarch	80 g	2.82 oz	5.37%
Milk 2	920 g	32.45 oz	61.74%
Egg yolks, at room temperature	200 g	7.05 oz	13.42%

Follow the procedure for pastry cream on page 6. Add the instant coffee crystals with the first amount of milk before boiling it.

NOTES *Do not hold this pastry cream for more than 2 days; because the egg yolks are not boiled, the enzymes will break down the gelatinized proteins in the cornstarch and result in a very unappealing custard.*

Do not make less than the quantity in this recipe. A smaller amount will not become hot enough to coagulate the proteins in the egg yolks and cornstarch, which is what thickens the custard.

PÂTE À CHOUX

YIELD: 1 KG/2 LB 3.52 OZ

INGREDIENT	METRIC	U.S.	%
Water	320 g	11.28 oz	31.75%
Sugar	5 g	.16 oz	.5%
Salt	5 g	.16 oz	.5%
Butter	150 g	5.28 oz	14.88%
Milk powder	28 g	.96 oz	2.78%
Bread flour	180 g	6.34 oz	17.86%
Eggs	320 g	11.36	31.75%

1. Preheat a hearth oven to 220°C/430°F.

2. Line a sheet pan with a nonstick rubber mat. Put a #808 tip inside a piping bag; this will be used for piping the cream puffs.

3. Boil the water with the sugar, salt, and butter over high heat. Add the milk powder and return to a boil. Turn off the heat and quickly stir in the flour. Turn the heat back on to medium-low (closer to low) and cook the paste for 2 minutes, stirring constantly. A film will develop at the base of the pot, and this is an indicator that the starch proteins are getting precooked (precoagulated); the 2 minutes of stirring time is to ensure that the entire mix is precooked.

4. Remove the pot from the heat and turn the paste into a mixer bowl. Mix on medium speed with the paddle attachment until the paste is at room temperature.

5. Add the eggs one at a time. Stop the mixer, drop the bowl, and scrape the sides in between each addition. You may not need to add the entire amount of eggs. Check the consistency. If the paddle is taken off the choux, the choux that is left in the bowl should not leave a peak, but rather, it should fall. If this recipe is done correctly, however, you will need to add the entire amount of eggs.

6. Pour the batter into the prepared piping bag. If piping large cream puffs, they will need to be 5 cm/2 in diameter. Small choux puffs will need to be 2.50 cm/ 1 in diameter. Once they are piped, spray a fine mist of water on them and place the craquelin topping dough on top of them (large disks on large puffs and small disks on small puffs).

7. Place the tray in the hearth oven and turn it off. After 25 minutes, open the vent and let them dry out for 10 to 12 more minutes.

8. Let them cool at room temperature. You can fill them at this point or freeze them. If freezing them, they should be refreshed in a hot oven for 5 minutes with the vent open.

CRAQUELIN TOPPING

YIELD: 510 G/1 LB 2 OZ

INGREDIENT	METRIC	U.S.	%
Soft butter	150 g	5.29 oz	29.41%
Brown sugar	180 g	6.35 oz	35.29%
All-purpose flour	180 g	6.35 oz	35.29%

1. Combine all of the ingredients in an electric mixer bowl. Using a paddle, mix on low speed until a homogenous mass is obtained.

2. Place the dough on a sheet of acetate and flatten with your hands as much as you can. Place another sheet of acetate on top of the dough, and sheet down to 2 2/3 mm/.1 in by using a sheeter or a rolling pin. Freeze the dough.

3. Once frozen, remove the top acetate sheet. Flip it over and pull the acetate sheet off, then place the sheeted dough back on. Doing this helps the dough release easily from the acetate. For the base of the nuns, cut out discs using a 5 cm/2 in ring cutter and for the top of the nuns use a 3 cm/1.25 in ring cutter. Reserve frozen and well wrapped. Discard after a month.

CHOCOLATE GLAZE DISKS

YIELD: 642 G/1 LB 6.56 OZ

INGREDIENT	METRIC	U.S	%
Water	240 g	8.47 oz	37.35%
Sugar	175 g	6.17 oz	27.24%
Cocoa powder	70 g	2.47 oz	10.89%
Heavy cream	150 g	5.29 oz	23.35%
Gelatin sheets, silver, bloomed, excess moisture squeezed out	8 oz	.26 oz	1.17%

1. Line a half sheet pan with a nonstick rubber mat. Place a 3-mm/.1-in-deep frame inside the sheet pan.

2. Boil the water and sugar in a 1.76-L/2-qt sauce pot over high heat until the sugar is dissolved.

3. Turn off the heat and stir in the cocoa powder with a whisk until dissolved.

4. Return the pot to high heat and bring to a boil again. Add the cream and turn the heat down to a simmer.

5. Cook until thickened, about 30 minutes, stirring frequently. Add the bloomed gelatin. Pour into the prepared frame and freeze.

6. Once frozen hard, flip the glaze over, peel off the rubber mat, and then put the glaze back on the mat again. This helps the glaze to keep from sticking.

7. Cut out the large disks with the 5-cm/2-in ring cutter and the small disks using the 3-cm/1.25-in ring cutter. Reserve frozen until needed. Discard after 1 month.

COCONUT DACQUOISE

YIELD: 800 G/1 LB 12.16 OZ

INGREDIENT	METRIC	U.S.	%
Egg whites	250 g	8.82 oz	31.25%
Superfine or bakers' sugar	80 g	2.82 oz	10%
Confectioners' sugar, sifted	250 g	8.82 oz	31.25%
Shredded coconut, finely ground	220 g	7.76 oz	27.5%

1. Preheat a convection oven to 160°C/325°F.

2. Lightly grease the border of a half sheet pan with a coat of nonstick oil spray. Line it with a nonstick rubber mat.

3. Make a French meringue out of the egg whites and superfine sugar using the method on page 12.

4. Fold the confectioners; sugar and shredded coconut into the meringue.

5. Spread onto the prepared sheet pan in an even layer.

6. Bake until the center is dry but the mixture is not colored, 8 to 10 minutes.

7. Cool at room temperature. Once cool, refrigerate to chill. Once chilled, cut out 7.5-cm/3-in squares.

8. Reserve refrigerated until ready to assemble the dessert. Discard after 3 days.

COCONUT CREAM

YIELD: 1.8 KG/4 LB 2.24 OZ

INGREDIENT	METRIC	U.S.	%
Coconut purée	1 kg	2 lb 3.2 oz	53.19%
Sugar 1	100 g	3.53 oz	5.32%
Egg whites	50 g	1.76 oz	2.66%
Heavy cream	550 g	1 lb 3.36 oz	29.26%
Sugar 2	150 g	5.29 oz	7.98%
Heavy cream stabilizer	8 g	.28 oz	.43%
Gelatin sheets, silver, bloomed in cold water, excess water squeezed out	22 g	.78 oz	1.17%

Follow the method for the Pink Guava Cream on page 309 (Steps 2 through 7); omit the instruction to fold in puffed rice. Use the coconut cream immediately to assemble the dessert.

CHOCOLATE STARS COATED IN EDIBLE COPPER LUSTER DUST

YIELD: 250 G/8.82 OZ

INGREDIENT	METRIC	U.S.
Dark chocolate, tempered	250 g	8.82 oz
Edible copper luster dust	2 g	.07 oz

1. Pour enough chocolate into the polycarbonate star mold (see Resources, page 520) to fill each mold to the top. Even it out with a chocolate knife.

2. Let set at room temperature. Once the chocolate is fully crystallized, after about 1 hour, turn the mold over to release the stars.

3. Brush each star with the luster dust using a soft art brush. Affix the dust with a mist of edible lacquer spray (see Resources, page 520).

4. Reserve in a cool, dry area, preferably enclosed. Discard after 1 year.

Ch 5

PASSED-AROUND DESSERTS

These desserts share one of the service qualities of buffet-type desserts: They are generally completely finished before service and ready to be displayed and eaten. There are, of course, exceptions to these guidelines in that some buffet desserts may be finished in front of the customer. This exception does not apply to passed-around desserts; they must be completely finished in the kitchen and never in the dining room, since the waitstaff must transport a tray or other service vessel with one hand or maybe two, leaving no room for manipulation of food. On the other hand, these desserts do not need to be completely stable at room temperature.

There is some room to work with items that are temperature sensitive. For example, a frozen ice pop tray can be sent out of the kitchen and into the dining room and make its rounds to a good amount of customers before the pops start to melt. There are also ways to make sure a frozen dessert does not melt quickly; see Chartreuse Ice Cream on page 379. These are all aspects that are in your control so long as you understand your desserts' storage and display requirements. They need to be preserved to their peak quality, so you need to know what the correct serving equipment is and how to communicate well with your waitstaff.

A passed-around dessert is typically served where people are standing or at least do not have much room to put a plate down to eat. Having said that, if they cannot put a plate down to eat, they cannot put what they are drinking down either, which means they may only have one free hand to eat. This has many implications. One of those is that the dessert must be easy to eat with one hand or it must otherwise require the least amount of effort put into eating it. It should also not make a mess. In most cases, these items are served at an event where people will not be dressing down, and you don't want the responsibility of getting stuck with a laundry bill. You can also consider serving these desserts with implements that can help a person eat them with ease, such as small envelopes, lollipop sticks, small cups, or large spoons. This leaves only one question: Where does the customer put the utensil when he or she is done with it? Again, it is important to communicate with the waitstaff so that they know to clear these items from your customers' hands not too long after they have been served. Otherwise, you will find a dining room with trash on the floor and in other unwelcome places.

Typically this type of service will require that you offer a good variety of desserts. There is no formula to calculate how many varieties of dessert to offer per number of people being served, but since you are serving basically canapé-size portions, one variety is not enough. You should consider making at least two desserts per person, so that the total number of desserts you make will be twice the amount of people you have for a particular event. You may make more, but you should not make less than that.

For some desserts, you should consider that you will generally finish "plating" your items on the service vessel that will be used by the waitstaff to carry the desserts into the dining room. Others can be completely finished ahead of time, but a last-minute garnish can make the dessert better by adding flavor or texture that is temperature and moisture sensitive (something with crunch or something frozen, for example). This allows you slightly more variety than with buffet-style desserts. These types of dessert also have points in common with other styles of dessert such as pre-desserts and mignardises, since they are small portions and plated desserts with *à la minute* finishes. For the most part, they are stand-alone pieces, meaning that they are not necessarily multi-flavored or multitextured. They are more simple and straightforward. Remember: These items are not plated desserts where there can be a variety of components playing off each other. It is a single piece that is held in the hand and should not be a challenge to eat.

ORANGE BLOSSOM CREAM POPS | WARM MADELEINES

YIELD: 10 SERVINGS

WHY THESE FLAVORS WORK	These items provide contrasts in textures and temperatures but are similar in flavor. This dessert explores what happens when one flavor is presented in two very different ways.
COMPONENTS	**Madeleine Batter** (page 364) **Orange blossom water** **Orange Blossom Cream Pops** (page 364)
SERVING INSTRUCTIONS	1. Preheat a convection oven to 160°C/325°F. 2. Lightly grease a tray of madeleine molds with a layer of nonstick oil spray. These trays come in two sizes, 12 pieces and 18 pieces. Use a 12-piece tray for each round of service. 3. Pipe the madeleine batter into the prepared mold. Bake until light golden brown, about 7 minutes. 4. Remove the tray from the oven and turn it over so that the baked madeleines come out. 5. On the scalloped side of the madeleines, brush 5 g/.17 oz orange blossom water per cookie. 6. Place the warm madeleines inside a folded napkin. 7. Place the cream pops on an ice pop stand. Serve immediately.

CARROT CAKE CUBES

YIELD: 10 SERVINGS

WHY THESE FLAVORS WORK

Carrots play to the savory side as well as the dessert side; their natural sweetness is more pronounced when they are cooked. On carrot cakes throughout the United States you will typically see a cream cheese frosting. Cream cheese is yet another ingredient that is used in both savory and sweet preparations. This may be the reason these ingredients have found a common ground in this dessert. The cream cheese in this case is combined with mascarpone to subdue its savory character. When cream cheese is properly sweetened and used in moderation, is a great wrapper for a good carrot cake, adding sour and salty notes to it. The chocolate shell adds a snap, a necessary texture to this dessert, and a neat little box to keep it all in. Chocolate works surprisingly well with these flavors.

COMPONENTS

Chocolate Cubes (page 365)

Cream Cheese and Mascarpone Cream (page 365)

Carrot Cake (page 366)

Orange Velvet Spray (page 252)

Carrot Foam (page 367)

SERVING INSTRUCTIONS

1. Fill each of the 10 chocolate cubes with 30 g/1.06 oz of the cream cheese and mascarpone cream.

2. Push a carrot cake rectangle into the cream; the cream should come up around the sides of the cake. Let it set in the refrigerator upside-down.

3. Set up a spray station, a surface that should be covered with plastic to keep the shop clean where you can spray the cubes.

4. Fill a compressor canister with the orange velvet spray and turn the cubes over. Spray the cubes with an even coating of spray on 2 of the 4 sides only. You need about 50 g/1.7 oz for all 10 cubes. Keep the compressor gun at least 60 cm/24 in from the cubes to obtain a velvety smooth look.

5. Place a 2.5-cm/1-in piece of the carrot foam on top of the cubes. Reserve refrigerated until ready to serve.

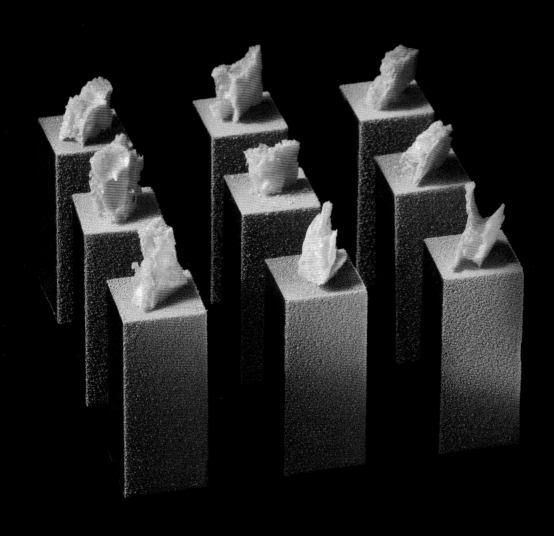

CRISPS

WHY THESE FLAVORS WORK	In this case we have a single flavor, but it is featured in an unusual texture that is not ordinarily used or eaten alone: crispy. These crisps should be eaten one at a time rather than in combination, since eating them together will muddle any unique flavors from each crisp.
COMPONENTS	**Naturally flavored potato starch crisps: peppermint, strawberry, peach, coconut, and lemon** (page 367)
SERVING INSTRUCTIONS	Arrange assorted flavors of fruit crisps in single-flavor stacks on a tray just before serving.

CHOCOLATE-RUM CANNELÉS

YIELD: 20 PIECES

WHY THESE FLAVORS WORK	Traditional cannelés are flavored with vanilla. This wonderful pastry is hard to describe, since if you didn't know better, you'd think something was wrong. It is crisp and firm on the crust as if it were burned but soft and moist on the inside, almost as if it were undercooked. Yet that is exactly how it is supposed to be. In this recipe, it is flavored with chocolate and rum. Both flavors enjoy an almost seamless symbiosis, even though you may not see them together in a cocktail (although, why not?). Rum and chocolate are meant to be together when it comes to pastries and desserts, but it needs to be dark rum, not white, because dark rum's flavors work with those from the chocolate to create a very pleasant combination.
COMPONENTS	**Mini Chocolate-Rum Cannelés** (page 368)
SERVING INSTRUCTIONS	Cannelés are baked and reserved at room temperature. They can be served anytime after they are baked and have cooled. Discard after 24 hours.
NOTE	*Avoid using flexible silicone mats to make cannelés if you can help it; I suggest using the traditional metallic (copper exterior) molds, which are expensive but yield the best results.*

INTRODUCTION TO MACARONS

First, do not confuse macarons with macaroons. They are two completely different cookies. The macaron is an almond meringue cookie that can be either French or Italian and the macaroon is a coconut cookie that is often dipped in chocolate. Notice also the difference in spelling.

The macaron is one of the best items to eat for a sweet fix. It is sweet enough to satisfy with only a few bites, and texturally it is crunchy, chewy, and soft at the same time; even when it is refrigerated for many days it retains the crunch in its outer shell. The variations on flavors and fillings that can be used are almost endless, and this includes savory fillings to an extent (see the items on pages 368 to 373). Think of what you are looking for in a macaron when deciding on the fillings you want to use. Use jams, marmalades, fruit preserves, or candied fruits, or you can mix these items with buttercream, for example. Buttercream has the advantage that it can be mixed with many ingredients and it is easy to pipe, but it may mute the flavor you are going for. It also holds very well inside a macaron since it is mostly fat. Using a small quantity certainly does not hurt, but if you can get away without using it, the resulting filling will be a more flavorful product.

The final texture of a macaron with a slightly raised dome with a hard shell and soft interior makes sense. But the thought process behind it is what I find brilliant. The macaron as we know it today exists thanks to Pierre Desfontaines, of the Ladurée pastry shops in Paris. He perfected the recipe and the method, and more important was the first to sandwich two of these cookies together close to the beginning of the 1900s.

There are three key moments in the process that can make or break a macaron:

1. **FOLDING. At the moment when you fold the meringue into the mixed and sifted almond flour mixture, it is easy to under- or overmix the batter. Getting the mix just right will determine the out-come. Undermixing will yield a chunky, grainy-looking macaron. An overmixed macaron will not hold its shape and will puddle once it is piped onto a sheet pan. A properly mixed macaron will hold its shape after being piped and will have a smooth surface.**

2. **PIPING. While piping will not necessarily determine the success or failure of the quality of the macaron, it will determine the uniformity of size of the finished pieces. The size is determined not only by the width or diameter of the piped macaron but also by the height at which it is piped. The higher above the sheet pan you pipe the batter, the bigger your macaron will be.**

3. **BAKING. Baking instructions are provided here, but chances are that they will have to be fine-tuned to your oven, since no two ovens are alike. The most important objectives are to fully bake the macarons and to do so without any Maillard reaction (coloring) on the macarons. Part of the success in this step is letting the macarons form a skin (or shell) on their surface before baking. This occurs after the macarons are piped and left to sit at room temperature to form said shell. This time may vary depending on environmental conditions in your shop. Is it a dry or humid day? Have other ovens been running (is the shop cool or warm)? Is it warm outside or is it cold? Regardless of the environment, you can always judge by touching the surface of the cookie. If it is dry, then they are ready to bake. If your finger leaves a dent or picks up some of the cookie batter, then they are not quite ready. There is also such a thing as overdrying. If the cookie dries for too long, it forms a thick, hard shell, and this will result in no "feet" at the bottom of the cookie. The foot is the grainy-looking belt around the base of the smooth dome. Those feet are a sign of quality in a macaron.**

BASE MACARON RECIPE

YIELD: 970 G/2 LB 2.08 OZ (ABOUT 70 SANDWICH COOKIES)

INGREDIENT	METRIC	U.S.	%
Egg whites	200 g	7.05 oz	20.62%
Powdered egg whites	10 g	.35 oz	1.03%
Superfine, fondant, or bakers' sugar	60 g	2.12 oz	6.19%
Almond flour	250 g	8.82 oz	25.77%
Confectioners' sugar	450 g	15.87 oz	46.39%
Natural food coloring, water based	as needed	as needed	

1. Combine the egg whites with the powdered egg whites by stirring in the powdered egg whites in a slow cascading motion with a whisk.

2. Grind the superfine sugar in a coffee grinder until very fine unless using fondant sugar, in which case you only need to sift it to remove any lumps.

3. Combine the almond flour with the confectioners' sugar in a bowl and then mix in a Robot Coupe for 30 seconds; pass through a drum sieve.

4. In an electric mixer fitted with the whip attachment, whip the egg whites on high speed. When they have reached medium peaks, sprinkle in the sugar, and then whip to stiff peaks. Add a few drops of food coloring if needed at this point. Whip for a few more seconds to fully incorporate the color. The amount of color depends on the type of coloring you use. Natural food coloring is expensive and requires a larger quantity to properly color a base than non-natural colors and they tend to fade with time. Always use liquid soluble colors, not fat-based colors. You may use powdered color as well, just make sure it is liquid soluble and not fat soluble). For the colors used in these macaron recipes, see page 520 for resources.

5. Fold the meringue into the dry ingredients until smooth using a rubber spatula. Do not over-mix (it will become very loose). It should puddle a little bit just after you stop stirring. You are not making a sponge cake here, so there will be some deflation in the meringue, but this is expected.

6. Pour into a piping bag fitted with a #6 plain tip.

7. Pipe onto a sheet pan lined with a thin, nonstick baking mat (preferably not the rubber mats, since these are too thick; see Resources, page 520). Using a perforated mat results in a more efficient heat transfer to the bottom of the macaron, which gives the cookie higher volume. The diameter of the macaron should be about 3.18 cm/1.25 in. Space them out leaving at least a 2.50-cm/1-in space between them. Let them air-dry for 30 to 40 minutes. Always check by touching the dome of the cookie to feel for a dry surface. Your finger should not leave a dent.

8. Meanwhile, preheat a convection oven to 150°C/300°F and set to fan speed 3. Bake for 2 minutes, then turn the fan speed down to 1 and bake for 2 more minutes. Turn off the oven and leave the macarons in the oven for 12 to 14 minutes more, or 8 to 10 minutes for small macarons. They are ready when they can be lifted up from the mat without sticking.

9. Cool at room temperature.

10. Fill with the appropriate filling. The filling should be placed in a piping bag with a small #2 plain tip. The average thickness of the filling should be about 3 mm/.1 in but can vary depending on the filling. Too little filling is not recommended; there should be enough in there to be able to tell what flavor it is, but there shouldn't be too much either. The consistency of the filling is important as well. It shouldn't be too wet, or it will make the cookie soggy and spill out of the cookie. Ideally, it should hold its shape once it is piped. This is where using a little buttercream can help to tighten up the filling, but remember to use it in moderation.

11. Place the cookies in a single layer on a sheet pan and cover with plastic wrap. It is crucial not to serve the cookies as soon as they are assembled, since they will need about 24 hours to get acquainted. This means that the filling will soften the base of the cookie it is in contact with and meld both the cookies to it. Some chefs recommend more than 24 hours, but this amount of time is just enough.

12. Reserve frozen for up to 3 months or refrigerate for up to 7 days, well wrapped in an airtight container.

13. They can be served straight from the refrigerator or left out to temper for 1 hour before serving. I enjoy them either way. They are even pleasant to eat frozen.

NOTE

Ideally fondant sugar should be used for the meringue component of the macarons; it is the finest consistency and thus dissolves more readily into the egg whites, which in turn produces a smoother, shinier macaron.

For specific macaron varieties, see pages 368–373.

HIERBA SANTA GELÉE | SASSAFRAS PANNA COTTA

YIELD: 30 SERVINGS

WHY THESE FLAVORS WORK	Hierba santa is not a very common ingredient. Some growers sell it under a different name: root beer leaf, because there are some flavor notes of root beer in there. Sassafras is one of the ingredients used to make root beer, and therefore these two flavors are well aligned without being identical.
COMPONENTS	**Hierba Santa Gelée** (page 374) **Sassafras Panna Cotta** (page 374)
SERVING INSTRUCTIONS	1. Place 30 Plexiglas tubes measuring 2.5 cm/1 in wide by 5 cm/2 in long on a very flat sheet pan lined with a sheet of acetate. Deep-freeze this setup. 2. Using a sauce gun, portion 5 g/.17 oz of the room-temperature gelée into each tube. It is crucial that they be frozen and the liquid tempered so that it sets on contact and does not spill out of the tubes. 3. Once the gelée is set, keep it refrigerated. and make the sassafras panna cotta. 4. Portion the room-temperature panna cotta into the tubes using a funnel gun, to within 3 mm/.1 in from the top of the tube. Let it set in the refrigerator. 5. Once set, portion the remaining gelée on top of the panna cotta to fill the tube to the top. Let this set as well. 6. Reserve in the refrigerator until needed. Temper this dessert for at least 30 minutes before serving.
NOTE	*To eat this dessert you need to suck it from one of the openings, like a giant straw.*

CHOCOLATE AND FRUIT POPS

YIELD: 10 OF EACH FLAVOR (TOTAL OF 80)

WHY THESE
FLAVORS WORK

Dark chocolate and açai: Açai has an intense berry flavor that almost tastes like fake berry flavor. The açai is intensified by the bitterness of the dark chocolate.

Dark chocolate and pomegranate: Pomegranate is a sour flavor that can be muted by most flavors, but the dark chocolate acts as an enhancer.

Dark chocolate and Steuben grapes: This grape is very similar to the Concord grape but with a concentrated flavor. When dry it is almost wine-like, which pairs well with a dark chocolate instead of a sweeter one.

Milk chocolate and lucuma: Lucuma is a fruit that is most common in Peru. It has a unique flavor that is very intense and on the sweet side, with an almost umami taste to it, which makes it a good balance for milk chocolate.

Milk chocolate and coffee: Coffee and all three chocolates (dark, milk, and white) go well together, but for different reasons. Milk chocolate tames the bitterness of the coffee—think of adding milk to a cup of coffee.

White chocolate and bayberry: This berry is very complex in flavor with a highly sour taste, which is why the sweetness of the white chocolate is an ideal balance for it. The species of bayberry called for here is commercially known as "Yumberry."

White chocolate and wild blueberry: Wild blueberries have a fruiter taste than cultivated blueberries, and they are also slightly more acidic. White chocolate enhances their flavor very well.

White chocolate and matcha: Matcha has a slightly fishy taste, which is unfortunate. Certain brands, though, somehow manage to circumvent that (see Resources, page 520). It still has a very green-vegetable/grassy flavor, which is kept in check by the dairy flavor of white chocolate, thus making them great companions in your mouth.

COMPONENTS

Dark chocolate

Milk chocolate

White chocolate

Freeze-dried fruit powders: bayberry, açai, wild blueberry, lucuma, pomegranate, Steuben grape

Other flavors: instant coffee powder, matcha green tea

Edible lacquer spray

SERVING INSTRUCTIONS

1. Place 80 lollipop sticks on a flat surface.

2. Temper one chocolate at a time. You will need about 400 g/14.1 oz per type of chocolate to make 20 lollipops (each pop is about 20 g/.7 oz).

3. Pour the chocolate into a parchment paper cornet. Pipe it into a swirled drizzle, making sure to pipe some over the lollipop stick. Let the chocolate crystallize.

4. Set up the freeze-dried fruit powders and other flavors by placing each one on a flat plate. You will need about 200 g/7.05 oz of each.

5. Spray each pop (only the chocolate part) with edible lacquer spray on both sides and dip it into the powder, making sure it is completely covered. Tap off the excess powder.

6. Reserve at room temperature in a cool, dry place, preferably enclosed. Discard after 2 months.

BERRY FOOL ENVELOPE

YIELD: 40 SERVINGS

WHY THESE FLAVORS WORK	A fool is a dessert that dates from the sixteenth century and is composed of fruit (sometimes puréed), whipped cream, and sugar, and sometimes an added flavor such as rose. It has that name because supposedly even a fool can make it. This dessert combines the flavors of cream and berries (raspberries, strawberries, and blackberries), which go so well together because each fruit has a certain sweetness but also acidic flavors that are tempered by the smooth richness of the cream and the sweetness of the sugar. In this case, heavy cream solids have been added and composed into a dry dessert that reconstitutes in the mouth.
COMPONENTS	**Berry Fool Envelope** (page 375)
SERVING INSTRUCTIONS	Place the berry fool envelopes inside a vellum envelope. Reserve in an airtight container in a cool, dry place. The meringues will keep for up to 1 month.

PUMPKIN SEED AND MILK CHOCOLATE MINI BARS

YIELD: 40 MINI-BARS

WHY THESE FLAVORS WORK

The original inspiration for this pairing was peanut butter and milk chocolate. Having tasted that pairing often and enjoyed it, it occurred to me that maybe different nut pastes might also work. And they do for the most part, but I also started thinking about seeds. Pumpkin seed paste works very well, almost for the same reason that peanut butter does. It is rich and smooth, but it also has a more pervasive flavor. The milk chocolate enhances that flavor, and the dark chocolate wraps the whole package tightly with its bitterness. As a side note, sesame paste and sunflower seeds also work very well with milk chocolate.

COMPONENTS

Pumpkin Seed and Milk Chocolate Ganache (page 375)

Tempered dark chocolate

Silver-green luster dust (see Resources, page 520)

Edible lacquer (see Resources, page 520)

SERVING INSTRUCTIONS

1. Dip each ganache oval in tempered dark chocolate.

2. Before the chocolate sets, apply compressed air to the surface of the bar to give it a rippled look. You will have to do this one at a time to keep the chocolate that the ovals are dipped in from setting too much. Otherwise there will be no rippled effect.

3. Once the chocolate has crystallized, apply a coat of edible lacquer to each chocolate mini bar to affix the luster dust. Brush each piece with silver-green luster dust. You will need about 20 g/.7 oz for all 40 pieces.

4. Reserve in a cool, dry, enclosed area. Discard after 1 month.

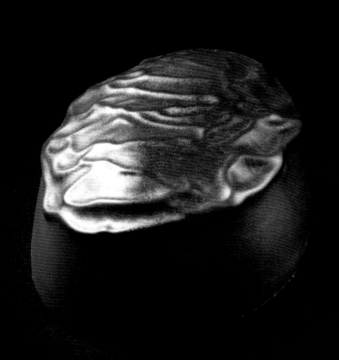

BLACK OLIVE RAISINS

YIELD: 40 SERVINGS

WHY THESE FLAVORS WORK	Spanish olives were chosen for their complexity and depth of flavor, which is very umami-like. They are also not sour and briny like most Italian olives. The final result will be like a raisin, except with the flavor of an olive and with a little crunch on the skin.
COMPONENTS	**Black Olive Raisins** (page 376)
SERVING INSTRUCTIONS	Fill forty 60-g/2.12-oz envelopes with 45 g/1.5 oz of black olive raisins.

LIQUID RED VELVET CAKE TRUFFLES

YIELD: 100 TRUFFLES

WHY THESE FLAVORS WORK	Since red velvet cake contains cocoa powder, chocolate and red velvet obviously have a very well-aligned flavor profile. However, red velvet cake has a particular, unique flavor all its own, which is only made more profound by the presence of dark chocolate. The crumbs on the surface add a third texture to this truffle.
COMPONENTS	**Red Velvet Cake Liquid Filling** (page 376) **Dark chocolate truffle shells** (see Resources, page 520) **Tempered dark chocolate** **Red Velvet Cake Crumbs** (page 376)
SERVING INSTRUCTIONS	1. Pour the red velvet cake purée into the dark chocolate truffle shells. 2. Freeze them until the purée has hardened. 3. Cap the top of the truffle shells with tempered chocolate. Let them thaw at room temperature. 4. Coat the truffles with tempered chocolate. You will need about 500 g/1 lb 1.64 oz of tempered dark chocolate to completely coat 100 truffles. Immediately after they are coated, toss them into the red velvet cake crumbs before the tempered chocolate sets so that the crumbs will adhere to the truffle shell. 5. Reserve in the refrigerator for up to 1 week. Temper the finished truffles at room temperature for at least 1 hour before serving.

LEMON VERBENA GELÉE | BLACKBERRY COULIS | ANISE HYSSOP

YIELD: 40 SERVINGS

WHY THESE FLAVORS WORK	Lemon verbena has a very subtle yet immediately recognizable flavor that, as its name indicates, is very citrus-like. This is what makes it very friendly with flavors like mint and blackberry.
COMPONENTS	**Lemon Verbena Gelée** (page 377) **Blackberry Coulis dots** (page 377) **Anise hyssop leaves**
SERVING INSTRUCTIONS	1. Remove the gelée from the molds by prying them out gently with a small offset spatula. 2. Using an eye dropper, squeeze a single drop of coulis onto the surface of the gelée. 3. Place a single small leaf of anise hyssop on the surface of the gelée. Serve immediately.

DOTS

YIELD: 40 SHEETS

WHY THESE FLAVORS WORK	This item is inspired by a classic American candy. The difference is that this is naturally flavored, with the added bonus of being able to eat the paper on which they are served.
COMPONENTS	**Rice paper rectangles** **Fig Royal Icing dots** (page 378)
SERVING INSTRUCTIONS	1. Cut five 8½ by 11-in sheets of rice paper into rectangles measuring 5 cm/2 in by 10 cm/4 in. You should get between 8 and 10 rectangles out of each sheet of rice paper. 3. Pipe the royal icing onto each rectangle, for a total of 11 evenly spaced dots on each sheet. 4. Let the royal icing set at room temperature for at least 8 hours. Reserve in an airtight container before serving. 5. They can be plated far ahead of time if needed, since they are shelf stable.

CHARTREUSE ICE CREAM BITES

YIELD: 40 SERVINGS

WHY THESE FLAVORS WORK

Chartreuse is a very complex-flavored liquor that is highly alcoholic and has strong herbal notes that are strengthened by the dark chocolate. Be sure to use the green variety here rather than the yellow. The dark chocolate shell also adds a grown-up twist to the chocolate shell often found in ice cream novelties, as well as a textural snap to a smooth ice cream.

COMPONENTS

Chartreuse Ice Cream (page 379)

Chocolate Shell (page 378)

SERVING INSTRUCTIONS

1. Line a full sheet pan with a nonstick rubber mat. Freeze this setup.

2. Once the chartreuse ice cream is churned, pour it into a piping bag fitted with a #8 plain round tip and pipe it onto the frozen sheet pan into tubes as long as the sheet pan. Do this with all of the ice cream base.

3. Freeze to harden the ice cream.

4. Once it has hardened, using an offset spatula (and not a knife on the nonstick rubber mat), cut out 3.75-cm/1.5–in-wide tubes.

5. Return the setup to the freezer while you make the chocolate shell.

6. Insert a stainless-steel pin (see Resources, page 520) into each ice cream tube and dip each one in the chocolate shell; keep it dipped for 10 seconds so that it forms a thick enough shell. Return to the freezer.

7. To serve, you can set up the ice cream on a bed of dry ice that's topped with a fine-mesh screen. This will keep them frozen for longer as they are being passed.

ORANGE BLOSSOM CREAM POPS

YIELD: 1.4 KG/3 LB 2.72 OZ

INGREDIENT	METRIC	U.S.	%
Whole milk	1.2 kg	2 lb 10.24 oz	83.33%
Fondant sugar or superfine sugar	225 g	7.94 oz	15.63%
Orange blossom water	10 g	.35 oz	.69%
Vanilla paste	5 g	.18 oz	.35%

1. Assemble 10 silicone ice pop molds (see Resources, page 520); slide the serving sticks into them at this point.

2. Combine all of the ingredients in a bowl and stir until the sugar has dissolved.

3. Pour the base into the prepared molds, filling them to the top, and place in the freezer.

4. Once completely hardened, remove them from the molds.

5. Reserve frozen, preferably in an airtight container. Thaw and re-freeze after 3 days.

MADELEINE BATTER

YIELD: 506 G/1 LB 1.87 OZ

INGREDIENT	METRIC	U.S.	%
Pastry flour	105 g	3.7 oz	20.73%
Baking powder	4 g	.14 oz	.79%
Salt	1 g	.02 oz	.1%
Sugar	90 g	3.17 oz	17.77%
Brown sugar	50 g	1.76 oz	9.87%
Eggs	115 g	4.06 oz	22.7%
Butter, melted but cool	105 g	3.7 oz	20.73%
Honey	12 g	.42 oz	2.37%
Milk	25 g	.88 oz	4.94%

1. Sift the pastry flour with the baking powder and salt.

2. Combine the sugars and eggs and whip using an electric mixer until they reach the ribbon stage.

3. Add the dry ingredients and mix until just combined. Add the melted butter, honey, and milk. Mix until just combined.

4. Reserve in the refrigerator for service. Bake to order, and discard after service.

NOTE *This recipe yields more than you will need for 10 orders. The remaining batter may be used for more madeleines. This recipe will yield 40 to 45 individual madeleines.*

CHOCOLATE CUBES

YIELD: 500 G/1 LB 1.64 OZ

INGREDIENT	METRIC	U.S.	%
Tempered dark chocolate	500 g	1 lb 1.64 oz	100%

1. You will need 10 plastic cube containers measuring 3 cm/1.25 in wide by 3 cm/1.25 in long by 7 cm/2.75 in high (see Resources, page 520).

2. Using a pastry brush, brush the inside of the containers with tempered chocolate (especially the corners of the molds).

3. Pour the tempered chocolate into the molds. Let the chocolate sit in the molds for about 1 minute, and then turn them over to let the excess chocolate drip out. Let the molds set in a freezer with direct cold air going into the molds.

4. Once the chocolate is completely set and it looks like it has released from the mold, let it warm up slightly, then try to slide the chocolate out of the mold with a gloved finger. Since these molds have straight sides, the release of chocolate can be challenging.

5. Reserve the cubes covered at room temperature. Discard after 1 year.

    NOTE *There will be chocolate left over, but the total amount is necessary in order to fill the molds completely and then empty them out to form a shell.*

CREAM CHEESE AND MASCARPONE CREAM

YIELD: 500 G/1 LB 1.64 OZ

INGREDIENT	METRIC	U.S.	%
Cream cheese	290 g	10.23 oz	58%
Mascarpone	145 g	5.11 oz	29%
Vanilla paste	5 g	.18 oz	1%
Confectioners' sugar	60 g	2.12 oz	12%

1. Soften the cream cheese in a microwave until soft but not melted.

2. Mix all of the ingredients together over a double boiler with an immersion blender until smooth.

3. Use while still fluid to build carrot cake cubes. Any remaining cream can be cooled, refrigerated, and used for other desserts; it will need to be rewarmed over a hot water bath. Discard after 1 week.

CARROT CAKE

YIELD: 1 KG/2 LB 3.2 OZ

INGREDIENT	METRIC	U.S.	%
Carrots	110 g	3.88 oz	11%
Bread flour	95 g	3.35 oz	9.5%
Pastry flour	65 g	2.29 oz	6.5%
Baking soda	8 g	.28 oz	.80%
Ground cinnamon	4 g	.14 oz	.4%
Salt	5 g	.18 oz	.5%
Butter, at 21°C/70°F	240 g	8.47 oz	24%
Sugar	260 g	9.17 oz	26%
Vanilla paste	3 g	.11 oz	.3%
Eggs, at 21°C/70°F	140 g	4.94 oz	14%
Walnuts, coarsely chopped	70 g	2.47 oz	7%

1. Preheat a convection oven to 160°C/325°F.

2. Lightly grease the internal border of a quarter sheet pan with nonstick oil spray. Line the pan with a nonstick rubber mat.

3. Wash, peel, and grate the carrots.

4. Sift both flours, the baking soda, cinnamon, and salt together.

5. In an electric mixer fitted with the paddle attachment, cream the butter, sugar, and vanilla paste until light and fluffy, about 4 minutes.

6. Slowly incorporate the eggs.

7. Stop the mixer and add the flour mixture. Mix on low speed just to incorporate completely, and then add the walnuts and carrots, mixing for a few more seconds until the nuts and carrots are evenly distributed.

8. Spread the batter onto the prepared sheet pan in an even layer using an offset spatula.

9. Bake until done, 8 to 12 minutes.

10. Cool to room temperature, and then chill in the refrigerator. It is easier to cut the cake once it is cold.

11. Cut the cake into rectangles measuring 2.5 cm/1 in wide by 5 cm/2 in long by 2.5 cm/1 in deep.

12. Freeze the rectangles to harden. This will make the process of pushing them into the chocolate cubes less complicated since they will be firm; they will be able to push into the mascarpone and cream cheese without being damaged.

NOTE *This recipe yields more than 10 orders, but it cannot be baked in a smaller pan with positive results.*

CARROT FOAM

YIELD: 420 G/14.84 OZ

INGREDIENT	METRIC	U.S.	%
Xanthan gum (.5%)	2 g	.07 oz	.5%
Methocel F50 (.85%)	4 g	.13 oz	.86%
Sugar	40 g	1.41 oz	9.51%
Carrot juice	375 g	13.23 oz	89.14%

1. Prepare a one-quarter sheet of silicone paper by poking it with a needle, making as many holes as you can. The silicone paper needs to be perforated because Methocel requires coming into contact with heat on its entire surface in order to gel. If you don't perforate the paper you will end up with a crisp surface but a soft base.

2. Turn a dehydrator on to 65°C/150°F.

3. Combine the xanthan gum, Methocel F50, and sugar in a coffee grinder and grind to obtain a fine homogenous mix.

4. Using a handheld immersion blender, shear the dry mix into the carrot juice in the bowl of an electric mixer, pouring the dry ingredients slowly to avoid clumping. You should have a thick, viscous mass.

5. Place the bowl on an electric mixer fitted with the whip attachment. Whip on high speed until the liquid increases in volume eightfold and looks like shaving cream.

6. Spread the foam into an even layer on the perforated silicone paper. It should be about 2.5 cm/1 in thick.

7. Place in the dehydrator and let it dry for at least 2 hours.

8. Once the foam has gelled, it will remain soft if it is warm, but when it cools it will be crisp. Reserve this foam warm in a dehydrator until ready to assemble the entremets. Discard after 1 week.

FRUIT CRISPS

YIELD: 250 G/8.82 OZ

INGREDIENT	METRIC	U.S.	%
Water	175 g	6.17 oz	70%
Freeze-dried fruit powder/ freeze-dried peppermint powder	50 g	1.76 oz	20%
Potato starch	25 g	.88 oz	10%

1. Turn a dehydrator on to 65°C/150°F.

2. Prepare each desired flavor of crisp separately. Combine the water with the freeze-dried powder (see Resources, page 520) in a small, shallow sauce pot; stir until dissolved.

3. Stir in the potato starch and turn the heat up to high. Stir constantly until you obtain a gelatinous mass.

4. Spread the mixture as thinly as possible onto a sheet of acetate that will fit into your dehydrator.

5. Let the mixture dry completely in the dehydrator for about 4 hours.

6. Once it is dry, it will stay soft and pliable while it is still warm, but when it cools it will become crispy. Break the crisps into organic pieces 5 cm/2 in to 7.5 cm/3 in (they don't have to be perfect squares or shapes).

7. Keep the pieces in the dehydrator until you are ready to serve them.

MINI CHOCOLATE-RUM CANNELÉS

YIELD: 1.15 KG/2 LB 8.64 OZ

INGREDIENT	METRIC	U.S.	%
Confectioners' sugar	225 g	7.94 oz	19.51%
All-purpose flour	85 g	3 oz	7.37%
Cocoa powder	8 g	.28 oz	.69%
Milk	500 g	1 lb 1.64 oz	43.37%
Butter	75 g	2.65 oz	6.5%
Dark chocolate coins (64%)	100 g	3.53 oz	8.67%
Eggs	100 g	3.53 oz	8.67%
Egg yolks	40 g	1.41 oz	3.47%
Dark rum	20 g	.71 oz	1.73%

1. Lightly grease the cannelé molds with nonstick oil spray (see Resources, page 520, for the molds).

2. Preheat a convection oven to 180°C/350°F.

3. Sift the confectioners' sugar, flour, and cocoa powder together.

4. Bring the milk to a boil and then pour it on top of the butter and chocolate in a bowl. Stir until both the butter and chocolate are melted and combined.

5. Combine the eggs and the yolks and then whisk them into the sifted sugar-flour mixture to form a paste.

6. Combine this mixture well with the milk mixture and then stir in the rum.

7. Fill the molds to within .5 cm/.2 in from the tops.

8. Bake for 45 to 50 minutes. The crown of the cannelés should feel firm when you press down with a fingertip. Remove the cannelés from the mold before they cool.

9. Reserve uncovered at room temperature.

GOAT CHEESE AND ACACIA HONEY MACARONS (GRAY)

YIELD: 550 G/1 LB 3.36 OZ

INGREDIENT	METRIC	U.S.	%
Color			
Vegetable ash powder	10 g	.35 oz	
Filling			
Goat cheese, smooth	425 g	14.99 oz	77.27%
Acacia honey	125 g	4.41 oz	22.73%

1. To color the macarons, add the vegetable ash powder to the flour-sugar mixture before placing it in the Robot Coupe.

2. **For the filling:** Place both ingredients inside an electric mixer bowl and mix with the paddle attachment until smooth.

3. Have half of the macarons flipped over and ready to be filled. Pipe the filling onto the macaron bases. Place the top macaron over the filling and gently push down. Reserve refrigerated.

SAGE AND FOIE GRAS MACARONS
(SPECKLED GREEN)

YIELD: 1 KG/2 LB 3.2 OZ

INGREDIENT	METRIC	U.S.	%
Color			
Sage leaves, dehydrated	10 g	.35 oz	
Filling			
Foie gras, deveined, soaked in milk overnight	930 g	2 lb .8 oz	93%
Pedro Ximénez sherry	50 g	1.76 oz	5%
Salt	15 g	.53 oz	1.5%
Black pepper, freshly ground	5 g	.18 oz	.5%

1. To color the macarons, grind the sage leaves in a coffee grinder.

2. Combine the sage leaves with the flour-sugar mixture before placing it in the Robot Coupe.

3. **For the filling:** Remove the foie gras from the milk and pat dry with a clean towel. Temper for 2 hours before making the mousse; this reduces the cooking time. Make sure to keep it well covered with plastic wrap to reduce oxidation. Prepare an ice water bath.

4. Have half of the macarons flipped over (flat side up) ready to be filled. Have a piping bag ready with a #2 tip.

5. Set the timer on a Thermomix for 5 minutes and the temperature to 80°C/175°F. Do not put the ingredients into the Thermomix cup until the machine reaches the right temperature, which will take about 2 minutes. Otherwise, it will make your foie gras too hot and it will break or separate.

6. Without delay, once the desired temperature is reached, turn the machine off and put all of the filling ingredients in the cup. Set the machine on speed 3 for 2 minutes. Turn the machine on and let it mix for the allotted time.

7. Pour the contents of the pitcher into a bowl that will fit comfortably inside the ice water bath. Remove the ice from the ice water bath and place the bowl with the foie gras inside the cold water bath. Stir until it has the consistency of a smooth ganache.

8. Transfer the filling into the prepared piping bag and pipe it onto the macaron bases. Place the top macaron over the filling and gently push down. Reserve refrigerated.

PUMPKIN BUTTER MACARONS (ORANGE-BROWN)

YIELD: 785 G/1 LB 11.68 OZ

INGREDIENT	METRIC	U.S.	%
Color			
Orange natural food coloring, water based	as needed	as needed	
Brown natural food coloring, water based	as needed	as needed	
Filling			
Sugar pumpkin, peeled, seeded, and cut into medium-dice chunks	500 g	1 lb 1.64 oz	63.69%
Butter	80 g	2.82 oz	10.19%
Maple sugar	200 g	7.05 oz	25.48%
Vanilla pod, split and seeds scraped	1	1	
Ground cinnamon	5 g	.18 oz	.64%

1. To color the macarons, add a few drops of orange coloring and a few drops of brown coloring in Step 4 of the master recipe to obtain a burnt orange hue.

2. **For the filling:** Combine all of the ingredients in a small sauce pot and cook over medium-low heat, stirring occasionally. Reduce the mix by 30 percent through evaporation. The base should weigh about 550 g/1 lb 3.4 oz.

3. Cool in an ice water bath before piping into the macarons.

4. Have half of the macarons flipped over (flat side up) and ready to be filled. Pipe the filling onto the macaron bases. Place the top macaron over the filling and gently push down. Reserve refrigerated.

LITCHI JELLY AND RASPBERRY JAM MACARONS (PINK AND RED)

YIELD: 800 G/1 LB 12.22 OZ

INGREDIENT	METRIC	U.S.	%
Color			
Pink natural food coloring, water based	as needed	as needed	
Red natural food coloring, water based	as needed	as needed	
Filling			
Litchi jelly (see Resources, page xxx)	300 g	10.58 oz	100%
Raspberry Jam			
Raspberries	250 g	8.82 oz	50%
Sugar	250 g	8.82 oz	50%
Tahitian vanilla pod, split and seeds scraped	1	1	

1. To color the macarons, you will need to make two separate batches simultaneously. Color one of them light pink and the other a deep red.

2. Pipe a 2.5-cm/1-in diameter disk of pink macaron batter onto the prepared sheet pans and, with the help of another person, immediately pipe a 1.25-cm/.5-in disk of deep red batter directly into the center of the pink macaron. Proceed as directed to finish the cookies.

3. **For the jelly:** Chop the jelly with a knife until small pieces are obtained.

4. Pipe into the center of half of the flipped-over macarons in a 1.25-cm/.5-in radius.

5. **For the jam:** Combine all of the ingredients in a small sauce pot and bring to a boil, then turn the heat down to medium so that the mixture is at a simmer. Cook to 65° Brix.

6. Cool over an ice water bath. Pipe a ring of jam around the litchi jelly on each macaron. Place the top macaron over the filling and gently push down. Reserve refrigerated.

APRICOT JAM AND SICILIAN PISTACHIO MACARONS (LIGHT ORANGE)

YIELD: 650 G/1 LB 13.92 OZ

INGREDIENT	METRIC	U.S.	%
Color			
Yellow natural food coloring, water based	as needed	as needed	
Orange natural food coloring, water based	as needed	as needed	
Filling			
Dried apricots	200 g	7.05 oz	23.53%
Water	400 g	14.11 oz	47.06%
Sugar	250 g	8.82 oz	29.41%
Vanilla pod, split and seeds scraped	1	1	
Sicilian pistachios	400 g	14.11 oz	

1. To color the macarons, add a few drops of yellow and orange food coloring in Step 4 of the master recipe, to resemble the color of an apricot.

2. **For the filling:** Combine the dried apricots with the water and bring them to a boil. Let the apricots reconstitute in the water for about 30 minutes, then drain the apricots. You will have about 300 g/10.58 oz or more of apricots; you can include them all in the recipe without a negative effect.

3. Combine the apricots, sugar, and vanilla pod and seeds in a pot. Bring to a boil, and then reduce to a simmer. Cook until the mixture reaches 68° Brix.

4. Discard the vanilla pod and cool the mixture over an ice water bath. Transfer the mixture to a piping bag fitted with an #802 straight tip.

5. Pipe a ring around the border of half of the macarons. The pistachios will go in the center of the macaron.

6. Preheat a convection oven to 160°C/325°F.

7. Chop the pistachios by hand as finely as possible. Don't use a Robot Coupe; you may obtain very uneven picccз.

8. Place the pistachios on a sheet pan lined with a non-stick rubber mat. Toast until aromatic, about 5 minutes. Cool to room temperature.

9. Fill the center of the piped macarons with the pistachios. Place the top macaron over the filling and gently push down. Reserve refrigerated.

NOTE *Dried apricots have a much more concentrated apricot flavor than fresh apricots. Fresh apricots are not really all that good; they are one of those fruits that gets better through the application of heat.*

CANDIED ANGELICA AND TOASTED ALMOND MACARONS (LIGHT GREEN)

YIELD: 700 G/1 LB 8.64 OZ

INGREDIENT	METRIC	U.S.	%
Color			
Light green natural food coloring, water based	as needed	as needed	
Filling			
Toasted marcona almonds	300 g	10.58 oz	42.86%
Candied angelica, cut into brunoise (see Resources, page 520)	400 g	14.11 oz	57.14%

1. To color the macarons, apply a few drops of food coloring in Step 4 of the master recipe.

2. **For the filling:** Place the almonds in a Robot Coupe while they are still warm and grind them to a smooth paste.

3. Pipe a 1.25-cm/.5-in diameter ring of the almond paste at the center of half of the cookies.

4. Spoon the candied angelica brunoise around the almond paste. Place the top macaron over the filling and gently push down. Reserve refrigerated.

VANILLA MACARONS (WHITE)

YIELD: 910 G/2 LB

INGREDIENT	METRIC	U.S.	%
Heavy cream	300 g	10.58 oz	32.97%
White chocolate coins	600 g	1 lb 5.12 oz	65.93%
Vanilla paste	10 g	.35 oz	1.1%

1. Bring the heavy cream to a rolling boil and pour it over the white chocolate. Stir to emulsify and melt the chocolate.

2. Stir in the vanilla paste and mix evenly.

3. Have half of the macarons flipped over (flat side up) and ready to be filled. Pipe the filling onto the macaron bases. Place the top macaron over the filling and gently push down. Reserve refrigerated.

NOTE *This is perhaps the most challenging macaron to bake since it is intended to be pure white.*

CHESTNUT AND CRÈME FRAÎCHE MACARONS (LIGHT BROWN)

YIELD: 380 G/13.4 OZ

INGREDIENT	METRIC	U.S.	%
Color			
Brown natural food coloring, water based	as needed	as needed	
Filling			
Chestnut cream (see Resources, page 520)	400 g	14.11 oz	51.28%
Crème fraîche	300 g	10.58 oz	38.46%
Vanilla paste	5 g	.18 oz	.64%
Superfine or bakers' sugar	75 g	2.65 oz	9.62%

1. To color the macarons, add a few drops of natural brown food coloring in Step 4 of the master recipe.

2. **For the filling:** Pipe a ring of chestnut cream around the border of half of the macarons using a piping bag and a #2 tip.

3. Combine the remaining ingredients in a bowl using a whisk. Stir until the sugar has dissolved. Transfer to a piping bag.

4. Have half of the macarons flipped over (flat side up) and ready to be filled. Pipe the filling onto the macaron bases. Place the top macaron over the filling and gently push down. Reserve refrigerated.

NOTE *The recommended brand of ready-made chestnut cream (see Resources, page 520) is of very high quality and is made from bits and pieces of marrons glacés. Were you to make this cream from scratch, you would have to spend a year making the marrons glacés.*

YUZU MACARONS (YELLOW)

YIELD: 650 G/1 LB 6.88 OZ

INGREDIENT	METRIC	U.S.
Color		
Yellow natural food coloring, water based	as needed	as needed
Filling		
Yuzu marmalade (see Resources, page xxx)	650 g	1 lb 6.88 oz

1. To color the macarons, add a few drops of bright yellow in Step 4 of the master recipe.

2. **For the filling:** Purée the marmalade in a Robot Coupe until smooth.

3. Have half of the macarons flipped over (flat side up) and ready to be filled. Pipe the filling onto the macaron bases. Place the top macaron over the filling and gently push down. Reserve refrigerated.

HIERBA SANTA GELÉE

YIELD: 773 G/1 LB 11.2 OZ

INGREDIENT	METRIC	U.S.	%
Blanched Hierba Santa Leaves			
Water	3 kg	6 lb 9.76 oz	71.09%
Ascorbic acid	10 g	.35 oz	.24%
Salt	10 g	.35 oz	.24%
Hierba santa leaves, stems removed	1.2 kg	2 lb 10.64 oz	28.44%
Infused Water			
Blanched Hierba Santa Leaves	1 kg	2 lb 3.2 oz	58.82%
Water, at room temperature	500 g	1 lb 1.64 oz	29.41%
Sugar	200 g	7.05 oz	11.76%
Gelée			
Gelatin sheets, silver, bloomed in cold water, excess water squeezed off	23 g	.79 oz	2.91%
Infused Water	750 g	1 lb 10.4 oz	97.09%

1. **For the blanched hierba santa leaves:** Bring the water, ascorbic acid, and salt to a rolling boil.

2. Meanwhile, set up an ice water bath large enough to hold all of the leaves.

3. Dip the leaves all at once into the boiling water. Make sure to fully submerge them in the water. Blanch the leaves for 7 to 10 seconds or until they are wilted.

4. Quickly remove the leaves from the boiling water and place them in the ice water bath, stirring them to cool them down quickly.

5. **For the infused water:** Blend all of the ingredients together. Adjust the sweetness if necessary by adding more sugar and stirring to dissolve.

6. Pass through a fine-mesh sieve and then through cheesecloth to obtain a liquid purée.

7. **For the gelée:** Melt the gelatin over a water bath or in a microwave, then stir it quickly into the infused water using a whisk. It is crucial that the water not be too cold; otherwise the gelatin will set quickly. Let the gelée cool to room temperature.

SASSAFRAS PANNA COTTA

YIELD: 1.34 KG/2 LB 15.36 OZ

INGREDIENT	METRIC	U.S.	%
Heavy cream	1.2 kg	2 lb 10.24 oz	89.39%
Sugar	120 g	4.23 oz	8.94%
Gelatin sheets, silver, bloomed in cold water, excess water squeezed off	13 g	.44 oz	.93%
Sassafras extract (safrole-free)	10 g	.35 oz	.74%

1. Combine the heavy cream and sugar in a sauce pot and bring to a simmer, stirring until the sugar has dissolved.

2. Remove from the heat and add the gelatin. Stir to dissolve.

3. Add the extract once the base has cooled at room temperature in a shallow hotel pan. Do not ice it down. Add more to taste if needed.

NOTE *Safrole is a harmful chemical component found in the sassafras root that can cause liver damage. This is why the extract should be used. A high-quality extract is as good as using the root itself, without the liver damage.*

BERRY FOOL ENVELOPE

YIELD: 810 G/1 LB 12.48 OZ

INGREDIENT	METRIC	U.S.	%
Egg whites	180 g	6.35 oz	22.22%
Sugar	360 g	12.7 oz	44.44%
Freeze-dried raspberries	50 g	1.76 oz	6.17%
Freeze-dried strawberries	50 g	1.76 oz	6.17%
Freeze-dried blackberries	50 g	1.76 oz	6.17%
Heavy cream solids	120 g	4.23 oz	14.81%

1. Turn a dehydrator on to 60°C/140°F.

2. Place a rubber chablon with rectangular perforations measuring 2.5 cm/1 in wide by 7.5 cm/3 in long by 3 mm/.1 in deep over a nonstick rubber mat. (A chablon is a stencil that you can make yourself out of rubber, or you can obtain one ready-made; see Resources, page 520.) These chablons typically have up to 72 perforations. You may have to use 2 half sheet nonstick rubber mats in order for the full yield to fit inside the dehydrator.

3. Make an Italian meringue with the egg whites and the sugar (see method on page 13). While the meringue is cooling in the mixer, coarsely chop the freeze-dried fruits and combine them together in a separate bowl.

4. Once the meringue has cooled, fold the heavy cream solids in by hand using a rubber spatula.

5. Spread the meringue over the chablon. Sprinkle the freeze-dried fruit to cover the surface of the meringue. Lift the chablon.

6. Dry the meringue in the dehydrator for at least 4 hours. Meringue is ideally stored in the dehydrator until the last moment if you can afford to give up the space. Any moisture will evaporate and the meringue will stay dry.

PUMPKIN SEED AND MILK CHOCOLATE GANACHE

YIELD: 3.4 KG/7 LB 7.84 OZ

INGREDIENT	METRIC	U.S.	%
Tempered milk chocolate	1.68 kg	3 lb 11.2 oz	49.41%
Pumpkin seed paste	720 g	1 lb 9.27 oz	21.18%

1. Have the oval silicone molds on a flat sheet pan ready for use (see Resources, page 520). Oval molds measure 12.5 cm/5 in long by 7.5 cm/3 in wide and 1.25 cm/.5 in deep.

2. Combine the tempered milk chocolate with the pumpkin seed paste in a bowl using a rubber spatula.

3. Pour the mixture into the silicone mold and even out the surface with an offset spatula.

4. Let the ganache crystallize at room temperature before unmolding them.

5. Reserve in a cool, dry, enclosed area. Discard after 2 months.

BLACK OLIVE RAISINS

YIELD: 40 SERVINGS

INGREDIENT	METRIC	U.S.	%
Black olives, Spanish, pitted	1.5 kg	3 lb 4.8 oz	55.56%
Water	200 g	7.05 oz	7.41%
Sugar	1 kg	2 lb 3.2 oz	37.04%

1. In a 3.76-L/4-qt sauce pot, combine the olives with enough water to cover them by 2.5 cm/1 inch. Bring them to a boil and then drain the olives. This is meant to remove excess brine and maintain the flavor and a slight amount of salt in the olives.

2. Dry the olives for 12 hours in a dehydrator set to 60°C/140°F.

3. Combine the blanched and dehydrated olives in a clean sauce pot with the water and the sugar.

4. Cook over high heat until the sugar reaches 120°C/250°F, stirring the olives frequently with a wooden spoon.

5. Drain the olives in a fine-mesh sieve to remove the excess cooked sugar, and then transfer the olives to a nonstick rubber mat to cool.

6. Reserve in an airtight container until needed. The olives will keep for up to 1 month.

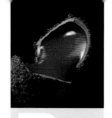

RED VELVET CAKE LIQUID FILLING

YIELD: 1.5 KG/3 LB 4.8 OZ

INGREDIENT	METRIC	U.S.	%
Red velvet cake, cut into cubes (see Note)	1 kg	2 lb 3.2 oz	66.67%
Water	350 g	12.35 oz	23.33%
Corn syrup	150 g	5.29 oz	10%

1. Combine all of the ingredients in a blender cup and blend until smooth. You may need to adjust the consistency if the liquid is too thick simply by adding more water. The final texture should be similar to that of crème anglaise.

2. Use the purée in truffles or store for later use. The purée may be stored in the refrigerator for up to 1 week.

NOTE *For the red velvet cake, see the recipe and method for the true red velvet cake on page 252. You will need a total of 2 kg/70.54 oz of baked cake. Bake all 2 kg/70.54 oz in a full sheet pan and cut the cake in half. Cut one half of the cake into medium cubes. They do not need to be perfect. Put them in a dehydrator set to 60°C/140°F to dry overnight. Once dry, grind the cake in a Robot Coupe and reserve the crumbs in the dehydrator until ready to use. Use the other half of the cake to make the liquid red velvet cake filling.*

LEMON VERBENA GELÉE

YIELD: 806 G/1 LB 12.32 OZ

INGREDIENT	METRIC	U.S.	%
Lemon Verbena Infusion			
Water	1.03 kg	2 lb 4.48 oz	86.25%
Fresh lemon verbena	40 g	1.41 oz	3.33%
Sugar	125 g	4.41 oz	10.42%
Gelée			
Lemon Verbena Infusion	800 g	1 lb 12.32 oz	99.3%
Gellan gum, low acyl	6 g	.2 oz	.7%

1. **For the infusion:** Bring the water up to just under a boil. Pour it over the verbena leaves. Let them steep for 5 minutes, then strain the leaves out of the infusion.

2. Stir in the sugar while the infusion is still hot so that it dissolves completely.

3. Cool in an ice water bath.

4. **For the gelée:** Set up forty 2.5-cm/1-in cube molds on a flat sheet pan.

5. Combine both ingredients in a 1.92-L/2-qt sauce pot using a whisk. Bring to a boil.

6. Pour the liquid into a funnel gun and pour the liquid into the prepared molds. Fill each mold up to 2.5 cm/1 in high (about 20 g/.7 oz).

7. Let set in the refrigerator. Discard after 2 days.

BLACKBERRY COULIS

YIELD: 400 G/14.11 OZ

INGREDIENT	METRIC	U.S.	%
Fresh blackberries	300 g	10.58 oz	75%
Sugar	100 g	3.53 oz	25%

1. Combine both ingredients in a small sauce pot and bring to a boil. Boil for 1 minute.

2. Purée while hot in a blender and then pass through a fine-mesh sieve.

3. Cool in an ice water bath. Reserve refrigerated. Discard after 3 days.

FIG ROYAL ICING

YIELD: 319 G/11.25 OZ

INGREDIENT	METRIC	U.S.	%
Confectioners' sugar	250 g	8.82 oz	78.37%
Egg whites, pasteurized	50 g	1.76 oz	15.67%
Cream of tartar	2 g	.07 oz	.63%
Natural fig compound	15 g	.53 oz	4.7%
Natural purple food coloring, alcohol based	2 g	.07 oz	.63%

1. Combine the confectioners' sugar, egg whites, and cream of tartar in the bowl of an electric mixer fitted with the paddle attachment. Mix until they form a smooth, homogeneous paste.

2. Add the fig compound and the food coloring. Adjust as needed.

3. Transfer to a piping bag or reserve in a container covered with plastic wrap directly over its surface to keep it from drying out.

4. Discard after 2 weeks.

   NOTE *You will need to use a high-quality fig compound (see Resources, page 520) in order for the flavor to remain true and not taste fake, and natural food coloring, which should be alcohol based, not fat based. You can adjust the quantities above as needed.*

CHOCOLATE SHELL

YIELD: 440 G/15.52 OZ

INGREDIENT	METRIC	U.S.	%
Dark chocolate	400 g	14.11 oz	90.91%
Canola oil	40 g	1.41 oz	9.09%

1. Combine both ingredients in a bowl and place over a hot water bath. Stir to melt the chocolate.

2. To use, the shell should be no hotter than 40°C/105°F.

CHARTREUSE ICE CREAM

YIELD: 1.83 KG/ 4 LB .48 OZ

INGREDIENT	METRIC	U.S.	%
Steeped milk	1.07 kg	2 lb 5.6 oz	58.47%
Heavy cream	140 g	4.94 oz	7.65%
Powdered milk	70 g	2.47 oz	3.83%
Sugar	270 g	9.52 oz	14.75%
Ice cream stabilizer	5 g	.18 oz	.27%
Egg yolks	115 g	4.06 oz	6.28%
Chartreuse verte	160 g	5.64 oz	8.74%

1. Follow the modern ice cream method on page 50; add the Chartreuse at the end of the churning process.

2. Let the base age for at least 4 hours before churning.

3. Churn the ice cream base. When it is completely frozen, add the Chartreuse as the machine is still spinning. Let it spin for a few more seconds so that the liquor is completely incorporated.

4. Pour into a piping bag fitted with a #8 tip.

Ch 6

CAKES (entremets)

Because finished patisserie cakes must be kept refrigerated for many hours, it limits the many opportunities that could be possible for serving them. This means that anything that goes on them must be moisture resistant, which eliminates any sugar garnishes, baked garnishes, and any other similarly sensitive products.

It also means that you are not responsible or in charge of cutting the cake, so whatever happens when the cake is gone is out of your hands.

All of that changes when the cake is in your territory and you control its destiny. A cake is most often ordered to celebrate a special occasion; it is rarely ordered "just because." This means that whoever ordered it highly likely placed the order for it well ahead of time. Many restaurants and hotels have a 48- or 72-hour advance-order policy on special cakes. However, many high-end hotels and restaurants always have cakes on hand for last-minute orders. Let's face it, we don't all have the foresight to order cakes, and often a reason to celebrate can come on suddenly from one moment to the next.

In most cases, such celebration cakes are for as many people as your largest table can hold (typically 10 to 12 people maximum), not for large banquets. Serving dozens of people requires much larger cakes, which in fact may require two to three days to prepare. In this chapter, all the cakes are small—for no more than 12 people—and the recipes do not include buttercream or fondant-finished cakes. That is a completely different category of cake.

What makes a good cake? The answer is subjective, since preference is often personal. However, there are a few guiding principles to making a good cake that are generally agreed upon. First, the cake must be texturally well balanced. What this means is that the cake should not be completely one-dimensional when it comes to texture. Contrast is highly appreciated in cakes, as with any other foods: smooth, crunchy, chewy. If you can incorporate smooth (which is always going to be a dominant and ever-present texture in cakes) with one more texture, you will have succeeded on that front.

Temper cakes for at least 30 minutes before they are served, since this will soften any cold components and make them more pleasurable in texture. Tempering will also mean that if the cake is warmer than refrigeration temperatures, it will be more flavorful; the colder the food, the harder it is to taste the flavors. Don't leave the cake out for too long, though; this might affect its structural integrity, especially if you work in a hot kitchen.

Flavor combinations can be good, but it is not a rule that you have to have a variety. The cake can have a theme, like dark chocolate or caramel, and the components can be different preparations made with that flavor.

COMPONENTS OF A CAKE

Cakes are composed of five basic elements:

- **Base:** This is the bottommost layer of the cake, and it can be a sponge cake, a tart shell, streusel, or anything that has a firm body and can support the components around it.

- **Body:** The body is usually the largest flavor component and makes up most of the cake. It is usually a creamy product, such as mousse or Bavarian cream.

- **Inclusion(s):** These are layered elements inside the body and above the base that can contribute texture and/or other flavors.

- **Coating:** This is the component that surrounds the cake and has the important function of protecting the cake, but it is also a textural/flavor component. Spraying a cake with chocolate velvet spray is better than coating it with glaze for two reasons: Velvet spray acts as a shell that does not absorb off flavors from refrigeration, and it also adds some texture.

- **Garnish:** This is what is used to make the cake visually attractive, but it should also have a functional use, and that is that it should be harmonious with the other elements of the cake. It is also an opportunity to add firm textures that would soften inside the cake.

ASSEMBLY GUIDELINES

These assembly instructions will apply to most cakes in this section and will be referenced throughout the chapter.

1. THE RECIPES IN THIS CHAPTER YIELD 4 CAKES. It is always a good idea to make larger quantities of product than smaller quantities, since many recipes cannot be made for individual quantities successfully. For example, a half sheet pan of sponge cake will yield four to six finished entremets, depending on their dimension. However, it is difficult to make just enough sponge cake for one cake. Freeze the remaining cakes, and this way they will always be available and ready for any last-minute orders. Finishing them is the easy part; assembling them is the time-consuming part.

2. PREPARE THE MOLD(S). The molds need to be lined with a strip of acetate that will fit inside them, meaning the band will be as deep as the cake and as long as its total length, overlapping slightly where both ends of the acetate meet. Lightly grease each cake mold with nonstick oil spray, wipe the excess off with a paper towel, and then line the mold with the previously cut strip of acetate. Make sure that it is flush with the mold.

- The molds will be placed on a sheet pan lined with a sheet of Plexiglas, which will also be lined with acetate. Lightly grease the Plexiglas with a coat of nonstick oil spray, remove the excess with a paper towel, and then adhere a sheet of acetate onto it. Smooth it out with a clean paper towel so that it has no air bubbles trapped between the acetate and the Plexiglas. Why use Plexiglas? Because sheet pans are seldom flat; even when they are brand-new, they tend to bow down the center. Plexiglas stays flat and even.

3. FREEZE ALL OF THE INCLUSIONS AND THE BASE OF THE CAKE. **This will make them easier to handle and push into the body of the cake. Have all of the previous steps completed before you make the body of the cake.**

4. MAKE THE BODY OF THE CAKE. **You are now ready to assemble the cake. Keep in mind that these cakes are assembled upside down.**

5. BEGIN BY PIPING A RING OF THE BODY AROUND THE BASE OF THE MOLD. **Start piping from the outside in, always keeping the tip of the piping bag inside the body, because this prevents air pocket formation. If you are only adding one inclusion, fill the body only one-third of the way up the mold. Place the frozen inclusion on top of the cream and push down so that the cream comes up around the inclusion; again, this prevents air pocket formation. If you have more inclusions, consider this when piping the body of the cake in; it means you will have to pipe less in at first if you want your layers to be evenly spaced.**

Place the mold onto a sheet of acetate. Pipe an even layer of mousse in the base of the mold.

Next, inserts and/or inclusions may be added. They should be frozen and gently pressed into the first mousse layer.

An additional layer of mousse is added, then the base is gently pressed into the mold. Be sure that this final layer makes a smooth surface even with the mold.

Once the cake has fully set, it can be pushed out of the mold. Applying heat with a torch can make this process easier.

Since this cake is being coated in velvet spray, it is placed on a flat sheet pan lined with a sheet of acetate.

Garnish the cake as desired.

6. FILL THE MOLD ALMOST TO THE TOP. **Place the base into the mold, pushing into the body so that it can come up the sides of the mold and prevent air pocket formation.**

7. USING AN OFFSET SPATULA, EVEN OUT THE CAKE. **Place a sheet of acetate on the filled cakes, and then a sheet of Plexiglas on top of it, and then a flat weight, such as heavy cutting board. This helps produce an evenly shaped cake.**

8. FREEZE UNTIL HARDENED. **Once hardened, push the cake out of the mold. You may need to apply some heat with a torch to help loosen the outer layer, but don't get too carried away; you don't want to melt the cake. Once the mold is off, return the cake to the freezer to re-harden the outer layer. Once hardened, wrap the cakes and reserve them frozen for up to 3 months, or take the strip of acetate off and finish the cake.**

9. COAT THE CAKE WITH GLAZE, VELVET SPRAY, OR MERINGUE. **It is mostly recommended to finish the cakes on a wire rack because it keeps things cleaner. If spraying the cake, melt the chocolate velvet spray and set up a spray area. Line the area with plastic; you can use clean, unused large trash-can liners). Fill the spray gun with the velvet spray and coat the cakes with an even mist of velvet, rotating the cake one-quarter of the way each time to ensure you are coating the entire surface. If you are using a glaze, make sure to melt the glaze to the appropriate temperature and coat the cakes while frozen. Move the cakes 5 cm/2 in any direction just after glazing and while on the wire rack to prevent formation of feet around the base of the cake. Transfer the glazed or sprayed cakes to the base on which they will be displayed.**

10. GARNISH THE CAKE. **Only place the non-temperature or non-moisture-sensitive garnishes.**

11. DEFROST IN THE REFRIGERATOR. **Temper for 30 minutes before serving for ideal texture.**

SERVICE

At this point, the cake has been ideally tempered for 30 minutes and is at its peak texture. Just before the cake is served and presented, apply the final garnishes, which may have been too fragile, temperature sensitive, or moisture sensitive to put on the cake previously. The service staff will then present the cake to the table. There are two possible scenarios: The service staff, if they are well trained and qualified (and confident) can cut the cake tableside and serve the individual portions. This is a nice touch for upscale service but is not indispensable. More typi-cally, the cake will be presented and then taken back to the chef to cut, plate, and garnish. If this is the case, you should prepare enough garnishes for each slice. If garnishing the cake with one or two components, such as a single chocolate curl and a single macaron, it is a good idea to have the correct number of curls and macarons available to place on each slice of the cake when you send it into the dining room.

To cut the cake, you will need to have a hot water bath that is deep enough for the entire blade of the knife to fit. Use a long, thin slicing knife. Dip it in the hot water bath, wipe it dry with a clean cloth towel or heavy-duty paper towel, and then cut straight down, pulling the knife toward you, not back up again. Every time you cut, dip the knife in hot water and wipe it dry.

You may choose to go further and serve the cake with a sauce and/or ice cream or other frozen components, which make more sense than a sauce.

GÂTEAU MAILLARD

YIELD: 4 CAKES

WHY THESE FLAVORS WORK	All of the components of this cake have been through the Maillard reaction, so they all share that as a common flavor thread. However, each component has its own distinct flavor and texture character that is clearly distinguishable but harmonizes with everything else.
COMPONENTS	BODY: **Caramelized White Chocolate Mousse** (page 317) INCLUSION 1: **Toasted Rye Bread Cream** (page 417) INCLUSION 2: **Brown Butter Génoise** (page 416) BASE: **Shortbread Toffee Base** (page 416) COATING: **Vegetable Ash Velvet Spray** (page 418) GARNISH: **Toasted Sourdough Sliver** (page 418)
ASSEMBLY INSTRUCTIONS	1. Pipe the first amount of caramelized white chocolate mousse up to 2.5 cm/1 in in a square mold measuring 15 cm/6 in on each side and 10 cm/4 in deep. Push in the frozen rye cream inclusion. 2. Pipe in additional caramelized white chocolate mousse to within 2.5 cm/1 in from the top of the mold. You will need a total of 4.5 kg/9 lb 15.36 oz of the mousse. Place the frozen génoise in, followed by the frozen shortbread toffee base. Fill in any gaps that may be around the génoise and shortbread base with additional white chocolate mousse. 3. Even out the top with an offset spatula and freeze to harden. 4. Set up a spray station, a surface that should be covered with plastic to keep the shop clean where you can spray the cake. 5. Once the cake is hardened, unmold. Fill a compressor canister with the vegetable ash velvet spray and spray the cake with an even coating of spray, taking care to spray mostly the sides of the mold. Keep the compressor gun at least 60 cm/24 in from the cake to obtain a velvety smooth look. 6. Apply the toasted sliver of sourdough.

COFFEE AND DOUGHNUTS

YIELD: 4 CAKES

WHY THESE FLAVORS WORK	Coffee and doughnuts. What is there to explain? Coffee has a distinct bitter flavor that cuts through the sweetness and richness of a doughnut. It is a flavor that is clear and present all on its own, but it is tamed by that of a doughnut without either flavor taking over the other.
COMPONENTS	BODY: **Doughnut Cream** (page 420) INCLUSION 2: **Brioche Doughnut** (page 420) INCLUSION 1: **Baked Espresso Custard** (page 419) BASE: **Espresso Sponge Cake** (page 418) COATING: **Espresso Velvet Spray** (page 421) GARNISH: **Chocolate Ring** (page 421), **doughnut hole**, **melted dark chocolate**

ASSEMBLY INSTRUCTIONS

1. Assemble 4 square cake molds measuring 20 cm/8 in long on each side by 6.25 cm/2.5 in deep. Line each mold with acetate.

2. Pipe the doughnut cream into the mold to fill them up to 1.25 cm/.5 in high. Place the brioche doughnut at the center of the doughnut cream and push in gently.

3. Pipe more of the doughnut cream into the mold to cover the doughnut completely. Place the frozen espresso custard on top of the cream and push it into the cream until it comes up the sides of the custard.

4. Pipe more of the doughnut cream around the custard, but not over it, to come to within 1.25 cm/.5 in of the border of the mold.

5. Place the espresso sponge cake on top of the espresso custard and push it into the cream. The cream should come up the sides of the sponge cake. Even out the top of the mold using an offset spatula and freeze to harden.

6. Set up a spray station, a surface that should be covered with plastic to keep the shop clean where you can spray the cake.

7. Once the cake is hardened, unmold. Fill a compressor canister with the espresso velvet spray and spray the cake with an even coating of spray to coat completely.

8. Adhere the chocolate ring to the cake using melted chocolate. Thaw in the refrigerator.

9. Place the doughnut hole on the cake just before it is displayed and served.

CHERRY AND CHOCOLATE GÂTEAU

YIELD: 4 CAKES

WHY THESE FLAVORS WORK	This is not a cake in the traditional sense. It is a shell of shortbread cookie base fully baked and then filled with cherry jam and a purée of chocolate mudslide cookie. It is coated in a red velvet spray and topped with an encapsulated cherry nectar sphere.
COMPONENTS	BASE (SHELL): **Flexible Shortbread** (page 421) INCLUSION 1: **Cherry Jam** (page 422) INCLUSION 2: **Mudslide Cookie Purée** (page 423) COATING: **Red Velvet Spray** (page 248) GARNISH: **Encapsulated Cherry Nectar Sphere** (page 423), **silver leaf**
ASSEMBLY INSTRUCTIONS	1. Line 4 rectangular molds measuring 10 cm/4 in wide by 20 cm/8 in long by 2.5 cm/1 in deep with an acetate strip. Place the molds on a Plexiglas base lined with acetate. 2. Cut the flexible shortbread into 4 tops, 4 bases, and 4 strips to go around the sides of the mold. The tops will measure 10 cm/4 in wide by 20 cm/8 in long. The strips will measure 2.5 cm/1 in wide by 60 cm/24 in long. The bases will measure 9 cm/3.5 in wide by 19 cm/7.5 in long. 3. Put a base rectangle of shortbread inside the mold. Place the strip of shortbread around the inside wall of the mold; the ends should not overlap, so trim them if needed so that they just meet. This type of dough can be manipulated like clay, so don't worry if the strip cracks or breaks; simply push it back into shape with your fingers. 4. Fill up to .5 cm/.2 in high with the cherry jam. 5. Fill to within 3 mm/.1 in from the top of the mold with the mudslide cookie purée. Top with a rectangle of shortbread. 6. Freeze to harden and then unmold. Set up a spray station, a surface that should be covered with plastic to keep the shop clean where you can spray the cake. 7. Fill a compressor canister with the red velvet spray and spray the cake with an even coating of spray to coat completely. Keep the compressor gun at least 60 cm/24 in from the cake to obtain a velvety smooth look. 8. Place an encapsulated cherry nectar sphere on top of the cake. Put a small piece of silver leaf over the sphere. Thaw in the refrigerator.

UNUSUALLY MOIST CHOCOLATE CAKE | CRÈME FRAÎCHE CREAM | CARAMEL MOUSSE | CHOCOLATE SHORTBREAD

YIELD: 4 CAKES

This is a different type of cake, where the body is a sponge cake that has been hollowed out and then filled. You could say that it is an inside-out cake. Caramel and crème fraîche are background flavors that are both connected by the dairy flavor factor, with a degree of acidity from the crème fraîche, that all serves to balance the frontal chocolate flavor. It is a very simple and straightforward composition of flavors, but they work very well together.

COMPONENTS

BODY: **Chocolate Blackout Sponge Cake** (page 424)

INCLUSION 1: **Caramel Mousse** (page 426)

INCLUSION 2: **Crème Fraîche Cream** (page 425)

BASE: **Chocolate Shortbread** (page 425)

COATING: **Dark Chocolate Velvet Spray** (page 223)

GARNISH: **Copper Luster Dust Paste** (page 426), **Chocolate Curved Triangle** (page 427)

ASSEMBLY INSTRUCTIONS

1. Once the blackout cake is baked, cooled down, and chilled in the refrigerator, you will need to hollow it out: Using a paring knife, cut into the cake 2.5 cm/1 in from the border. Do not cut all the way down; cut to 3.75 cm/1.5 in from the base. Carve out a cube from the inside of the cake using the paring knife. You are looking to create a cavity that will fit the inclusions and the shortbread base.

2. Place the frozen caramel mousse inside the cavity.

3. Pipe the crème fraîche cream around the caramel mousse and over it to fill the cavity up to within 3 mm/.1 in from the top of the cake.

4. Place the frozen chocolate shortbread on top of the crème fraîche cream. Push down gently. The shortbread should be flush with the top border of the cake.

5. Freeze the entire cake. Set up a spray station, a surface that should be covered with plastic to keep the shop clean where you can spray the cake.

6. Fill a compressor canister with the dark chocolate velvet spray and spray the cake with an even coating of spray to coat completely. Keep the compressor gun at least 60 cm/24 in from the cake to obtain a velvety smooth look.

7. Place the cake on the base on which it will be presented. Apply a dollop of copper luster dust paste and adhere the chocolate curved triangle to the cake. Thaw the cake in the refrigerator.

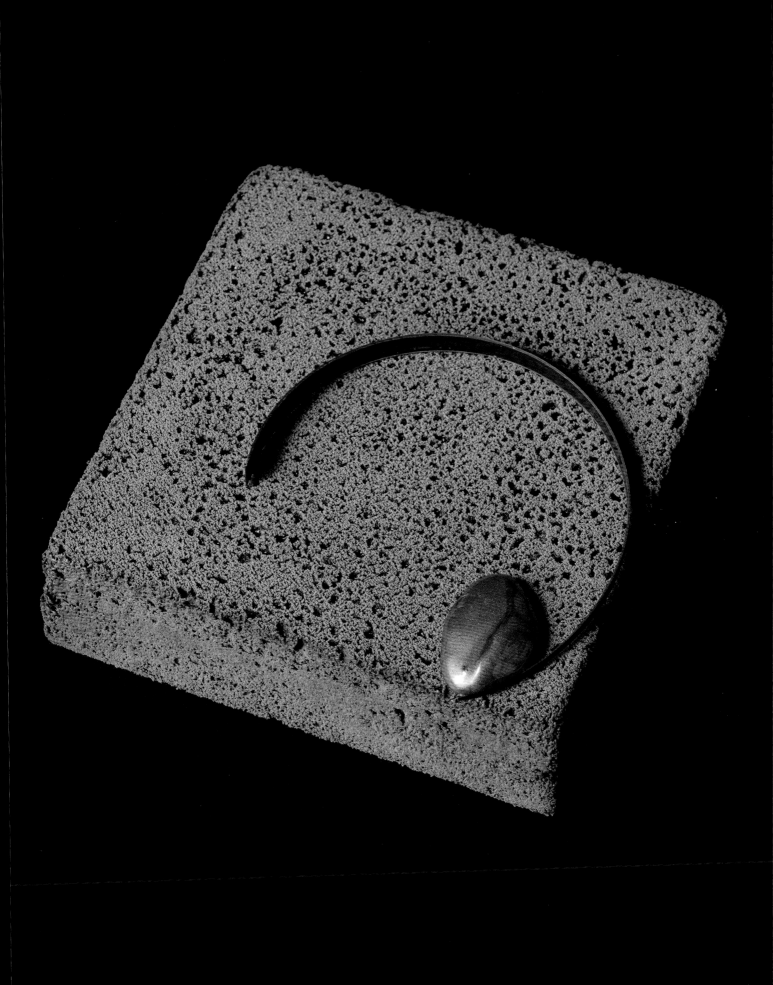

YUZU CREAM | PASSION FRUIT CURD | GREEN TEA GÉNOISE | HIBISCUS VEIL

YIELD: 4 CAKES

WHY THESE FLAVORS WORK

Yuzu is a Japanese citrus fruit that is very floral and aromatic, in the same profile as passion fruit. Both are very intense, present flavors, but they are clearly distinguishable even when they are together. The main flavor in this cake is yuzu, with passion fruit lending a secondary role. The green tea génoise is meant to add an herbal note that surrounds both flavors without overwhelming them. The hibiscus adds a note of acidity and a very floral flavor that surrounds the other components of the cake to enhance their flavors; it can be very powerful, which is why it is used in such small quantities in this cake.

COMPONENTS

BASE: **Green Tea Génoise** (page 427)
BODY: **Yuzu Cream** (page 428)
COATING: **White Velvet Spray** (page 429)
GARNISH: **Passion Fruit Curd** (page 428), **Hibiscus Veil** (page 429)

ASSEMBLY INSTRUCTIONS

1. Line 4 rectangular molds measuring 9 cm/3.5 in wide by 20 cm/8 in long by 9 cm/3.5 in high with a strip of acetate.

2. Place the green tea génoise against one side of the mold. It will be facing the mold directly on the right side so it will be exposed, but it will be covered in the yuzu cream on the left side and at the fore and aft of the cake.

3. Make the yuzu cream and pipe it into the mold, around the cake and up to the top of the mold. This is one of the few cakes that is not assembled upside down.

4. Even out the top of the mold with an offset spatula and freeze it until it is hardened. Once the cake is frozen, if the yuzu cream has dipped, pour some yuzu cream on top of the cake and even it out again. This will correct the dip in the cake.

5. Once it is hardened, remove the cake from the mold. Take off the acetate strip.

6. Set up a spray station, a surface that should be covered with plastic to keep the shop clean where you can spray the cake.

7. Fill a compressor canister with the white velvet spray. Place a rectangle of cardboard directly in front of the exposed green tea génoise and coat the cake with an even coating. Keep the compressor gun at least 60 cm/24 in from the cake to obtain a velvety smooth look.

8. Transfer the cake to the tray on which it will be presented. Wrap the tube of passion fruit curd with the hibiscus veil. Place it on top of the cake. Thaw the cake in the refrigerator.

EARTH

WHY THESE FLAVORS WORK

There are three frontal flavors here: lemon, and chocolate. They are all bitter, but the subtleties of their particular flavors make them good companions in food.. Lemon and chocolate have a particular affinity for each other. Because of this, it is only natural to combine these two elements. The wild card is the litchi. What on earth does litchi have to do with the other flavors? Litchi is a background flavor that is easily identifiable, but if used in the right quantities it can really enhance the other flavors present in this dessert without fully taking over.

COMPONENTS

BODY: **Dark Chocolate Mousse** (page 444)

INCLUSION 1: **Lemon Curd** (page 431)

INCLUSION 2: **Litchi Gelée** (page 431)

BASE: **Brownie** (page 430)

COATING: **Dark Chocolate Ganache** (page 432), **Dark Chocolate Velvet Spray** (page 223), **Green Velvet Spray** (page 302)

GARNISH: **Chocolate Soil** (page 432), **Lemon "Dew Drops"** (page 432)

20 edible flowers, 20 microgreens

ASSEMBLY INSTRUCTIONS

1. Line 4 rectangular molds measuring 10 cm/4 in wide by 20 cm/8 in long by 10 cm/4 in wide with acetate sheets. Place on a piece of Plexiglas lined with acetate as well.

2. Make the dark chocolate mousse and pipe it in to fill up to about 2.5 cm/1 in. You will need a total of 6 kg/13 lb 3.52 oz of dark chocolate mousse.

3. Place the frozen lemon curd inclusion on top of the mousse and push down gently so the mousse comes up the sides of the curd.

4. Spoon an even layer of litchi gelée on top of the lemon curd. You will need about 200 g/7.05 oz per cake.

5. Pipe more mousse around the gelée and the curd as well as over the gelée, up to within about 2.5 cm/1 in from the top of the cake mold.

6. Put the brownie base on top of the mousse and push in gently so that the mousse comes up the sides of the brownie.

7. Even out the top and freeze the cake to harden it.

8. Once it has frozen, take the cake out of the mold and make the chocolate ganache.

continued on page 398

9. When the ganache is firm but still soft enough to pipe, pipe it on top of the cake in a random pattern. The intention is to make it look like a slice of earth. Smooth out the areas that look too abrupt with an offset spatula.

10. Apply the soil on top of the ganache while it is still not fully set (you will need 190 g/6.70 oz per cake). The soil needs to adhere to the ganache.

11. Set up a spray station, a surface that should be covered with plastic to keep the shop clean where you can spray the cake.

12. Fill a compressor canister with the green velvet spray and spray the only on the top of the cake. Keep the compressor gun at least 60 cm/24 in from the cake to obtain a velvety smooth look. Then spray the sides with the dark chocolate velvet spray. You will need 300 g/10.58 oz of green velvet spray and 500 g/1 lb 1.63 oz of dark chocolate velvet spray.

13. Apply a few lemon "dew drops" over the top of the cake, again, in a random pattern.

14. Apply edible flowers and microgreens on the day the cake will be served. Let the cake temper in the refrigerator.

coffee

Coffee and coffee drinks are arguably one of the weakest points many restaurants have, no matter how great they are. There are a few simple reasons for this:

- **Coffee and coffee drinks are often served at the very end of the meal. The front of the house is often pressured into turning a table quickly to seat the next party; therefore great care and attention may not be given to every single cup of coffee.**

- **Waitstaff may be highly qualified to serve tables and care for the customers' needs, but that does not automatically made them baristas. Some high-end restaurants have a person or two exclusively making coffee and coffee drinks, but this can get expensive in terms of labor cost. More often than not, the person who tends to a table will be the same person making coffee.**

- **A good coffee-making machine and grinder can be outrageously expensive. When you consider the profit margin on a cup of coffee, it is very high, but then how many cups of coffee do you need to sell to earn back your investment? And how many until you actually start making money off of it?**

- **Caring for the coffee beans takes time, work, and space. Ideally there is enough rotation of coffee bean inventory that this is not even an issue. Coffee beans begin to oxidize as soon as the bag they come in is opened.**

These are just a few key points to consider when it comes to coffee, because if your establishment can make great food, have great service, and also offer a great coffee drink, you will ensure success and repeat customers. As pastry chef, you are not necessarily in charge of a coffee program, but keep in mind that coffee is served around your desserts and therefore you must develop an interest in the drinks' production, because the last thing you want to happen is the staff making a bad cup of coffee after you have worked so hard on your desserts. And really, what is worse than a bad cup of coffee?

tea and infusions

While tea and infusion sales are dwarfed by coffee and coffee drinks, it doesn't mean that they don't require special care and attention to prepare properly. These are items that can be very easily made very well but are often not done that way. There are many intricacies in making a good cup or pot of tea, and they are all well within your control. It is not rocket science, really. First you must know that the difference between tea and infusions is that all tea comes from the same tree, *Camellia sinensis,* and anything else that does not come from this tree is called an infusion, or tisane.

There are four major categories of tea: white, green, oolong, and black, and these have subcategories of their own. What puts them each in a different category is the level of fermentation and oxidation. White and green teas are not fermented, oolong is semi-fermented, and black is completely fermented. White and green are not oxidized, oolong is partially oxidized, and black is fully oxidized. One of the most important steps in making tea is the time the leaves spend brewing in the water; it should be 2 to 7 minutes depending on the tea. Additional important factors are the quantity of leaves used (use 1 to 2 teaspoons per cup of water, plus 1 teaspoon "for the pot" if you are brewing a pot) and the temperature of the water used to brew the tea (93°C/203°F). Preserving that heat is key as well; therefore, keep tea cups and pots warm at all times to ensure that the tea will stay warm for longer periods of time. Also note that loose-leaf teas will always be better in quality than bagged teas. Keep in mind that they also take longer to brew.

Infusions can be many things, like spices, herbs, citrus fruits, dried fruits, and even flowers. They follow similar brewing principles as tea, but they are not as fragile or sensitive to overbrewing. A general ratio for brewing tisanes is 1 tablespoon of tisane ingredient per 1 cup of water. The problem with this is that the size of the tisane components can vary wildly. If using cinnamon sticks, whole litchis, or rosemary stems, for example, they can't be measured in a spoon measure. A better way to measure the amount needed to make a tisane is to weigh out 10 or 11 g/.35 to .39 oz of tisane ingredient per 250 g/8.82 oz of water, or roughly 1 cup.

TOASTED MILK CREAM | CHOCOLATE SHORTBREAD | BUBBLE CHOCOLATE | FLOURLESS CHOCOLATE CAKE

YIELD: 4 CAKES

WHY THESE FLAVORS WORK

This cake is inspired mostly by milk and cookies, which is a generally well-liked combination. This cake combines those flavors and add other ingredients that go well with milk, like chocolate and cake. The two main flavors are milk and chocolate, where the toasted milk is there to lend its dairy creaminess support through it all, keeping the chocolate in check.

COMPONENTS

BODY: **Toasted Milk Cream** (page 434)
INCLUSION 1: **Chocolate Shortbread** (page 425)
INCLUSION 2: **Bubble Chocolate** (page 433)
BASE: **Flourless Chocolate Cake** (page 433)
Tempered white chocolate
COATING: **Shiny Chocolate Glaze** (page 304)
GARNISH: **Gold Spray** (see Resources, page 520), **Dark Chocolate Plaque** (page 435), **Chocolate Ginkgo Leaf** (page 435)

ASSEMBLY INSTRUCTIONS

1. Line 4 square molds measuring 15 cm/6 in on each side by 10 cm/4 in high with acetate.

2. Make the toasted milk cream. Fill the mold 3.75 cm/1.5 in up with the toasted milk cream. Place the chocolate shortbread inclusion on top of the cream and push it down lightly.

3. Fill the mold with more cream to within 3.75 cm/1.5 in of the top of the mold.

4. Insert the bubble chocolate inclusion, pushing it in lightly. Place the flourless chocolate base into the mold and push it in lightly as well. Pipe more cream around the cake if necessary to fill in any gaps. Freeze to harden.

5. Once hardened, flip the mold over and unmold the cakes. Freeze to harden again.

6. Meanwhile, temper 500 g/1 lb 1.63 oz of white chocolate.

7. Drizzle it over the tops of all the cakes in a random pattern. Transfer the frozen cakes to a wire rack and hold in the freezer.

8. Meanwhile, warm up 2 kg/4 lb 6.4 oz of the shiny chocolate glaze to 40°C/105°F.

9. Pour over the cakes. There is always extra that pours down the sides of the cake; therefore you will always need to start with more than you absolutely need to cover the cake.

10. Coat one side of the cake with gold spray. Place a chocolate plaque on the surface of the cake and a golden chocolate ginkgo leaf over the plaque. Thaw in the refrigerator.

WHIPPED VANILLA MILK AND PASTRY CREAM | RASPBERRY CAKE | GREEN TEA GELÉE

YIELD: 1 CAKE

WHY THESE FLAVORS WORK

This is a very simple flavor profile: vanilla, raspberries, and green tea. Vanilla, forever in harmony with all things sweet, has a way of tying in the raspberry and green tea, two seemingly odd flavors to put together but well harmonized in the presence of the vanilla and dairy flavors.

This cake is not assembled as a classic cake. In fact, there is really nothing classic about it. It is assembled into cubes, which are the individual servings themselves. The portion may look large, but the whipped milk and pastry cream are as light as air.

COMPONENTS

Wafer paper rectangles

Cocoa butter spray (see Resources, page 520)

Raspberry Sponge Cake (page 435)

Whipped Vanilla Milk and Pastry Cream (page 436)

Green Tea Gelée (page 437)

Raspberry Chocolate Pinecones (page 436)

ASSEMBLY INSTRUCTIONS

1. Assemble 6 rectangular Plexiglas cubes measuring 10 cm/4 in wide by 12.5 cm/5 in long by 5 cm/2 in thick. Lightly spray each wafer paper square with a mist of cocoa butter and immediately adhere it to the interior of the cube. Repeat with the other wafer paper squares.

2. Put a square of raspberry sponge cake behind the wafer paper.

3. Make the whipped vanilla milk and pastry cream. Pipe into the rectangular cubes and let set in the refrigerator.

4. Once they are set, you can coat the top of the cubes with the green tea gelée and 1 raspberry pinecone half per cube.

NOTES

This recipe is for one cake only (in six segments), since the whipped vanilla milk does not stay fluid for long and sets rather quickly, making it impossible to make more than one cake at a time.

You will need a full sheet of wafer paper, cut into squares that measure 7.5 cm/3 in on each side. Using a rubber stamp (see Resources, page 520) and black edible ink soaked into a sponge stamp pad, apply images onto the paper. Reserve in an envelope until ready to use.

CAKE FOR TWO: CASSIS AND ALMOND

YIELD: 4 CAKES

WHY THESE FLAVORS WORK	This is a very simple cake made by alternating layers of cassis (black currant) cake and almond cream that is optionally scented with vanilla bean; this requires the use of the Volcano Vaporizer. The flavor of cassis is very straightforward but very complex at the same time, with intense berry fruit flavor along with a less intense floral note. Highly acidic, it benefits from the mellow flavor that the almond provides along with the dairy component, which tames that acidity and keeps it in check without hiding it. The vanilla is simply a scent that enhances all the flavors in the cake and adds a special touch.
COMPONENTS	**Cassis Sponge Cake** (page 437) **Almond Cream** (page 438) **Vanilla scent**
ASSEMBLY INSTRUCTIONS	1. Each cake is to be assembled in a 15-cm/6-in tall apothecary jar (see Resources, page 520). The cake should be assembled to order since it contains freshly whipped cream that can deflate over time. 2. Alternate 6 layers of cake with the cream, starting with cake and ending with cream. Pipe 100 g/3.53 oz of cream per layer, and then 200 g/7.05 oz in the top layer. The cream layers should be about 1 cm/.4 in thick. The last layer of cream should be piped into peaks. 3. Once the cake is assembled and just before it is sent out, it is scented with vanilla beans using the Volcano Vaporizer (see the process photos on page 209). To scent 1 cake, 20 g/.7 oz of vanilla powder is sufficient.

CHOCOLATE BAR CAKE

YIELD: 4 CAKES

WHY THESE
FLAVORS WORK

This cake is really a candy bar disguised as a cake. This item was developed with the intention of having a shelf-stable cake with components that would emulate a cake but not be perishable. For example, the bubble chocolate acts as a texture component but also as if it were a light mousse. The praline cream is also acting as a creamy component but without the water content that would make it perishable.

The richness of the hazelnut praline can be cut with acidic flavors such as those of citrus fruit, in this case Meyer lemon. The citrus with the nuts and the chocolate make for an organized "randomness" of flavors that connect well to each other. Even though they are each very distinct, they all benefit from each other's presence.

COMPONENTS

COATING: **Chocolate Shell** (page 438)

BODY: **Bubble Chocolate** (page 433)

INCLUSION 1: **Praline Cream** (page 439)

INCLUSION 2: **Meyer Lemon Pâte de Fruit** (page 439)

BASE: **Angel Food Cake** (page 440)

Tempered dark chocolate

GARNISH: **Royal Icing** (page 440)**, antique gold–colored cocoa butter**

ASSEMBLY INSTRUCTIONS

1. Once the shell has been cast into the mold and the chocolate has crystallized, make the bubble chocolate. See page 435 for the recipe and procedure; make a half recipe or one 1-L/1.04-quart canister for all 4 entremets. Portion the bubble chocolate into the mold to fill up to 1.25 cm/.5 in. Let it crystallize before applying the next layer.

2. Pipe about 200 g/7.05 oz of the praline cream on top of the bubble chocolate to fill each bar 5 mm/.2 in.

3. Place the triangle of Meyer lemon pâte de fruit on top of the praline cream. Place the triangle of angel food cake on top of the pâte de fruit. Cap the mold with tempered chocolate.

4. Apply the royal icing using a stencil (see Resources, page 520); spread the royal icing over the stencil and even it out using an offset spatula. Lift the stencil away carefully.

5. Allow the royal icing to dry at room temperature for about 2 hours.

6. Melt 30 g/1.06 oz of antique gold–colored cocoa butter and pour it into the canister of an airbrush. Airbrush the bar with the cocoa butter, spraying on one side only (you do not need to coat the entire bar).

7. Reserve in a cool dry place, preferably enclosed. Discard after 2 weeks.

NOTE   *The best way to present this bar is on a cutting board with a knife so that you can let your customers cut it as they see fit.*

CRÈME BRÛLÉE CAKE

YIELD: 4 CAKES

WHY THESE FLAVORS WORK	Vanilla acts as the general background flavor that ties in the maple (another background flavor) with the praline, which is the frontal flavor in this dessert. It is a very simple cake that is full of textures (soft, crispy, chewy) but must be finished just before it is to be eaten to maintain the integrity of those textures.
COMPONENTS	**Crisp Maple Feuilles de Brick** (page 441) **Praline Genoa Bread** (page 442) **Crème Brûlée** (page 441) **Turbinado sugar**
ASSEMBLY INSTRUCTIONS	1. This cake is assembled *à la minute*. Place the crispy feuilles de brick on top of the Genoa bread. 2. Push the crème brûlée out of the mold directly onto the feuilles de brick. 3. Sprinkle an even layer of turbinado sugar on top of the crème brûlée and caramelize it using a torch. Serve immediately.

BIG RED CAKE

YIELD: 4 CAKES

WHY THESE FLAVORS WORK	This cake is inspired by a traditional French dessert called *Fraisier*. The strawberries are the frontal flavor here, and the vanilla and cream help to modulate any acidic intensity that may be out of control. This cake, like its inspiration, is all smooth and soft textures.

COMPONENTS

BASE: **Vanilla Chiffon Cake** (page 442)
INCLUSION: **Fresh ripe strawberries** (see Note)
BODY: **Vanilla Diplomat Cream** (page 443)
COATING: **Red Velvet Spray** (page 248)
GARNISH: **Gelled Cream Letters ([spelling FRESA] (strawberry); page 443)**
Melted white chocolate

ASSEMBLY INSTRUCTIONS

1. This cake will be assembled right side up instead of upside down in a slanted oval mold measuring 12.5 cm/5 in wide by 20 cm/8 in long by 3.75 cm/1.5 in high on its narrowest side and 10 cm/4 in high on its highest side. Line it with a sheet of acetate and place it on a flat sheet pan lined with acetate as well.

2. Place the chiffon cake at the center of the base of the mold.

3. Put about 300 g/10.58 oz of quartered strawberries on top of the chiffon cake, in a standing position. There should be enough strawberries to cover the chiffon cake in its entirety.

4. Pipe the diplomat cream around and on top of the strawberries to the top of the mold. Even out the surface of the mold with an offset spatula.

5. Freeze the cake until it has hardened. Unmold the cake and set up a spray station, a surface that should be covered with plastic to keep the shop clean where you can spray the cake.

6. Fill a compressor canister with the red velvet spray and spray the cake with an even coating of spray to coat completely. Keep the compressor gun at least 60 cm/24 in from the cake to obtain a velvety smooth look.

7. Place the cake on the base on which it will be displayed.

8. Attach the letters F/R/E/S/A to the surface of the cake using a few dots of melted white chocolate (you will need no more than 10 g/.35 oz of chocolate for this). Thaw in the refrigerator.

NOTE

Stem, hull, and quarter 1.2 kg/2 lb 10.24 oz strawberries just before you need them. Otherwise they will discolor.

CHOCOLATE AND RASPBERRY LIPS

YIELD: 4 CAKES

WHY THESE FLAVORS WORK

Chocolate and raspberry is a combination that you either like or you don't. Raspberries by themselves are not particularly sweet in the strict sense. They tend to be more sour, but with red fruit flavors that work well with certain types of dark chocolate, particularly those with low percentages of cacao. The savarin is more of a background flavor. It is a yeasted cake (but not a bread) and therefore will have a certain flavor of fermentation and Maillard, which are also background flavors. The cake is soaked in a Chambord syrup, which is a liqueur made with black raspberries, which are close in flavor to red raspberries.

COMPONENTS

BODY: **Dark Chocolate Mousse** (page 444)

INCLUSION: **Preserved Raspberries in Raspberry Jelly** (page 444)

BASE: **Savarin** (page 445)

COATING: **Shiny Chocolate Glaze** (page 304)

GARNISH: **Raspberry Chocolate Lips** (page 445)

ASSEMBLY INSTRUCTIONS

1. Place 4 half-sphere molds measuring 14 cm/5.5 in diameter by 5 cm/2 in deep on smaller ring molds in order to keep them in place.

2. Pipe the chocolate mousse into the molds to fill them up to within 2.5 cm/1 in from the top.

3. Push the half-sphere of preserved raspberry jelly into the mousse and then place the savarin on top of the raspberry jelly.

4. Pipe more mousse around the savarin if necessary to fill any gaps around it. Make sure that the savarin and the mousse are at the same level as the top of the mold.

5. Freeze the cake to harden it.

6. Once hardened, unmold the cake onto a wire rack. Pour the shiny chocolate glaze on top of the cake. Let set for a few seconds, and then slide it with the help of an offset spatula a few inches in any direction to prevent feet from forming at the bottom of the cake.

7. Transfer the cake to the base on which it will be presented. Attach a total of 21 raspberry lips onto the cake. Let the cake thaw in the refrigerator.

HAZELNUT GIANDUJA CAKE

YIELD: 4 CAKES

WHY THESE FLAVORS WORK	Gianduja could be loosely described as a combination of chocolate and a nut paste, typically hazelnut. The main and really only flavor is hazelnut, but it is presented in a variety of textures: soft, smooth, crispy/crunchy.
COMPONENTS	BODY: **Gianduja Mousse** (page 447) INCLUSION 1: **Hazelnut Praline** (page 447) INCLUSION 2: **Gianduja Feuilletine** (page 446) BASE: **Hazelnut Dacquoise** (page 446) COATING: **Dark Chocolate Velvet Spray** (page 223), **White Chocolate Velvet Spray** (page 429) GARNISH: **Gianduja Décor** (page 447)
ASSEMBLY INSTRUCTIONS	1. This cake was made with a custom-made silicone mold of 4 offset disks (see Resources, page 520). The dimensions are 20 cm/8 in diameter by 5 cm/2 in deep. Fill the mold with hazelnut gianduja mousse up to 1.25 cm/.5 in high.
	2. Put a disk of hazelnut praline over the mousse and push gently down. Pipe a thin layer of mousse around and over the hazelnut praline. Fill the mold with more mousse up to within 1.25 cm/.5 in from the top of the mold.
	3. Put the gianduja feuilletine with the hazelnut dacquoise disk over the mousse with the feuilletine side down and push gently down. The dacquoise disk should be at the same level as the top of the mold. Fill in any empty gaps if necessary with additional mousse.
	4. Freeze the cake to harden. For a mold like this, the only way to get the cake out cleanly is to get it as frozen as possible in a blast freezer (-38°C/-37°F). Unmold the cake once completely hardened. You can opt to leave it in a regular freezer until the day you need to finish the cake, but, if possible, blast-freeze it for at least 1 hour before you plan to finish the cake. If you are using a regular stainless-steel mold to assemble this cake, you will not need to go through the trouble of freezing in a blast freezer; just make sure it is hard enough to unmold cleanly.
	5. Set up a spray station, a surface that should be covered with plastic to keep the shop clean where you can spray the cake. Fill a compressor canister with the dark chocolate velvet spray and spray the cake with an even coating of spray to coat completely. Keep the compressor gun at least 60 cm/24 in from the cake to obtain a velvety smooth look.
	6. Spray one side of the cake with white chocolate velvet spray. Apply the gianduja chocolate décor on top of the cake. Thaw in the refrigerator.

SHORTBREAD TOFFEE BASE

YIELD: 1.41 KG/3 LB 1.6 OZ

INGREDIENT	METRIC	U.S.	%
Toffee			
Salted butter	100 g	3.53 oz	33.9%
Sugar	170 g	5.98 oz	57.63%
Water	25 g	.88 oz	8.47%
Shortbread Base			
All-purpose flour	360 g	12.7 oz	25.53%
Almond flour	220 g	7.76 oz	15.6%
Confectioners' sugar	180 g	6.35 oz	12.77%
Salt	10 g	.35 oz	.71%
Butter	220 g	7.76 oz	15.6%
Butter, melted but cool	120 g	4.23 oz	8.51%
Toffee pieces	300 g	10.58 oz	21.28%

1. **For the toffee:** Line a half sheet pan with a nonstick rubber mat.

2. Combine the butter, sugar, and water in a sauce pot and cook over medium-high heat until the mixture reaches 152°C/305°F. Immediately pour onto the prepared sheet pan. Let it cool and break into small pieces, about 3 mm/.12 in size, using a knife.

3. If not using immediately, place inside a zip-top bag or an airtight container. The toffee will keep indefinitely if stored in a cool, dry place in an airtight container.

4. **For the shortbread base:** Line a flat sheet pan with a nonstick rubber mat. Place a 6-mm/.25-in-deep frame over the mat.

5. Follow the procedure for the shortbread cookie on page 421. Once the second amount of butter has been added, mix in the toffee pieces by hand in a bowl.

6. Pour the contents of the bowl into the frame and even it out using a rolling pin. Freeze.

7. Cut out 4 squares measuring 14 cm/5.5 in on each side.

8. Reserve the squares frozen until needed. Save any remaining shortbread for future use.

BROWN BUTTER GÉNOISE

YIELD: 1.51 KG/3 LB 5.28 OZ

INGREDIENT	METRIC	U.S.	%
Eggs	680 g	1 lb 8 oz	44.96%
Sugar	350 g	12.35 oz	23.14%
Salt	3 g	.09 oz	.17%
All-purpose flour	350 g	12.35 oz	23.14%
Milk powder	70 g	2.47 oz	4.63%
Butter, melted but cool	60 g	2.12 oz	3.97%

1. Follow the warm foaming method on page 11. Prepare a full sheet pan for this quantity.

2. Once the génoise is chilled, cut it into a square that measures 14 cm/5.5 in on each side by 1.25 cm/.5 in thick.

3. Freeze to harden. Reserve frozen until ready to assemble the cake.

TOASTED RYE BREAD CREAM

YIELD: 2 KG/4 LB 6.55 OZ

INGREDIENT	METRIC	U.S.	%
Infused Cream			
Rye bread (seedless)	900 g	1 lb 15.68 oz	27.27%
Heavy cream	2.4 kg	5 lb 4.64 oz	72.73%
Inclusion			
Infused Cream	1.2 kg	2 lb 10.24 oz	60%
Gelatin, sheets, silver, bloomed in cold water, excess water squeezed off	24 g	.85 oz	1.2%
Heavy cream	760 g	1 lb 10.72 oz	38%
Heavy cream stabilizer, liquid	16 g	.56 oz	.8%

1. **For the infused cream:** Dice the rye bread and toast it in a 160°C/325°F oven until golden brown. Make sure to use rye bread without caraway seeds.

2. Meanwhile, bring the heavy cream to a simmer.

3. Stir the hot toasted rye bread into the hot cream. Let steep for 10 minutes.

4. Strain the cream as much as possible and then blend the resulting cream with a Ber (immersion) mixer. Pass through cheesecloth; discard any leftover bread.

5. Cool in an ice water bath and proceed with the cream inclusion.

6. **For the inclusion:** Line a sheet pan with a nonstick rubber mat. Using caramel bars (heavy stainless-steel bars), create a square frame that measures 28 cm/11in on each side by 2.5 cm/1 in deep.

7. Make the cream according to the aerated desserts method on page 14. The stabilizer must be added to the heavy cream before it is whipped.

8. Pour the resulting cream into the prepared frame and even out the top. Freeze to harden.

9. Once hardened, remove the frame, remove the mat, and cut the cream into 4 equal-size squares using a hot knife.

10. Reserve frozen until ready to assemble the cake.

NOTE *This recipe will yield less than the total weight of the recipe ingredients, since the bread will absorb much of the cream and it will be strained out. The yield will be about half the total weight.*

VEGETABLE ASH VELVET SPRAY

YIELD: 465 G/1 LB .4 OZ

INGREDIENT	METRIC	U.S.	%
Caramelized White Chocolate (page 316)	200 g	7.05 oz	43.01%
Cocoa butter	250 g	8.82 oz	53.76%
Vegetable ash	15 g	.53 oz	3.23%

1. Combine all of the ingredients in a bowl over a hot water bath and melt. Stir to combine uniformly.

2. Fill the spray gun canister or reserve for later use. It will harden at room temperature. Use either a microwave or a hot water bath to melt it.

TOASTED SOURDOUGH SLIVER

YIELD: ONE 454-G/1-LB SOURDOUGH BÂTARD LOAF

INGREDIENT	METRIC	U.S.	%
Sourdough bâtard loaf	454 g	1 lb	100%

1. Refrigerate the loaf until completely chilled.

2. Tear the loaf into 7.5-cm/3-in pieces by hand. The size is approximate; this is an organic and imprecise shape. The idea is to show the bread as naturally as possible.

3. Using a heat gun (paint stripper) on the lowest setting, toast each slice on both sides.

4. Reserve exposed until just before displaying the cake; do not wrap or place in an airtight container.

ESPRESSO SPONGE CAKE

YIELD: 1.5 KG/3 LB 4.8 OZ

INGREDIENT	METRIC	U.S.	%
Cake flour	280 g	9.88 oz	18.67%
Almond flour	130 g	4.59 oz	8.67%
Baking powder	20 g	.71 oz	1.33%
Eggs	320 g	11.29 oz	21.33%
Brown sugar	275 g	9.7 oz	18.33%
Instant coffee powder	10 g	.35 oz	.67%
Milk	210 g	7.41 oz	14%
Canola oil	255 g	8.99 oz	17%
Dark chocolate	300 g	10.58 oz	

1. Preheat a convection oven to 160°C/325°F.

2. Lightly grease the inner border of a full sheet pan with nonstick oil spray and then line it with a nonstick rubber mat.

3. Sift the cake flour, almond flour, and baking powder together.

4. Combine the eggs, brown sugar, and instant coffee powder in the bowl of an electric mixer fitted with the whip attachment. Whip until the mixture reaches the ribbon stage (see page 11).

5. Stop the mixer and add one-quarter of the milk. Mix for a few seconds on low speed, and then add one-quarter of the dry ingredients and mix on low speed for a few seconds. Continue this way, alternating both items until they are both completely mixed.

6. Slowly stir in the canola oil. Pour into the prepared sheet pan and, using an offset spatula, spread to even it out.

7. Bake until done, 12 to 15 minutes or until it springs back at the center of the cake when gentle pressure is applied with the fingertips.

8. Cool at room temperature and then freeze the cake.

9. Once hardened, turn it onto a cutting board, remove the rubber mat, and apply a thin layer of dark chocolate using a paint roller. Let the chocolate harden and then cut out 4 squares measuring 17.5 cm/7 in on each side by 1.25 cm/.5 in thick.

10. Reserve frozen until ready to assemble the cake.

BAKED ESPRESSO CUSTARD

YIELD: 2.73 KG/6 LB .32 OZ

INGREDIENT	METRIC	U.S.	%
Heavy cream	1.9 kg	4 lb 3 oz	69.55%
Instant coffee powder	30 g	1.06 oz	1.1%
Sugar	400 g	14.11 oz	14.64%
Salt	2 g	.07 oz	.07%
Egg yolks	400 g	14.11 oz	14.64%

1. Lightly grease four 5-cm/2-in deep half hotel pans with a coat of nonstick oil spray. Line them with plastic wrap.

2. Preheat a convection oven to 135°C/275°F.

3. Assemble four full-size hotel pans (one for each half hotel pan) and 2 gallons of very hot water.

4. Put the heavy cream, coffee powder, half the sugar, and the salt in a pot over high heat.

5. Put the other half of the sugar in a bowl with the egg yolks. The bowl should be large enough to hold all of the ingredients.

6. Once the heavy cream mixture boils, slowly pour it into the yolk mixture while stirring with a whisk. Incorporate all of the heavy cream mixture.

7. Portion 680 g/1 lb 8 oz into each prepared half hotel pan.

8. Put each half hotel pan inside a large hotel pan.

9. Place each setup in the oven. Pour 2 L/2 qt of hot water into each large hotel pan.

10. Bake until the custards are just set, about 20 minutes. Check them by tapping on the pan. Look for a gelatinous jiggle, which means the custard is just set. If the custard base sloshes around the pan, the custard is not yet set and needs to bake further.

11. Cool the custards out of the large hotel pans at room temperature. Once cool, freeze the custards to harden them.

12. Once hardened, remove them from their baking pans. Remove the plastic and cut each custard into a square that measures 17.5 cm/7 in on each side. Reserve the custards frozen until ready to assemble the cake. Discard after 1 month.

BRIOCHE DOUGHNUT

YIELD: 1 KG/2 LB 3.27 OZ

INGREDIENT	METRIC	U.S.
Brioche Dough (page 156)	1 kg	2 lb 3.27 oz

1. Once the dough has rested and is firm and cold, roll it down to 1.25 cm/.5 in using either a sheeter or a rolling pin. Let the dough relax for 30 minutes in the refrigerator.

2. Using a 7.5-cm/3-in doughnut cutter dipped in flour, cut out as many doughnuts as possible and place them on a sheet pan lined with silicone paper. Proof the dough at room temperature in a large plastic bag for 2 hours or until doubled in size. You will only need 4 doughnuts and 4 doughnut centers for 4 cakes. Eat the remaining doughnuts (or see the Note).

3. Set a fryer filled with peanut oil to 180°C/355°F.

4. Fry 4 doughnuts at a time until golden brown, about 30 seconds on each side.

5. Once fried, toss them in granulated sugar as soon as they come out of the fryer to completely coat them; repeat this procedure with the doughnut centers. Keep in mind that these will fry faster. Turn them constantly in the frying oil so that they color evenly and stay round. This takes about a total of 30 seconds.

6. Let them cool on a sheet pan at room temperature. Freeze the doughnuts to assemble the cakes. Save the doughnut centers to garnish the cake.

NOTE *This recipe will yield more doughnuts than you need; it is not recommended to make smaller recipes with brioche since the final result may not be very good. If you wish, reserve the extra doughnuts in the freezer before proofing them and frying them.*

DOUGHNUT CREAM

YIELD: 4.99 KG/11 LB .02 OZ

INGREDIENT	METRIC	U.S.	%
Doughnut Purée			
Cake doughnuts	650 g	1 lb 6.92 oz	28.02%
Heavy cream	1.5 kg	3 lb 4.8 oz	64.66%
Sugar	170 g	6 oz	7.33%
Doughnut Cream			
Doughnut Purée	3 kg	6 lb 9.76 oz	60.12%
Gelatin sheets, silver, bloomed in cold water, excess water squeezed off	60 g	2.12 oz	1.2%
Heavy cream	1.90 kg	4 lb 3 oz	38.08%
Heavy cream stabilizer, liquid	30 g	1.06 oz	.6%

1. **For the doughnut purée:** Break the doughnuts into small morsels.

2. Combine the doughnuts, cream, and sugar in a pot, bring the cream to a boil, and then turn off the heat. Let the doughnuts soak up the cream and become completely soft.

3. Purée the mixture until smooth using a handheld immersion blender.

4. Reserve warm to make the cream.

5. Make sure you have the mold ready as well as all of the inclusions frozen and ready to assemble the cake.

6. **For the doughnut cream:** Follow with the aerated desserts method on page 14. The doughnut purée will act as the custard (crème anglaise). Assemble the cake.

NOTE *This is a cream made in the way of a Bavarian cream, where the base is a doughnut purée instead of a crème anglaise or fruit purée. It is important to use cake doughnuts that are store-bought, since they have an intense "doughnut" flavor that is hard to replicate. See Resources on page 520 for the most doughnut-flavored doughnuts.*

ESPRESSO VELVET SPRAY

YIELD: 1.02 KG/2 LB 3.84 OZ

INGREDIENT	METRIC	U.S.	%
Dark chocolate	500 g	1 lb 1.64 oz	49.02%
Instant coffee powder	20 g	.71 oz	1.96%
Cocoa butter	500 g	1 lb 1.64 oz	49.02%

1. Combine all of the ingredients in a bowl and melt over a hot water bath. Coffee powder dissolves faster in water than in fat, so it will take a few minutes of stirring to fully dissolve the crystals.

2. Fill the spray paint canister and spray the cakes, or reserve at room temperature in an airtight container. Discard after 6 months.

CHOCOLATE RING

YIELD: 300 G/10.58 OZ

INGREDIENT	METRIC	U.S.	%
Tempered dark chocolate	300 g	10.58 oz	100%

1. See Resources on page 520 for the rubber ring molds. Pipe the tempered chocolate into the rings and let it crystallize in the molds.

2. Once it has fully crystallized, push it out of the molds. Reserve in a cool, dry place, preferably enclosed. Discard after 1 year.

FLEXIBLE SHORTBREAD

YIELD: 2.2 KG/4 LB 14.24 OZ

INGREDIENT	METRIC	U.S.	%
All-purpose flour	720 g	1 lb 9.28 oz	32.43%
Almond flour	440 g	15.52 oz	19.82%
Confectioners' sugar	360 g	12.7 oz	16.22%
Salt	20 g	.71 oz	.9%
Butter, cut into 1.25-cm/ .5-in cubes	440 g	15.52 oz	19.82%
Butter, melted but cool	240 g	8.47 oz	10.81%

1. Preheat a convection oven to 160°C/325°F. Line a full sheet pan with a nonstick rubber mat.

2. In a Robot Coupe, combine the flours, sugar, and salt, and mix. Stop, add the cubed butter, and mix until fully incorporated.

3. Spread the mixture out on the prepared sheet pan and bake until golden brown, 15 to 20 minutes.

4. Let it cool; transfer to a Robot Coupe and grind to a fine powder. Pour in the melted butter and let the mixture come together into a solid mass.

5. Spread it out in a 3-mm/.1-in-thick frame. Reserve in the refrigerator until hardened. You may cut the dough to the sizes you need after the dough has chilled in order to get a clean cut. Any unused dough may be frozen. When shaping the tart, keep the top and bottom rectangles frozen, and the strip that will be the middle of the cake in the refrigerator so that it stays flexible.

CHERRY JAM

YIELD: 406 G/14.32 OZ

INGREDIENT	METRIC	U.S.	%
Calcium Solution			
Calcium lactate	2 g	.07 g	1.8%
Water	120 g	4.23 oz	98.2%
Cherry Jam			
Cherry purée (see Notes)	350 g	12.35	86.21%
Sugar	50 g	1.76 oz	12.32%
Calcium Solution	4 g	.07 oz	.99%
Universal pectin (pectin NH 95)	2 g	.14 oz	.49%

1. **For the calcium solution:** Combine both ingredients using a handheld immersion blender to dissolve the calcium. Reserve refrigerated.

2. **For the cherry jam:** Boil the cherry purée, 80 percent of the sugar, and the calcium solution in a small sauce pot. In the meantime, combine the remaining sugar with the pectin to obtain an even mixture.

3. Add the pectin-sugar mixture to the cherry mixture by shearing it in with a handheld immersion blender.

4. Return to a boil for 1 minute while stirring with a whisk.

5. Pour the hot jam onto a half hotel pan to cool at room temperature.

6. Once it is cool you may pipe it into the dough-lined molds. If not using right away, keep refrigerated for up to 2 weeks.

   NOTES *Make the calcium solution first. This jam is gelled with universal pectin (pectin NH 95), which requires calcium to gel. The recipe for the solution makes much more than what you need, but it is not reasonable to make only the 4 g/.07oz that you need. The rest keeps very well in the refrigerator and may be used later.*

   You can make your own cherry purée by pitting cherries and puréeing them in a blender.

MUDSLIDE COOKIES

YIELD: 2 KG/4 LB 6.4 OZ

INGREDIENT	METRIC	U.S.	%
Chocolate liquor	170 g	6 oz	8.5%
Dark chocolate coins (55%)	220 g	7.76 oz	11%
Butter	85 g	3 oz	4.25%
Eggs, at room temperature	300 g	10.58 oz	15%
Sugar	520 g	1 lb 2.24 oz	26%
Vanilla paste	5 g	.18 oz	.25%
Coffee extract	5 g	.18 oz	.25%
Pastry flour	85 g	3 oz	4.25%
Salt	3 g	.11 oz	.15%
Baking powder	7 g	.25 oz	.35%
Chocolate chunks	600 g	1 lb 5.12 oz	30%

1. Line 3 full sheet pans with parchment paper.

2. Combine the chocolate liquor, dark chocolate, and butter and melt it slowly in the microwave. It must not be too hot; 43°C/110°F is warm enough.

3. In a 4.73-L/5-quart electric mixer whip the eggs, sugar, vanilla, and coffee extract for 10 minutes on medium-high speed, until the mixture reaches the ribbon stage (see page 11).

4. Once the eggs have achieved maximum volume (quadrupled from its original volume), turn the mixer to low speed and add the melted chocolate mixture.

5. Take the mixture off the mixer, scrape down the bowl well, and insert the paddle attachment.

6. Mix in the flour, salt, and baking powder on speed 1 and scrape to thoroughly incorporate all of the ingredients.

7. Add the chocolate chunks and mix thoroughly.

8. Let the batter cool and firm up before scooping. Scoop the cookies when a scoop of batter doesn't spread any longer.

9. Scoop all of the batter onto the prepared sheet pans using a #10 scoop. Leave about 5 cm/2 in between each scoop.

10. Freeze the cookies before baking them.

11. Preheat a convection oven to 160°C/325° F. Bake the cookies until firm, 12 to 14 minutes.

12. Cool at room temperature. Reserve the cookies for the cookie purée. If not using soon, reserve in an airtight container at room temperature for up to 2 days or frozen for up to 1 month.

MUDSLIDE COOKIE PURÉE

YIELD: 2.5 KG/5 LB 8.16 OZ

INGREDIENT	METRIC	U.S.	%
Mudslide Cookies (page 422)	2 kg	4 lb 6.4 oz	80%
Water	500 g	1 lb 1.64 oz	20%

1. Break the cookies into small pieces.

2. Combine both ingredients in a blender and purée till smooth. You may need to add more water. The consistency should be similar to ganache.

3. Pour the cookie purée into the rectangular tart molds (see Resources, page 520) lined with the flexible shortbread as per the instructions on page 421 or reserve refrigerated until needed.

ENCAPSULATED CHERRY NECTAR SPHERE

YIELD: 380 G/13.4 OZ

INGREDIENT	METRIC	U.S.	%
Black cherry purée	300 g	10.58 oz	78.95%
Sugar	75 g	2.65 oz	19.74%
Gelatin, sheets, silver, bloomed in cold water, excess water squeezed off	5 g	.18 oz	1.32%

1. Combine the cherry purée and sugar in a bowl. Add the bloomed gelatin and place the bowl over a hot water bath.

2. Stir until the gelatin and sugar have dissolved.

3. Pour into a silicone hemisphere mold mat with a base diameter of 2.5 cm/1 in. You will have more than the 4 spheres you need; making less than this recipe is not recommended for practical purposes. The extras can be reserved frozen.

4. Freeze the spheres until hardened. Once hardened, they can be unmolded and dipped in the encapsulating bath. See the recipe for lemon soda spheres on page 135 for directions and amounts for the encapsulating bath.

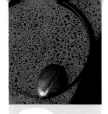

CHOCOLATE BLACKOUT SPONGE CAKE

YIELD: 6.55 KG/14 LB 7.2 OZ

INGREDIENT	METRIC	U.S.	%
Chocolate Shortbread (page 425; see Note)	454 g	1 lb	
All-purpose flour	900 g	1 lb 15.68 oz	13.72%
Cocoa powder	360 g	12.7 oz	5.49%
Salt	27 g	.95 oz	.41%
Baking soda	45 g	1.59 oz	.69%
Baking powder	36 g	1.27 oz	.55%
Sugar	1.8 kg	3 lb 15.36 oz	27.45%
Eggs	750 g	1 lb 10.4 oz	11.44%
Buttermilk	1.11 kg	2 lb 7.04 oz	16.93%
Brewed coffee, cold	1.02 kg	2 lb 3.84 oz	15.55%
Butter, melted but cool	510 g	1 lb 1.99 oz	7.78%

1. Preheat a convection oven to 162°C/325°F.

2. Lightly grease 4 square frames measuring 20 cm/8 in on each side by 5 cm/2 in high with nonstick oil spray and then coat them with flour. Line 2 sheet pans with nonstick rubber mats. Place 2 frames in each sheet pan.

3. Roll the chocolate shortbread out into a 1.25 cm/.5 in thick tube with your hands and wrap it around the outside of the frame at the base where it comes in contact with the non-stick rubber mat. Flatten it with your fingertips against the frame and the rubber mat. This is to prevent the batter, which is very loose, from seeping out of the frame.

4. Sift the flour, cocoa powder, salt, baking soda, and baking powder together and place in the bowl of an electric mixer.

5. Combine the eggs, buttermilk, and coffee in another bowl and whisk together to obtain a homogeneous mix.

6. Place the bowl with the dry ingredients on a mixer with the paddle attachment on low speed and slowly pour in the egg mixture.

7. Once the liquid has been completely incorporated, pour in the butter and mix until it has combined completely.

8. Divide the batter into the prepared frames (about 1.6 kg/4 lb 2.4 oz per frame). Bake until the cake springs back when it yields to gentle pressure, 25 to 35 minutes. Or perform a knife test by introducing the tip of a knife down the center of the cake; if it comes out dry, it is done baking.

9. Let the cakes cool at room temperature. Wrap tightly. If refrigerated, it will keep in peak condition for 3 to 4 days. If frozen, no more than 1 month is recommended.

CRÈME FRAÎCHE CREAM

YIELD: 2.98 KG/6 LB 9.12 OZ

INGREDIENT	METRIC	U.S.	%
Crème fraîche	2 kg	4 lb 6.4 oz	67.11%
Heavy cream	750 g	1 lb 10.4 oz	25.17%
Sugar	200 g	7.05 oz	6.71%
Heavy cream stabilizer, liquid	30 g	1.06 oz	1.01%

1. Combine all of the ingredients in the bowl of an electric mixer. Whip until stiff.

2. Pipe into the cake's cavity as per the assembly instructions.

   NOTE *This cream should be made just before you are ready to use it.*

CHOCOLATE SHORTBREAD

YIELD: 1.25 KG/2 LB 12 OZ

INGREDIENT	METRIC	U.S.	%
Butter	385 g	13.58 oz	30.8%
Sugar	230 g	8.11 oz	18.4%
All-purpose flour	380 g	13.4 oz	30.4%
Cocoa powder	140 g	4.94 oz	11.2%
Baking powder	4 g	.14 oz	.32%
Salt	1 g	.04 oz	.08%
Butter, melted but cool	110 g	3.88 oz	8.8%

1. See the method for shortbread on page 421 to make the dough. Chill the dough for at least 1 hour.

2. Roll the dough to 3 mm/.1 in thick on a sheeter or by hand using a rolling pin. Chill the dough again and then dock it with a fork.

3. Preheat a convection oven to 160°C/325°F.

4. Bake the shortbread until firm, about 10 minutes. Cool at room temperature.

5. Grind in a Robot Coupe until uniform, fine crumbs are obtained.

6. Pour in the melted butter to form a uniform mass.

7. Sheet the dough out to 3 mm/.1 in thick. Freeze to harden. Once hard, cut out 4 squares measuring 17.5 cm/7 in long on each side.

8. Reserve frozen until ready to assemble the cake. Discard after 1 month.

   NOTE *For the Chocolate Blackout Sponge Cake on page 424, reserve 454 g/1 lb of the crumbs without the addition of melted butter.*

CARAMEL MOUSSE

YIELD: 2.43 KG/5 LB 5.76 OZ

INGREDIENT	METRIC	U.S.	%
Heavy cream 1	350 g	12.35 oz	14.39%
Sugar	450 g	15.87 oz	18.5%
Butter	150 g	5.29 oz	6.17%
Eggs	300 g	10.58 oz	12.33%
Gelatin, sheets, silver, bloomed in cold water, excess water squeezed off	21 g	.74 oz	.86%
Heavy cream 2	1.15 kg	2 lb 8.48 oz	47.27%
Heavy cream stabilizer, liquid	12 g	.42 oz	.49%

1. Using caramel bars (heavy stainless-steel bars), make a square frame measuring 30 cm/12 in long on each side by 2.5 cm/1 in deep over a flat sheet pan lined with a nonstick rubber mat . Freeze this setup.

2. Warm up the first amount of heavy cream in a sauce pot.

3. In 3.76-L/4-qt sauce pot, cook the sugar over high heat, stirring constantly until it turns a medium amber brown, 170°C/338°F. Stir in the butter completely, then add the warm heavy cream. Remove the caramel from the heat.

4. Place the eggs over a hot water bath and warm them to 60°C/140°F while stirring constantly. Transfer them to the bowl of an electric mixer and whip until they have cooled to room temperature. While the eggs are whipping, stream in the caramel. Add the gelatin and whip until the gelatin dissolves and the mixture has cooled to 21°C/70°F.

5. Whip the second amount of heavy cream and the stabilizer in an electric mixer to medium-soft peaks. Fold the whipped cream into the caramel in 2 additions.

6. Pour into the prepared frame. Even out the top of the frame. Freeze to harden.

7. Once hardened completely, remove the frame and then flip the mousse over onto a cutting board lined with parchment paper. Cut the mousse into 4 even squares measuring 15 cm/6 in long on each size using a warm slicing knife. Dip the knife in hot water and then dry it to get a clean cut.

8. Reserve frozen until ready to assemble the cake.

COPPER LUSTER DUST PASTE

YIELD: 102 G/3.6 OZ

INGREDIENT	METRIC	U.S.	%
Copper luster dust	2 g	.07 oz	1.96%
Mirror glaze	100 g	3.53 oz	98.04%

1. Combine both ingredients in a bowl.

2. Stir to combine evenly. Reserve at room temperature, covered, until ready to finish the cake. This paste can be made well in advance and will keep for at least 1 month at room temperature.

CHOCOLATE CURVED TRIANGLE

YIELD: 300 G/10.58 OZ

INGREDIENT	METRIC	U.S.	%
Tempered dark chocolate	300 g	10.58 oz	100%

1. Cut a sheet of acetate into a 17.5-cm/7-in square.

2. Spread the tempered chocolate on the acetate.

3. When the chocolate has semi-crystallized, cut out 12 triangles measuring 1.25 cm/.5 in wide by 15 cm/6 in long.

4. Wrap parchment paper around a 10-cm/4-in diameter PVC tube to prevent the chocolate from sticking, and then wrap the acetate sheet around the tube. Wrap the acetate with parchment as well to keep it in place, and tape it closed.

5. Let the chocolate set on the tube. Reserve in a cool, dry place.

GREEN TEA GÉNOISE

YIELD: 1.98 KG/4 LB 5.92 OZ

INGREDIENT	METRIC	U.S.	%
Eggs	880 g	1 lb 15.04 oz	44.35%
Sugar	500 g	1 lb 1.64 oz	25.2%
Salt	4 g	.14 oz	.2%
All-purpose flour	500 g	1 lb 1.64 oz	25.2%
Matcha green tea powder	20 g	.71 oz	1.01%
Butter, melted but cool	80 g	2.82 oz	4.03%

1. Lightly grease a half sheet pan with nonstick oil spray. Line it with a half-size nonstick rubber mat.

2. Preheat a steam oven to 100°C/212°F.

3. Follow the method for the Earl Grey Génoise (under Jasmine Tea Cake) on page 218.

4. Steam the génoise for 10 to 12 minutes.

5. Once the cake has cooled, refrigerate it to chill (it cuts better when cold). Cut into rectangles measuring 7.5 cm/3 in wide by 15 cm/6 in long by 2.5 cm/1 in high.

6. Reserve covered and refrigerated until ready to assemble the cake.

PASSION FRUIT CURD

YIELD: 515 G/1 LB 2.17 OZ

INGREDIENT	METRIC	U.S	%
Passion fruit purée (see Note)	90 g	3.17 oz	17.48%
Lemon juice	10 g	.35 oz	1.94%
Sugar	120 g	4.23 oz	23.3%
Yolks	120 g	4.23 oz	23.3%
Butter, diced	165 g	5.82 oz	32.04%
Gelatin sheets, silver, bloomed in cold water, excess water squeezed off	10 g	.35 oz	1.94%

1. Line 10 PVC tubes measuring 20 cm/8 in long by 1.25 cm/.5 in diameter with acetate plastic. It should be about 2.5 cm/1 in longer than the tube; pinch one end of the acetate that protrudes from the PVC tube shut with a paper clip to prevent the curd from pouring out.

2. Follow the method for the passion fruit curd on page 321. The gelatin is added at the end of the process but while the base is still hot in order for it to melt.

3. Pipe the curd into the tubes and allow it to harden in the freezer.

4. Once the curd is hard, cut both ends that protrude from the PVC tube with a knife. Push the curd out and remove the acetate plastic. Reserve frozen until ready to assemble the cake.

    NOTE *If the passion fruit purée is concentrated, use a mixture of half passion fruit purée and half orange juice.*

YUZU CREAM

YIELD: 2.63 KG/5 LB 12.64 OZ

INGREDIENT	METRIC	U.S.	%
Heavy cream	1 kg	2 lb 3.2 oz	38.02%
Yuzu juice	320 g	11.29 oz	12.17%
Sugar	480 g	1 lb .93 oz	18.25%
Eggs	400 g	14.11 oz	15.21%
Butter	400 g	14.11 oz	15.21%
Gelatin sheets, silver, bloomed in cold water, excess water squeezed off	30 g	1.06 oz	1.14%

1. Make sure the molds are prepared before making the cream.

2. Whip the heavy cream to medium peaks and reserve in refrigeration.

3. Combine the yuzu juice, sugar, and eggs in a bowl and cook over a hot water bath until thickened.

4. Take off the heat and stir in the butter; dissolve completely.

5. Add the bloomed gelatin to the above mixture while it is hot so that it dissolves completely.

6. Fold in one-quarter of the cold whipped heavy cream. Then fold in half of the remaining whipped cream and then the other half of the whipped cream. Pour into a piping bag and pipe into the cake molds all the way to the top.

7. Even out the top with an offset spatula.

8. Freeze and reserve leftover yuzu cream. At this point, the cream will dip inside the mold. It always happens, which is why I prefer to assemble cakes upside down. Once the cake is frozen, pour some yuzu cream on top of the cake and even it out again. This will correct the dip in the cake.

9. Reserve frozen until ready to finish the cake.

HIBISCUS VEIL

YIELD: 203 G/7.19 OZ

INGREDIENT	METRIC	U.S.	%
Hibiscus Infusion			
Dried hibiscus leaves	50 g	1.76 oz	11.11%
Water, at 95°C/205°F	400 g	14.11 oz	88.89%
Hibiscus Veil			
Hibiscus Infusion	75 g	2.65 oz	36.82%
Water	75 g	2.65 oz	36.82%
Simple syrup, at 50° Brix	50 g	1.76 oz	24.55%
Agar-agar	3 g	.11 oz	1.47%
Gellan gum, high acyl	1 g	.02 oz	.34%

1. **For the infusion:** Combine the hibiscus leaves and water and infuse for 5 minutes.

2. Strain out the hibiscus flowers and cool the infusion to room temperature. Reserve in the refrigerator for up to 1 week.

3. **For the veil:** Combine all of the ingredients in a small sauce pot and bring to a boil while stirring with a whisk.

4. Pour into a very flat tray and let it set there.

5. Using a ruler and the back of a paring knife, cut the veil into rectangles measuring 5 cm/2 in wide by 20 cm/8 in long.

6. Reserve the tray wrapped in plastic wrap in the refrigerator until ready to assemble the cake.

WHITE VELVET SPRAY

YIELD: 670 G/1 LB 7.52 OZ

INGREDIENT	METRIC	U.S.	%
White chocolate	300 g	10.58 oz	44.78%
Cocoa butter	300 g	10.58 oz	44.78%
Titanium white cocoa butter	70 g	2.47 oz	10.45%

1. Combine the white chocolate and both cocoa butters in a bowl and melt over a hot water bath.

2. Transfer to an airtight container and reserve at room temperature for up to 1 year.

BROWNIE

YIELD: 2.08 KG/4 LB 6.72 OZ

INGREDIENT	METRIC	U.S.	%
Cake flour	220 g	7.76 oz	10.96%
Salt	3 g	.11 oz	.15%
Dark chocolate	280 g	9.88 oz	13.94%
Butter	340 g	11.99 oz	16.93%
Eggs	300 g	10.58 oz	14.94%
Sugar	400 g	14.11 oz	19.92%
Brown sugar	145 g	5.11 oz	7.22%
Walnuts, chopped and toasted	160 g	5.64 oz	7.97%
Chocolate chips	160 g	5.64 oz	7.97%

1. Lightly grease the border of a half sheet pan with non-stick oil spray. Line it with a nonstick rubber mat.

2. Preheat a convection oven to 160°C/325°F. Sift the cake flour and salt together.

3. Melt the chocolate and butter together over a hot water bath.

4. Whip the eggs and sugars to the ribbon stage in the bowl of an electric mixer on high speed.

5. Stir the melted chocolate and butter into the whipped egg mixture. Stir in the dry ingredients and then fold in the walnuts and chocolate chips.

6. Spread evenly onto the prepared sheet pan. Bake until set, 12 to 18 minutes.

7. Cool at room temperature and then refrigerate the cake to cut it (it cuts easier and cleaner when cold; do not freeze it, though, as it will be too hard to cut). Cut out 4 rectangles measuring 7.5 cm/3 in wide by 17.5 cm/7 in long. Reserve cold until ready to assemble the cake.

the front of the house

Developing a good relationship with the people who are in charge of describing and serving your desserts is absolutely crucial to your success and also to the customer's positive experience. There are many degrees of service, ranging from bad to excellent, but for the most part it falls into a category of "average" for a very simple reason: Not too many waiters are waiters by profession. Many waiters wait on tables while they are in college or while they wait for their other careers to take off. There are many great waiters and managers out there, but not as many as those who are not qualified to serve food. Good service staff is hard to come by, so if you find them, do everything you can to keep them. This type of person does care if you used crème fraîche instead of sour cream, and wants to know why you did it and if the crème fraîche is local or not, and why you chose to switch.

Personally, my relationship with the front of the house has often left me with a feeling of powerlessness since, once the dessert leaves my kitchen, I have really no way of knowing what happens to the food, how it is being served, or how the customer is being cared for. Because of this, it is so crucial to work with the front of the house instead of against them. It doesn't mean that you have to be best friends and have drinks after work, but it does mean that you have a lot riding on their competence and willingness to do the right thing for you, your food, and your customers. It doesn't take that much to build a positive work environment. A terrific way to build this relationship is by doing tastings with them on a frequent basis. It helps if your restaurant has preservice meetings. If you are enthusiastic and positive about your food, it can be contagious.

LEMON CURD

YIELD: 1.2 KG/2 LB 10.24 OZ

INGREDIENT	METRIC	U.S.	%
Gelled lemon curd (page 223)	1.2 kg	2 lb 10.24 oz	100%

1. Line a half sheet pan with a nonstick rubber mat. Place a 1.25-cm/.5–in-deep frame inside the sheet pan.

2. Pour the warm curd into the frame.

3. Let it set in the freezer.

4. Once set, remove the frame. Flip the curd over onto a sheet of parchment paper and peel off the nonstick rubber mat.

5. Cut out 4 rectangles measuring 7.5 cm wide by 17.5 cm/7 in long.

6. Reserve the rectangles frozen until ready to assemble the cake.

LITCHI GELÉE

YIELD: 840 G/1 LB 13.6 OZ

INGREDIENT	METRIC	U.S.	%
Litchi purée	800 g	1 lb 12.16 oz	95.24%
Gelatin, sheets, silver, bloomed in cold water, excess water squeezed off	40 g	1.41 oz	4.76%

1. Warm the litchi purée to 40°C/105°F over a hot water bath. Add the gelatin and stir until it has dissolved completely.

2. Pour into a hot pan and let set completely in the refrigerator.

3. Unmold the set gelée onto a cutting board (turn the hotel pan over onto a cutting board and apply heat to the pan with a blow dryer; it will release onto the cutting board). Cut into medium-dice pieces (the shape does not need to be perfect) with a knife.

4. Reserve refrigerated until ready to assemble the cake.

CHOCOLATE SOIL

YIELD: 760 G/1 LB 10.8 OZ

INGREDIENT	METRIC	U.S.	%
Sugar	200 g	7.05 oz	26.32%
Almond flour	200 g	7.05 oz	26.32%
All-purpose flour	120 g	4.23 oz	15.79%
Cocoa powder	88 g	3.10 oz	11.58%
Butter, melted but cool	140 g	4.94 oz	18.42%
Salt	12 g	0.42 oz	1.58%

1. Preheat a convection oven to 160° C/320° F

2. Mix all of the ingredients in a mixer bowl using the paddle attachment until you obtain a homogenous mix and spread onto a sheet pan lined with a nonstick rubber mat in an even layer.

3. Bake for 15 minutes or until aromatic (you can't tell by its color because it is already brown); you may also be able to tell by tasting it. Spoon a small amount out and cool it down; it should taste like a baked almond cookie).

4. Cool down at room temperature. Reserve in an airtight container in the refrigerator for up to 1 week, or freeze for up to 1 month.

DARK CHOCOLATE GANACHE

YIELD: 1.2 KG/2 LB 10.24 OZ

INGREDIENT	METRIC	U.S.	%
Heavy cream	600 g	1 lb 5.15 oz	50%
Dark chocolate	500 g	1 lb 1.64 oz	41.67%
Butter, soft	100 g	3.53 oz	8.33%

1. Bring the heavy cream to a boil and pour it over the dark chocolate.

2. Let sit for 10 seconds, and then stir the cream into the chocolate to create a homogeneous mix.

3. When the mixture cools to about 30°C/86°F, stir in the soft butter. You will need to "push" it into the ganache with the rubber spatula, pressing against the side of the bowl. At this temperature the butter does not dissolve or melt; it will merely be mixed in.

4. Once you do not see any butter pieces, the ganache is ready to use.

LEMON "DEW DROPS"

YIELD: 120 G/4.23 OZ

INGREDIENT	METRIC	U.S.	%
Lemon juice	20 g	.71 oz	16.67%
Clear or mirror glaze (see Resources, page 520)	100 g	3.53 oz	83.33%

Combine both ingredients and stir well until homogenous. Reserve refrigerated until ready to use.

BUBBLE CHOCOLATE

YIELD: 2.4 KG/5 LB 4.64 OZ

INGREDIENT	METRIC	U.S.	%
Dark chocolate coins	2 kg	4 lb 6.4 oz	83.33%
Canola oil	400 g	14.11 oz	16.67%

1. You will need two 1-L/1.05-qt heavy cream whippers and 4 CO$_2$ charges; alternatively, make half the recipe at a time, because 1-L/1.05-qt whippers cannot hold the entire recipe.

2. Prepare a 25-cm/10-in square frame using 2.5-cm/1-in-thick caramel bars (heavy stainless-steel bars).

3. Melt the chocolate with the oil over a hot water bath. Divide the mixture equally between the two whipper canisters.

4. Charge each canister with 2 cartridges, shaking vigorously after each charge.

5. Immediately after, extrude the chocolate into the prepared frame. Both canisters should fill the frame and there should be excess; pour the excess into a sheet pan lined with a nonstick rubber mat and let it set in the refrigerator. Cut this piece into 4 smaller pieces about 5 cm/2 in long; they will be used to garnish the cake.

6. Let set at room temperature. Once set, cut the chocolate into four 10-cm/5-in squares.

7. Reserve in the refrigerator until ready to assemble the cake.

FLOURLESS CHOCOLATE CAKE

YIELD: 2 KG/4 LB 6.4 OZ

INGREDIENT	METRIC	U.S.	%
Dark chocolate coins 64%	680 g	1 lb 7.84 oz	34%
Butter	340 g	11.99 oz	17%
Egg yolks	300 g	10.58 oz	15%
Sugar 1	180 g	6.35 oz	9%
Egg whites	450 g	15.87 oz	22.5%
Sugar 2	50 g	1.76 oz	2.5%

1. Lightly grease the border of a half sheet pan with nonstick oil spray. Line the sheet pan with a nonstick rubber mat.

2. Preheat a convection oven to 160°C/320°F.

3. Melt the chocolate with the butter over a hot water bath or in the microwave.

4. While melting, whip the egg yolks and the first amount of sugar to ribbon stage and then make a French meringue with the egg whites and the second amount of sugar using the method on page 12.

5. Mix the egg yolk mixture into the melted chocolate using a whisk.

6. Fold in the meringue in 2 additions.

7. Spread onto the prepared sheet pan and bake until done, 12 to 16 minutes, or until the cake feels firm to the touch. If it feels wet, it is still not fully baked.

8. Cool to room temperature and then chill in the refrigerator.

9. Once cold, cut the cake into four 12.5-cm/5-in squares. Freeze to harden and reserve frozen until ready to assemble the cake. This can be stored frozen for up to 1 month.

TOASTED MILK CREAM

YIELD: 6.84 KG/15 LB 1.28 OZ

INGREDIENT	METRIC	U.S.	%
Milk powder	420 g	14.82 oz	6.14%
Heavy cream	4.2 kg	9 lb 4 oz	61.38%
Sugar	1.05 kg	2 lb 5.04 oz	15.35%
Egg yolks	1.05 kg	2 lb 5.04 oz	15.35%
Gelatin, sheets, silver, bloomed in cold water, excess water squeezed off	123 g	4.32 oz	1.79%

1. Assemble the molds and the components of the cake. You will need to use this cream right after you have made it.

2. In a small rondeau, toast the milk powder over medium-high heat, stirring with a wooden spoon to evenly toast the milk.

3. Once the powder is evenly browned, add the heavy cream and half of the sugar. Proceed with the anglaise method on page 8.

4. Once the anglaise has completely cooled, place one-fifth of it in a bowl with the bloomed gelatin over a hot water bath. Stir to dissolve the gelatin.

5. Meanwhile, in the bowl of an electric mixer, whip the remaining anglaise on high speed until it has quadrupled in volume.

6. Whisk one-quarter of the whipped anglaise into the warm anglaise-gelatin mixture.

7. Fold half of the whipped anglaise into the previous mixture, and then fold the remaining amount of whipped anglaise.

8. Assemble the cakes.

NOTE *This is a very interesting method, which I cannot in good conscience claim as my brainchild. Essentially it questions the whole Bavarian cream method in which we take a base (anglaise and/or fruit purée, or pastry cream), add gelatin to it, and then fold the whipped cream into it to make it light and airy. There are two basic problems with the classic Bavarian cream method. One is that it extends the time it takes to make the product and, most important, the addition of the whipped cream will dilute the flavor of the base. In this method, we make an anglaise with heavy cream only (instead of heavy cream and milk), and we add nothing else but gelatin. The heavy cream in the anglaise alone is sufficient to be able to take in air when whipped, obtaining the desired lightness and airiness of a Bavarian cream.*

DARK CHOCOLATE PLAQUE AND GINKGO LEAF

YIELD: APPROXIMATELY 4 PLAQUES AND 4 GINKGO LEAVES

INGREDIENT	METRIC	U.S.
Dark chocolate, tempered	400 g	14.11 oz
Gold luster dust	as needed	as needed

1. You will need to have an acetate sheet available, as well as 4 silicone ginkgo leaf molds (see Resources, page 520).

2. Brush the ginkgo molds with tempered chocolate first to help prevent air pockets from forming, and then pour the tempered chocolate into the mold to fill to the top. Allow to crystallize at room temperature.

3. Meanwhile, pour tempered chocolate onto the acetate and spread in a thin, even layer using an offset spatula.

4. When the chocolate is semi-crystallized, cut out rectangles measuring 7.5 cm/3 in wide by 10 cm/4 in long using a ruler and the back of a paring knife.

5. Flip the acetate over a flat sheet pan and place a flat weight such as a cutting board on top of it, and allow to set at room temperature.

6. Once the leaves and the plaques have fully crystallized, remove the leaves from the molds and peel the acetate off the chocolate plaques.

7. Using a brush, brush a strip of gold luster dust on one side of the chocolate plaques.

8. Brush the gold luster dust on the ginkgo leaves, coating them completely. Make sure to remove all excess dust with the brush; it should be an even coat.

9. Reserve in a cool, dry area, preferably enclosed. Discard after 1 year.

NOTE *Try to get all of the tempered dark chocolate work done in one step to save time.*

RASPBERRY SPONGE CAKE

YIELD: 1.51 KG/3 LB 5.44 OZ

INGREDIENT	METRIC	U.S.	%
All-purpose flour	330 g	11.64 oz	21.78%
Beet powder	45 g	1.59 oz	2.97%
Sugar	360 g	12.7 oz	23.76%
Baking powder	15 g	.53 oz	.99%
Eggs, at room temperature	150 g	5.29 oz	9.9%
Butter, melted but cool	165 g	5.82 oz	10.89%
Raspberry purée, at room temperature	330 g	11.64 oz	21.78%
Sour cream, at room temperature	45 g	1.59 oz	2.97%
Chambord liqueur	75 g	2.65 oz	4.95%

1. Lightly grease the interior border of a half sheet pan. Line it with a nonstick rubber mat.

2. Preheat a convection oven to 160°C/320F.

3. Combine the flour, beet powder, sugar and baking powder, and sift them.

4. Place the eggs in a bowl. Slowly pour the butter in while whisking to create an emulsion. Repeat with the raspberry purée, sour cream, and Chambord.

5. Stir in the dry ingredients and whisk until just combined.

6. Pour the batter into the prepared sheet pan.

7. Bake until done, 10 to 15 minutes. It will spring back when gentle pressure is applied with your fingertips to the center of the sponge cake.

8. Cool to room temperature and then chill in the refrigerator.

9. Cut out squares measuring 7.5 cm/3 in on each side by 1.25 cm/.5 in thick.

10. Reserve well covered in the refrigerator until ready to assemble the cakes.

WHIPPED VANILLA MILK AND PASTRY CREAM

YIELD: 750 G/1 LB 10.26 OZ

INGREDIENT	METRIC	U.S.	%
Pastry Cream (page 6)	1.1 kg	2 lb 6.72 oz	59.46%
Lecithin powder	8 g	.28 oz	.43%
Egg white powder	11 g	.39 oz	.59%
Skim milk	580 g	1 lb 4.46 oz	31.35%
Gelatin sheets, silver, bloomed in cold water, excess water squeezed off	20 g	.71 oz	1.08%
Sugar	125 g	4.41 oz	6.76%
Vanilla paste	6 g	.21 oz	.32%

1. Stir the pastry cream with a whisk to loosen it up. Make sure the molds are assembled with the cake and the wafer paper.

2. Ber mix the lecithin powder and egg white powder with 60 percent of the milk, and then place it in a mixer bowl with the whip attachment.

3. Combine the remaining milk with the gelatin and sugar. Warm the mixture up just enough to melt the gelatin.

4. Add to the mixture in the bowl and whip on high speed; wrap the mixer with plastic or else you will have a mess on your hands.

5. Place a bowl with ice water under the bowl as it whips to cool the gelatin and so that it starts foaming the mix. This takes a very long time to whip, so be patient. Whip until it looks like egg whites whipped to stiff peaks; then add the vanilla paste and remove from the mixer. Fold the whipped milk foam into the loosened pastry cream in 2 additions. Pour into a piping bag.

6. Fill the Plexiglas cubes to the top. Even out the top and set in the refrigerator.

NOTE *This recipe and method came from an idea to have a glass of cake and a slice of milk. But how do you slice milk? You could add gelatin to milk and call it good, but I was compelled to have an item that resembled a cake; therefore, it had to be airy and light, and a gelled slice of milk is not. Folding the milk foam into the pastry cream makes for an extremely lighter-than-air preparation full of flavor and smooth texture. This particular method is inspired by the classic Bavarian cream method, inasmuch as two separate components are folded in together.*

RASPBERRY CHOCOLATE PINECONES

NOTE *See the recipe and method for making beet couverture on page 511. Replace the amount of beet powder with freeze-dried raspberry powder. You will need polycarbonate pinecone molds (see Resources, page 520). Proceed with the molded chocolate method. These pinecones are not solid pieces of chocolate, just shells. You will need to make at least a 2-kg/4 lb 6.55 oz batch to fit in the melangeur, but to make the pinecones you will need 600 g/ 1 lb 5.16 oz.*

GREEN TEA GELÉE

YIELD: 251 G/8.87 OZ

INGREDIENT	METRIC	U.S.	%
Matcha green tea powder	40 g	1.41 oz	15.9%
Water	160 g	5.64 oz	63.59%
Sugar	50 g	1.76 oz	19.87%
Gellan gum, low acyl	2 g	.06 oz	.64%

1. Combine all of the ingredients in a small sauce pot and stir well to dissolve the sugar and the matcha and to hydrate the gellan gum.

2. Bring to a quick boil, and then pour into a 30-cm/12-in square tray.

3. Let set without moving the tray, and then refrigerate.

4. Once cold, cut the gelée into rectangles that will cover the top of the Plexiglas cubes. They need to measure 5 cm/2 in wide by 12.5 cm/5 in long.

5. Keep well covered and refrigerated until needed. Discard after 2 days.

CASSIS SPONGE CAKE

YIELD: 3.03 KG/6 LB 10.88 OZ

INGREDIENT	METRIC	U.S.	%
All-purpose flour	660 g	1 lb 7.28 oz	21.78%
Freeze-dried black currant powder	90 g	3.17 oz	2.97%
Baking powder	30 g	1.06 oz	.99%
Eggs, at room temperature	300 g	10.58 oz	9.9%
Butter, melted but cool	330 g	11.64 oz	10.89%
Cassis purée (see Resources, page 520)	660 g	1 lb 7.28 oz	21.78%
Crème fraîche, at room temperature	90 g	3.17 oz	2.97%
Crème de cassis liqueur	150 g	5.29 oz	4.95%
Sugar	720 g	25.4 oz	23.76%

1. Lightly grease the inside frame of a full sheet pan with nonstick oil spray. Line it with a nonstick rubber mat.

2. Follow the method for raspberry sponge cake on page 435. Substitute cassis purée for the raspberry purée.

3. Once the cake has cooled, cut out 7.5-cm/3-in diameter disks. Each sheet of cake yields between 24 and 28 disks, and each finished entremet requires 6 disks. Reserve any left over for future cakes.

4. Reserve the sponge cake at room temperature if it is to be assembled soon; otherwise reserve frozen until needed for up to 1 month. The cake tastes better and has a better texture if it is tempered and not cold.

ALMOND CREAM

YIELD: 4.25 KG/9 LB 5.92 OZ

INGREDIENT	METRIC	U.S.	%
Heavy cream	3.2 kg	7 lb .8 oz	75.29%
Almonds, slivered and blanched	750 g	1 lb 10.4 oz	17.65%
Sugar	270 g	9.52 oz	6.35%
Heavy cream stabilizer	30 g	1.06 oz	.71%

1. Bring the cream to a simmer in a rondeau.

2. Meanwhile, toast the almonds as dark as possible without burning them in a 160°C/320°F oven. Add the hot toasted almonds to the hot cream. Stir. Cover with plastic wrap and let steep for 2 hours.

3. Reheat the cream and then strain out the almonds. Reheating prevents the almonds from holding on to too much cream when you strain it. There should be about 2.8 kg/6 lb 2.72 oz of cream left after straining the almonds out. Add the sugar while the cream is hot so that it dissolves. Cool over an ice water bath and then reserve in the refrigerator until needed.

4. When you are ready to assemble the cake, whip 700 g/ 1 lb 8.64 oz of cream with the stabilizer in the bowl of an electric mixer until stiff. Pour into a piping bag fitted with a #4 fluted piping tip and assemble the cakes.

CHOCOLATE SHELL

YIELD: 750 G/1 LB 10.46 OZ

INGREDIENT	METRIC	U.S.	%
Tempered dark chocolate	750 g	1 lb 10.46 oz	100%

1. You will need triangular rubber molds measuring 6.25 cm/2.5 in wide by 30 cm/12 in long by 3 cm/1.2 in deep (see Resources, page 520).

2. Fill the molds with the tempered dark chocolate and proceed with the molded chocolate method (see page 421) to create shells in which to assemble the entremets.

3. Let the chocolate crystallize at room temperature. Leave the bars inside the mold (you need to assemble this cake while it is in the mold). You are now ready to assemble the bars.

MEYER LEMON PÂTE DE FRUIT

YIELD: 790 G/1 LB 11.87 OZ

INGREDIENT	METRIC	U.S.	%
Water	88 g	3.09 oz	11.08%
Glucose syrup 1	80 g	2.82 oz	10.13%
Sugar 1	40 g	1.41 oz	5.06%
Pectin	10 g	.35 oz	1.27%
Glucose syrup 2	155 g	5.47 oz	19.62%
Sugar 2	330 g	11.64 oz	41.77%
Meyer lemon juice	88 g	3.09 oz	11.08%
Superfine sugar	as needed	as needed	

1. Using caramel bars (heavy stainless-steel bars), make a frame measuring 20 cm/8 in wide by 27.5 cm/11 in long by 5 mm/.2 in deep over a nonstick rubber mat.

2. Sprinkle superfine sugar over the surface of the mat.

3. Combine the water and the first amount of the glucose syrup in a sauce pot. Mix until the glucose has dissolved.

4. Combine the first amount of sugar and the pectin and slowly pour into the glucose mixture while whisking constantly.

5. Bring the mixture to a boil, and then add the second amount of glucose syrup. Add the second amount of sugar.

6. Cook the mixture to 107°C/225°F. Remove the pot from the heat and stir in the Meyer lemon juice until a homogenous mass is achieved.

7. Pour the pâte de fruit into the prepared frame. Let it set for a few minutes, and then sprinkle the entire surface with superfine sugar.

8. Once the pâte de fruit has set, cut it into triangles measuring 5 cm/2 in wide by 27.5 cm/11 in long. Discard after 1 month or after the outer layers start to dry out.

PRALINE CREAM

YIELD: 800 G/1 LB 12.22 OZ

INGREDIENT	METRIC	U.S.	%
Butter, soft	200 g	7.05 oz	25%
Praline paste	200 g	7.05 oz	25%
Milk chocolate, tempered	400 g	14.11 oz	50%

1. Combine the soft butter with the praline paste in a bowl using a rubber spatula.

2. Stir in the tempered milk chocolate. Mix until homogeneous.

3. Pour into a piping bag and pipe into the candy bar on top of the bubble chocolate.

NOTE *This item should be made just before it is needed. If you make it in advance and store it, the chocolate will harden and will be hard to re-temper it with the other components.*

ANGEL FOOD CAKE

YIELD: 1 KG/2 LB 3.36 OZ

INGREDIENT	METRIC	U.S.	%
Pastry flour	160 g	5.64 oz	15.94%
Sugar	210 g	7.41 oz	20.93%
Egg whites	420 g	14.82 oz	41.85%
Superfine or bakers' sugar	210 g	7.41 oz	20.93%
Cream of tartar	1 g	.04 oz	.1%
Salt	3 g	.09 oz	.25%

1. Line a half sheet pan with a nonstick rubber mat. Do not spray the border of the sheet pan, since angel food cake needs something to adhere to as it bakes; otherwise it will pancake while it cools.

2. Preheat a convection oven to 160°C/320°F. Sift the pastry flour and sugar together.

3. Whip the egg whites on high speed with the superfine sugar, cream of tartar, and salt.

4. Fold in the sifted dry ingredients by hand.

5. Pour the batter into the prepared pan and spread it out in an even layer using an offset spatula.

6. Bake until the surface turns golden brown, 12 to 15 minutes.

7. Let the angel food cake cool at room temperature.

8. Once the cake has cooled, freeze it. This cake cuts much easier once it is frozen.

9. Cut the cake into 4 triangles measuring 5 cm/2 in wide by 27.5 cm/11 in long, and freeze them until needed. The cakes will keep for up to 3 months in the freezer.

ROYAL ICING

YIELD: 323 G/11.39 OZ

INGREDIENT	METRIC	U.S.	%
Confectioner's sugar	270 g	9.52 oz	83.59%
Egg whites	51 g	1.80 oz	15.79%
Cream of tartar	2 g	0.07 oz	0.62%

1. Whip all of the ingredients together in a mixer until well combined, light, and fluffy.

2. Use right away or reserve in an airtight container in refrigeration for up to 1 month.

CRÈME BRÛLÉE

YIELD: 794 G/1 LB 12.02 OZ

INGREDIENT	METRIC	U.S.	%
Heavy cream, at room temperature	690 g	1 lb 8.34 oz	86.86%
Vanilla paste	20 g	.71 oz	2.52%
Sugar	80 g	2.82 oz	10.07%
Agar-agar	3 g	.1 oz	.35%
Locust bean gum	2 g	.06 oz	.21%

1. Place 4 oval tubes measuring 5 cm/2 in wide by 25 cm/10 in long in a standing position over a flat sheet pan lined with a 3-mm/.12-in thick sheet of rolling fondant. The dimensions should be a square that measures 15 cm/6 in on each side; roll it out by hand or using a sheeter. Push the molds gently into the fondant and then tape the molds together so that they don't tilt or fall over. This will ensure that the liquid does not seep through the tubes. It also helps to keep the tubes in place. The tubes do not need to be lined because once the cream sets, it can be gently pushed out without it sticking to the tube.

2. Combine the heavy cream and the vanilla paste in a small sauce pot. Combine the sugar, agar-agar, and locust bean gum in a small bowl using a whisk. Shear this mixture into the cream using a handheld immersion blender. Since it is cream, it needs to be tempered; otherwise when you shear the agar and locust bean gum in, it will whip. Tempered cream does not whip.

3. Bring the liquid to a boil while shearing. Let it boil for 5 seconds, then turn off the heat.

4. Pour the cream into the prepared tubes and refrigerate.

5. Once the cream has set, it can gently be pushed out of the tubes or reserved in the refrigerator for up to 3 days.

NOTE *This is not a crème brûlée in the strict sense of the term. It is crème brûlée–like, because the cream, which is gelled with agar-agar and locust bean gum and contains no eggs, has a similar texture to crème brûlée. It is also different in the fact that it is not baked, but rather is cooked on the stove and then poured into a mold to set. This recipe was adapted from Chef Michael Laiskonis, Executive Pastry Chef at Le Bernardin in New York City.*

CRISP MAPLE FEUILLES DE BRICK

YIELD: 200 G/7.05 OZ

INGREDIENT	METRIC	U.S.	%
Clarified butter, melted	100 g	3.53 oz	50%
Maple syrup	100 g	3.53 oz	50%
Feuille de brick sheets	6	6	

1. Combine the clarified butter and maple syrup in a small sauce pot. Keep warm over very low heat.

2. Stack the sheets of feuille de brick. Feuille de brick comes in disk-shaped sheets; they are separated by parchment paper. Using a ruler and a very sharp cutter, cut out 2 sets of rectangles side by side that measure 7.5 cm/3 in wide by 27.5 cm/11 in long, to obtain a total of 12 rectangles. Keep them covered with plastic wrap so they don't dry out.

3. Preheat a convection oven to 160°C/320°F.

4. Line a flat half sheet pan with a nonstick rubber mat.

5. Put 4 rectangles of feuille de brick evenly separated onto the rubber mat.

6. Brush a light coat of the maple-butter mixture on top of each rectangle.

7. Place a second rectangle of feuille de brick on top of each brushed rectangle. Make sure that they are evenly stacked. Brush another coat of the maple-butter mixture and repeat with the last set of feuille de brick rectangles.

8. Place a second nonstick rubber mat over the stacked rectangles and put the sheet pan in the oven.

9. Bake until golden brown, about 7 minutes.

10. Once they are baked, remove the top rubber mat and let the feuilles de brick cool at room temperature. Reserve in an airtight container until needed. If holding for more than 1 day, refresh in a warm oven for 2 minutes. Discard after 1 week.

PRALINE GENOA BREAD

YIELD: 1.28 KG/2 LB 13.28 OZ

INGREDIENT	METRIC	U.S.	%
Almond paste	480 g	1 lb 1.93 oz	37.3%
Praline paste	120 g	4.23 oz	9.32%
Eggs	375 g	13.23 oz	29.14%
Invert sugar	53 g	1.85 oz	4.08%
Salt	5 g	.16 oz	.35%
All-purpose flour	90 g	3.17 oz	6.99%
Butter, melted but cool	165 g	5.82 oz	12.82%

1. See the procedure for black sesame Genoa bread on page 243. Substitute praline paste for black sesame paste.

2. Once the cake has cooled, cut it into rectangles measuring 5 cm/2 in wide by 25 cm/10 in long by 1.25 cm/.5 in deep.

3. Reserve in an airtight container in the refrigerator until needed. Discard after 3 days.

VANILLA CHIFFON CAKE

YIELD: 1.5 KG/3 LB 4.8 OZ

INGREDIENT	METRIC	U.S.	%
Cake flour	370 g	13.05 oz	24.67%
Sugar	320 g	11.29 oz	21.33%
Baking powder	15 g	.53 oz	1%
Salt	5 g	.18 oz	.33%
Vanilla paste	10 g	.35 oz	.67%
Egg yolks	230 g	8.11 oz	15.33%
Canola oil	35 g	1.23 oz	2.33%
Water	180 g	6.35 oz	12%
Egg whites	230 g	8.11 oz	15.33%
Sugar	90 g	3.17 oz	6%
Lemon juice	15 g	.53 oz	1%
White chocolate, melted	150 g	5.29 oz	

1. Follow the procedure for the chiffon cake on page 310.

2. Once the cake has cooled, freeze it for about 1 hour. It is easier to cut when it is firm.

3. Once firm, flip it onto a cutting board and peel the rubber mat off. Using a paint roller, coat the base of the cake with a thin layer of white chocolate.

4. Once it sets, turn the cake over and cut it into ovals measuring 10 cm/4 in wide by 17.5 cm/7 in long.

5. Keep the cakes frozen until you are ready to use them. Discard them after 1 month.

VANILLA DIPLOMAT CREAM

YIELD: 5.1 KG/11 LB 3.84 OZ

INGREDIENT	METRIC	U.S.	%
Vanilla Pastry Cream (page 436)	3 kg	6 lb 9.76 oz	58.82%
Heavy cream	2 kg	4 lb 6.4 oz	39.22%
Liquid heavy cream stabilizer	40 g	1.41 oz	.78%
Gelatin, sheets, silver, bloomed in cold water, excess water squeezed off	60 g	2.12 oz	1.18%

1. Make sure to have the chiffon cake and the strawberries inside the mold and ready to go.

2. Use a whisk to soften and break down the pastry cream. It should be smooth and soft.

3. Combine the heavy cream and liquid cream stabilizer in the bowl of an electric mixer. Whip on medium speed until the mixture reaches medium-stiff peaks. Reserve in the refrigerator until needed.

4. Add one-fifth of the pastry cream to the bloomed gelatin in a bowl and place it over a hot water bath to melt the gelatin.

5. Once the gelatin has melted, stir all the pastry cream into the mixture using a whisk.

6. Working quickly, stir one-quarter of the whipped cream into the pastry cream. Fold half of the remaining whipped cream into the pastry cream, and then fold the remaining whipped cream.

7. Pipe into the prepared molds.

GELLED CREAM LETTERS

YIELD: 559 G/1 LB 3.73 OZ

INGREDIENT	METRIC	U.S.	%
Heavy cream, at room temperature	500 g	1 lb 1.64 oz	89.38%
Sugar	50 g	1.76 oz	8.94%
Agar-agar	8 g	.28 oz	1.43%
Gellan gum, low acyl	2 g	.05 oz	.25%

1. Combine the heavy cream and sugar in a sauce pot. Shear in the agar-agar and the gellan gum using a handheld blender.

2. Switch to a whisk and bring the mixture to a boil. Boil for 5 seconds, and then take off the heat. Let sit for about 1 minute. This helps reduce the amount of bubbles in the cream. Portion into the letter molds (see Resources, page 520) and let set in the refrigerator. Keep in the molds until ready to finish the cake. Discard after 3 days.

PRESERVED RASPBERRIES IN RASPBERRY JELLY

YIELD: 821 G/1 LB 12.96 OZ

INGREDIENT	METRIC	U.S.	%
Preserved whole raspberries (see Resources, page 520)	400 g	14.11 oz	48.72%
Sugar	65 g	2.29 oz	7.92%
Universal pectin (pectin NH 95)	4 g	.14 oz	.49%
Raspberry purée	350 g	12.35 oz	42.63%
Calcium lactate	2 g	.07 oz	.24%

1. Assemble 4 silicone molds measuring 7.5 cm/3 in diameter by 2.5 cm/1 in deep. Fill each mold with 100 g/3.53 oz of preserved whole raspberries.

2. Combine the sugar with the universal pectin.

3. Combine the raspberry purée with the calcium lactate in a small sauce pot. Bring to a boil.

4. Once it reaches a boil, whisk in the pectin-sugar mixture and boil for 1 more minute while stirring.

5. Pour into the silicone molds and fill to the top.

6. Allow the jelly to set in the refrigerator. Freeze to unmold. Reserve frozen to assemble the cake. Discard after 2 months.

DARK CHOCOLATE MOUSSE

YIELD: 2.1 KG/4 LB 10.4 OZ

INGREDIENT	METRIC	U.S.	%
Eggs	425 g	14.99 oz	20.14%
Sugar	180 g	6.35 oz	8.53%
Dark chocolate coins 64%	565 g	1 lb 3.93 oz	26.78%
Heavy cream	940 g	2 lb 1. 12 oz	44.55%

Follow the method for the dark chocolate mousse on page 304.

NOTE *For the Earth entremet, add 100 g/3.53 oz of soluble coffee powder with the egg yolks and sugar before they are warmed over a hot water bath.*

SAVARIN

YIELD: 648 G/1 LB 6.72 OZ

INGREDIENT	METRIC	U.S.	%
All-purpose flour	250 g	8.82 oz	38.58%
Salt	5 g	.18 oz	.77%
Yeast, instant dry	3 g	.11 oz	.46%
Sugar	25 g	.88 oz	3.86%
Milk, at 21°C/70°F	125 g	4.41 oz	19.29%
Butter, melted but cool	90 g	3.17 oz	13.89%
Eggs	150 g	5.29 oz	23.15%
Chambord Syrup (below)	400 g	14.11 oz	

1. Assemble four 7.5-cm/3-in diameter silicone savarin molds (see Resources, page 520) on a flat sheet pan.

2. Combine the flour, salt, yeast, and sugar in a bowl.

3. Pour the milk into the bowl of an electric mixer fitted with the paddle attachment. Start mixing on low speed. Add the melted butter and then the mixed dry ingredients.

4. Turn the speed to medium and then add the eggs one at a time. Continue to mix until a smooth, elastic mixture is obtained.

5. Turn off the mixer and cover the bowl with a damp towel.

6. Proof the dough for about 30 minutes, and then punch it down.

7. Meanwhile, preheat a convection oven to 160°C/ 320°F.

8. Pour the dough into a piping bag and pipe into the savarin molds to fill two-thirds of the way. Let it proof until it reaches the top of the mold, about 30 minutes.

9. Bake the savarin for 12 to 15 minutes, or until they are a light golden brown.

10. Once cool, turn them out of the molds and soak them in the Chambord syrup for at least 1 hour before assembling the cakes.

CHAMBORD SYRUP

YIELD: 400 G/14.11 OZ

INGREDIENT	METRIC	U.S.	%
Simple syrup, at 50° Brix	300 g	10.58 oz	75%
Chambord liqueur	100 g	3.53 oz	25%

Combine all of the ingredients in a bowl. Reserve in an airtight container in refrigeration for up to 6 months or longer.

RASPBERRY CHOCOLATE LIPS

Follow the method for the raspberry chocolate on page 436.

Follow the method for molded chocolates on page 42, using a lips mold to shape the chocolate.

Reserve in a cool, dry area, preferably enclosed.

HAZELNUT DACQUOISE

YIELD: 1.2 KG/2 LB 10.24 OZ

INGREDIENT	METRIC	U.S.	%
Dacquoise			
Confectioners' sugar	370 g	13.05 oz	30.83%
Hazelnut flour	335 g	11.82 oz	27.92%
Egg whites	370 g	13.05 oz	30.83%
Sugar	125 g	4.41 oz	10.42%
Hazelnut gianduja, melted	100 g	3.53 oz	

1. **For the dacquoise:** Preheat a convection oven to 160°C/320°F.

2. Lightly grease the interior borders of a half sheet pan with nonstick oil spray. Line it with a nonstick rubber mat.

3. Sift the confectioners' sugar and hazelnut flour together. Make a French meringue out of the egg whites and the sugar following the method on page 12.

4. Fold the sifted dry ingredients into the meringue. Spread onto the prepared sheet pan.

5. Bake until the surface is a light golden brown, 9 to 12 minutes. Cool to room temperature.

6. Once cool, freeze the cake until hardened. Once hard, turn it over onto a cutting board.

7. Using a paint roller, paint the base of the dacquoise with a thin layer of the melted gianduja. Work quickly so that it doesn't harden while applying the gianduja.

8. Flip the cake over again and cut out 4 disks with a 17.5-cm/7-in diameter ring cutter.

9. Place the disks inside four 17.5-cm/7-in round stainless-steel cake molds over a flat sheet pan lined with a nonstick rubber mat. Reserve refrigerated for up to 1 week.

GIANDUJA FEUILLETINE

YIELD: 1.26 KG/2 LB 12.32 OZ

INGREDIENT	METRIC	U.S.	%
Gianduja, chopped	1 kg	2 lb 3.2 oz	79.37%
Sugar	200 g	7.05 oz	15.87%
Water	50 g	1.76 oz	3.97%
Canola oil	10 g	.35 oz	.79%

1. Put the gianduja in the bowl of an electric mixer fitted with the paddle attachment.

2. Combine the sugar and water in a small pot and cook over high heat to obtain a medium-dark caramel. The quantity is too small to use a thermometer; there is no thermometer that has a probe that could be submerged into such a small amount of sugar, so go by the color.

3. Turn the mixer on medium speed and carefully pour the sugar down the sides of the bowl; avoid pouring on the paddle since it can splatter and be dangerous. Once all of the sugar has been poured in and the gianduja has melted, pour in the oil and mix thoroughly.

4. Divide the feuilletine in equal parts by pouring about 300 g/10.58 oz over each of the dacquoise disks. Make sure it spread out evenly over the cake.

5. Allow to set in the refrigerator.

6. Once the feuilletine is set, remove the cake rings and reserve this set (the dacquoise with the feuilletine disks) in the freezer until ready to assemble the cakes.

HAZELNUT PRALINE

INGREDIENT	METRIC	U.S.	%
Hazelnuts, blanched	500 g	1 lb 1.64 oz	46.73%
Sugar	450 g	15.87 oz	42.06%
Cocoa butter, melted	120 g	4.23 oz	11.21%

1. Assemble 4 stainless-steel cake rings measuring 17.5 cm/7 in diameter and at least 1.25 cm/.5 in high and place them over a flat sheet pan lined with a nonstick rubber mat.

2. Follow the method for the peanut praline on page 306.

3. Once the praline is made and is still fluid, pour it into the rings. Divide the mixture into equal parts and spread it out evenly.

4. Let set in the refrigerator. Remove the rings and reserve the praline in the freezer until ready to assemble the cake. Discard after 1 month.

GIANDUJA MOUSSE

YIELD: 4.56 KG/10 LB .8 OZ

INGREDIENT	METRIC	U.S.	%
Eggs	800 g	1 lb 12.16 oz	17.54%
Sugar	320 g	11.29 oz	7.02%
Gianduja	1.6 kg	3 lb 8.32 oz	35.09%
Heavy cream	1.8 kg	3 lb 15.36 oz	39.47%
Gelatin sheets, silver, bloomed in cold water, excess water squeezed off	40 g	1.41 oz	.88%

1. Make sure you have the inclusions and the base frozen and ready to go.

2. Follow the method for the caramelized white chocolate mousse on page 317. Assemble the cake immediately.

GIANDUJA DÉCOR

YIELD: 250 G/8.82 OZ

INGREDIENT	METRIC	U.S.	%
Gianduja, tempered	250 g	8.82 oz	100%

1. Pour the tempered gianduja into the letter "G" molds (see Resources, page 520).

2. Let crystallize in the mold. Reserve in a cool, dry place, preferably enclosed. If stored in these conditions, the décor will keep for more than 1 year.

ch

PETITS FOURS (mignardises)

Petits fours are generally defined as small confections that are served and eaten at the very end of a meal, after the main dessert. Translated from the French language, the term *petit four* means "small oven," meaning an oven at a low temperature. This term dates back to the eighteenth century to Marie-Antoine Carême (1784–1833), who was the first to mention these items. The petits fours had to be baked after the larger cakes, as the coal oven was starting to cool down. The cost of coal was so high at the time that the chef did not want to waste any of its precious heat.

Classic petits fours are divided into two primary categories: petits fours secs (*sec* means "dry"; some examples are cookies, macarons, and tuiles), which should not contain any "wet" components such as cream or jam, and petits fours frais—*frais* means "fresh," and this category includes petits fours that contain a temperature-sensitive element such as pastry cream, jam, or whipped cream. Within this second category, there is a subcategory of petits fours glacés, or glazed petits fours, which are items that are coated in a glaze (such as fondant) and can be filled with a cream. Technically, items such as éclairs would fit under the glacés subcategory, which gets unnecessarily complicated and which is why the term *frais* is more commonly used. The final petit four category is petits fours salés, or savory petits fours—bite-size savory appetizers served at cocktail parties and buffets. They share only a first and middle name with sweet petits fours and technically are not even connected, except for the fact that they are small items that are eaten with one's hands.

There is an actual petit four that is called a "petit four," and many think that this was the original petit four, if only because of its name. It consists of alternating layers of frangipane, apricot jam, frangipane, raspberry jam, and marzipan. This is wrapped and weighed down to compress the layers and bind them. It is then frozen and cut into different shapes, such as disks, squares, diamonds, or triangles. The cake is then coated with pouring fondant, which can be colored and mixed with some simple syrup to make it more fluid, and then decorated with a piped chocolate design.

Petits fours is a term with a wider range, and it can encompass a very large variety of products. What puts them in a category all their own is:

- They are eaten at the end of the meal.

- They are eaten without utensils (they should be able to be eaten with one hand).

- They are served with coffee, tea, or liquor service.

Mignardises are often confused with petits fours. If a tray is made up of a single type of petit four, regardless of its ornate complexity, it cannot be considered a mignardise. A mixed tray of different types of petits fours is considered mignardise. The term *mignard* is a French word that can be used in two ways: as an adjective, in which case it is used to describe something precious, pretty and delicate; and as a noun, to refer to a small child. Mignardises can also be referred to as *friandises.*

Before deciding whether or not to offer mignardises, you also have to consider the restaurant's environment and style of service and food. Does it make sense? Is it necessary? Consider that, although making all of these small-size items will have an impact on your labor cost, you can't really charge a customer for them. The cost for mignardises should be built into the cost of your desserts or into the prix fixe menu. Keep in mind that every single table will receive a tray of mignardises; it's not as if it is an actual dessert option. The variety and the type of petits fours you offer are up to you. Don't forget that by this point in the meal, not too many people have room left to eat more, which is why the products should be small or at least be something that can be cut and shared by the table (see the chocolate bars on page 478). It is something small to have along with an espresso or glass of port.

Mignardises that are meant to be shared are somewhat large if you compare them side by side with an individually portioned petit four, but they serve a truly special purpose. It goes completely against the definition of *petit four,* with the *petit* part being overlooked, but when you have something larger for a group of people to share, it is a really special service offering. It may not be for all types of customers, though. With more familiar groups, it makes sense and it is a great way to bring people together, especially because each person gets to cut a piece off and then pass it around. We never really think of a chocolate bar as something that is necessarily served at a restaurant regardless of the moment, but it is a very special item that is visually impressive and has so much potential.

This chapter features mainly chocolate (bonbons and bars), since that is truly the best way to end a meal. There are a few mini tarts and a few other confections as well, but the focus is on chocolate.

CHOCOLATE BONBONS AS PETITS FOURS

Before starting any of the recipes in this section, please review the process for tempering chocolate on pages 27 to 29 and the method for molded chocolates and dipped chocolates on pages 42 to 46. In this section, molded chocolates are more prevalent than dipped chocolates because many molded chocolates can be made in a consistent manner without an enrober. Enrobers are great machines that can produce many chocolates at one time, thus making it very convenient. However, many people who will use this book might not own one. Therefore this section will stick to molded chocolates, which are more plausible in a common kitchen environment. Molded chocolates also have a shine that is impossible to replicate with dipped chocolates, unless you cover the surface of an enrobed chocolate with a transfer sheet, and their shapes are also much more versatile.

In this section, the bonbons will be presented in the following way:

- NAME: **This is the name of the filling of the bonbon. In other words, what is the shell filled with? The flavor(s) give the name to the chocolate piece.**

- SHELL: **This refers to the type of chocolate used to make the shell (white, milk, dark, caramelized white chocolate, Earl Grey couverture, and so forth).**

- GARNISH: **How was the chocolate finished? What were the decorative elements added? Keep in mind that, to an extent, the exterior of the chocolate informs of the interior of the chocolate. In other words, the garnishes should reflect what is inside. If the chocolate has a red miso paste ganache, there should be a red element on the outside. Sometimes you can use a component of the ganache on the surface of the chocolate; for example, if you make a lavender ganache, affix a lavender flower to the surface of the chocolate. Or there is always the option of doing whatever you want to do to make the chocolate visually attractive. Nothing is written in stone.**

- SHELF LIFE: **This is an approximate shelf life for each filling. It could be longer or shorter. It will be shorter if the chocolates are kept in unfriendly environmental conditions, such as high temperatures and humidity. An ideal temperature to reserve chocolates is 15°C/59°F or a maximum of 22°C/72°F with 60 percent environmental humidity. This latter temperature also happens to be a comfortable temperature to work with chocolates. Any colder and the tempered chocolate bowl will start setting very quickly, giving you a shorter window to work with. Of course you can re-warm the chocolate in a microwave or chocolate bath, but in colder shops, you will have to stop and do this more frequently.**

- RECIPE: **This is the actual recipe for the filling. The recipes are for a single mold, which on average has 24 cavities (24 pieces). The recipes will yield that approximate amount.**

For resources on where to obtain these molds, see page 520.

POPCORN

YIELD: ABOUT 24 PIECES

COMPONENTS

GARNISH: **white cocoa butter**

SHELL: **tempered dark chocolate**

FILLING: **Popcorn Filling** (page 504)

ASSEMBLY INSTRUCTIONS

1. Spray the interior of the mold with white cocoa butter using an airbrush.

2. Cast the molds using tempered dark chocolate according to the Molded Chocolates method on page 44.

3. Spoon the filling into the chocolate cast molds to just under the top rim and cap the molds. The chocolates have a shelf life of more than 2 months.

FRENCH TOAST | PINEAPPLE JAM

YIELD: ABOUT 24 PIECES

COMPONENTS	
	SHELL: **tempered milk chocolate**
	FILLING: **Pineapple Jam** (page 504), **French Toast Filling** (page 505)
	GARNISH: **tempered white chocolate, yellow cocoa butter, brown cocoa butter**

ASSEMBLY INSTRUCTIONS

1. Cast the molds using tempered milk chocolate according to the Molded Chocolates method on page 44.

2. Fill the molds halfway up with pineapple jam.

3. Insert the disks of brioche into the molds on top of the jam, pushing them in gently. Cap the molds. Once they are set, unmold them.

4. Once the chocolates are unmolded, cut out 10 squares of plastic wrap measuring 7.5 cm/3 in on each side. Spread them out.

5. Pour about 10 g/.35 oz of tempered white chocolate in the center of each one, and then place a finished chocolate bonbon on top of each dot, pushing down so that the base of the chocolate comes into contact with the plastic wrap and the fluid white chocolate pushes out around the mold.

6. Bring the corners of the plastic wrap together and twist them closed. Let the chocolate set in the plastic wrap tent.

7. Once the chocolate has crystallized, remove the plastic, airbrush the chocolates completely with yellow cocoa butter, and then airbrush with brown cocoa butter on one side only. The chocolates have a shelf life of about 1 month.

DOUGHNUT

YIELD: 24 PIECES

COMPONENTS	SHELL: **tempered dark chocolate** FILLING: **Doughnut Ganache** (page 505) GARNISH: **white cocoa butter**
ASSEMBLY INSTRUCTIONS	1. Cast the molds using tempered dark chocolate according to the Molded Chocolates method on page 44. · 2. Pipe the ganache into the mold to just under the top rim once it reaches 30°C/86°F. Cap the molds. 3. Unmold the chocolate halves and attached them using tempered dark chocolate. 4. Once the chocolates are unmolded and attached (this is a two-sided mold), the pieces are airbrushed lightly with a white cocoa butter spray. The chocolates have a shelf life of up to 2 months.

CANDIED APPLES | SAFFRON COUVERTURE

COMPONENTS	SHELL: **Saffron Couverture** (page 511) FILLING: **Candied Apples** (page 513)
ASSEMBLY INSTRUCTIONS	1. Cast the molds using saffron couverture according to the Molded Chocolates method on page 44. 2. Fill the molds with candied apples to just under the top rim. Cap the molds. 3. The chocolates have a shelf life of about 2 months.

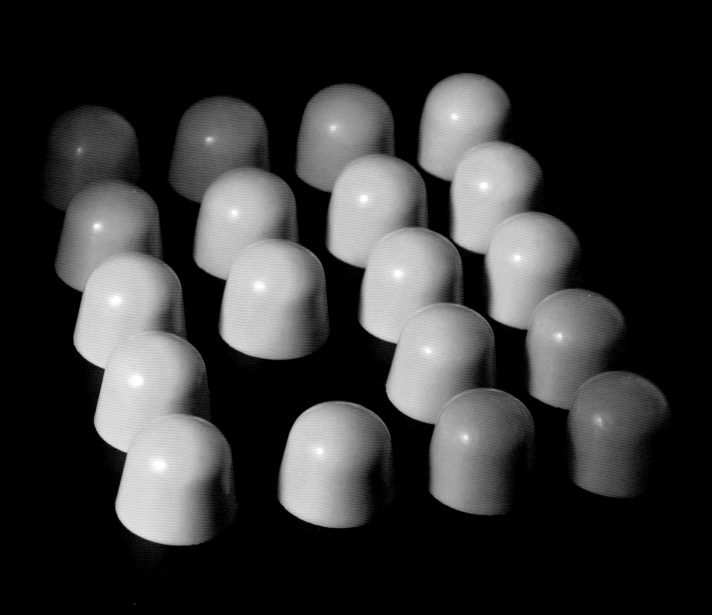

BLACK TRUFFLE BUBBLE CHOCOLATE

YIELD: ABOUT 24 PIECES

COMPONENTS	GARNISH: **black cocoa butter**
	SHELL: **tempered dark chocolate**
	FILLING: **Bubble Chocolate** (page 506)

ASSEMBLY INSTRUCTIONS	1. Airbrush the interior of the mold with black cocoa butter using an air brush.
	2. Cast the molds using tempered dark chocolate according to the Molded Chocolates method on page 44.
	3. Portion the chocolate into each mold, filling it all the way to the top. Using a chocolate scraper, scrape any excess off the top of the mold. Allow to crystallize at room temperature. This chocolate does not need to be capped.
	4. The chocolates have a shelf life of about 6 months (the filling is just chocolate and oil that has been aerated).

YOGURT | RASPBERRY

YIELD: ABOUT 24 PIECES

COMPONENTS	
	GARNISH: **red cocoa butter**
	SHELL: **tempered white chocolate**
	FILLING: **freeze-dried yogurt powder, freeze-dried whole raspberries**

ASSEMBLY INSTRUCTIONS

1. Airbrush the interior of one side of each mold with red cocoa butter using an air brush.

2. Cast the molds using tempered white chocolate according to the Molded Chocolates method on page 44.

3. Spoon 5 g/.17 oz of freeze-dried yogurt powder into each mold.

4. Place a whole freeze-dried raspberry inside each mold.

5. Spoon another 5 g/.17 oz freeze-dried powder on top of each raspberry.

6. Cap the mold. The chocolates have a shelf life of about 6 months.

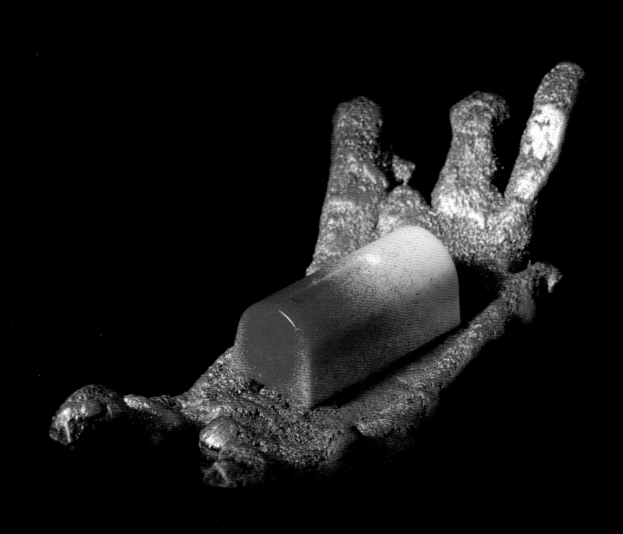

FIG | PASSION FRUIT | TOFFEE

YIELD: ABOUT 24 PIECES

COMPONENTS	SHELL: **tempered dark chocolate**
	FILLING: **Fig, Passion Fruit, and Toffee Filling** (page 506)
	GARNISH: **gold luster dust**

ASSEMBLY INSTRUCTIONS

1. Cast the molds using tempered dark chocolate according to the Molded Chocolates method on page 44. The chocolate "pillow" shells must be out of the mold before filling, since this will make it easier to assemble them once they are filled.

2. Pipe the filling into both parts of the mold. For molds like this, go a little higher up than the top of the mold so that both sides can be "glued" together. The ganache is the glue that will keep them attached.

3. Attach both sides of the pillow before the ganache has crystallized completely.

4. Once both halves are attached, brush the surface of the chocolate with gold luster dust and then spray them with edible lacquer to affix the dust to the mold.

5. The chocolates have a shelf life of more than 2 months.

APRICOT | RICE PUDDING

YIELD: ABOUT 24 PIECES

COMPONENTS	SHELL: **tempered dark chocolate** FILLING: **Rice Pudding Ganache** (page 508) GARNISH: **tempered milk chocolate, Apricot Foam** (page 507)
ASSEMBLY INSTRUCTIONS	1. Cast the molds using tempered dark chocolate according to the Molded Chocolates method on page 44. 2. Wait for ganache to reach 30°C/86°F before piping into the mold to just under the top rim. Cap the mold. 3. Attach the apricot foam to each finished chocolate with a dot of tempered milk chocolate. The chocolates have a shelf life of 2 weeks

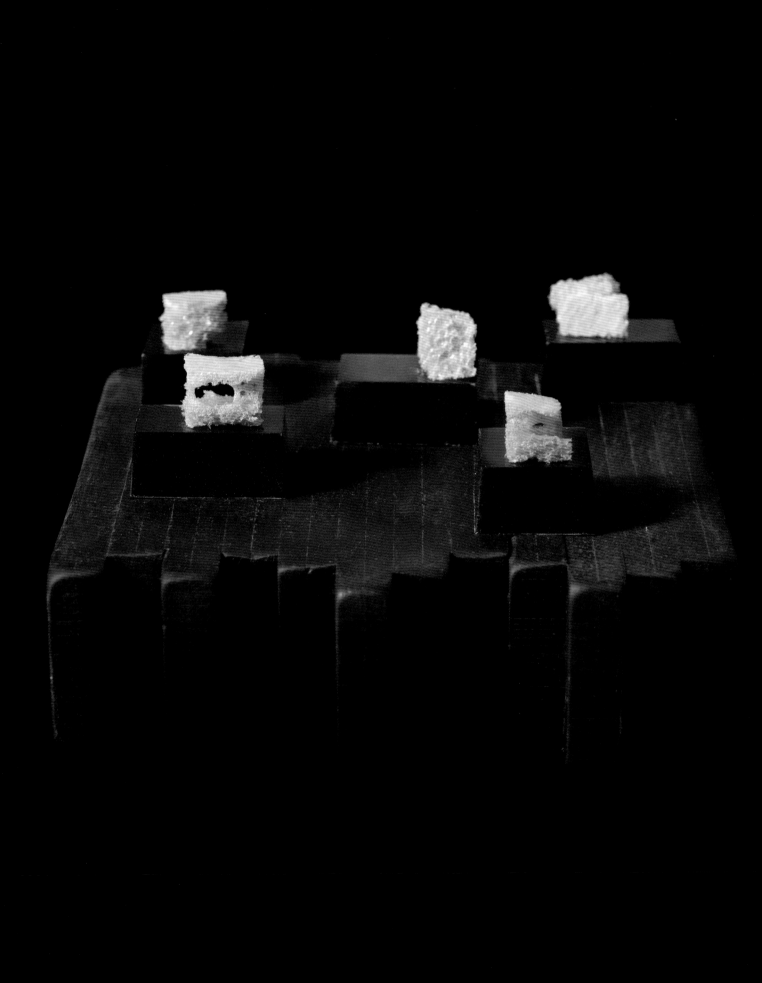

CILANTRO | TANGERINE | LITCHI

YIELD: ABOUT 24 PIECES

COMPONENTS	SHELL: **tempered white chocolate** FILLING: **Cilantro, Tangerine, and Litchi Filling** (page 508) GARNISH: **green luster dust**
ASSEMBLY INSTRUCTIONS	1. Cast the molds using tempered white chocolate according to the Molded Chocolates method on page 44. 2. When the ganache reaches 30°C/89°F, pipe it into the mold to fill it halfway. 3. Insert 1 piece of litchi jelly into each mold, pushing it into the piped ganache. Fill the rest of the mold to almost the top with the cilantro and tangerine ganache. 4. Cap the mold. One the chocolate has set, remove from the mold. 5. Brush each unmolded piece with green luster dust. Affix the dust with a light coating of edible lacquer spray. The chocolates have a shelf life of 2 weeks.

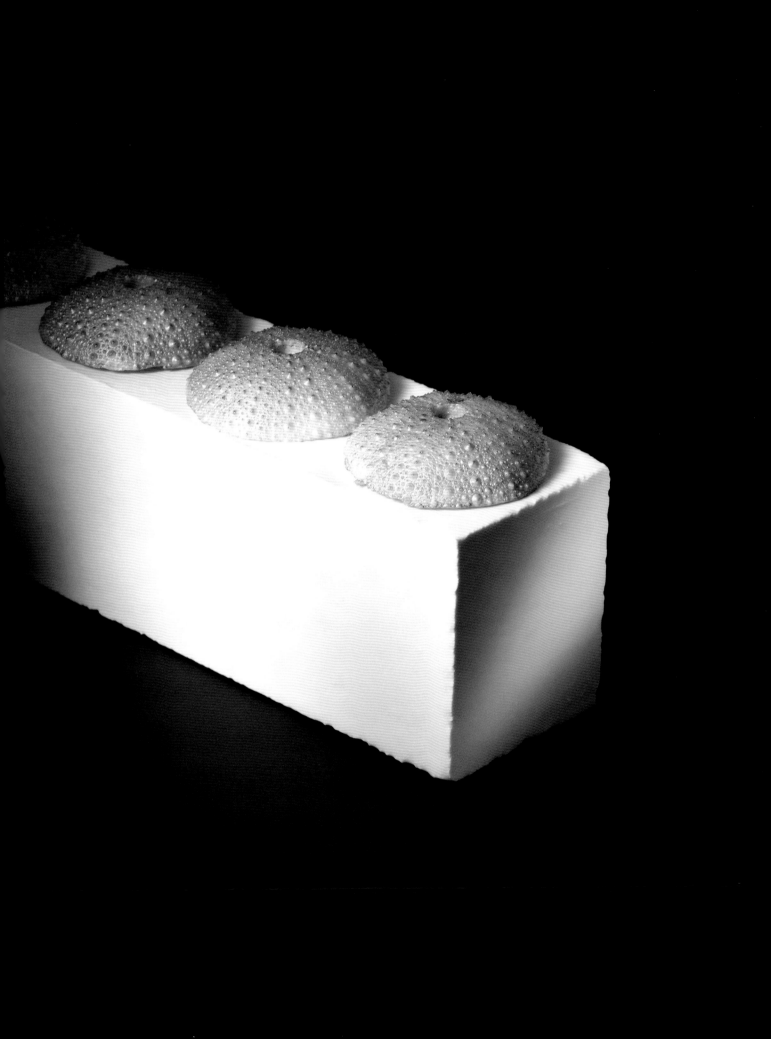

MISO | SHISO

YIELD: ABOUT 24 PIECES

COMPONENTS	GARNISH: **emerald green cocoa butter** SHELL: **tempered white chocolate colored with red cocoa butter** FILLING: **Dehydrated Shiso Leaves** (page 509), **Red Miso Ganache** (page 509)
ASSEMBLY INSTRUCTIONS	1. Spray the emerald green cocoa butter into the mold using an airbrush. 2. Cast the molds using the tempered red chocolate according to the Molded Chocolates method on page 44. 3. Spoon 1 g/.04 oz of ground shiso leaves into each mold. 5. Once the red miso ganache reaches 30°C/89°F, pipe it into the mold, filling it just under the top. 6. Cap the mold. The chocolates have a shelf life of 2 months.

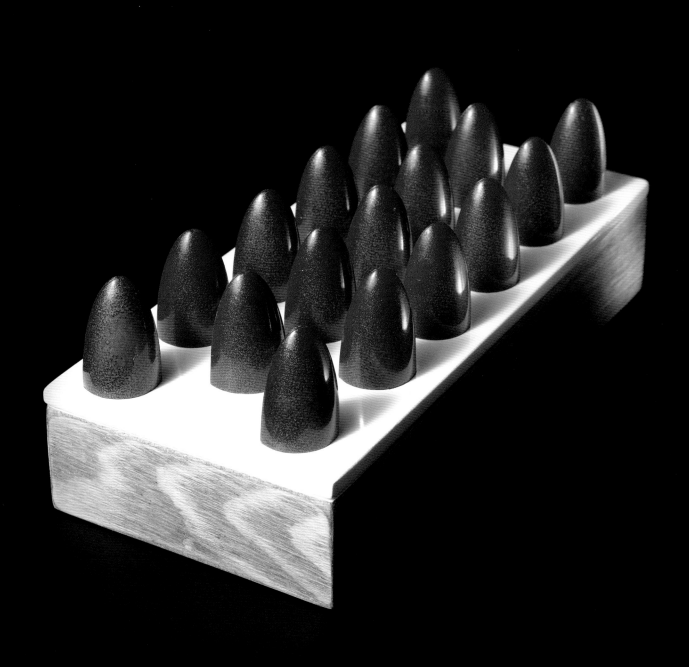

FOIE GRAS INGOT

YIELD: ABOUT 35 PIECES

COMPONENTS	SHELL: **dark chocolate**
	FILLING: **Foie Gras Filling** (page 510)
	GARNISH: **gold leaf**

ASSEMBLY INSTRUCTIONS

1. Temper the dark chocolate and dip the foie squares.

2. Once the pieces are dipped and the chocolate has crystallized, spray each piece with edible lacquer spray one at a time and wrap each piece with a sheet of gold, very carefully so as to wrap the piece completely with one sheet. The lacquer spray is the only way to attach the gold leaf to the ingot.

3. The chocolates must be refrigerated since the foie gras is not shelf stable. Keep the chocolates in the refrigerator for a maximum of 4 days.

CHOCOLATE BARS: BEET | BLACK OLIVE | SAFFRON | EARL GREY | MATCHA TEA

YIELD: ABOUT 40 BARS

COMPONENTS	**Individual chocolate bars, assorted flavors** (pages 511–512)
SERVING INSTRUCTIONS	Bars are stored in a cool, dry place, preferably enclosed, for up to 1 year. They should be served at room temperature.

CINNAMON-SCENTED FRENCH TOAST AND BACON PRALINE BAR

YIELD: ABOUT 9 BARS

COMPONENTS	SHELL: **tempered dark chocolate** FILLING: **French Toast Ganache** (page 513), **Bacon Praline** (page 512), **fleur de sel** GARNISH: **cinnamon scent**
ASSEMBLY INSTRUCTIONS	1. Cast the molds using tempered dark chocolate according to the Molded Chocolates method on page 44. 2. Once the French Toast Ganache is cold, cut out 6.5-cm/2.5-in squares and put them inside each bar mold. 3. To cap the bars, have the bacon praline available. Pour tempered dark chocolate over the bar mold and scrape the excess chocolate off with a chocolate scraper. 4. Immediately after scraping and before the chocolate crystallizes, sprinkle an even amount of bacon praline over the fluid chocolate to coat it as much as possible. Push down gently on the praline so that it attaches itself well to the chocolate. Sprinkle the fleur de sel over the top of the praline. 5. Allow the chocolate to fully crystallize before unmolding. Once unmolded, package them into the plastic zip-top bags. 6. Apply cinnamon scent using the Volcano Vaporizer. The recipe is for nine candy bars, which is how many shells are in a mold; therefore you will only need to fill the chamber of the Volcano Vaporizer with 10 g/.35 oz of ground cinnamon. Turn the machine on and allow it to get warm. 7. Insert the tube from the Vaporizer into the bag and let it inflate the bag completely. Remove the tube quickly and close the zip-top quickly as well. 8. When you are done, use a heat-sealing device to seal the bags shut and thus conserve the scent of the cinnamon inside the bag. The bars have a shelf life of about 1 month.

EKTE GJETOST | TOFFEE | CANDIED APPLES

YIELD: ABOUT 10 BARS

COMPONENTS	GARNISH: **black cocoa butter** SHELL: **tempered Caramelized White Chocolate** (page 316) FILLING: **Ekte Gjetost, Toffee** (page 513), **Candied Apples** (page 513)
ASSEMBLY INSTRUCTIONS	1. Airbrush the interior of the mold with black cocoa butter using an air brush. 2. Cast the molds using tempered caramelized white chocolate according to the Molded Chocolates method on page 44. 3. Using a mixer and the paddle attachment, soften 150 g/5.3 oz of the cheese by turning the mixer on to low speed. Paddle until the cheese is soft enough to pipe. 4. Transfer the cheese to a piping bag and pipe it into each of 5 domes in the bar to fill them halfway. 5. Place a piece of toffee inside each dome as well as a piece of candied apple, pushing it into the cheese as much as possible. 6. Cap the mold with tempered caramelized white chocolate. The shelf life of the bars is 1 week because the Ekte Gjetost, a caramelized goat's milk cheese, is not shelf stable for long.
NOTE	*The flavor of Ekte Gjetost, a Danish goat cheese, is similar to dulce de leche, but it is goat-y and lightly salted, with a texture vaguely reminiscent of very firm peanut butter. This cheese is generally polarizing in that people either really like it or don't like it at all.*

BAGUETTE GANACHE

YIELD: ABOUT 2 LARGE BARS

COMPONENTS	SHELL: **tempered Sourdough Couverture** (page 514) FILLING: **Baguette Ganache** (page 514) GARNISH: **Dark Chocolate Spray** (page 223)
ASSEMBLY INSTRUCTIONS	1. Cast the molds using tempered sourdough couverture according to the Molded Chocolates method on page 44. 2. Pipe the ganache into the mold to just under the top rim. Cap the mold. When the chocolate has set, unmold the bars. 3. Using a spray painter, spray about 100 g/3.53 oz of dark chocolate spray in a light mist over the top of the mold only; you are not looking to coat the mold completely. The shelf life of the bars is up to 2 months.

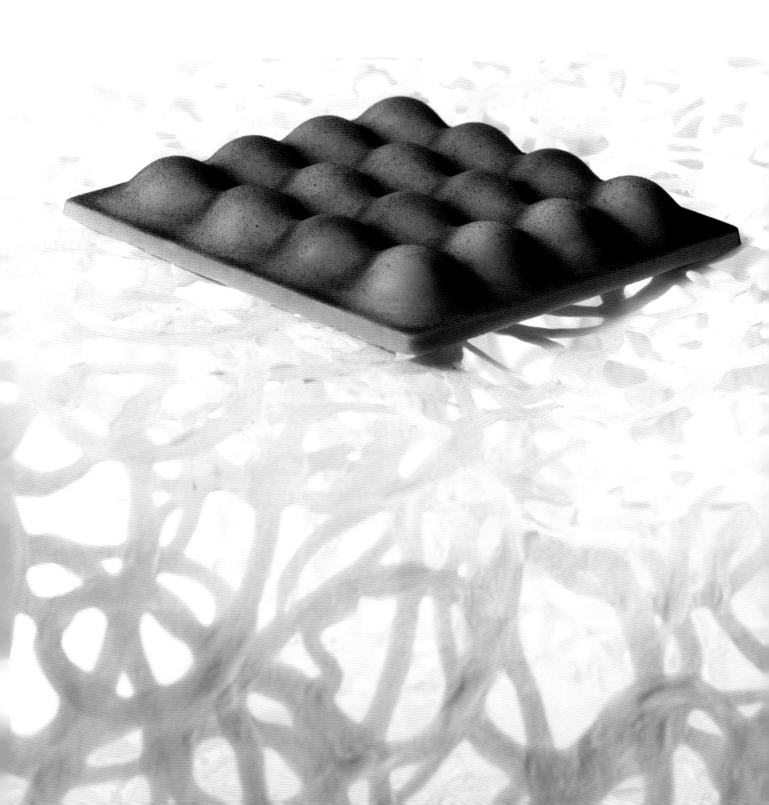

OLIVE OIL CARAMEL AND TOASTED PINE NUTS

YIELD: ABOUT 24 PIECES

COMPONENTS	
	GARNISH: **green olive–colored cocoa butter**
	SHELL: **tempered dark chocolate**
	FILLING: **Olive Oil Caramel with Toasted Pine Nuts** (page 515)

ASSEMBLY INSTRUCTIONS	
	1. Airbrush the interior of the mold with green olive-colored cocoa butter using an air brush.
	2. Cast the molds using tempered dark chocolate according to the Molded Chocolates method on page 44.
	3. Pipe into the mold to just under the top rim of the cavity. Cap the mold with tempered dark chocolate.
	4. The shelf life of the bars is 1 month because pine nuts get stale or rancid easily.

MARIGOLD TARTS

YIELD: ABOUT 40 TARTS

COMPONENTS	**Marigold Caramel** (page 516) **Sablé Tart Shells** (page 515) **Crushed candied green marigolds** (see Resources, page 520) **Silver oval dragées** (see Resources, page 520)
ASSEMBLY INSTRUCTIONS	1. Pour the marigold caramel into the baked tart shells as soon as it is made. Allow the caramel to set at room temperature. 2. Sprinkle a pinch of candied green marigolds over the caramel. You will need only about 45 g/1.5 oz for all 40 tarts. 3. Place a single oval dragée on one side of the tart. 4. Discard after 24 hours.

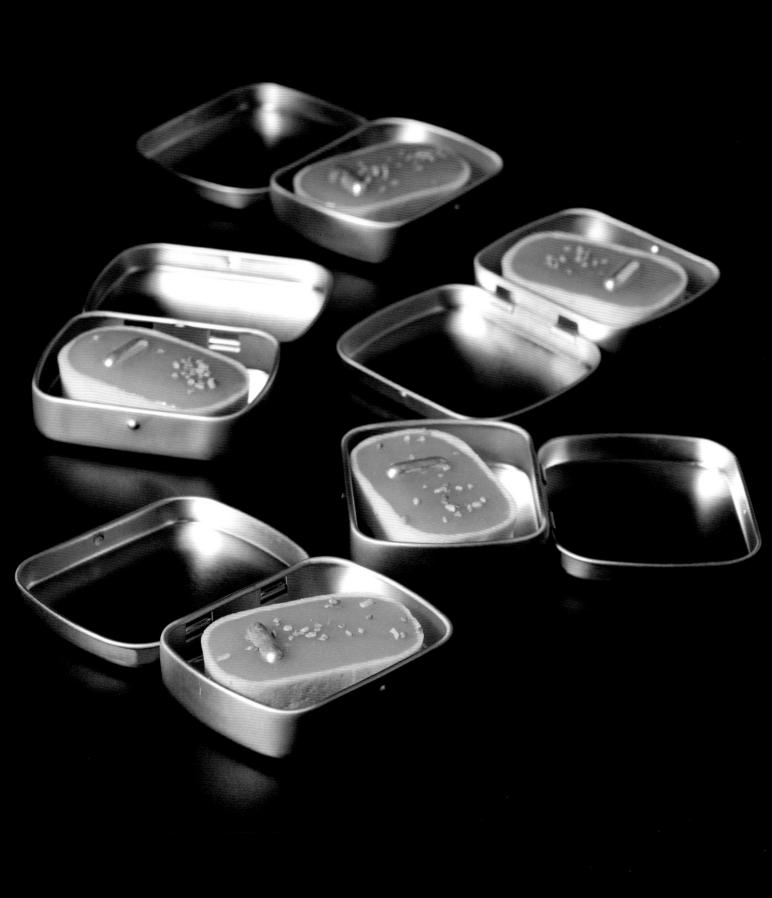

PEPPERMINT LOZENGES

YIELD: 334 G/11.78 OZ

INGREDIENT	METRIC	U.S.	%
Gelatin powder	5 g	.18 oz	1.5%
Water	28 g	.99 oz	8.38%
Confectioners' sugar	300 g	10.58 oz	89.82%
Peppermint extract	1 g	.04 oz	.3%

1. Bloom the gelatin in the water. Melt over a warm—not hot—water bath; heat just enough to dissolve the gelatin so that it is not hot, just melted.

2. Combine with the confectioners' sugar and peppermint extract, mixing to obtain a dough-like mass. You may want to add more extract since the flavor tends to dissipate when the lozenge dries. It is up to personal taste, but it is better to overcompensate for this fact. You may also replace the peppermint with other flavors, but they may taste too artificial. Peppermint is an extract that people are accustomed to tasting in its artificial form.

3. Roll out the dough as thin as possible using a pasta machine.

4. Cut the dough into 2.5-cm/1-in squares.

5. Allow to air-dry for at least 24 hours, or dry in a dehydrator set to 50°C/122°F for at least 2 hours.

6. Once dry, you may apply a graphic image to the surface by using a rubber stamp and natural food coloring in a sponge pad.

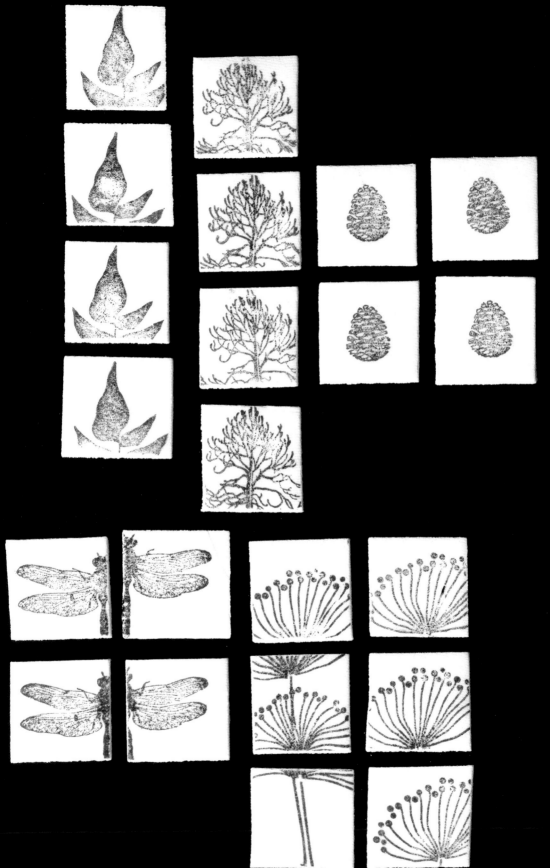

YUZU JELLIES

YIELD: ABOUT 144 JELLIES

INGREDIENT	METRIC	U.S.	%
Calcium Solution			
Monocalcium chloride	2 g	.07 oz	1.8%
Water	120 g	4.23 oz	98.2%
Jellies			
Yuzu purée (see Resources, page 520)	900 g	1 lb 15.75 oz	71.77%
Sugar	300 g	10.58 oz	23.92%
Calcium Solution	12 g	.42 oz	.96%
Universal pectin (aka pectin NH 95 or low-acyl pectin)	12 g	.42 oz	.96%
Gelatin sheets, silver, bloomed in cold water, excess water squeezed off	30 g	1.06 oz	2.39%
Sugar	1 kg	2 lb 3.27 oz	

1. **For the solution:** Combine both ingredients. Reserve in the refrigerator.

2. Prepare a frame using caramel bars (heavy stainless-steel bars) measuring 30 cm/12 in wide by 45 cm/18 in long 1.25 cm/.5 in deep. Place it over a flat sheet pan lined with a nonstick rubber mat.

3. Combine the yuzu purée with the sugar and the calcium solution in a 3.84-L/4-qt sauce pot. Bring to a boil over high heat while whisking. Turn off the heat and stir in the pectin as quickly as possible using the whisk. Boil over medium heat for 1 minute to fully hydrate the pectin.

4. Turn off the heat and add the bloomed gelatin sheets, stirring to completely dissolve them.

5. Pour the jelly into the prepared frame. Allow to cool to room temperature without moving the sheet pan. Once it has cooled, allow the mixture to gel completely in the refrigerator.

6. Once it has set completely, cover the surface of the jelly with a thin, even layer of sugar. Remove the caramel bars; you may need to separate them from the jelly with an offset spatula. Place a nonstick rubber mat over the jelly and flip it over carefully. Sprinkle the surface with a thin, even coat of sugar.

7. Using a guitar cutter (if available; otherwise use a knife and a ruler), cut out 2.5-cm/1-in squares. Toss them in sugar to coat them completely. Shake off the excess by placing the jellies in a drum sieve and shaking the sieve gently. Place them in a single layer on a sheet pan lined with parchment paper. Allow them to dry for 2 to 3 hours at room temperature; turn each piece over and allow to dry for 2 to 3 more hours. Wrap tightly and reserve in a cool, dry area at room temperature. Discard after 1 week.

MARSHMALLOWS: LILLET BLANC (yellow) | PORT (light purple) | ROSÉ CHAMPAGNE (light pink) | STOUT BEER (light brown)

YIELD: 20 MARSHMALLOW "TUBES"

INGREDIENT	METRIC	U.S.	%
Glutinous rice flour	as needed	as needed	
Gelatin powder	32 g	1.11 oz	2.36%
Liquor 1	188 g	6.61 oz	14.03%
Liquor 2	98 g	3.44 oz	7.3%
Sugar	450 g	15.87 oz	33.67%
Corn syrup	480 g	1 lb .93	35.91%
Water	90 g	3.17 oz	6.73%
Natural food coloring	as needed	as needed	

1. Lightly dust 2 sheet pans lined with silicone paper with glutinous rice flour. Use a sifter to obtain a thin, even layer. Assemble a piping bag fitted with a #6 plain piping tip.

2. Combine the gelatin powder with the first quantity of liquor in a small mixer bowl and let it bloom. Once bloomed, place on an electric mixer fitted with the whip attachment on low speed.

3. Meanwhile, combine the second amount of liquor, the sugar, corn syrup, and water in a pot. Cook to between 114 and 115°C/238 and 240°F.

4. Pour this mixture into the mixer as it mixes on slow speed. Turn the speed up to 2 or 3 once all the liquid has been poured in; any faster and it will splatter everywhere.

5. Once the mixture has cooled down, turn the speed up to high. At this point, it shouldn't splatter out of the bowl. If it does, then it needs to cool a little more before you turn the speed up.

6. Whip until thick, 8 to 10 minutes. You can add the food coloring at this point and whip until the color has completely mixed in. Pour into the piping bag. Pipe out tubes that are the length of the sheet pan. Dust the surface of the marshmallows with a light coat of glutinous rice flour, using a sifter to get a thin, even layer on the surface.

7. Let the tubes dry overnight, then coat the entire tubes with glutinous rice flour and dust off the excess flour. Reserve in glass jars or other airtight containers.

8. The marshmallows are presented whole and then cut to order at the customer's table using a sharp pair of scissors. Make sure the server wears gloves while doing this. The shelf life for the marshmallows is about 1 week if stored in airtight containers.

NOTE

This is a general recipe for all the marshmallows; replace the liquid amount with the respective alcohol type (Lillet Blanc, port, rosé Champagne, stout beer) to make different flavors. Again, you may add a few drops of natural, water-based food coloring toward the end of the whipping process.

DARK CHOCOLATE AND CARAMEL TARTS

YIELD: ABOUT 40 TARTS

COMPONENTS	**Caramel** (page 517)
	Sablé Tart Shells (see Note)
	Ganache (page 517)
	Specks of gold leaf

ASSEMBLY INSTRUCTIONS

1. Pour about 10 g/.35 oz of caramel into each tart shell.

2. Make the ganache and let it cool to 27°C/80°F. Pipe it into the tart shells, filling them until they dome slightly above the rim of the tart.

3. Let set completely at room temperature. Apply a small piece of gold leaf on top of the tart. Two sheets of gold leaf will be enough for all the tarts.

4. Discard after 24 hours. Do not refrigerate; the ganache tastes best if it is at room temperature.

NOTE

For the sablé tart shells, assemble 40 oval ring molds measuring 7 cm/2.75 in long by 5 mm/.2 in high. Follow the method for the tart shells on page 518. Once the dough is sheeted (to 2 mm/.08 in as well), cut it into disks that measure 7.5 cm/3 in diameter.

AÇAI LOLLIPOPS

YIELD: ABOUT 50 LOLLIPOPS

INGREDIENT	METRIC	U.S	%
Sugar	1.15.kg	2 lb 8.48 oz	65.49%
Glucose	360 g	12.7 oz	20.5%
Water	240 g	8.47 oz	13.67%
Cream of tartar	6 g	.21 oz	.34%
Açai berry extract (oil based), or as needed	2 or 3 drops	2 or 3 drops	
Natural food coloring (alcohol based or water based), or as needed	2 or 3 drops	2 or 3 drops	
Gold Spray (optional; page 466)	as needed	as needed	

1. Assemble the lollipop molds. You can make your own molds by cutting rectangles out of a 1-cm/.4-in thick neoprene mat (see Resources, page 520) that measures 1 cm/.4 in wide by 12.5 cm/5 in long using an X-Acto knife and a ruler. There are molds that are specific for making lollipops, which you can use as well. However, the neoprene mat allows you to cut out any shape or size you want.

2. Place the lollipop sticks down the center of the cut-out rectangles. Use tape to anchor the sticks, since they might move when the cooked sugar is poured into the molds.

3. You will also need a funnel gun to dispense the cooked sugar into the molds. Keep the funnel warm by keeping it filled with very hot water before pouring in the sugar. This will prevent the sugar from setting inside the funnel, especially at the tip.

4. Combine the sugar, glucose, water, and cream of tartar thoroughly in a sauce pot. Clean the inside of the pot with a clean brush and water. The brush should be used for this purpose only.

5. Cook over high heat, preferably over an induction burner, stirring until the mixture starts to boil. Stop stirring and continue to cook until the sugar reaches 156°C/313°F.

6. Remove the pot from the heat and add the flavoring and the coloring as needed, swirling the pot to mix the ingredients evenly.

7. Empty the funnel gun and dry it out thoroughly before pouring the cooked sugar into it. When the mixture stops bubbling, transfer it to the funnel gun.

8. Dispense the cooked sugar into the prepared molds. Let the lollipops set at room temperature.

9. Spray a mist of gold spray over them. This is simply a decorative element; you can do without it if you wish. Reserve the lollipops in an airtight container with silica gel packs at room temperature. They will keep indefinitely if stored in a cool, dry environment.

MAPLE COTTON CANDY

YIELD: ABOUT 20 BOXES

INGREDIENT	METRIC	U.S.	%
Superfine sugar	400 g	14.11 oz	50%
Maple sugar	400 g	14.11 oz	50%
Gold leaf sheets	20	20	
Chocolate Stars (see method on page 329)	100	100	

1. Use a commercial cotton candy machine to make this recipe (these machines can be rented). Small machines are not recommended for large quantities, but they'll work in a pinch.

2. Combine both sugars and mix well in a Robot Coupe. Pass through a drum sieve.

3. Make the cotton candy in the machine. Fill the central hopper halfway with the sugar mixture, and turn on the spinner and heat elements; when it starts to "spit" out the sugar floss, carefully grab it with your hands and place the cotton candy inside the boxes (see Note). Slide a gold leaf sheet on top of the cotton candy as well as 5 to 7 chocolate stars before closing the box. Cotton candy will keep fully expanded for about 1 day. After that, it starts to collapse onto itself.

NOTE

The boxes measure 10 cm/4 in wide by 25 cm/10 in long 2.5 cm/1 in high. It is hard to measure or weigh how much cotton candy should go into each box. Therefore, you will have to keep in mind that you don't want to put too much in, because it will get compressed when the box is closed. It should be enough to fill the box, but you should be able to close the lid of the box without compressing the cotton candy too much. Do not make this recipe in humid environments.

TANGERINE MOCHI

YIELD: ABOUT 100 PIECES (1.32 KG/2 LB 14.4 OZ)

INGREDIENT	METRIC	U.S.	%
Glutinous sweet rice flour	400 g	14.08 oz	30.3%
Superfine or other fine crystal sugar	440 g	15.52 oz	33.33%
Tangerine juice, hot	480 g	1 lb .96 oz	36.36%

1. Mix all of the ingredients and strain through a fine-mesh sieve into a plastic tub large enough to hold the mixture.

2. Microwave in 2-minute intervals on medium power 4 or 5 times, stirring after each interval using a wooden spoon. At first it will look like something is wrong because the mixture will look chunky and some spots will be fluid while other have cooked. Keep microwaving and stirring until you obtain a smooth, homogenous, elastic dough.

3. Transfer the dough onto a surface dusted with rice flour. Sprinkle some rice flour on top and roll the dough out to about a 1.25-cm/.5-in thickness using a rolling pin. Keep adding rice flour under it and on top to keep it from sticking; turn it over frequently.

4. Let it cool, rest, and relax, covered with plastic.

5. Once the mochi has cooled, cut out disks using the dull end of a 2.5-cm/1-in ring cutter dipped in rice flour first. If you use the sharp end, the mochi won't look very good; the dull end gives it that rounded "hamburger patty" look.

NOTE

The traditional mochi method takes about 2 hours of physically pounding the dough to obtain the chewy consistency associated with mochi. This method cuts the process down to a fraction of the time.

CHOCOLATE AND MALT POPS

YIELD: 900 G/1 LB 15.75 OZ (ABOUT 40 POPS)

INGREDIENT	METRIC	U.S.	%
Tempered dark chocolate	750 g	1 lb 10.4 oz	83.33%
Malt powder	150 g	5.29 oz	16.67%

1. Pour one-quarter of the tempered chocolate into button-shaped chocolate molds. Follow the molded chocolate method on page 44.

2. Insert a lollipop stick into each mold.

3. Stir the malt powder into the remaining tempered chocolate and pour into this the molds, filling them to the top.

4. Allow to crystallize at room temperature before unmolding.

5. Reserve in a cool, dry place, preferably enclosed. Discard after 6 months.

POPCORN FILLING

YIELD: 280 G/9.88 OZ

INGREDIENT	METRIC	U.S.	%
Popping corn	200 g	7.05 oz	71.43%
Canola oil	5 g	.18 oz	1.79%
Freeze-dried salted butter powder	30 g	1.06 oz	10.71%
Anhydrous butter, melted	45 g	1.59 oz	16.07%

1. Combine the popping corn with the canola oil in a deep pot.

2. Pop the popping corn over medium-high heat, stirring the pot frequently, until all of the kernels are popped.

3. Let the popcorn cool completely out of the pot and then grind it in a Robot Coupe as finely as possible. Pass the popcorn through a fine-mesh sieve.

4. Combine the popcorn with the freeze-dried butter powder.

5. Gently stir in the melted anhydrous butter. Add a little at a time; you may not need all of the butter. There should be just enough so that the popcorn is still loose but holds together when compressed.

NOTE *Anhydrous butter is water-free butter (not to be confused with clarified butter) that has the flavor of butter without the moisture, thus extending the shelf life of the filling.*

PINEAPPLE JAM

YIELD: 560 G/1 LB 3.71 OZ

INGREDIENT	METRIC	U.S.	%
Peeled, cored, and finely diced pineapple	350 g	12.35 oz	62.5%
Sugar	200 g	7.05 oz	35.71%
Lemon juice	10 g	.35 oz	1.79%

1. Combine all of the ingredients in a small sauce pot. Cook over medium-high heat until the mixture reaches 68° Brix.

2. Cool to room temperature.

FRENCH TOAST FILLING

YIELD: 453 G/15.98 OZ

INGREDIENT	METRIC	U.S.	%
Brioche Pullman loaf slice, 1.25 cm/.5 in thick by 30 cm/12 in long, crust trimmed	1	1	
Heavy cream	200 g	7.05 oz	44.15%
Vodka	50 g	1.76 oz	11.04%
Ground cinnamon	1 g	.04 oz	.22%
Vanilla paste	2 g	.07 oz	.44%
White chocolate coins	200 g	7.05 oz	44.15%

1. Place the slice of brioche on a half hotel pan lined with plastic wrap.

2. Combine the heavy cream, vodka, cinnamon, and vanilla paste in a small saucepot. Bring to a boil and then pour over the white chocolate. Stir until the chocolate has dissolved.

3. Pour on top of the brioche slice while warm.

4. Wrap the brioche with the plastic wrap it is laying on and refrigerate.

5. Once the ganache has crystallized, cut it out into disks that are smaller than the diameter of the mold.

NOTE *The vodka is added to this recipe to reduce the a_w (water activity) of the ganache and thus extend its shelf life. It doesn't really add much flavor, since vodka is flavorless for the most part. The ganache is a light, fluid ganache that is meant to give a certain texture to the brioche that is similar to if it had been soaked in a custard for French toast.*

DOUGHNUT GANACHE

YIELD: 635 G/1 LB 4.8 OZ

INGREDIENT	METRIC	U.S.	%
Cake doughnuts	50 g	1.76 oz	7.87%
Heavy cream	115 g	4.06 oz	18.11%
Sugar	25 g	.88 oz	3.94%
Glucose syrup	45 g	1.59 oz	7.09%
White chocolate coins	325 g	11.46 oz	51.18%
Butter, soft	40 g	1.41 oz	6.3%
Chocolate liqueur	35 g	1.23 oz	5.51%

1. Purée the doughnuts with the heavy cream and sugar until completely smooth.

2. Bring the doughnut purée and glucose syrup to a boil in a sauce pot. Pour over the white chocolate.

3. Stir to emulsify, then incorporate the butter, and stream in the chocolate liqueur.

4. Allow to cool, covered in plastic. Pipe into the mold once it reaches 30°C/86°F.

BUBBLE CHOCOLATE

YIELD: 550 G/1 LB 3.4 OZ

INGREDIENT	METRIC	U.S.	%
Dark chocolate	500 g	17.64 oz	90.91%
Black truffle oil	15 g	.53 oz	2.73%
Canola oil	35 g	1.23 oz	6.36%

1. Make sure the molds have been cast before making this filling.

2. Combine all of the ingredients in a bowl and melt over a hot water bath. Stir to combine evenly.

3. Fill a 1-L/1.06-quart heavy cream whipper canister with the mixture and fill it with 2 charges of CO_2. Shake the whipper vigorously after each charge.

FIG, PASSION FRUIT, AND TOFFEE FILLING

YIELD: 490 G/1 LB 1.28 OZ

INGREDIENT	METRIC	U.S.	%
Passion fruit purée, concentrated	100 g	3.53 oz	20.41%
White chocolate coins	300 g	10.58 oz	61.22%
Dried figs, finely chopped	45 g	1.59 oz	9.18%
Toffee (page 513), finely chopped	45 g	1.59 oz	9.18%

1. Combine the passion fruit purée and the white chocolate in a bowl. Stir over a hot water bath until they become a homogenous mix.

2. Remove from the heat and cool to 30°C/86°F. Stir in the chopped figs and toffee.

APRICOT FOAM

YIELD: 421 G/14.88 OZ

INGREDIENT	METRIC	U.S.	%
Xanthan gum	2 g	.07 oz	.5%
Methocel F50	4 g	.13 oz	.85%
Sugar	40 g	1.41 oz	9.49%
Lemon juice	6 g	.21 oz	1.42%
Water	95 g	3.35 oz	22.53%
Apricot purée	275 g	9.7 oz	65.21%

1. Set a dehydrator to 60°C/140°F.

2. Cut out a square of silicone that will fit flat inside of the dehydrator. Poke a good amount of holes in it using a scribe. (In order for Methocel F50 to gel, it needs to completely come in contact with heat.)

3. Combine the xanthan gum, Methocel F50, and sugar and mix well. Combine the lemon juice, water, and apricot purée in a blender cup and mix well. Shear the sugar mixture into the blender on medium-low speed and mix for 1 minute.

4. Transfer the mixture to the bowl of a mixer fitted with the whip attachment and whip on high speed until full volume is obtained (seven or eight times the original volume).

5. Spread it out in an even layer over the prepared silicone and then put it in the dehydrator. Allow to set for at least 3 hours or until crispy. When the mixture is warm, it does not feel crisp; it is only when it cools down that it will harden.

6. Reserve in the dehydrator until needed.

NOTE *The crispness of this foam is only temporary, even in the driest environments. Once it is attached to the finished chocolate with a dot of tempered milk chocolate, the foam will soften. It will look like a foam and feel like a foam, albeit a permanent foam.*

RICE PUDDING GANACHE

YIELD: 495 G/1 LB 1.46 OZ

INGREDIENT	METRIC	U.S. (OZ)	%
Rice Milk			
Milk	500 g	1 lb 1.64 oz	
Arborio rice	75 g	2.65 oz	
Ganache			
Rice Milk	140 g	4.94 oz	28.28%
Heavy cream	40 g	1.41 oz	8.08%
Glucose	50 g	1.76 oz	10.1%
White chocolate coins	240 g	8.47 oz	48.48%
Butter	25 g	.88 oz	5.05%

1. **For the rice milk:** Cook the milk and rice in a sauce pot over medium heat until the rice is very tender and falling apart.

2. Blend until very smooth.

3. Cool over an ice water bath.

4. **For the ganache:** Bring the cooled rice milk, cream, and glucose to a boil in a sauce pot.

5. Pour over the white chocolate and emulsify. Stir in the butter.

6. Wait for ganache to reach 30°C/86°F before piping into the mold.

CILANTRO, TANGERINE, AND LITCHI FILLING

YIELD: 439 G/15.49 OZ

INGREDIENT	METRIC	U.S.	%
Cilantro Cream			
Heavy cream	150 g	5.29 oz	90.91%
Cilantro leaves	15 g	.53 oz	9.09%
Ganache			
Tangerine zest	1 g	.04	.26%
Cilantro Cream	115 g	4.06	29.41%
Glucose syrup	15 g	.53	3.84%
White chocolate coins	250 g	8.82	63.94%
Butter, soft	10 g	.35	2.56%
Litchi jelly (see Resources, page 520; each piece is about 2 g)	24	24	

1. **For the cilantro cream:** Combine the cream and cilantro in a small sauce pot and bring to a boil over high heat. Turn off the heat and cover the pot with plastic wrap. Let steep for 10 minutes.

2. Strain the cream and let cool.

3. **For the ganache:** Zest the tangerine directly into the pot.

4. Add the cream and glucose syrup to the pot. Bring to a boil.

5. Pour over the white chocolate and let sit for about 1 minute, then stir to emulsify. Stir in the butter.

6. Pat the litchi jelly dry. This litchi jelly is firm and full of flavor and comes in rectangular strips that are from 2.5 cm/1 in to 3.75 cm/1.5 in long.

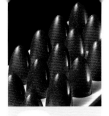

DEHYDRATED SHISO LEAVES

YIELD: 300 G/10.58 OZ

INGREDIENT	METRIC	U.S.	%
Shiso leaves	300 g	10.58 oz	100%

1. Set a dehydrator to 45°C/113°F. Place the leaves in the dehydrator for 12 hours or until they have completely dried.

2. Once they are dried, pulverize them in a coffee grinder.

3. Reserve in an airtight container in a cool, dry place. Discard after 1 year.

RED MISO GANACHE

YIELD: 420 G/14.82 OZ

INGREDIENT	METRIC	U.S.	%
Heavy cream	100 g	3.53 oz	23.81%
Red miso paste	20 g	.71 oz	4.76%
Glucose	25 g	.88 oz	5.95%
Butter	50 g	1.76 oz	11.9%
Milk chocolate coins	200 g	7.05 oz	47.62%
Trimoline	25 g	.88 oz	5.95%

	METRIC	U.S.	
Ground Dehydrated Shiso Leaves (page 509)	25 g	.88 oz	

1. Combine the cream, miso paste, glucose, and butter in a sauce pot and bring to a boil.

2. Pour over the milk chocolate, let sit for 30 seconds, and stir to emulsify.

3. Stir in the trimoline until a homogeneous mass is obtained. Let cool.

FOIE GRAS FILLING

YIELD: 707 G/1 LB 8.8 OZ

INGREDIENT	METRIC	U.S.	%
Foie gras	660 g	1 lb 7.28 oz	93.35%
Armagnac	40 g	1.41 oz	5.66%
Salt	7 g	.25 oz	.99%

1. Devein the foie gras and soak in milk overnight.

2. Remove the foie gras from the milk and pat dry with a clean towel. Temper for 2 hours before making the mousse; this reduces the cooking time. Make sure to keep it well covered with plastic wrap to reduce oxidation. Prepare an ice water bath.

3. Make a frame using caramel bars (heavy stainless-steel bars) measuring 30 cm/12 in long x 1.25 cm/.5 in thick. Place over a flat sheet pan lined with a nonstick rubber mat.

4. Set the timer on a Thermomix for 5 minutes and the temperature to 80°C/175°F. Do not put the ingredients into the Thermomix cup until the machine reaches the right temperature, which will take about 2 minutes. If you do, it will make your foie gras too hot and it will break or separate.

5. Without delay, once the desired temperature is reached, turn the machine off and put all of the ingredients into the cup. Set the machine on speed 3 for 2 minutes. Turn the machine on and let it mix for the allotted time.

6. Once the time is up, pour the contents of the pitcher into a bowl that fits comfortably inside the ice water bath. Remove the ice from the ice bath and place the bowl with the foie gras inside the cold water bath. Stir with a rubber spatula until it has the consistency of a smooth ganache.

7. Transfer the foie gras mixture into the prepared frame and even out the top. Cover with plastic wrap and refrigerate.

8. Once it has firmed up, spread 100 g/3.53 oz of melted dark chocolate over the surface of the mixture using a paint roller. Let it set. Turn the foie gras over onto a guitar with a 2.5-cm/1-in cutter. Cut out squares of the mixture.

9. Reserve the mixture well covered in the refrigerator. Temper dark chocolate and dip the foie gras squares before coating with the gold leaf.

BEET BARS

YIELD: 600 G/1 LB 5.12 OZ

INGREDIENT	METRIC	U.S.	%
Sugar	232 g	8.18 oz	38.67%
Cocoa butter coins	245 g	8.64 oz	40.83%
Beet powder	120 g	4.23 oz	20%
Lecithin powder	3 g	.11 oz	.5%

1. Grind the sugar in a coffee grinder.

2. Melt the cocoa butter to 45°C/110°F and place it inside the mélangeur (see Resources, page 520); turn it on.

3. As soon as the mélangeur starts moving, start adding the sugar in 4 additions, and then add the beet powder in 4 additions.

4. Let the mélangeur run for at least 12 and up to 18 hours.

5. Add the lecithin powder toward the end of the process and let it grind for about 2 more hours.

6. Transfer the couverture to a sheet pan lined with parchment paper and let it cool to set.

7. Temper the couverture with regular white chocolate and proceed with the molded chocolate method on page 44. Do not turn the molds over once they have been filled with the couverture. The bars are solid chocolate; therefore, fill the mold and then scrape off the excess.

8. Allow to crystallize at room temperature before unmolding.

BLACK OLIVE BARS

YIELD: 620 G/1 LB 5.76 OZ

INGREDIENT	METRIC	U.S.	%
White chocolate coins	550 g	1 lb 3.36 oz	88.71%
Freeze-dried black olives	35 g	1.23 oz	5.65%
Cocoa butter	35 g	1.23 oz	5.65%

1. Melt the chocolate to 45°C/110°F and place it in the mélangeur.

2. Grind the freeze-dried olives in a coffee grinder and add to the white chocolate in the mélangeur.

3. Let the mélangeur run for at least 12 and up to 18 hours.

4. Melt the cocoa butter to 45°C/110°F and add it to the mélangeur. Let it mix until just incorporated.

5. Transfer the couverture to a sheet pan lined with parchment paper and let it cool to set.

6. Temper the couverture with regular white chocolate and proceed with the molded chocolate method on page 44. Do not turn the molds over once they have been filled with the couverture; the bars are solid, therefore, fill the mold and then scrape the excess off.

7. Allow to crystallize at room temperature before unmolding.

SAFFRON BARS

YIELD: 616 G/1 LB 5.6 OZ

INGREDIENT	METRIC	U.S.	%
White chocolate	600 g	1 lb 5.12 oz	97.4%
Saffron	6 g	.21 oz	.97%
Cocoa butter	10 g	.35 oz	1.62%

See the method for Black Olive Bars. Substitute the saffron for the black olives.

EARL GREY BARS

YIELD: 605 G/1 LB 5.28 OZ

INGREDIENT	METRIC	U.S.	%
White chocolate	575 g	1 lb 4.16 oz	95.04%
Earl Grey tea	15 g	.53 oz	2.48%
Cocoa butter	15 g	.53 oz	2.48%

See the method for Black Olive Bars on page 511; substitute the Earl Grey tea leaves for the black olives.

MATCHA TEA BARS

YIELD: 600 G/1 LB 5.12 OZ

INGREDIENT	METRIC	U.S.	%
White chocolate	570 g	1 lb 4 oz	95%
Matcha tea powder	15 g	.53 oz	2.5%
Cocoa butter	15 g	.53 oz	2.5%

See the method for Black Olive Bars on page 511; substitute the matcha tea powder for the black olives.

BACON PRALINE

YIELD: 200 G/7.05 OZ

INGREDIENT	METRIC	U.S.	%
High-quality bacon, cooked	100 g	3.53 oz	50%
Sugar	75 g	2.65 oz	37.5%
Maple sugar	25 g	.88 oz	12.5%

1. Place the previously rendered bacon in a hot oven, inside a dehydrator set to 60°C/140°F over a wire rack, for at least 6 hours. There are two reasons for doing this: rendering the fat as much as possible and drying the bacon as much as possible to extend its shelf life.

2. Chop the bacon into small pieces and keep hot in the dehydrator.

3. Combine the sugar and maple sugar in a sauce pot and make a dry caramel over high heat, stirring constantly.

4. Once the sugar reaches a medium-dark brown, take the pot off the heat and add the bacon, stirring vigorously.

5. Pour the mixture onto a nonstick rubber mat and cool completely.

6. Chop finely with a knife. Reserve in a cool, dry place until ready to use. Discard after 1 month.

FRENCH TOAST GANACHE

YIELD: 453 G/15.98 OZ

INGREDIENT	METRIC	U.S.	%
Brioche Pullman loaf slice, 1.25 cm/.5 in thick by 30 cm/12 in long, crust removed	2	2	
Heavy cream	200 g	7.05 oz	36.17%
Rum	50 g	1.76 oz	9.04%
Ground cinnamon	3 g	.11 oz	.54%
Maple syrup	50 g	1.76 oz	9.04%
White chocolate coins	250 g	8.82 oz	45.21%
Fleur de sel	10 g	.35 oz	

1. Line a half sheet pan with plastic wrap. Place both slices of brioche inside the pan side by side.

2. Bring the heavy cream, rum, cinnamon, and maple syrup to a boil in a sauce pot and then pour over the white chocolate. Let sit for 1 minute and then stir to emulsify. Pour the mixture while it is still warm over the brioche, making sure to saturate it. Fold the flaps of plastic wrap over the brioche and refrigerate to firm up the ganache, about 2 hours.

3. Once cold, cut out 6.5-cm/2.5-in squares and put them inside each bar mold.

TOFFEE

See the toffee recipe on page 416. You will need about 150 g/5.3 oz for all 10 bars.

CANDIED APPLES

YIELD: 251 G/8.85 OZ

INGREDIENT	METRIC	U.S.	%
Granny Smith apple	1	1	
Sugar	200 g	7.05 oz	79.68%
Water	50 g	1.76 oz	19.92%
Lemon juice	1 g	.04 oz	.4%

1. Peel and cut the apple into small dice.

2. Combine the sugar, water, and lemon juice in a small sauce pot and cook over high heat. Once the sugar turns medium amber brown, add the apples and stir. Bring back to a simmer, then turn the heat down to low.

3. Cook the apples until they are translucent and dark amber brown, about 30 minutes.

4. Strain the apples, place them in a hotel pan, and cool to room temperature. Once they are cool, they can be placed inside the candy bar.

NOTES *Cooking apples this way is a way of preserving them, since most of their moisture (water content) evaporates during the cooking process and the sugar is absorbed. The lemon juice helps activate the natural pectin in the apples, which gives them somewhat of a chewy jelly consistency and helps them keep their shape after they are cooked. In other words, they should not turn to mush. They will turn to mush if they are old apples or apples with low pectin content. Ideally, use Granny Smith apples, but McIntosh and Ginger Gold apples also work well.*

SOURDOUGH COUVERTURE

YIELD: 2.01 KG/4 LB 6.88 OZ

INGREDIENT	METRIC	U.S.	%
Sourdough loaf, day-old	500 g	1 lb 1.63 oz	19.9%
Cocoa butter, heated to 45°C/115°F	820 g	1 lb 12.92 oz	40.8%
Superfine or bakers' sugar	780 g	1 lb 11.51 oz	38.81%
Lecithin powder	10 g	.35 oz	.5%

1. Cut the sourdough into small cubes and dry it in a low-temperature oven until it has no moisture whatsoever.

2. Grind it in a Robot Coupe to obtain crumbs, and then grind it even finer using a coffee grinder.

3. Proceed with the white chocolate method on page 38.

BAGUETTE GANACHE

YIELD: 635 G/1 LB 6.4 OZ

INGREDIENT	METRIC	U.S.	%
Baguette, toasted dark	50 g	1.76 oz	7.87%
Heavy cream	115 g	4.06 oz	18.11%
Sugar	25 g	.88 oz	3.94%
Glucose syrup	45 g	1.59 oz	7.09%
White chocolate	325 g	11.46 oz	51.18%
Butter, soft	40 g	1.41 oz	6.3%
Vodka	35 g	1.23 oz	5.51%

Follow the method for Doughnut Ganache on page 505. Replace the doughnuts with the toasted baguette and the chocolate liquor with the vodka.

OLIVE OIL CARAMEL WITH TOASTED PINE NUTS

YIELD: 952 G/2 LB 1.44 OZ

INGREDIENT	METRIC	U.S.	%
Sugar	260 g	9.17 oz	27.31%
Glucose	130 g	4.59 oz	13.66%
Lemon juice	2 g	.07 oz	.21%
Water	100 g	3.53 oz	10.5%
Heavy cream	220 g	7.76 oz	23.11%
Extra-virgin olive oil	40 g	1.41 oz	4.2%
Toasted pine nuts, coarsely chopped	200 g	7.05 oz	21.01%

1. Cook the sugar, glucose, lemon juice, and water in a small sauce pot over high heat.

2. Heat the cream and olive oil in a microwave, just enough to warm the mixture up to about 65°C/150°F.

3. When the sugar turns to a deep, dark caramel color (go by color, since taking the temperature of something so shallow is practically impossible), turn off the heat and add the hot cream and olive oil mixture, carefully whisking it in. Take great care and thoroughly whisk the caramel or it will separate while cooling.

4. Pour the mixture into a half hotel pan and allow it to cool before folding in the pine nuts.

5. Fold in the pine nuts and then pipe into the mold to just under the top of the cavity.

SABLÉ TART SHELLS

YIELD: 2.1 KG/4 LB 10.24 OZ

INGREDIENT	METRIC	U.S.	%
All-purpose flour	290 g	10.23 oz	13.76%
Cake flour	700 g	1 lb 8.64 oz	33.22%
Butter, at room temperature	480 g	1 lb .93 oz	22.78%
Salt	7 g	.25 oz	.33%
Confectioners' sugar	360 g	12.7 oz	17.09%
Almond flour	70 g	2.47 oz	3.32%
Eggs	200 g	7.05 oz	9.49%

1. Sift the all-purpose flour and cake flour together.

2. Cream the butter, salt, confectioners' sugar, and almond flour together on medium speed in an electric mixer bowl fitted with the paddle attachment until a homogenous mass is obtained, about 2 minutes.

3. Stop the mixer, add the eggs and mix for a few seconds on low speed until the eggs are completely incorporated.

4. Stop the mixer, add the sifted flour, and mix for a few seconds, pulsing the mixer at first to keep the flour in the bowl. Mix just to obtain a homogenous mass.

5. Shape the dough into a flat square and wrap with plastic. Chill for about 1 hour.

6. Grease the interior of 40 oval tart molds measuring 3.75 cm/1.5 in wide by 7.5 cm/3 in long by 5 mm/.2 in high with a small amount of butter. Place the molds over a flat sheet pan lined with a nonstick rubber mat.

7. Preheat a convection oven to 160°C/320°F.

8. Sheet the dough out to 2 mm/.08 in using a sheeter or by hand. Cut out ovals that are slightly larger than the mold that are 6.5 cm/2.5 in wide by 9 cm/3.5 in long.

9. Chill the dough in the freezer until slightly firm to shape the tarts.

10. Shape the tart shells by placing a piece of dough on top of each mold. Gently push the dough in with your fingertips until it conforms to the shape of the mold. Make sure that the dough is lined up with the mold. There will be some that protrudes from the rim of the mold. Do not cut it yet. Freeze the tarts until the dough hardens.

11. Once the dough is hard, use a paring knife to trim the excess off the top of the molds.

12. Dock the dough with a fork and, if the dough is still frozen, bake it; otherwise, re-freeze it. Bake until golden brown, about 7 minutes.

13. Cool at room temperature. Reserve in an airtight container at room temperature until needed. Discard after 2 weeks.

MARIGOLD CARAMEL

YIELD: 1.33 KG/2 LB 14.91 OZ

INGREDIENT	METRIC	U.S.	%
Marigold Syrup			
Crystallized marigolds	600 g	1 lb 5.12 oz	49.88%
Water	600 g	1 lb 5.12 oz	49.88%
Malic acid	3 g	.11 oz	.25%
Marigold Caramel			
Marigold Syrup	1.05 kg	2 lb 4.96 oz	78.95%
Butter	105 g	3.7 oz	7.89%
Heavy cream	105 g	3.7 oz	7.89%
Invert sugar	70 g	2.47 oz	5.26%

1. **For the marigold syrup:** Purée all of the ingredients together using a handheld immersion blender.

2. Reserve in an airtight container and refrigerate overnight.

3. Pass through a fine-mesh sieve before making the marigold caramel.

4. **For the marigold caramel:** Combine all of the ingredients in a 960-mL/1-qt saucepot. Bring to a boil, and then quickly reduce to a simmer.

5. Cook until the mixture reaches 112°C/234°F. Take off the heat and emulsify using a handheld immersion blender for 2 minutes, or until emulsified. Make sure to keep the head of the blender submerged in the caramel to prevent bubbles from forming.

6. Pour into the baked tart shells to fill until the caramel domes slightly over the top of the mold but not so much that it pours out of the tart shell. You will have some caramel left over, which may be used for more tarts made at a different time. The caramel has a shelf life of 2 months.

NOTE *The marigold caramel recipe was adapted from the recipe for the violet caramel from* The Big Fat Duck Cookbook *by Heston Blumenthal.*

CARAMEL

YIELD: 1.1 KG/2 LB 6.72 OZ

INGREDIENT	METRIC	U.S.	%
Sugar	400 g	14.11 oz	36.36%
Glucose	200 g	7.05 oz	18.18%
Water	100 g	3.53 oz	9.09%
Heavy cream	250 g	8.82 oz	22.73%
Butter	135 g	4.76 oz	12.27%
Fleur de sel	15 g	.53 oz	1.36%

1. Cook the sugar, glucose, and water in a 960-mL/1-qt saucepot over high heat.

2. Heat the cream, butter, and fleur de sel in a microwave, enough to warm the mixture up to about 65°C/150°F.

3. When the sugar turns a deep, dark caramel color, between 178 and 180°C/355 and 360°F, turn off the heat and slowly stream in the hot cream mixture, carefully whisking it in. Take great care and whisk the caramel thoroughly or it will separate while cooling.

4. Once cool, fill the tarts. There will be caramel left over after filling the tarts. Use it to make more tarts when necessary. This will keep for more than 6 months.

GANACHE

YIELD: 1.05 KG/2 LB 4.96 OZ

INGREDIENT	METRIC	U.S.	%
Heavy cream	500 g	1 lb 1.64 oz	47.62%
Dark chocolate coins (64%)	450 g	15.87 oz	42.86%
Butter, soft	100 g	3.53 oz	9.52%

1. Bring the heavy cream to a boil and pour it over the chocolate.

2. Let sit for 30 seconds before stirring with a rubber spatula. Stir to emulsify, and then add the butter. Stir until it has dissolved completely.

3. Dispense into tarts when it cools to 27°C/80°F. Discard the ganache after 1 week.

I cannot think of a way to enhance the customer's experience more than by providing him or her with a small take-home gift of food. It is a very special place that can pull this off. The first time I went to a restaurant that actually did this, I felt like the most important and special customer in the world. I am exaggerating only slightly, but when the maitre d' handed me a paper bag with a loaf of walnut bread, I was ecstatic, beside myself with joy at a gift of bread. In the days that followed I enjoyed this loaf, and each time I had a piece I thought about my experience there and how terrific it all had been. Years later, I remember that meal and that loaf of bread. That restaurant has since gone through many changes and adjustments, but my experience is intact. Perhaps I have romanticized it a bit, but I am quite sure that that loaf of bread made a difference and put the experience into a category all its own.

Since then I have always wanted to implement that experience at the restaurants I have worked at, but I didn't, except for one of them and then it was only for VIPs. In retrospect, I am very grateful that things happened this way. The logistics of adding on one more item multiplied by however many guests you are expecting are daunting. If you have the manpower and space and the advantage of a not-so-rigid food cost, then by all means, do it. This is the thing that can set you apart. This is the extra thing that can make people feel special and hold on to that feeling for many days—and in my case, years. Just make sure what you offer actually tastes good, because that warm, fuzzy feeling can completely turn around and have the opposite effect if it doesn't.

Some items that work well for this experience are cooked sugar confections such as hard candy and lollipops, chocolate, cookies, cannelés, hot chocolate mixes, and most confections, because their lifespan extends well beyond a day. Other items that can also work but have a short lifespan are cotton candy, breads, and other similar baked goods such as brioche. The latter is in fact a great item to give out with a small jar of jam or marmalade for breakfast the next day, especially for people who are from out of town. Always keep in mind, though, that once you start doing this, you shouldn't stop, because your customers will expect it every time they return. If you stop, they will wonder why, regardless of how good a meal they had.

BIBLIOGRAPHY

Beckett, Stephen T. *The Science of Chocolate*. London: RSC Paperbacks, 2000.

Bilheux, Roland; Escoffier, Alain; and Michalet, Pierre. *French Professional Pastry Series*. Paris: CICEM (Compagnie Internationale de Consultation Education et Media), 1988.

Calvel, Raymond; Wirtz, Ronald L.; and MacGuire, James J. *The Taste of Bread*. Gaithersburg, Maryland: Aspen Publishers, Inc., 2001.

Christian, Elizabeth W., and Vaclavik, Vickie A. *Essentials of Food Science (Second Edition)*. London: Kluwer Academic/Plenum Publishers, 2003.

Coultate, T.P. *Food: The Chemistry of its Components (Fourth Edition)*. Cambridge, UK: The Royal Society of Chemistry, 2003.

Davidson, Alan; Davidson, Jane; Jaine, Tom; and Saberi, Helen. *The Oxford Companion to Food (Second Edition)*. New York: Oxford University Press, 2006.

Dickinson, Eric and Miller, Reinhard. *Food Colloids*. Cambridge, UK: The Royal Society of Chemistry, 2001.

Edwards, W.P. *The Science of Sugar and Confectionery*. Cambridge, UK: The Royal Society of Chemistry, 2000.

Figoni, Paula. *How Baking Works*. Hoboken, New Jersey: John Wiley & Sons, Inc., 2008.

Hamelman, Jeffrey. *Bread: A Baker's Book of Techniques and Recipes*. Hoboken, New Jersey: John Wiley & Sons, Inc., 2004.

Jackson, E.B. *Sugar Confectionery Manufacture*. Gaithersburg, Maryland: Aspen Publishers, 1995.

Jenkins, Steven. *The Cheese Primer*. New York: Workman Publishing Company, Inc., 1996.

Larousse Gastronomique. New York: Clarkson Potter Publishers, 2001.

Loiseau, Bernard and Gilbert, Gérard. *Trucs de Pâtissier*. France: Marabout, 2000.

McGee, Harold. *On Food and Cooking*. New York: Scribner, 2004.

Meiselman, Herbert L. and MacFie, H.J.H. *Food Choice, Acceptance and Consumption*. London: Chapman and Hall, 1996.

Meiselman, Herbert L. *Dimensions of the Meal*. Gaithersburg, Maryland: Aspen Publishers, 2000.

Migoya, Francisco. *Frozen Desserts*. Hoboken, New Jersey: John Wiley & Sons, Inc., 2008.

——————————. *The Modern Café*. Hoboken, New Jersey: John Wiley & Sons, Inc., 2010.

Morato, Ramón. *Chocolate*. Barcelona: Grupo Editorial Vilbo, 2007.

Poilâne, Lionel and Poilâne, Apollonia. *Le Pain par Poilâne*. Paris: Le Cherche Midi Éditeur, 2005.

Rock, David. *Quiet Leadership*. New York: HarperCollins, 2006.

Roux, Michel. *Finest Desserts*. New York: Rizzoli, 1995.

The Culinary Institute of America. *Baking and Pastry: Mastering the Craft*. Hoboken, New Jersey: John Wiley & Sons, Inc., 2004.

Webb Young, James. *A Technique for Producing Ideas*. New York: McGraw-Hill, 2003.

Wrolstad, Ronald E.; Acree, Terry E.; Decker, Eric A.; Penner, Michael H.; Reid, David S.; Schwartz, Stephen J.; Shoemaker, Charles E.; Smith, Denise M.; and Sporns, Peter. *Handbook of Food Analytical Chemistry*. Hoboken, New Jersey: John Wiley & Sons, Inc., 2005.

Wybauw, Jean-Pierre. *Chocolate Without Borders*. Tielt, Belgium: Lannoo Uitgeverij, 2007.

Online Conversion Tools

www.onlineconversion.com

RESOURCES

HYDROCOLLOIDS
www.le-sanctuaire.com (including Genutine 400-C)

www.lepicerie.com

www.cpkelco.com

UNIVERSAL PECTIN (AKA PECTIN NH 95/LOW-ACYL PECTIN/
CITRUS PECTIN) AND MONOCALCIUM PHOSPHATE
www.pomonapectin.com

VOLCANO VAPORIZER
www.storz-bickel.com

AGAROID RS-507
www.ticgums.com

COCOA BEANS, CHOCOLATE-MAKING SUPPLIES
(COCOA NIB MILL, MELANGEUR, JUICER)
www.chocolatealchemy.com

VACUUM-SEALED CANISTER (QUICK MARINATOR)
www.foodsaver.com

SUPERBAG
www.le-sanctuaire.com

DISTILLER (COUNTERTOP)
www.freshwatersystems.com

HEAVY CREAM WHIPPER, SODA SIPHON
www.isinorthamerica.com

CUSTOM-MADE SILICONE MOLDS, SPECIALTY SILICONE MOLDS
www.chicagomoldschool.com

SPECIALTY CHEESES
www.murrayscheese.com

CUSTOM-CUT PLEXIGLAS
www.eplastics.com

DULCE DE LECHE/CAJETA (GOAT'S MILK CARAMEL)
www.mexgrocer.com

SMOKING GUN
www.cuisinetechnology.com

ANTIQUE CHOCOLATE MOLDS
www.ebay.com

KATAIFI (SHREDDED FILO DOUGH)
www.parthenonfoods.net

ALOE JUICE (SHIRAKIKU)
www.marukaiestore.com

HIBISCUS EXTRACT
www.lepicerie.com

HIBISCUS SYRUP
www.wildhibiscus.com

CUSTOM-MADE ALUMINUM MOLDS
Frank Longmore
e-mail: frank@frankencutters.com

FREEZE-DRIED BUTTER POWDER
www.usaemergencysupply.com

PLASTIC CUBE MOLDS AND BOXES
www.amacplastics.com

FREEZE-DRIED FRUITS (WHOLE AND POWDERED)
www.nutsonline.com

PUMPKIN SEED PASTE, PEANUT PASTE
www.le-sanctuaire.com

PETER'S CHOCOLATE
www.peterschocolate.com

TEXTURED ACETATE MATS, TRANSFER SHEETS
www.chefrubber.com

www.pcb-creation.fr

SILICONE ICE POP MOLDS, GOLD SPRAY, NATURAL FOOD COLORING,
NATURAL COCOA BUTTER COLORS, NEOPRENE MATS
www.chefrubber.com

FRUIT PURÉES
www.parisgourmet.com

CHOCOLATE MOLDS
www.tomric.com

INSTANT VIETNAMESE COFFEE
www.amazon.com

ICE CREAM AND SORBET STABILIZERS
www.parisgourmet.com

THERMOMIX
www.vorwerk.com/thermomix

PANDAN LEAVES
www.philamfood.com

QUARK POWDER
www.kanegrade.com

CANNELÉ MOLDS, SILICONE MOLDS, BAKING MATS
www.matfer.com

www.jbprince.com

SPECIALTY SPICES (INCLUDING REINE DES PRES)
www.le-sanctuaire.com

www.kalustyans.com

CHOCOLATE-COATED PUFFED RICE, SPECIALTY PASTRY MOLDS, SILVER LUSTER DUST–
COATED FEUILLETINE, RUBBER CHABLONS, DE-MOLD SPRAY, CANDIED GREEN MARIGOLDS
www.pcb-creation.fr

"Lego" mold
www.lego.com

COCONUT MILK POWDER
www.willpowder.com

EDIBLE LACQUER SPRAY, TRUFFLE SHELLS
www.auiswisscatalogue.com

LITCHI JELLY
www.bobateadirect.com

CANDIED ANGELICA, YELLOW MARIGOLDS, LILACS, ROSE PETALS,
AND VIOLETS; PRESERVED WHOLE RASPBERRIES
www.markethallfoods.com

ZIP-TOP BAGS
www.wholesalesuppliesplus.com

CHESTNUT CREAM/JAM
www.moreluxuries.com

YUZU MARMALADE
www.amazon.com

MATCHA TEA POWDER
www.matchasource.com

STAINLESS-STEEL PINS
www.jbprince.com

CAKE DOUGHNUTS
www.freihofers.com

WAFER PAPER, ROYAL ICING STENCILS
www.fancyflours.com

COCOA BUTTER SPRAY
www.pastrychef.com

RUBBER STAMPS
www.rubberstamps.com

APOTHECARY JARS
www.globaltable.com

SUBJECT INDEX

Ingredients
  flavor/flavor compatibility for, 60–84
  sources for, 520–521
Italian buttercream, 13
Italian meringue (cooked), 13

J

Joconde, 11
Juicer, 32, 33
Juniper berries, flavor/flavor compatibility,
  76

K

Kaffir limes/leaves, flavor/flavor
  compatibility, 63
Key limes, flavor/flavor compatibility, 63
Kumquats, flavor/flavor compatibility, 63

L

Laiskonis, Michael, 243, 441
Lamination pastry method, 22–24, 26
Lavender, flavor/flavor compatibility, 71
Lean dough, 26, 92
Lecithin, 34
Legumes, flavor/flavor compatibility, 83
Lemon balm, flavor/flavor compatibility, 71
Lemons, flavor/flavor compatibility, 63
Lemongrass, flavor/flavor compatibility,
  71
Lemon verbena, flavor/flavor compatibility,
  72
Licorice, flavor/flavor compatibility, 76
Limes, flavor/flavor compatibility, 63
Liquors, dessert, 311
Litchis, flavor/flavor compatibility, 65
Locust bean gum (LBG), 20

M

Macadamia nuts, flavor/flavor
  compatibility, 82
Macarons, 10, 12, 13, 342
  macarons vs. macaroons, 342
Mace, flavor/flavor compatibility, 76
Madagascar cocoa beans, 30
Maillard reaction, 89
Mangoes, flavor/flavor compatibility, 65
Marzipan, flavor/flavor compatibility, 82
Mélangeur, 29, 31, 32, 520
Melons, flavor/flavor compatibility, 65
Menu
  composition principles for, 86–87
  enunciation of desserts, 88–89
Meringue
  cake coating, 385

foaming egg whites, 10
French method (uncooked), 12
Italian method (cooked), 13
macarons, 342
in mousses, 15
preparation types, 57
Swiss method, 13
Methocel, 19
Meyer lemons, flavor/flavor compatibility,
  63
Microwave, melting chocolate in, 29
Mignardises, 451
Milk chocolate
  flavor/flavor compatibility, 79
  formulation, 37
Mint, flavor/flavor compatibility, 72
Molded chocolates, 42–45, 47, 452
Molds
  cake, 383
  chocolate, 42, 44, 210, 452
Mousses, 15

N

Nectarines, flavor/flavor compatibility, 66
Nothnagel, Michael, 34
Nutmeg, flavor/flavor compatibility, 77
Nuts
  flavor/flavor compatibility, 80–83
  preparations of, 56–57
  toasting, 80

O

Outdoor service, buffet, 262

P

Papayas, flavor/flavor compatibility, 66
Parfaits, 16
Passed-around desserts, guidelines for,
  332–333
Passion fruit, flavor/flavor compatibility, 66
Pastry chef–server relationship, 85, 430
Pastry cream (boiled custard) method,
  5–7, 236
Pastry methods
  blending, 3–4
  chocolate making. See Chocolate
    making
  chocolate tempering, 27–29
    seeding, 28–29
  creaming, 4–5
  custard, 5–9
    baked, 6, 7–8
    boiled (pastry cream), 5–7
    stirred (Anglaise method), 6, 8–9

foamed. See Aerated desserts;
    Foaming method
  gelling agents, 18–21
  lamination, 22–24
  meringue, 12–13
    French (uncooked), 12
    Italian (cooked), 13
    Swiss, 13
  pâte à choux ("precooked"), 24–25
  rubbed dough (cut-in), 25–26
  straight dough mixing, 26–27
  sugar cooking, 47–48
    dry method, 48
    stages/temperatures, 48
    wet method, 47
Pastry preparations, types of, 54–57
Pâte à bombe, 15
Pâte à choux ("precooked") method,
  24–25
Peaches, flavor/flavor compatibility, 66
Peanut butter, flavor/flavor compatibility,
  83
Peanuts
  flavor/flavor compatibility, 83
  toasting, 80
Pears, flavor/flavor compatibility, 67
Pecans, flavor/flavor compatibility, 82
Pectin, 20–21
  universal, 21, 154, 214, 305
Peppermint, flavor/flavor compatibility, 72
Persimmons, flavor/flavor compatibility, 67
Petits fours
  categories of, 450
  chocolate bonbons as, 452
  and mignardises, 451
Pineapple, flavor/flavor compatibility, 67
Pine nuts, flavor/flavor compatibility, 82
Piping bag, 384
Pistachios, flavor/flavor compatibility, 83
Plastic bowls, 10
Plated desserts, general guidelines,
  164–165
Plates, serving, 85
Plating, 107, 164
Plums, flavor/flavor compatibility, 67
Polycarbonate molds, 42
Pomegranates, flavor/flavor compatibility,
  68
Pomelos, flavor/flavor compatibility, 63
Poolish (pre-ferment), 89
Portion size, 84, 263
Praline, flavor/flavor compatibility, 83
Pre-desserts
  cheese carts/plates, 107, 150

RECIPE INDEX

Page numbers in *italics* indicate illustrations; page numbers in **bold** indicate recipes.